THE
POLITICS
OF
POWER

THE
POLITICS
OF
POWER

A Critical Introduction to American Government

SEVENTH EDITION

IRA KATZNELSON
Columbia University

MARK KESSELMAN
Columbia University

ALAN DRAPER
St. Lawrence University

 W. W. NORTON & COMPANY ▪ NEW YORK ▪ LONDON

W. W. Norton & Company has been independent since its founding in 1923, when William Warder Norton and Mary D. Herter Norton first published lectures delivered at the People's Institute, the adult education division of New York City's Cooper Union. The firm soon expanded its program beyond the Institute, publishing books by celebrated academics from America and abroad. By midcentury, the two major pillars of Norton's publishing program—trade books and college texts—were firmly established. In the 1950s, the Norton family transferred control of the company to its employees, and today—with a staff of four hundred and a comparable number of trade, college, and professional titles published each year—W. W. Norton & Company stands as the largest and oldest publishing house owned wholly by its employees.

Editor: Jake Schindel
Project Editor: Amy Weintraub
Electronic Media Editor: Lorraine Klimowich
Editorial Assistant: Sarah Wolf
Marketing Manager, Political Science: Sasha Levitt
Production Manager: Ashley Horna
Photo Editor: Evan Luberger
Permissions Manager: Megan Jackson
Text Design: Jo Anne Metsch
Composition: Cenveo® Publisher Services
Manufacturing: Maple-Vail Book Group

The text of this book is composed in Minion with the display set in Minion.

Library of Congress Cataloging-in-Publication Data has been applied for.
9780393919448

W. W. Norton & Company, Inc., 500 Fifth Avenue, New York, NY 10110-0017
wwnorton.com
W. W. Norton & Company Ltd., Castle House, 75/76 Wells Street, London
W1T 3QT

3 4 5 6 7 8 9 0

To Robert and Clarice Draper, and in memory of Ephraim and Sylvia Katznelson, and Paul and Anne Kesselman.

BRIEF CONTENTS

CONTENTS

PART III: POLITICAL INSTITUTIONS

CHAPTER 6

The Presidency

CHAPTER 7

The Congress

WHAT DO YOU THINK? BOXES

PREFACE

Within the subfield of comparative politics, scholars studying democratic transitions and consolidations stress the importance of holding a free, fair, and competitive election. Scholars add that an important test of a successful transition is the conduct of a *second* competitive election. One might transpose this reasoning to contemporary American politics, in order to observe that, as noteworthy as the election of America's first African American president was in 2008, the question of Barack Obama's racial background received very little attention and seemingly played very little role during the 2012 election. While the U.S. has a long way to go before achieving racial justice, it is worth celebrating the quiet symbolism of what a relative non-story the reelection of an African American president was.

Since the sixth edition of *The Politics of Power* was published, in 2009, there have been many other changes in American politics and society. Two examples: first, when Obama took office in 2009, the U.S. was mired in a severe recession and the economy was on the brink of free fall. Many of the nation's largest banks, insurance companies, and corporations were close to bankruptcy. During Obama's first term, a robust federal program to bail out the financial industry and corporate America, as well as stimulate the economy, helped stave off financial and economic collapse. By the time Obama was reelected in 2012, corporate America was experiencing an upswing. Although unemployment remained unacceptably high, there was steady job creation and sustained economic growth. The years since the publication of this book's sixth edition have therefore witnessed significant progress on the economic front—though several chapters in this new edition highlight the relatively low priority given by the federal government to job creation and improving the plight of the tens of millions left on the sidelines by the economic recovery.

A second change during President Obama's first term involved an improvement in the international position of the U.S. When Obama took office, the U.S. was internationally isolated, in large part because of the Bush administration's unilateral and heavy-handed actions, epitomized by the costly and apparently never-ending wars in Iraq and Afghanistan. During Obama's first term, U.S. standing in the world markedly improved. Although the world remains chaotic and dangerous, the U.S. has coordinated its actions with allies to confront a series of momentous changes. The U.S. ended its military presence in Iraq, and, following the dispatch of over 90,000 American troops to Afghanistan by presidents Bush and Obama, Obama arranged for a withdrawal of most U.S. troops by 2014.

The seventh edition of *The Politics of Power* charts these and other changes in American politics and political economy. All chapters have been thoroughly revised, both to reflect new scholarship and to keep abreast of recent events. The most important change, in response to reviewers' suggestions, is a rich and extended description in the first chapter of the nation's founding. Readers will also discover an in-depth analysis of the Obama presidency, including a discussion of the passage of the Affordable Care Act, the major domestic achievement of Obama's first term, and the Supreme Court's surprising ruling that upheld the constitutional validity of the act. This edition further provides a detailed analysis of Obama's distinctive presidential style, the innovative features of his successful reelection campaign, and his more audacious use of presidential power at the outset of his second term. Several chapters provide in-depth analyses of government policies and reforms aimed at ending the recession that began in 2008 and promoting economic growth, including tax cuts, increased federal spending, and innovative actions by the Federal Reserve Board. The book details the institutional gridlock of Obama's first term and the budget battles and compromises that followed the 2012 elections. A new case study of the Tea Party joins descriptions of the labor, feminist, and environmental movements. The seventh edition also analyzes the complexities and contradictions of Obama's foreign policy: on the one hand, an attempt to build multilateral alliances rather than engage in unilateral military intervention in response to turbulence in Libya, Syria, and Afghanistan; on the other hand, increased unilateral lethal actions involving special forces and unmanned aerial vehicles (UAVs)—that is, drones.

While *The Politics of Power* has been thoroughly updated, its aim remains the same: to introduce students to a critical perspective on American politics by highlighting how political conflicts, institutions, and processes are influenced by deep inequalities generated by the country's political economy. The text underscores the mutually supportive but uneasy relationship joining American democracy and American capitalism. We try to clarify this multifaceted association in the hope that our perspective and analytic framework will provoke thoughtful discussion. In so doing, we aim to help students develop their own approaches to the study of American politics, and to reflect on their role as citizens and participants.

Following the Introduction, which provides a framework that analyzes key issues in democratic theory, the book is divided into four parts. Part I explores ties linking economics and politics. We show how economic power impacts political power by influencing who gets what, where, and how. Part II examines the political participation of citizens by looking at the diverse ways they organize to promote their views, as well as how collective organization is affected by the structural power of business intertwined with economic inequality. Key topics include political parties, political finance, voting, and elections, in Chapter 4, and interest groups and social movements, in Chapter 5. Part III investigates the federal government's executive, legislative, and judicial institutions, focusing on the politics of power in operation, the institutional gridlock of recent years, and the relationship between core political institutions and America's political economy. Part IV turns to how social, economic, and foreign policies have been shaped by the economy, political participation, and political institutions. It also reviews the impact these policies have had on American political and social life. The conclusion, in Chapter 12, reviews the main points developed in the text and points to future possibilities in American politics.

This edition also updates pedagogical features that were introduced in the sixth edition. "What Do You Think?" boxes are sprinkled throughout the text. "Critical Thinking Questions" appear at the end of each chapter, prodding students to think for themselves about the material and arguments we have presented. A summary organized by subheadings also appears at the end of each chapter, and a glossary of key terms is included at the close of the book. A Test Bank, with new and updated multiple-choice and essay questions for each chapter, has been authored by Peter Kolozi of Bronx Community College and can be accessed, along with art PowerPoints from the book, at www.wwnorton.com/instructors.

Throughout, we have tried to be direct without being simplistic, engaging without being flippant, critical without being cynical. We will be pleased if our writing animates students new to the study of American politics, engages more-advanced students, and challenges professors who assign the book.

We are most grateful for the invaluable help we have received. Librarians at Columbia and St. Lawrence universities were enormously helpful in locating difficult sources and information. Reviewers of individual chapters were critical in offering advice that improved the book's argument and presentation. Our special thanks to Taylor Dark at California State University, Los Angeles;

Jeffrey Hilmer at Arizona State University; Peter Kolozi at Bronx Community College; Geoffrey Kurtz at Borough of Manhattan Community College; and Nicky González Yuen at De Anza College. In addition, we were supported by friends and family who offered encouragement and diversion. Ira Katznelson and Mark Kesselman recognize the help they received from students and colleagues at Columbia University, especially Amy Semet, as well as from their families. Alan Draper would like to thank Pat Ellis and their extended family of children, including Sam, Rachel, Bryan, and Trevor. Ira and Mark also gratefully acknowledge Alan's exceptional contribution to this edition. Collectively, we appreciate and acknowledge the gifted professionalism of Roby Harrington, Ann Shin, Jake Schindel, and Amy Weintraub at W. W. Norton. We are especially grateful for Jake Schindel's incisive editorial suggestions.

DEMOCRACY'S CHALLENGE

INTRODUCTION

It took three years to build at a cost of $7.5 million dollars—the equivalent of about $400 million today. It was almost 900 feet long—three football fields put end to end—weighed about 46,000 tons, and was 175 feet high from its keel to the top. Its owners said it was unsinkable. When it left the dock, the *Titanic* was the biggest, fastest, most luxurious ocean liner ever constructed.

The *Titanic* set sail on its maiden voyage from England bound for New York on April 10, 1912. On board were 2,228 people, as were 40,000 fresh eggs, 12,000 dinner plates, 6,000 tablecloths, and 1,000 finger bowls. As the boat cruised toward New York, first-class passengers spent their days swimming in a pool, exercising in a gymnasium, relaxing in a reading room, or exchanging pleasant-ries in a lounge reserved for them. In the evening they enjoyed elegant parties, drank fine wine, and ate sumptuous meals before retiring to their spacious staterooms. Many of the first-class passengers on board were familiar names from high society, such as John Jacob Astor IV, whose grandfather had struck it rich in lumber and real estate; George Widener, whose family had made its fortune in streetcars; and members of British nobility, such as the Countess of Rothes and Sir Cosmo Duff Gordon.

Passengers in third class did not have it as good. Families in third class were crowded into small rooms, which could barely accommodate two bunk beds and a toilet. Single men and women were housed in separate, congested, unpleasant holds below on opposite ends of the ship. There were only two bathtubs for use by the seven hundred passengers in third class. In addition, they were restricted from moving about the ship and from using the amenities reserved for first-class passengers. Many brought food for the duration of the trip across the ocean because they could not afford to dine on board. The price of the ticket had exhausted their savings. Unlike the Anglo-American

The *Titanic* sailing from Southampton, England, April 10, 1912.

aristocracy in first class, many third-class passengers were non-British immi-grants from such distant places as Poland, Italy, and Russia. They were fleeing persecution and poverty in the countries they had left behind in hopes of find-ing freedom and prosperity in America.

As the ship crossed the Atlantic, everything first appeared calm. Anxious to gain a competitive edge in the ruthlessly competitive steamship business—then the only means of transatlantic travel—the owners of the *Titanic* instructed the captain to increase the ship's speed. Dismissing the risks involved, the owners hoped to break the record for transatlantic travel and arrive in New York a day early. This would attract even more publicity for the ship's arrival and humble the competition. With its engines at full throttle, the *Titanic* entered treacherous waters off Newfoundland. Then disaster struck. An iceberg tore a 200-foot hole along the ship's hull. The *Titanic* began to sink. Bedlam broke out on board. The *Titanic* was equipped with all sorts of luxurious facilities, but the owners had outfitted the ship with only enough lifeboats to evacuate half the passen-gers. When the *Titanic* began to sink, the ship's owners ordered that first-class passengers be evacuated first. Meanwhile, third-class passengers trying to reach the lifeboats sometimes found the doors to the deck locked or blocked. Those fortunate enough to reach the deck found that first-class passengers were given priority on the lifeboats. Two-thirds of the first-class passengers were saved.

The results of that tragic night were quite different, however, for the passengers in steerage: two-thirds froze to death in the icy waters of the Atlantic. Just as wealth, income, and social standing influenced how people lived on board ship, so it influenced who would die.

In many ways, the tale of the *Titanic* offers a powerful metaphor for key features of American society and politics even a century after the disaster. The United States remains the wealthiest and strongest nation in the world. It is the biggest, fastest, most luxurious ocean liner around. Like the *Titanic*, it is also characterized by massive disparities in wealth and income that separate first- and third-class passengers. The richest 20 percent of American households earn more than half the country's income; the poorest quintile earn just 3 percent. Since 1980, increases in earnings have been concentrated at the top. During the past thirty years, the average income of the top 1 percent of wage earners tripled, while the wages of middle-class Americans increased by just 40 percent, barely keeping pace with inflation. The 2010 U.S. Census recently reported that the top 5 percent of households earned a median income of just over $180,000, the top 20 percent earned about $100,000, and the median income for the remaining 80 percent was approximately $50,000. Disparities in wealth are far greater. Wealth—including housing, stocks, and bonds—is remarkably uneven. The best recent measures indicate that the top 20 percent hold 84 percent of wealth in America. Much of that wealth is concentrated in the hands of the highest 1 percent of income earners, who, in 2011, held about 40 percent of the nation's wealth compared to 33 percent a quarter-century ago.

The deep recession of the late 2000s had a real impact on most Americans. A 2009 survey found that the net worth of the average family declined 23 percent in just two years between 2007 and 2009. By contrast, the pay packages—combinations of salaries, perks, and bonuses—for those at the highest rungs of large firms remained astonishing. In 2011, the CEO of McKesson Pharmaceuticals, who was the highest paid chief executive in the country, earned $131 million. Other CEOs in the top five included the heads of Ralph Lauren ($67 million), Vornado Realty ($64 million), Walt Disney ($53 million), and Express Scripts ($52 million). These packages included attractive stock options, generous retirement funds, and other benefits. Just before the steep economic downturn of the 2008 recession, those in the top one-tenth of 1 percent earned 976 times more income than those in the bottom 90 percent. Hedge-fund compensation was even more remarkable. The top 25 hedge-fund managers in 2011 earned an average of $576 million. The highest earner, Ray Dalio of Bridgewater Associates, took home a jaw-dropping $3.9 billion.[1] It is not surprising that growing inequality led to the emergence of a protest movement. In September 2011, a group called "Occupy Wall Street" organized to rally against income and wealth disparities. The group's slogan, "We are the 99 percent," underscored how disenchanted many Americans felt and continue to feel about the lopsided nature of the distribution of resources.

Gaps in wealth and income are greater in the United States than in any other economically developed country. High-income people have more purchasing power than the rich anywhere else—while the poor—the bottom 10 percent, can buy less than the equivalent group in Canada and Western Europe. Differences in wealth are also noteworthy. The top 20 percent of households own only about 69 percent of the wealth in Canada, and 74 percent in Sweden. At the bottom of the social order, the number of poor Americans increased by more than 5 million between 2000 and 2008, and nearly one in five children under the age of 18 falls below the government's standard for poverty. Indeed, according to the 2010 Census, the number of Americans living below the poverty line has become higher than at any time in the three decades that the Census has been collecting such information.[2]

Americans may all be passengers on the same ship, but they have very different experiences of the journey based upon their class position. Citizens who are at the top of the income and wealth distributions can afford first-class tickets. They have bigger homes, drive nicer cars, live in finer neighborhoods, and send their children to better schools than do citizens who can afford only third-class tickets. As on the *Titanic*, deep inequality also influences who lives at all. Membership in a higher social class reduces the risk of heart attack, diabetes, infectious disease, arthritis, and some cancers, and it is a more powerful predictor of health and mortality than genetics, exposure to carcinogens, and smoking.[3]

WHAT DO YOU THINK?

Capitalism and Equality

As an economic system based on private enterprise and markets, capitalism has been widely interpreted both as productive, for the way it produces wealth and well-being, and as a supporter of economic and political freedom. Others have argued that capitalism is a system of exploitation because it generates significant benefits for some at the expense of others, and thus curtails individual freedom for those at the bottom of the distribution of wealth and income. Which of these positions is more convincing?

Another system of inequality overlaps that of class. Even after the election of Barack Obama, the country's first African American president, and even after the longer-term growth of the black middle class of which he is a member, first- and third-class passengers often continue to be distinguished by the color of their skin. Whites earn more, are more fully employed, are more educated, are less victimized by crime, and live longer than racial minorities. A 2011 study reported the median, or midpoint, of white earnings to be $54,620 per household. For African Americans the equivalent figure is $32,068, and for Latinos it is $37,759. There is also a racial disparity with respect to wealth. A 2009 report from the Pew Research Center reported that the median net worth for whites was $113,000; for African Americans, it was $5,500; and for Latinos the sum was $6,300. These numbers reflect a significant decline since 2005, when the net worth of whites had reached $135,000, compared to $12,000 for African Americans and $18,000 for Latinos. Much of the decline has been due to a collapse in housing values. Today, the total net worth of white households is 20 times that of African American households and 18 times that of Latino households. Only 1 in 10 whites has less than a high school diploma, compared to nearly 2 in 10 African Americans and almost 4 in 10 Latinos. Further, there is a persistent gender gap. The median income for a man working full time in 2011 was almost $48,000; for a woman, less than $37,000.[4]

The example of the *Titanic* even extends beyond how class, racial, and gender inequalities shape and distort the quality of life. The opulence on board while the ship's owners skimped on lifeboats is all too reminiscent of the immense resources society devotes to satisfying extravagant consumer desires while investments in the public sector, such as schools, the environment, and the safety net—especially in difficult economic times—are stretched thin and under-funded. Historically, the American **welfare state** has not provided enough lifeboats to those who need medical care, child care, or income support. Millions of Americans would fall below the poverty line without the aid of government programs. In 2010, 3.2 million persons escaped falling below the poverty threshold by receiving unemployment insurance. Further, almost 4 million people receiving food stamps to supplement their income would have been considered poor had they not received those benefits. Another 5.4 million were boosted above poverty by tax credits. Yet despite these programs, the poverty rate grew from 11 percent in 2000 to 15 percent in 2010. All told, the 2010 Census reported that 46.2 million Americans are living in poverty. Elsewhere, governments do much more to counter inequality. Although their poverty rates are equivalent, or even higher, before public policies kick in, welfare-state programs in other rich industrialized nations have a bigger impact on poverty. In Great Britain, the welfare state reduces the number of poor people significantly; only 6 percent of the population earn an income that is under 40 percent of the country's median income. In the Netherlands, just over 4 percent do, and in Sweden merely 2 percent of the population earn that little.[5]

Further, the degree to which businesses put profits above other values is eerily similar to the way the owners of the *Titanic* recklessly endangered the lives of their passengers. The tragedy off the Newfoundland coast occurred in part because the *Titanic's* owners were intent on arriving early to gain favorable publicity and overshadow the competition. Regrettably, there are all too many examples of corporations seeking profits at the expense of their customers' welfare. Recent examples include Medtronic-implanted heart devices that malfunctioned in hundreds of patients and contributed to at least five deaths, Peanut Corporation of America (PCA) products infected by salmonella, and Philip Morris cigarettes that, like all cigarettes, cause cancer. In 2010, an offshore drilling platform exploded in the Gulf of Mexico, resulting in one of the worst environmental disasters in American history. In the haste to clean up the mess and repair the company's reputation, BP Oil, the owner of the wells, used dispersants that were much more toxic to wildlife than costlier and more environmentally friendly alternatives. Manufacturers who knew of the dangers they were causing decided it was cheaper not to make changes that were needed to enhance safety. Sometimes the price of greed can be more widespread and more systematic. Financial firms sought to take advantage of the housing frenzy of the early years of this century by creating new forms of debt instruments based on pools of mortgages. As a result, they became vastly overextended. When many borrowers could not afford the loans they had been encouraged to take, the whole financial system was put at risk and saved only by a massive bailout by the federal government.

CONSTITUTIONAL DEMOCRACY: THE FOUNDING

Although powerful, the *Titanic* as a metaphor breaks down at a crucial point. The United States is a constitutional **democracy**. The *Titanic* was not. The captain of the *Titanic* was accountable to the owners who employed him; the passengers did not elect him. By contrast, Americans can choose the people who govern. All adult American citizens today (except for prisoners and, in some states, ex-felons) have the right to vote, and each citizen gets the same single vote. Democrats and Republicans, as well as a host of minor political parties, compete actively to win the support of the electorate. Compared to those in most other countries, public authorities in the United States tend to be accessible and responsive. Because it is limited by the country's constitutional system, their rule is not arbitrary or unaccountable. Citizens are free to engage in political debate, criticize the government, and make demands for change. Newspapers, television, and the Internet provide regular reports of government activities, debate the wisdom of public policies, and expose wrongdoing by high government officials, including presidents.

These rights and liberties developed over time, often as the result of conflict and struggle. When the country was founded, American democracy was limited and constrained because the majority was not permitted to participate in political life. Initially, many states and localities imposed property restrictions on voting, which were not fully eliminated until the early 1830s. Women lacked the right to vote before the Nineteenth Amendment brought them into the electorate in 1920. African Americans, including ex-slaves, were formally guaranteed the franchise by the Fifteenth Amendment in 1870, five years after the end of the Civil War. But in practice they were largely prevented from voting by a host of devices—including literacy tests, poll taxes, discrimination by electoral registrars, and a good deal of violence—until the Voting Rights Act of 1965.

Over the course of the history of the republic, American constitutional government has become increasingly democratic; struggles to widen the franchise have brought more and more citizens into the political system as participants and voters. With the passage of the Twenty-Sixth Amendment in 1971, nearly all adults over the age of 18 became formally eligible to participate in American politics. As the country became more democratic, it also became a global beacon. Tens of millions of people fleeing oppressive conditions and seeking economic opportunity flocked to the United States, producing an increasingly varied population. Others were incorporated less willingly, as the result of the conquest of northern Mexico in the Mexican-American War, which ended in 1848, and of Hawaii, which was annexed to the United States in 1898. At first, the population was divided between a majority of whites, mainly Protestants from northern Europe (especially Great Britain) and a minority of African slaves and Native Americans. Over time, immigrant streams from Ireland and Germany, then from southern and eastern Europe, and most recently from Mexico, the Caribbean, South Asia, East Asia, Africa, and Latin America, have fashioned a population that is remarkably heterogeneous racially and ethnically, comprising the world's most diverse country in terms of religion, culture, and place of origin.

American constitutional government was first fashioned at a time when other nations were ruled by kings and emperors, not by elected officials whose actions were constrained by citizen rights. This revolutionary development came 11 years after the Second Continental Congress unanimously adopted the Declaration of Independence in 1776, rejecting British rule of the 13 colonies and declaring that all human beings are owed the "unalienable rights" of life, liberty, and the pursuit of happiness. Justifying separation from Britain, the July 4 Declaration moved from an elaboration of this philosophical statement of universal principles to the claim that the people possess the right to abolish a government that does not work to achieve these principles. It then turned to an enumeration of grievances against British rule and ended by declaiming that the connection between Britain and the colonies had been dissolved. Having experienced a long set of abuses, the document argued, the people had earned the right to rebel.

The government the Continental Congress first fashioned under the **Articles of Confederation** was relatively weak because each state retained its sovereignty and independence. There was no president; Congress was placed at the center of government and had the power to make war, sign treaties, borrow or coin money, and manage relations with Native American Indians.

It soon became clear that this design for the nation's government was insufficient. The weak national government was effectively paralyzed. It could not levy taxes, but could only request that the various states provide revenues to the national government. As former Supreme Court Justice John Paul Stevens has observed, "a failure to replace the Articles of Confederation would have exacerbated the problem of state restraints on free commerce that provided the primary motivation for framing a new government"—a motivation to create a common national market within which **capitalism** could develop. The 13 states were much more powerful than the central government. Each had its own currency. Each had its own rules about international trade. Each had its own militia, and some even had their own navy. The Confederate Congress—the country's only national institution, in which each state was granted a single vote—was unable to grapple with the wide range of economic problems, internal unrest, and military challenges facing the new republic. Passing laws that concerned important defense and spending policies required the approval of a supermajority of nine states, while even ordinary legislation could not be passed without large majorities.[6] Another Constitutional Convention, gathered in May 1787 in Philadelphia and concluding four months later, was called to invent a better, more practical, and more effective government.

With disappointment rife, the Constitutional Convention's 55 delegates sought to design a government based on the consent of the people that could actually govern a complex nation. To do so, they had to reconcile a wide variety of different interests, and find a balance between those who wanted a much stronger national government and those who sought to protect the powers of the states. They had to negotiate among diverse interests, most notably those that distinguished large from small states, and especially those that divided the South, with its slave-based economy, from the North, where free farming and commercial interests dominated. Without compromise, some delegates worried, the United States might even split into countries based in New England, the Middle Atlantic states, and the South.

Following months of difficult negotiations lasting through the summer of 1787, compromises were found that created a durable constitutional republic based on the principles of a government elected by the people. Powers were divided—not, as in most political regimes in human history, concentrated in specific offices or persons. The national government would be characterized by a **separation of powers**, and the capacity to govern shared by the executive branch (led by the president), by the legislative branch (a Congress with two chambers—the House of Representatives and the Senate), and by the judicial branch (the Supreme Court). These branches were placed in a relationship of **checks and balances** with one another. The president was granted power to veto congressional legislation; the Senate would have to approve key presidential appointments; and the Supreme Court could review laws passed by Congress and signed by the president. Further, the political system would be characterized by **federalism**, a system that limits national power by reserving many powers and functions to the governments of the country's states. Government, in short, was designed to be accountable to the people, who were invited into the political process as participants. To be sure, the framers did not invite the people to rule directly. They were concerned, as James Madison described in several of the Federalist essays, that simply allowing decisions to be reached by popular majorities might result in the poor, the greater part of the population, appropriating the wealth of the rich—what Madison regarded as a form of tyranny. Fresh in the minds of the founders was "Shays's Rebellion"—an uprising of farmers in central and western Massachusetts who sought to cancel their debts by seizing control of the federal arsenal at Springfield. Notwithstanding, it was a hallmark of the **Constitution** that, in the last resort, the people were sovereign.

Overall, the result was a wholly new set of institutions that were designed to adjudicate among conflicting interests while advancing a public interest.

None of this proved easy to do. The Convention had to decide how to reconcile two different plans for government representation of the people. The

Virginia Plan proposed a strong national government and a president who would be selected by a Congress in which each state's representation in both the House and the Senate would be determined by the size of its population. The **New Jersey Plan**, favoring the smaller states, would have continued the Confederate Congress with small adjustments to increase some national powers while keeping more policy making in the hands of the states. And each state would have the same number of representatives in the House and Senate, an advantage for states with smaller populations.

The solution of this dispute lay in developing different rules for the two independent and coequal chambers of Congress. The Connecticut Compromise—also known as the **Great Compromise**—placed legislative power in a Congress with both a Senate and a House of Representatives. The number of representatives elected from each state to the House would be based on population. Further, when new states would be admitted to the Union, their standing would be equal to the original 13 in the selection of congressmen and senators. The Senate, however, would be different. Each state would have just two senators, a measure that protected the smaller states from being dominated by a coalition of the larger states. As a result, Virginia, with a free population of 691,000 in 1790, had the same representation as Delaware, whose population numbered only 59,000. Counterbalancing this victory for the smaller states, however, was the proviso, demanded by the larger states, that all bills that raised or appropriated monies should be initiated in the House. With these agreements, all House members came to be chosen by direct election every two years. Senators, by contrast, have been elected directly only since 1913 (until then, they were selected by state legislatures); their six-year terms are staggered so that one-third of the Senate is up for election every two years,

WHAT DO YOU THINK?

From Confederation to Union

The Constitution created a form of government that stands midway between the weaker system that prevailed under the Articles of Confederation and stronger fully centralized systems lacking in federalism. Keeping in mind today's debates about the scope and scale of the federal government, how do you assess the advantages of the constitutional system the United States possesses against these two alternatives?

another stricture intended to guard against hasty shifts in public attitudes. Congress was given significant power to regulate commerce, borrow money, collect taxes, and maintain the armed forces.

The president, in turn, headed the executive branch of government. The central challenge was one of making the office strong enough to direct an effective government independent of Congress but not so strong as to resemble an all-powerful monarchy. The president, it was determined, would be elected by an **Electoral College** in which each state would have as many electors as the sum of its members of the House and Senate. The people would vote for a president every four years state by state, and these results would determine which electors would come together to actually pick the president. The holder of this office would manage foreign affairs, serve as commander-in-chief of the armed forces, oversee the federal bureaucracy, and veto congressional legislation. While the president was granted many critical powers, governing effectively would depend on coordinating with Congress and gaining its agreement both for new laws and for key appointments.

The judicial branch designated by the Constitution was to be headed by a Supreme Court, whose members, appointed by the president and approved by the Senate, would serve for lifetime terms, a provision that was adopted to guard their independence. The main task of the Court was to resolve constitutional controversies, including the ability to determine when federal and when state law would apply, and the capacity to judge how citizen rights should be understood and protected. The Court was also granted authority to settle disputes about land and territory.

As this system was shaped, one of the most divisive questions was what to do about slavery. This fundamental issue concerning the status of enslaved and often brutalized human beings made it nearly impossible to write a national constitution. Should slaves count as persons for the purpose of determining the number of representatives each state would have in the House of Representatives? Could the slave states continue to import slaves from overseas? What should the status be of a slave who had escaped to a free state? No constitution could be agreed to unless these contentious issues were resolved. The Convention adapted to the existence of slavery by deciding to count every five slaves as three persons for the purposes of apportioning seats in the House of Representatives, even though slaves were not citizens and could not vote. In this way, and by prohibiting Congress from abolishing the importation of slaves until 1808 (though slaves were taxed up to $10 a head) and including a fugitive-slave clause that provided for the return of escaped slaves to their owners, the Constitution recognized slavery as legitimate within the country's constitutional democracy. Together with the provision that each state would have two senators, these arrangements effectively protected slavery by giving southern states blocking power until the middle of the nineteenth century. Strikingly, the world "slave" did not appear in the Constitution, which referred instead to "such persons as the several States now existing shall think proper to admit."

This new government was granted considerable capacity to shape key features of economic life. It could raise taxes for the federal government (except on exports) without any limit, including revenue from tariffs on goods imported into the country. It could regulate commerce between states and with foreign countries, including commercial treaties, while leaving internal commerce in the hands of individual states. The Convention also insured that the United States would have a secure currency and credible financial standing, in part by assuming the debts of the Confederation government and those of the individual states. It also gave power to Congress and the courts to adjudicate existing land disputes between the federal government and individual states. The new government also was granted the powers to develop the infrastructure needed for economic development, including the right to establish common standards for weights and measures, to authorize patents and copyrights, and, most important, to build a national network of post offices.

The Constitution also fashioned a national state that could defend itself and act vigorously on the international stage. When the delegates met in Philadelphia, they were worried both about overseas enemies, especially Great Britain, the country the United States had recently defeated but which was still the world's strongest naval power. They approved the creation of a national army and navy, and commissioned private ships to seize those belonging to an enemy. Congress was granted the power to declare war, and the Senate the responsibility to approve treaties negotiated by the president with other nations with two-thirds vote. As the delegates created these arrangements, they worried about the potential loss of liberty for American citizens should the government be too zealous in pursuing national security.

The Constitution became the supreme law of the land once it was ratified by the states, following a massive campaign to convince the public to approve the new constitutional system. A great debate ensued between **Federalists**, who supported the new, stronger government, and the **Anti-Federalists**, who believed that its augmented powers threatened the prerogatives of the states as well as individual liberties. After ratifying conventions backed the new constitution in nine states by mid-June 1788, bringing the new government into being, votes had not yet been taken in the key states of Virginia or New York, whose approval would make the new government acceptable to their populations. *The Federalist Papers*, the remarkable collection of essays by Alexander Hamilton, John Jay, and James Madison, geared toward explaining the meaning of the Constitution to a still doubtful public, helped push approval over the line by narrow margins in both states, in late June and July. The last two states to back the new political system were North Carolina, which waited until the next year, and Rhode Island, which did not approve the Constitution until 1790, after George Washington had been elected president and Congress was meeting in its first session.

The founding moment was not yet complete. As originally drafted and ratified, the Constitution—based on the idea of consent by "We the People" and on political representation, the separation of powers, checks and balances, and a federal system—lacked an explicit statement of the **civil liberties** of American citizens, something the Anti-Federalists advocated as a further check against possible government tyranny. At the time of the Constitutional Convention, the delegates believed that these liberties did not need to be explicitly stated, as they would be guaranteed by the type of republican government they were creating. But when the document was placed before the states for ratification, it soon became clear that approval might not be forthcoming unless an understanding was reached that soon after ratification the Constitution would be amended to guarantee individual rights.

In 1791, the ten amendments called the **Bill of Rights** were added. These amendments, which assured American citizens that they possessed rights that could not be infringed, prevented public authorities from acting in arbitrary ways by placing limits on what government could do. These ten amendments fall into distinct categories. The First insures that Congress is not free to designate any single religion as official or established and may not limit religious freedom or freedom of speech, assembly, and petition. The Second, Third, and Fourth prevent the executive branch from infringing on the right of the people to keep and bear arms, from arbitrarily taking homes for use by the military, and from searching for or seizing evidence without getting a court order on the basis of the probable existence of a crime. The Fifth through the Eight constrain the judiciary. Citizens cannot be indicted for serious crimes without a grand jury. Courts must offer speedy justice, provide trials by jury, and let the accused know the charges and evidence against them and confront witnesses. Courts also cannot compel people to testify against themselves, nor can they try people more than once for the same offense. Punishment cannot be excessive, bail must be reasonably set, and property cannot be taken without proper compensation. An imprisoned person has the right of *habeas corpus*, that is, the capacity to file a petition demanding that the courts determine whether the imprisonment is lawful. The last two amendments, the Ninth and the Tenth, reserve to the people and to the states any powers not explicitly assigned to the federal government.

Democracy cannot be judged, however, only by these cherished rights and formal procedures. It must be evaluated based on how well these procedures work. Trials, for example, are often not speedy, and evidence is sometimes withheld from defendants who are not adequately represented by defense lawyers. Governmental power is at times arbitrary. Checks and balances do not always constrain the abuse of power. The substance of democracy, moreover, is also deeply affected when the democratic features of American government are combined with deep inequalities, and when the unequal distribution of wealth and prospects between first-class and third-class passengers affects the majority's ability to influence public policy. To what extent is **popular sovereignty** possible in a society characterized by large inequalities of resources?

We explore these issues in the pages that follow. We ask whether and how American democracy is distorted by large inequalities. When do political institutions permit, even promote, inequalities and when do they enable ordinary citizens to shape public policies and effect social, economic, and political change? We have two starting points—the country's democratic institutions that are grounded in the Constitution that has governed the United States since it was ratified in 1789, and the character of the capitalist economic system, including the special informal status of the country's major business firms.

WHAT DO YOU THINK?

Poverty and a Minimum Standard

The Constitution is silent about economic inequality. Yet in setting out to enhance "life, liberty, and the pursuit of happiness," it seems to imply that good government should not tolerate too much inequality and should be concerned about poverty because too few resources make it difficult, and sometimes impossible, for citizens to achieve these goals. Should the Constitution have done more—or do more today—to mandate equality, such as setting a minimum level of income and wealth for each citizen?

STANDARDS OF DEMOCRACY

Like the *Titanic*, the country's capitalist **market** economy—an economy that has produced great prosperity and economic development as well as inequality, insecurity, and cycles of boom and bust—is inherently not democratic. It is based on the capacity of some persons and firms to invest capital in order to gain the largest returns. They take risks to maximize profits. When things go well, markets generate productive investments, create jobs, and correct economic imbalances. When things go poorly, the sum of business decisions helps produce circumstances that put the whole economy in crisis. But in good times and bad, the basic economic decisions are made by those who own the means to produce goods and services, well outside the sphere of popular sovereignty.

Leaders in the marketplace have disproportionate power, not only because they have more money and the ability to secure access and influence through lobbying and campaign donations, but also because governments must act in ways that promote the prosperity of the private economy, the country's great engine of wealth and employment. The well-being of everyone, as measured by jobs and income, has come to depend on the investment decisions and the profits of private firms, and on corporate executives who decide about the organization of work, where firms and factories will be located, how resources should be allocated, and how much executives and workers are paid. The political economist Charles Lindblom shrewdly observed how "business leaders thus become a kind of public official and exercise what, on a broad view of their role, are public functions."[7] Because leaders of the private economy cannot be ordered to invest or perform effectively for the greater good, they sometimes have to be prompted and persuaded to do so. Public policies concerned with taxation, trade, and regulation, among other matters, are the instruments the government uses to achieve this goal.

Business thus commands a privileged position in public life. "In the eyes of government officials," Lindblom notes, "businessmen do not appear simply as the representatives of a special interest, as representatives of interest groups do. They appear as functionaries performing functions that government officials regard as indispensable."[8] Business leaders in general, but especially the leaders of major corporate firms, have a double advantage in the country's democracy. With more money, they can afford to hire lobbyists, contribute to campaigns, create organizations, gain access to decision makers, and thereby influence debates about public policy. Even more important, they hold a key structural position—the jobs and income of many Americans depend upon corporate investment strategies and decisions. Consequently, they informally become key partners of government in what might be called a **corporate complex**. When key sectors of the private economy fail spectacularly, as the automobile industry recently did, government may decide to step in to shepherd them back to self-sustaining health. Thus, when Chrysler and General Motors collapsed into bankruptcy in May and June 2009, the government spent over $60 billion, and temporarily took control of General Motors, in order to restore the companies to profitability while also overseeing a process that reduced the wages of automobile workers, laid off a third of the auto industry workforce, and cut the health benefits of retirees as well as current employees. Chrysler and General Motors repaid the government, and by 2012 the companies posted profits of $183 million and $7.6 billion respectively. Even under emergency conditions, these firms were able to shape the terms of their rescue.[9]

One consequence of the close relationship between business and government is that political views are unevenly represented in public debate. Key issues of manifest public significance—such as what to produce, where and how to produce it, and what to do with the resources generated by production—are decided by CEOs, managers, and governing boards with little public discussion, at least until a crisis occurs. The result is a public sphere more limited than the cacophony of debate between liberals and conservatives might suggest. The principle of "majority rule," the centerpiece of representative democracy, often applies to a confined range of questions. Some of the most important issues affecting the welfare of citizens are decided in corporate boardrooms that are well outside the reach of majority rule.

It is impossible to understand the politics of power in the United States without paying attention to the many ways democracy and inequality intertwine to affect virtually every aspect of American life, including economic opportunities across lines of race and gender, the quality of city neighborhoods, the provision of services, the health of the environment, and the scope and character of political choices made by government officials and citizens. These are the issues we place front and center in this critical introduction to American government, which highlights both the exemplary aspects of American political democracy and the recurring problems that distort it to make the country's political system less democratic than it might be.

When we judge American democracy, we have to start with the rights, institutions, and procedures that enable individuals and groups to make their views known and fairly select their leaders and public officials. These include civil liberties, such as freedom of speech, freedom of assembly, freedom of the press, and **civil rights**, including the absence of discriminatory barriers to participation. Without such procedural guarantees, it is extraordinarily difficult for people to formulate and express their interests. We have to consider the structure of government, the character of its institutions, and the mechanisms by which public policy is made. But we also must direct attention to the impact of deep and persistent patterns of inequality and investigate how, and with what consequences, valued features of democracy are affected by disparities in income, wealth, and life chances.

Efforts to assess American democracy by examining how popular influence and control are affected by the uneven distribution of income, wealth, and other assets have produced some of the best work by political scientists on American politics. In 1961, the political scientist Robert Dahl published a brilliant and influential study of politics in New Haven, Connecticut; his book *Who Governs?* has become a classic in political science. By commonly accepted standards, he argued, the city was a democracy. Virtually all of its adult citizens were legally entitled to vote; voters had a choice of candidates, and their votes were honestly counted in free elections. In New Haven, Dahl found that "two political parties contest elections, offer rival slates of candidates, and thus present the voters with at least some outward show of choice." Yet, he observed, although the city's residents were legally equal at the ballot box, they were unequal in other ways that contrasted sharply with their formal political equality. Less than one-sixteenth of the taxpayers owned one-third of the city's property. In the wealthiest ward, one family out of four had an income three times the city average; most of the families in the poorest ward earned under $2,000 per year, or $15,000 today. Only one out of thirty adults in the poorest ward had attended college, in contrast to nearly half of those in the richest ward.[10]

Can this combination of legal equality and class inequality be designated as democratic? Dahl put the question this way: "In a system where nearly every adult may vote but where knowledge, wealth, social position, access to officials, and other resources are unequally distributed, who actually governs? . . . How does a 'democratic' system work amid inequality of resources?"[11] He placed quotation marks around the term *democratic* because its meaning in this situation is unclear. Should a democratic system be measured only by such matters as fair and open elections, or should it be measured by the control and distribution of resources? What, in short, is the relationship between capitalism and democracy?

In New Haven, Dahl was heartened to find that no single elite group made all the city's key political decisions. Rather, different groups determined policy in matters of urban renewal, public education, and the nomination of candidates for office. However, there was one feature that ran across different aspects of New Haven's life. In each area, there was a wide disparity between the ability to make decisions by politically and economically powerful people, on the one hand, and average citizens, on the other. As a result of such disparities, Dahl noted, New Haven was "a long way from achieving the goal of political equality advocated by the philosophers of democracy and incorporated into the creed of democracy and equality practically every American professes to uphold." Nevertheless, he concluded that "New Haven is an example of a democratic system, warts and all."[12]

Like New Haven a half-century ago, the United States can be considered a democracy. But our understanding of American politics would be incomplete and inaccurate if we treated its limitations and flaws as minor or unfortunate exceptions, for these features of American democracy shape the life chances of citizens, the character of communities, and the operation of the country's politics of power. This book not only invites us to think about American democracy in terms of formal rules and rights but also asks whether and when citizens have equal chances to influence and control the making of decisions that affect them. Democratic procedures and institutions are essential to democracy. However, they do not guarantee it. What matters as well is the substance of democracy. The right to free speech is precious. But even in an age when the Internet and its blogs have opened up new means of communication, information can become distorted when those who own the media use it to express their views to millions while most Americans lack the equivalent means to disseminate their opinions to even a few. Political rights, such as the right to vote, are an essential part of any democracy. But these rights are undermined when candidates shape policies favorable to the wealthy, who can provide them with campaign contributions that ordinary citizens cannot afford. Civil liberties are to be cherished. But these are perverted when, for example, some people can afford to hire expensive lawyers to take advantage of the right to a fair trial when others must rely on overworked and underpaid court-appointed attorneys to defend them. The point of these examples is that procedural rights are important, but they are also not enough. A successful working democracy requires (1) widespread participation in decision making, (2) an absence of restrictions on who gets to participate and on the fair terms of their participation, (3) access to relevant and accurate information, (4) inclusive representation of the interests, values, and beliefs of citizens, and (5) patterns of decision making that do not give undue influence to various forms of privilege.

Democracy implies rule by the many, not the privileged few. Effective and extensive citizen involvement in decision making has long been regarded as a centerpiece of democracy. In the famous view of the eighteenth-century French political theorist Jean-Jacques Rousseau, people develop political skills as active citizens when they can exercise real control over how political life is conducted and when they help shape the content of public policy. As the political theorist Carole Pateman put it in her interpretation of Rousseau's *The Social Contract*, "the more the individual citizen participates, the better he is able to do so. . . . He learns to be a public as well as a private citizen."[13]

Direct political participation is much easier to achieve in small groups and settings like juries, town meetings, or face-to-face community organizations than it is in societies as a whole, especially in a society as large and complex as the United States. For this reason, when we gauge whether the interests, values, and beliefs of citizens are present in an inclusive manner, we have to think not only about their ability and propensity to vote in elections, join campaigns, belong to political parties, take part in interest groups, or mobilize as activists in social movements but also about how the country's system of political representation actually works.

It is impossible for all citizens to participate simultaneously in making political and policy decisions. As a result, they depend on having their preferences literally "re-presented" by others inside the political process. This is what happens in legislatures—Congress, state legislatures, and city councils—which are democracy's core institutions. We elect persons who represent our views, who seek to make laws that serve both particular and general interests, and who are periodically judged by their constituents.

As we assess how well representative democracy is working, some key questions come to the fore. First, do the country's representatives—the people who make the laws and decide the policies—reflect the characteristics of the people they formally represent, or is there a systematic bias that limits the presence of representatives based on class, race, ethnicity, sex, or religion? Having a diverse body of representatives is important because the more they reflect the range of the population, the more likely it is that the interests of different types of citizens will be adequately represented. Group members are much more likely than others to vigorously represent their own interests.[14]

Second, are representatives aware of, and responsive to, their constituents' concerns? In practice, ordinary citizens often find it difficult to achieve a representation of their interests, since persons with more resources tend to perceive and promote their own interests more accurately and effectively than those of other citizens. Thus, a key issue in a representative democracy is not who rules, but how those who rule use their power. How well do representatives perceive the preferences of their constituents, and how do they act on their behalf? Further, do they do so effectively?

Third, and broadest, is the question posed by Robert Dahl: "How does a 'democratic' system work amid inequality of resources?" As capitalism and democracy coexist in varied and changing ways, their character and content now, as in the past, are contested. Extreme inequality blocks the full achievement of a fully realized democracy, in which all citizens have equal chances to influence the making of decisions that affect them. In turn, the openness of democratic political life invites and even promotes persistent challenges to the various dimensions of inequality that limit the meaningful scope of political life. By coming to understand the politics of power, we can better grasp the current limits of and opportunities for American democracy.

POLITICAL CHANGE

These issues are not new. They date to the earliest days of the Republic and have taken different form at different moments in American history. Within the ambit of the country's representative democracy, Americans have weighed and debated the proper role for government in the economy, the extent to which inequalities of wealth and income are acceptable, and what, if anything, government should do to manage and limit these differences. The political system has been the focus of great debates about how foreign affairs dovetail with domestic concerns and about who should qualify to be a citizen and who should not. The meaning of federalism (how much power the federal government should have as compared to the states) and the character of the separation of powers (what balance should be struck between the president, Congress, and the Supreme Court) have also been contested. So, too, have the ways capitalism should be managed and regulated by the government, and how the operation of the economy affects the daily lives and opportunities of Americans.

WHAT DO YOU THINK?

Patterns of Political Representation

Before the ratification of the Nineteenth Amendment to the Constitution in 1920, most women could not vote. Before the Voting Rights Act of 1965, most African Americans were excluded from the franchise. These landmark legal changes widened democracy. How important is office holding, in proportion to their numbers in the population, by women, African Americans, and other historically marginalized groups for the democratic potential of voting to be realized?

The particular situations and conditions within which such matters have been debated and resolved have never been constant or static. Each generation confronts these matters in a particular way. Each generation thus must reassess American politics as it grapples with large-scale patterns of change that affect the character and contours of the country's democracy. In the current era, three matters have come to the fore that have dramatically reshaped the character and agenda of American politics. As we explore the politics of power, we need to bear in mind these issues of great significance.

As the Lone Superpower, the United States Confronts a More Interconnected and More Unpredictable World

After the Cold War ended in 1989 and the Soviet Union collapsed in 1991, the United States was left as the only **superpower** in the world. Its military power is unrivaled. The United States has at least one military member present in 148 countries, and hundreds of thousands of American troops equipped with the most advanced weaponry are stationed in over 600 military bases located in 38 countries. In 13 of these locations, more than 1,000 American military personnel are in place.[15] Spending more on defense than the next 15 highest-spending nations combined, the United States has the most technologically sophisticated, best-equipped military in the world. The United States launched the Iraq War on March 20, 2003, and subdued the military forces of Saddam Hussein within weeks. Sophisticated pilotless drone airplanes that no other country possesses have targeted the Taliban and Al-Qaeda in Afghanistan and Pakistan.

The biggest and most powerful military helps serve and protect the biggest and most powerful economy in the world. The United States is the largest national market, home to more leading corporations than any other country. Although it contains just under 5 percent of the world's population, the American economy accounts for about a quarter of the world's gross domestic product (GDP).[16] Even in difficult economic times, the dollar continues to be the principal international medium of exchange, the currency in which the rest of the world does business.

This combined military and economic power underpins the country's extraordinary influence in international affairs. There are few significant places or issues around the world where the United States does not project its power, from sending humanitarian aid to fight against the AIDS epidemic in Africa to negotiating trade agreements with China; from attempting to mediate the Arab-Israeli conflict to sending tens of thousands of troops to Afghanistan;

from confining people designated as enemy combatants to confronting drug smugglers in South America. Yet the more the United States has outdistanced all other rivals, the more it has become clear that world security after the Cold War is difficult to guarantee, that military power alone does not assure the United States will be unchallenged, and that a proper balance between liberty and security is not easy to find. The most visible instances of this uncertainty and vulnerability remain the shockingly successful terrorist attacks on the World Trade Center and Pentagon in September 2001, and the failure of the American occupation of Iraq to bring peace or order to the country over the course of many years. Despite the killing of Osama Bin Laden, the mastermind behind the 9/11 attacks, other key personnel involved in planning the attack and other terrorist actions remain at large; the closing phase of the Iraq War has brought uncertain prospects; and the region encompassing Iran, Afghanistan, and Pakistan remains persistently—even increasingly—dangerous.

In all, the world has become a more complicated stage. There are now more countries with more weapons of mass destruction, including growing nuclear arsenals, which can cause vast damage. Small conflicts now have a greater chance of escalating into larger ones that draw surrounding countries into the turmoil. The threat of terrorism remains and continues to haunt American society. With the nation's economy more integrated with the rest of the world, it is subject not only to deep challenges at home but also to market changes that occur beyond its borders and over which it has little control. Further, the globe faces multiple environmental challenges, including climate changes that threaten crops, livelihoods, and the sustainability of life in some parts of the planet. As the world has become more interdependent, domestic politics has become less insulated than ever before. Throughout American history, the country has been shaped by war and trade; but the scope and velocity of today's movements of people, ideas, money, goods, and weapons across national boundaries are unprecedented. Greater global interdependence increases American power and vulnerability at one and the same time. As a result, the politics of power is not crisply divided between domestic and international affairs. Issues that concern the interplay of democracy and capitalism cannot be confined to domestic politics.

Politics Has Become More Polarized

It used to be a truism of American political life that ideology was muted, that party differences were relatively small. Over the past thirty years, these patterns have been upset, even reversed. The Democratic and Republican parties have increasingly moved apart, both in their mass appeal and in their behavior in

Washington. During this period, more and more Americans have recognized ever starker differences between the conservatism of Republicans and the liberalism of Democrats. More and more voters have become fixed in their partisan positions and ideological preferences, and elections are determined by relatively small shifts in the middle of the spectrum. Many Americans remain disengaged from politics, but those who participate tend to line up reliably on opposing sides.

From the 1910s to the early 1960s, the Democratic Party housed liberal and progressive politicians who supported unions, civil rights, and social equality. It also sheltered the country's leading segregationist politicians from the South, where Jim Crow defined the law of the land. The Republican Party likewise was quite heterogeneous; it included internationally minded, relatively liberal members and isolationist, more conservative party leaders. But conservative Democrats and moderate Republicans have become endangered political species. The most significant cause of these developments has been the partisan realignment of the South since the 1960s. Although the South was once solidly Democratic in its voting patterns, today it usually votes Republican in national elections and, increasingly, in local contests as well. This leveling of the party landscape, such that neither party holds an overwhelming national mandate anymore, has resulted in increased partisan combat, which in turn has produced over the past few decades less civility, more party unity, and less willingness to compromise.

This gulf has been shaped by divisions of class and race, gender and culture. In 1956 and 1960, those in the top income quintile were only slightly more likely than those in the bottom quintile to identify themselves as Republicans; today they are more than twice as likely to do so. American politics is even more sharply divided by race. With the mass departure of southern whites from the Democratic Party after Congress passed civil rights legislation in the 1960s, the majority of the country's white voters became reliably Republican. By contrast, African Americans, Latinos, and Asian-Pacific Americans support Democratic candidates by significant margins, especially in national elections. Black voters in particular rarely give less than 80 or 90 percent of their votes to Democrats. In recent elections, the divide in voting preferences by men and women has been stark, with women more often voting Democratic. There has also been a growing religious division in the electorate. Evangelical Protestants heavily tilt Republican. Mainline Protestants and Catholics are closely divided. Jews and secular persons heavily lean Democratic.[17]

Both as a cause and as a reflection of these developments, differences *within* the parties have gotten smaller at the same time as differences *between* the parties have become larger. The Republican triumph in 1994, in which, led by Newt Gingrich, the party took back control of the House, brought into the fold committed conservatives who sought to govern on the basis of a common platform they called the Contract with America. The return of the House to the Democratic Party's control in 2006 was part of a strong liberal tilt that was reinforced in 2008, only to be changed once again when the Republicans regained control of the House in the 2010 elections.[18] Votes in Congress today are more divided between the two parties than at any time in the past six decades; liberals are grouped almost exclusively in the Democratic Party and conservatives in the Republican Party.

Economic Crises Returned, Calling into Question Both the Virtues of Markets and the Promise of Government

During the Great Depression of the 1930s, the New Deal program dealt with the collapse of many industries and widespread unemployment by transforming the role of government and extending its reach into the economy. As markets failed, they were resurrected by bold legislation and public programs. As a result, many Americans came to think increasingly of the federal government as their ally in creating a more fair society in which people had economic opportunity and were cushioned against disaster. For the four decades that followed, democracy and capitalism learned to coexist on terms that extended the scope of governmental responsibility.

The election of Ronald Reagan as president in 1980, after a decade of economic difficulties culminating in high inflation rates, signaled the triumph of a more conservative ideology that called the role of big government into question.

WHAT DO YOU THINK?

Is Political Conflict Damaging to the Public Interest?

In 1950, a committee of the American Political Science Association criticized American political parties for being too alike and insufficiently committed to distinctive ideologies that could act as a check on one another and provide the public a true choice in policy decisions. Today, politics has become more polarized between Democrats and Republicans, liberals and conservatives. There is concern that this polarization places politics ahead of a search for the public interest. Who has the better argument—the advocates of more or less polarization?

Four years before the election, Robert Bartley, then in charge of the editorial page of the politically conservative *Wall Street Journal*, observed that liberalism as an "establishment . . . has ordered our political and intellectual lives for the past two generations." He predicted that "over the next few years we will see an increasing challenge to the very heart of liberal . . . thinking."[19] The new ideology that Bartley and other conservative intellectuals advocated, as a distinctly minority position, was thought to be well outside the political mainstream. It held that government should do less, not more; that government should be smaller, not bigger; that more decisions should be left to the marketplace, not elected officials; and that society should provide more opportunity, not more equality. After 1980, President Reagan drew on the ideas of a new generation of conservative intellectuals to implement this design for a more modest government and more reliance on the marketplace. As a result of the Reagan revolution, conservatives came to set the main terms of public debate. The political center shifted to the right. Democrats, including President Bill Clinton, also invoked the virtues of smaller government, balanced budgets, and the marketplace. President George W. Bush and the Republican Party invoked these ideas and successfully appealed to a strong belief in the virtues of markets as they gained control over all three branches of government following the 2002 and 2004 elections.

The huge global crisis of 2008 and the slump in economic performance that followed called into question the ideology and practice of a less regulated capitalism. Even some of the most notable advocates of free-market capitalism had second thoughts. Alan Greenspan, who served as chairman of the Federal Reserve from 1987 to 1996 and who had been one of the country's most articulate and important advocates of a smaller role for government and reduced regulation, found himself "in a state of shocked disbelief" that caused him to rethink his free-market ideology. Asked during congressional testimony in October 2008 whether "your view of the world, your ideology, was not right . . . was not working," he replied, "absolutely, precisely. . . . I have found a flaw [in that view]. . . . I have been very distressed by that fact."[20] Late in the Bush administration, and especially in the early period of the Obama presidency, government was called on to save the banking system, restore faith in Wall Street, stimulate the economy by massive public-works spending, and initiate new ways to regulate reckless and speculative economic behavior.

Big government—as an idea and as a set of public policies—had returned. If the pro-market ideology of the past three decades had been a response to what were seen as failures of heavy-handed policies and bloated bureaucracies, the financial collapse and steep recession that began in 2008 undercut the idea that markets on their own can effectively correct themselves. And the administration of President

Obama proposed an active role for the federal government in protecting the environment and regulating the banking industry, as well as reshaping and extending the system of health care in the United States. But the return of a strong role for government came with doubts and uncertainties about its capacities, programs, and choices. Both the polarized political system and public opinion divided sharply over whether policy makers should advance large-scale changes or shore up an older system. There was much disagreement about whether strong regulation of business helped or hindered the economy and the creation of jobs. Americans also debated whether tax policies should aim to reduce inequality and how new laws might transform the character of American capitalism. In all, Americans argued about the links that connect capitalism and democracy.

CONCLUSION

The tension between democracy and capitalism, the manner in which formal, legal equality and real, substantive inequality interact, is the principal subject of this book. Capturing how the interplay of democracy and capitalism shape the politics of the United States is its task.

In Part I, "American Political Economy," we consider the close relationship between the national government and the country's market economy at a time of growing economic globalization. We do so in Chapters 2 and 3 by examining the changing role of government in advancing, regulating, and counteracting market forces.

Part II, "Political Participation," analyzes how citizens interact with their government. Chapter 4, treating parties and elections, studies polarization and new patterns of electoral mobilization, as well as the strategies used to affect outcomes. Interest groups and social movements are the subjects of Chapter 5, which analyzes how associations and patterns of activity in civil society shape American politics and open possibilities for change.

Having described how political preferences are transmitted to policy makers, Part III, "Political Institutions," turns in Chapters 6, 7, and 8 to the interplay of political economy, political culture, and political participation in the institutional settings of the presidency, Congress, and the courts.

Part IV, "Public Policy," treats the public-policy outcomes that these processes produce. Chapters 9, 10, and 11 reflect, respectively, on economic, social, and foreign policy. Finally, our conclusion, Chapter 12, reviews the main points of the text and discusses possible futures for American politics and society.

CHAPTER SUMMARY

Introduction

Like the *Titanic*, the United States has different social classes. The capitalist market economy has produced economic progress and much prosperity, but also a significant degree of poverty and disparities in wealth and income that are wider than those found in other economically developed countries.

Constitutional Democracy: The Founding

The United States is a constitutional democracy, a form of government that is designed to prevent public authorities from acting in arbitrary ways and that is based on formal procedures for electing officials, making laws, and implementing policies. American democracy guarantees citizens the right to vote, to participate in political debate, to criticize leaders, and to mobilize and organize for desired ends. Key questions are how American government and politics either reinforce or modify the country's patterns of inequality in wealth and income, and which citizens have more power to influence these outcomes.

Standards of Democracy

American democracy can be judged by a number of criteria. First is the extent to which all citizens can participate in selecting leaders and making decisions. Second is whether elected officials reflect the characteristics of the people who select them. Third is whether these leaders are responsive to the concerns of their constituents. Fourth is how democracy reduces the inequalities that make it difficult for citizens to have equal chances to wield influence.

Political Change

The character of American democracy is not static; it is vitally affected by large-scale change. Three recent changes have reshaped the content of American politics: as the lone superpower, the United States confronts a more interconnected and more unpredictable world; politics has become more polarized; and with the return of economic crises, both the virtues of markets and the promise of government have been called into question. In light of these circumstances, the book probes the following questions about the politics of power: How do deep inequalities affect the operation of American democracy? When does democracy heighten these disparities, and when does it become a tool to moderate these differences among its citizens?

Critical Thinking Questions

1. How much inequality based on class, race, or gender is consistent with democracy?

2. Does citizenship include only civil and political rights, or does it also contain social rights, such as a minimum standard of health? If so, what are other such social rights bestowed by citizenship?

3. Should we think about power as the capacity of some to get others to do what they want, or as the ability of the whole society to achieve goals citizens have in common?

Suggested Readings

Larry M. Bartels, *Unequal Democracy: The Political Economy of the New Gilded Age.* Princeton, NJ: Princeton University Press, 2008.

Robert A. Dahl, *Democracy and Its Critics.* New Haven, CT: Yale University Press, 1989.

Robert A. Dahl, *On Democracy.* New Haven, CT: Yale University Press, 1998.

Charles E. Lindblom, *Politics and Markets.* New York: Basic Books, 1977.

Nolan McCarty, Keith T. Poole, and Howard Rosenthal, *Polarized America: The Dance of Ideology and Unequal Riches.* Cambridge, MA: MIT Press, 2006.

Carole Pateman, *Participation and Democratic Theory.* New York: Cambridge University Press, 1970.

PART I

AMERICAN POLITICAL ECONOMY

n the 1960s, Flint, Michigan was a prosperous town. General Motors (GM), the world's largest corporation at the time, employed over 40,000 workers in auto plants throughout the city. Flint and GM were so entwined that roads in town bore such names as Chevrolet Highway and Buick Freeway in tribute to two of GM's automotive divisions. Work on the GM assembly lines in Flint was hard, but the union, the United Automobile Workers (UAW), helped to ensure that workers were rewarded for their efforts.[1] In 1969, average earnings in Genesee County, where Flint is located, were roughly $2,000 above those in the rest of Michigan and $7,000 higher than the average income throughout the United States.[2] Unemployment was low and poverty was negligible. In one of the first quality-of-urban-life surveys ever conducted, Flint ranked 18th out of 66 medium-sized cities.

Fast-forward to 1980. In that year, Flint led the nation's cities in joblessness with an unemployment rate of 20.7 percent. Unemployment in Flint remained twice as high as in the rest of Michigan throughout the decade. By the turn of the century, in 2000, Flint led almost all metropolitan areas nationwide in terms of jobs lost.

As jobs disappeared, so did people. Flint's population fell from 190,000 in 1970 to 125,000 in 2000. Depopulation left its mark on Flint as once proud, stable neighborhoods were defaced by abandoned buildings and dilapidated housing. Public services declined. The city was beset by the indignities of poverty, unemployment, crime, and urban decay. Flint ranked dead last in *Money Magazine's* 1987 quality-of-life survey of 300 cities.[3]

What transformed Flint from one of the most pleasant to one of the least attractive cities in the country? The answer can be summed up in two words: General Motors. Beginning in the 1980s, GM decided to disinvest, closing factories and moving product lines out of the city. GM closed plants in Flint not out of malevolence, but because its share of the U.S. auto market tumbled—from 46 percent in 1980 to just 28 percent by 2002. GM lost market share because

A shuttered GM plant in Flint, Michigan.

it responded too late to the challenge of more efficient cars imported from Japan, experienced turmoil within the ranks of its board of directors, had the worst labor relations of the Big Three car companies, had greater administrative overhead than any of its competitors, and pursued an expensive and failed strategy of replacing workers with robots.

The documentary filmmaker Michael Moore, who grew up in Flint, left home in the 1970s to pursue a career in journalism and filmmaking. When he returned to Flint years later, he found a city on its knees. To capture and explain Flint's demise, Moore went looking for the person whose decisions helped produce the tragedy afflicting his beloved hometown. He did not go looking for the mayor of Flint or the city council. Nor did he go looking for the governor of Michigan or any other public official. Instead, he went looking for Roger Smith, the chairman and CEO of General Motors. Moore believed that decisions made by GM had more consequences for the city than any action taken by any public official. Moore's film *Roger & Me* (1990) provides a graphic and tragicomic description of how Flint's dependence on its corporate sponsor led to the city's ruin and portrays Moore's futile attempt to impress on Roger Smith the tragic consequences that GM's plant closures had on Flint and its citizens.[4]

But Roger Smith's decision to close plants in Flint was not the result of venality or callousness on his part. GM's decisions were dictated more by the imperatives of profit-seeking in a capitalist economy than by the moral character of management. The costs that GM's decisions imposed on Flint and its citizens were invisible from the perspective of GM's balance sheet. They were an unfortunate, unintended by-product of management's attempt to maximize earnings. The movie ends with Roger Smith presiding over a lavish Christmas celebration in Detroit while Moore is back in Flint filming the sheriff evicting another family from its home during the holiday season.

The story of GM, and its relationship with Flint and GM autoworkers, persisted long after Michael Moore produced *Roger & Me*. GM continued to decline throughout the new century; its market share has now dipped below 20 percent. From a peak of 80,000 GM workers employed in Flint in 1970, only 5,000 were left by 2008. The effects on Flint have been devastating. According to the 2010 census, this once prosperous city of 200,000 had shrunk to almost half its size, with only 102,000 citizens. A quarter of its families live in poverty. Foreclosures and abandoned homes were so numerous that the city began a process of planned shrinkage that involved demolishing whole neighborhoods. People would be congregated in the areas that remained viable so that city services could be concentrated among them, and the rest of the city would be left to return to nature.[5] By 2009, over 1,000 abandoned homes had been demolished, and plans had been made to tear down 3,000 more. One union leader poignantly captured the sense of neglect and depletion that went far beyond mere plant closures in Flint when he said, "People talk about closing a plant. We closed a city here."[6]

As Flint receded so did its tax base. In 2012, it was $25 million in debt and was placed in receivership by Michigan's governor, Rick Snyder. This meant that powers formerly wielded by elected officials would now be exercised by an appointed Emergency Manager, who proceeded to increase taxes and cut city services. Even worse than the specific policies imposed on Flint, perhaps the greatest indignity was that Flint had lost the right to rule itself. Flint's citizens protested that they were now the victims of taxation without representation. An unelected, unaccountable manager now ruled Flint, rendering their votes meaningless and their elected city officials powerless.

Analyzing how GM controlled the fate of Flint illuminates basic features of the way power is exercised in the United States. Part I of *The Politics of Power* examines the **political economy** of the United States, that is, the interaction between the economy and government. Chapter 2 highlights the impact that corporations, such as GM, have on politics. Chapter 3 provides a history of the American political economy, analyzes government's role in sustaining capitalism, and describes the sometimes tense, sometimes smooth relationship between political and economic power.

CAPITALISM AND DEMOCRACY

INTRODUCTION

This chapter explores the contrast between America's political and economic systems. Whereas democratic procedures govern the political sphere, they are largely absent from the economic sphere; and whereas equality typifies political relations, inequality epitomizes the economic sphere.

The American economic system is organized along capitalist lines. That is, business is privately owned and produces commodities for sale on the market. Firms produce goods and services for sale in the hope of achieving the greatest return on their investment, that is, profit. To earn profits, firms must outcompete their rivals in the marketplace. The competitive drive for profits requires firms to become more efficient and explore new markets, making capitalism dynamic and innovative.

A production system based on markets is decentralized and largely self-regulating. No central institution directs the process. The exchange between buyers and sellers is voluntary. But markets are never wholly free, nor do they order themselves. They always require states to create rules that structure markets so that creativity and investments will pay off. Consider, for example, the board game "Monopoly." Players are given money to buy, sell, and trade different properties. Now consider playing "Monopoly" if there were no rules stipulating what happens when you land on someone else's property; no rules about how you can build houses and hotels to increase the value of your property; or no rules about how you can mortgage your property to raise cash. "Monopoly" is unplayable without rules. Similarly, market freedom requires state compulsion in order to thrive. The visible hand of the state is required for the invisible hand of the market to work.

A final characteristic of capitalism, alongside firms seeking profits through production for the market, is wage labor. While a small proportion of people obtain income through owning a business, most people earn their living by working for others—by selling their labor to employers in exchange for a wage. Unlike feudalism, where peasants were tied to a lord's domain, capitalism allows workers to contract for work with any employer. This shift from the former to the latter represented a real increase in freedom, but it also obscured a necessity. Unless workers found a buyer for their labor, they had no means of supporting themselves. As Adam Smith—an 18th-century economist who was a passionate advocate of capitalism—acknowledged, "Many workmen could not subsist a week, few could subsist a month, and scarce any subsist a year without employment."[1]

Capitalism, the system based on private ownership of the means of production, on wage labor, and on production for the market, has proved remarkably dynamic, productive, innovative, and efficient. It has vanquished its rivals, such as communist planned economies, which involved centralized and authoritarian control of the economy by the state. Capitalism was nimble, while planned economies were all thumbs. In 1990, the average citizen's living standard in the former Soviet Union—the United States' communist rival during the Cold War—was one-third that of the average American's. The Soviet Union lost the Cold War not on the battlefield but in the war of production between planned economies and market-based capitalism. Capitalism has been so successful that there are few alternatives to it anymore, and those that do exist, such as the economies of North Korea and Cuba, are hardly models that other countries want to emulate.

THE DILEMMAS OF MARKETS

Market-based production is a superb mechanism for encouraging innovation, promoting efficiency, and increasing productivity. These are desirable by-products of competition among business firms to reduce their costs of production, thereby enabling them to lower prices, increase profits, and expand market shares. However, the same factor that accounts for the dynamism of capitalism—the search for profits—also produces undesirable outcomes that undermine, as opposed to promote, public interests. Market systems have their benefits, but they also have their dark side.

For example, capitalist market systems are volatile. Capitalism's dynamism, its revolutionary thrust, is also the source of its instability. Supply and demand are not coordinated. Investment, production, and consumption fail to maintain balance. Consequently, business cycles occur in which periods of economic growth measured by output, employment, and profits are followed by periods of contraction in which production declines, unemployment increases, and bankruptcies rise. Each period of expansion and contraction is pregnant with the conditions that produce its opposite. Just as a recession sets the stage for a new period of profitable investment by weeding out inefficient firms, expansion creates the conditions for contraction by promoting overproduction.

A recent example of volatility and the wrath of business cycles is, of course, the Great Recession that began in 2008. Housing prices rose throughout the beginning of the twenty-first century, as people rushed to take advantage of rising property values. But when investors became skeptical of the values underlying the mortgage securities they bought, the money to finance new mortgages dried up. Housing prices began to plummet. Just as rising demand for houses had once pushed prices higher, now a glut of unsold homes created momentum in the opposite direction, causing housing prices to fall. The pricking of the housing bubble then set off the deepest and most prolonged downturn since the Great Depression of the 1930s. Banks failed, firms closed, and people lost their homes and their jobs. Such tragedies have social costs. When plants are idle and workers are unemployed, vital resources that could be employed productively are wasted. But market volatility has more personal, more intimate costs that can't be measured by unemployment statistics or bankruptcies alone. When markets move capriciously, people feel they do not control their own fate, which contributes to feelings of powerlessness and insecurity.

Another drawback of capitalism is that its constant need to increase production and consumption collides with the realities of a world that has finite resources and fragile ecosystems. Capitalism suffers from "affluenza," which is defined as an unsustainable addiction to economic growth that threatens to strain and overwhelm the environment.[2] The environment has enough problems sustaining affluence among developed countries like the United States. But with less developed countries wanting to become affluent, too—by increasing their per capita GDP the same way we do—the world's ecosystem will be overwhelmed. Citizens in developing countries, of course, are entitled to enjoy the benefits of development as much as Americans do. But if everyone were to catch up to American rates of consumption, the economic geographer Larry Diamond estimates it "would be as if the world population ballooned to 72 billion people," which is 64 billion more than it has now.[3]

A third problem with capitalist production is its tendency to create harmful spillover effects, or what economists call "**externalities.**" These are costs that firms create but taxpayers and individuals pay for. For instance, the spectacular profits of the energy industry don't take into account the costs of climate change due to the greenhouse gases that energy companies produce. One estimate calculated the overall costs and risks of climate change equivalent "to losing at least 5% of global GDP each year, now and forever."[4] Utilities create air pollution that contributes to respiratory diseases, lung cancer, asthma, and emphysema. But the cost of doctor visits and hospital admissions to treat these ailments is not charged against corporate profits but rather ends up being paid by individuals and taxpayers. Finally, the bets that aggressive traders on Wall Street make, according to Jacob S. Hacker and Paul Pierson, "create huge risks for the economy as a whole. Yet, these risks are largely not taken into account in the prices paid in financial markets."[5] In all these circumstances, business's financial statement looks better but society's balance sheet looks worse.

Capitalism also comes into conflict with the public interest when profits create incentives that divert business from meeting public needs. What is profitable for individual companies may not also be rewarding to society. Pharmaceutical companies, for example, have an interest in developing products for consumers who can afford to purchase them but have no interest in meeting public needs for which they cannot obtain adequate profits. Consequently, pharmaceutical companies develop more profitable "copycat" drugs that are similar to those already on the market as opposed to new drugs that could address more pressing and life-threatening medical needs. Or take the example of efforts in the recent recession to help homeowners who faced foreclosure renegotiate their mortgages so they could stay in their homes. The government allocated $75 billion in assistance to help homeowners stave off foreclosure. However, many mortgage companies were reluctant to help strapped homeowners because they collect lucrative fees from delinquent loans. The New York Times reported that "[e]ven when borrowers stop paying, mortgage companies that service the loans collect fees out of the proceeds when homes are ultimately sold in foreclosure. So the longer the borrowers remain delinquent, the greater the opportunities for these mortgage companies to extract revenues."[6] The behavior of these firms makes perfect sense from the point of view of their profits. But it makes no sense from the point of view of the wider community's welfare.

Finally, capitalism justifies an inherently undemocratic form of production. Employers have the right to hire and fire, set wages and salaries, and tell workers what to do and how to do it because they own and control the means of production. The workplace is an authoritarian political system in which employers rule. The only protections workers have from the unilateral power of management are government regulations and collective-bargaining agreements, if they are lucky enough to belong to a union. Consider the simple case of using the restroom. College students think nothing of getting up in the middle of class to go to the bathroom. Imagine the outcry if faculty announced that students could not leave class to do so and that those who did would be penalized with reduced grades or even dismissal from the course! Yet such restrictions apply frequently at work. No federal law requires supervisors to allow workers to take a restroom break. Management can restrict the number of restroom trips employees make, regulate their duration, specify when they will occur, and penalize workers for violating these rules.[7]

Employers, of course, make more important decisions than regulating workers' trips to the bathroom. Those who own and control the means of production decide what to produce, where production should take place, and how it should occur. This is especially true of large corporations who play an outsize role in the economy. As we will see shortly, a small number of large corporations account for much of the entire American economy's output. For this reason, we refer to these corporations as *private governments*. They are *private* in the sense that those who own and control them—the financial resources, factories, machines, offices, and raw materials used to produce commodities for sale—are not elected by the public through democratic procedures. The public does not get to vote on, for example, where corporate factories and offices are located, how their profits are invested, or how their workers are deployed. Political parties and candidates do not offer different views on these issues for voters to consider. They are off the table, not debated politically, because we have turned these issues over to private corporations to decide. But these corporations resemble *governments* because their decisions on these issues have profound consequences for the public. More than almost any action taken by government, the decisions corporations make regarding whether to invest, where to invest, and how work should be organized affect people's lives and their communities. Just ask the people in Flint.

Some people argue that capitalists, far from being powerful, are themselves slaves to the marketplace. The consumer is king, not the capitalist. If capitalists do not produce what consumers want, their businesses will fail. A consumer democracy rules. All must bow to the market, even large corporations. Just ask General Motors, which used to be the largest corporation in the world but due to declining market share and profits had to be bailed out by the government.

But there are several problems with this argument. First, the marketplace is not a democracy where everyone has an equal vote. In the political arena, one person is entitled to one vote. In the market, one dollar equals one vote, permitting the affluent to cast more votes than the poor. Consumer democracy violates the principle of political equality and replaces it with a new principle whereby votes are distributed according to the size of someone's wallet. Second, consumers may register their unequal number of votes when it comes to their preferences for specific products on the market. But they do not vote on where production takes place, how it is organized, or where profits are invested. These decisions are made behind the backs of consumers in corporate boardrooms. Finally, business spends enormous amounts of money on advertising and marketing to shape consumer preferences. Consumers enjoy the illusion of democratic choice in a marketplace that is contrived and manipulated.

The marketplace is not a consumer democracy. To the contrary, corporations have extraordinary influence over the entire political economy. The day-to-day strategic decisions corporations make affect the fate of local communities such as Flint and, in the case of reckless banks and an irresponsible financial sector, the entire nation. Such strategic decisions include where to invest, what to invest in, and how to organize production. These decisions, which have extensive consequences for society and every citizen's well-being, are the prerogative of capitalists because they own and control the means of production. A fuller picture of capitalism as a system of private government can be gained by analyzing the rights conferred on capitalists by their control of capital.

Whether to Invest

Investment decisions by industrial corporations and financial institutions—investment banks, stockbrokers, private-equity firms, and hedge funds—determine the level of goods and services produced in the United States. When investment lags, production slows, wages stagnate, and employment declines. When investment booms, production grows, jobs increase, and wages rise as employers compete for workers.

With society dependent upon the level of business investment that creates jobs, citizens tend to identify their personal welfare with the welfare of business. It appears as if the interests of business and society are aligned and consistent with each other. Hence all the talk from both Democrats and Republicans about reviving the American economy by meeting the needs of "job creators," the business community. In his 2011 State of the Union address, President Obama tried to sell his jobs proposal, which included tax breaks for business, by proclaiming, "For everyone who speaks so passionately about making life easier for job creators, this plan's for you."[8] His Republican opponent in the 2012 election, Mitt Romney, was not to be outdone, promising that his plan to reduce tax rates would encourage job creators, who would then put unemployed Americans back to work.

At one level, Obama and Romney are right: business is the goose that lays the golden eggs. And if you want the goose to produce, business demands you provide it with the right incentives: lower labor costs, lower taxes, and fewer regulations so that it will invest, create jobs, and keep the wheels of commerce turning. When Charles Wilson, the president of GM, was appointed by President Eisenhower in 1953 to become Secretary of Defense, he was asked at his nomination hearings by a member of the Senate Armed Services Committee whether he would be able to make a decision against GM in his new capacity as head of the Defense Department. Wilson replied famously that he could not conceive of such a situation because "[w]hat is good for General Motors is good for the U.S. and vice-versa." While this is not so much the case today as it was sixty years ago, when GM was the largest corporation in the world, the logic of his statement still holds. If corporations, like GM, don't make money and invest, the American economy suffers and unemployment ensues. This connection between corporate profits and a strong economy helps explain the widespread support for capitalism in the United States, a view that does not simply result from ideological manipulation but has a rational, objective basis.

But the interests of citizens are opposed to business as much as they are aligned with it. Just as it is rational for people to perceive their interests as consistent with business, it is equally rational for them to define their interests against it. A paradox is at work: their jobs may depend on the profits of their firm, but, perversely, sustaining those profits comes at the expense of their welfare. For business to make higher profits, workers must accept lower wages; agree to pay higher taxes so that business can pay less; and reduce regulations that protect the environment and ensure product safety so that business can lower its costs. The wealth creators have interests that diverge from those of the job creators. Workers in Flint recognized the horns of this dilemma when, in the midst of GM's crisis, they joked, "The only thing worse than working for General Motors is not working for General Motors."

One way Americans resolve this paradox is by generally supporting capitalist values, such as individualism and minimum state interference, only in the abstract. When asked about specific government programs to assist the poor, Americans tend to express broad approval for such activities. The political scientist Elizabeth Sanders writes that "whatever their reservations about government power," non-elite Americans "have shared a powerful belief in community, collective action, and the government's responsibility to remedy market 'defects.'"[9] Even during the heyday of conservatism in the 1980s, when Republican presidents Ronald Reagan and George H. W. Bush were regularly denouncing the sins of big government, large majorities of the public continued to support social programs like Social Security.

Where to Invest

In a capitalist system, corporate leaders are free to decide where they will locate their facilities. Business firms take into account such factors as proximity to suppliers, raw materials, and markets when they decide where to locate an office or factory. They try to choose sites that will minimize costs and maximize sales. Corporations also consider whether the local community is sympathetic to their needs. Consequently, states and local governments compete with each other by offering tax exemptions, loans, property tax abatements, free services, anti-union laws, and weak environmental regulations to attract investment and the jobs it brings.[10] Taxpayers are, in many instances, subsidizing business expenses in order to attract investment. For example, in 2000 Mississippi beat other states in attracting a Nissan plant that would employ 5,300 people by offering the company over $377 million in incentives—or over $83,000 per job the Nissan facility was expected to create. One 2012 study found that Texas led the nation by providing businesses with $19 billion a year in incentives, while Oklahoma and West Virginia offered incentives to businesses that were equal to one-third of their entire state budget.[11] According to one analyst, "State and local governments give away seventy billion dollars annually in tax breaks and subsidies in order to lure (or keep) companies. The strategies make sense for local communities keen to generate new jobs, but, from a national perspective, since they usually just reward companies moving from one state to another, they're simply giveaways."[12]

This is exactly what happened in the case of Curt Schilling, a former major-league baseball pitcher who had an illustrious career with the Philadelphia Phillies, Arizona Diamondbacks, and Boston Red Sox but saved his best pitch in retirement for the Governor of Rhode Island. In 2011, Schilling moved his company that produced computer games from Massachusetts to Rhode Island in return for $475 million in loan guarantees from the Ocean State. According to Schilling's agreement with Rhode Island, the more jobs his firm, 38 Studios, created, the more access to the loan guarantees it would receive. Shilling's company proceeded to hire more workers in order to get access to loans guaranteed by the state, but the company hardly had any product to sell. By 2012, 350 people were on staff, but with hardly any revenues coming in the door, 38 Studios missed payroll, could not pay its vendors, and had to file for bankruptcy, leaving Rhode Island to pay off $112 million in loans it guaranteed to the company's lenders.[13]

Ironically, tax abatements, loan guarantees, and other financial incentives to attract corporate investment may actually retard local economic development instead of promoting it. The loss of tax revenue may leave communities without enough money to support basic services and amenities that make it attractive to homeowners and other potential businesses. After an exhaustive analysis of these incentives, the political scientist Peter Eisenger concluded, "The positive effects of such incentives have not been established incontrovertibly, and there are even potentially perverse effects."[14]

Corporations that produce technical and specialized goods have to consider the skills of local workers when they decide where to locate. But if highly skilled and specialized labor is not required, corporations also consider how compliant a workforce is and how easy it would be to avoid unions. In 2010, Toyota closed its unionized plant in California that made Corollas and opened a new, non-union plant to build them in Mississippi. While the Midwest rust belt has bled automaking jobs recently—Michigan alone accounting for 40 percent of the net job loss in the industry since 2003—southern states with so-called right-to-work laws, which discourage union organizing, have fared much better. Alabama and Mississippi have actually added auto-manufacturing jobs as the industry as a whole has contracted, while Tennessee and Kentucky have held steady. Two labor economists attribute the southern migration of auto-manufacturing jobs to the "low-cost land and labor" in Dixie, where states "promote more flexible labor regulations and do not appear to have strong union sentiment."[15]

But corporations can consider not only the fifty states but the whole world when deciding where to build their offices and factories. They can invest offshore and set up call centers in India, assembly plants in China, and research facilities in Europe. For example, from 1920 to 1950 the textile industry moved from New England to the South, which offered tax incentives, lower wages, and an anti-union climate to firms that relocated. But in a trend beginning in the 1960s and continuing to the present, those same firms left the South to invest in poor, developing countries that offered still lower wages, more subsidies, and a more anti-union climate than even southern states could offer.

An alternative to offshore production is outsourcing, which occurs when companies contract out production overseas to other companies that used to be done, or could be done, in-house in the U.S. Take the case of Apple. It employs only 43,000 people nationally, but it outsources work to companies in Asia that employ over 700,000 workers to produce and assemble iPads, iPhones, and other Apple products. During the 2012 presidential campaign, Democrats and Republicans traded charges over outsourcing. Obama accused Romney of outsourcing jobs as a way to make profits while he was head of the private-equity firm Bain Capital, while Romney charged Obama with sending stimulus money to firms that used it to create jobs overseas.

What to Invest In

Investment decisions also determine the kinds of goods available in society. As with other business decisions, companies decide to invest in what they judge will be most profitable. For example, pharmaceutical companies devote more resources to devising medications for relatively harmless ailments for consumers in affluent countries than to creating drugs to treat or prevent tropical diseases found among low-income groups in the global South. In one instance, researchers accidentally found the cure for sleeping sickness, a fatal disease prevalent in Africa. But it was unprofitable for pharmaceutical companies to produce the antidote because so few people who suffered from the disease in Africa could afford to buy it. However, the patent holder resumed production when it was discovered that the medicine could prevent the growth of facial hair on women. It then became profitable to produce the drug and market it as a cosmetic to women in the West as opposed to a lifesaving drug in Africa.[16] Talent and money are diverted to develop drugs that have commercial as opposed to medical value. One study found that two-thirds of new drugs were simply modified versions of existing drugs that did not provide significant benefits over those already on the market.[17] The development of "copycat" drugs hardly qualifies as a medical breakthrough, but it is more profitable to invest in them than in new areas of medical research whose results are uncertain but may also be more medically useful.

How Production Is Organized

New recruits at a Springfield, Arkansas, poultry plant receive orientation in a classroom with a prominently displayed sign: "Democracies depend on the political participation of its citizens, but not in the workplace." The sign is printed in Spanish and English, "but the message is clear in any language."[18]

The political structure of the workplace is very different from the democratic rules that govern the political arena. Employers decide who will be hired, fired, and promoted; what tasks employees will perform; and what kind of technology will be utilized. The British historian R. H. Tawney put it this way: "[T]he man who employs, governs. . . . He occupies what is really a public office. He has power, not of pit and gallows . . . but of overtime and short-time, full bellies and empty bellies, health and sickness."[19]

Management seeks to fully control the process of production because profits depend on how efficiently labor can be managed. While executives want to manage workers and design work so as to increase productivity and lower production costs, their employees want to conserve their energy and preserve their autonomy. Consequently, a tug of war ensues in which capitalists try to exert control over the labor process in order to maximize production, while workers try to deflect it in order to maximize their freedom at work. One way workers resist the power of management over their work lives is by forming labor unions. Collective-bargaining agreements between employers and unions often include work rules that restrict management's power on the shop floor and in offices. The contract signed by unions and employers is the rule of law at work, setting limits on what would otherwise be the unilateral power of management. Workers have also exercised their power as citizens to enact laws that limit the power of employers at work. Laws require employers to meet safety standards; pay minimum wages; limit hours; not discriminate in hiring, firing, and promotions; and not interfere in union-organizing drives. But in recent years, unions have grown weaker. Fewer workers are covered by collective-bargaining agreements, and enforcement of workplace standards has become lax. The result, according to two labor experts, is that private employers in the United States "have more authority in deciding how to treat their workers than do employers in other advanced countries."[20]

THE STRUCTURAL ADVANTAGE OF BUSINESS

The decisions made by business firms—whether to invest, where to invest, what to invest in, and how to organize production—are usually regarded as private. Congress does not consider them, and they do not appear on the political agenda. Yet, because they deeply affect the entire society, they are preeminently political. Their consequences are wide, including the entire nation, and deep, influencing the quality of our lives.

American democracy is truncated when the most important decisions are off the table, beyond the reach of government. Instead, decisions that have profound consequences for the entire community—from the anguish of Flint to the affluence of Silicon Valley—are decided by business, which is unaccountable and guided by profit. As the political economist Charles Lindblom observed, "Because public functions in the market system rest in the hands of businessmen, it follows that jobs, prices, production, growth, the standard of living, and the economic security of everyone all rest in their hands."[21] The New York Times provided a vivid illustration of Lindblom's point when it reported, in the midst of an economic slump during President George W. Bush's first term, "that the course of the American economy . . . rests with corporate managers.

The choices they make about . . . fresh investments in factories, computers, telecommunications equipment and other capital goods will go a long way in determining whether the United States limps along at a modest rate of growth or restores itself to robust economic health."[22]

The party in office changed but the economic strategy was still the same when President Obama took office in 2008. Vice President Joseph Biden's chief economist, Jared Bernstein, explained the Obama administration's approach to reducing unemployment in the midst of a deep recession: "We have to help stoke the private-sector engine of job growth. Government cannot by itself create the employment necessary to fully offset the millions of jobs lost. What we can do is help to create the conditions fertile for robust hiring by the private sector."[23] During the 2008 recession, economists, business executives, talk-show hosts, and citizens eagerly scrutinized reports of business investment, hiring, and sales for clues about where the country was heading. These were far more important indicators of whether unemployment was abating and the recession was lifting than any statistic about government.

Because society depends on what only capitalists can deliver, and capitalists will deliver only if they can profit, they enjoy a unique advantage in the political arena. As we argued earlier, business is the goose that lays the golden egg, and politicians have an interest in helping the goose produce. In the nineteenth century, the federal government gave railroad companies more land than the entire area of France to encourage the construction of the transcontinental railroad. Typically, the government offers business more prosaic inducements, such as patent protection, tariffs, tax breaks, research-and-development subsidies, vocational training, loan guarantees, and military protection in order to promote investment and commerce. Government generosity is especially great during crises. In the recession of 2008–09, despite widespread popular opposition to bailing out banks and other firms, the government provided hundreds of billions of dollars to stabilize the system of private production and finance.

Politicians often offer incentives to inspire that intangible but vital phenomenon called "business confidence." Firms need to be confident that their ventures will be profitable and pay off if they are going to invest, and banks need to be confident that loans will be repaid if they are going to extend credit. Politicians have an interest in stoking such confidence, in encouraging investment and lending, because their own interests, their own careers, depend on it. If business lacks confidence and does not invest, the resulting downturn in employment and incomes can wreak havoc with politicians' electoral prospects. In the 2012 campaign, for example, pundits wondered whether President Obama would be able to overcome the drag of a weak economic recovery to win reelection. Conversely, when business leaders are confident that good times lie ahead, they are likely to invest, hire, and increase wages. Politicians' careers are then buoyed by the resulting prosperity because they can take credit for the good times that citizens enjoy.

Politicians' careers are dependent on the collective decisions of business in a second way. When the economy is booming—when business is investing and creating jobs—tax revenues flow into government coffers. The more revenue that is at the disposal of government, the more programs and services politicians can offer to earn credit with voters. The opposite is also true. Tax revenues decline in a recession, leading to service cutbacks that citizens blame on politicians, hurting their chances for reelection. A growing economy increases tax revenues that politicians can use to curry favor with voters. Similarly, a decline in investment and employment jeopardizes politicians' careers. Tax revenues fall, inducing service cutbacks that voters blame on their elected officials.

Thus, politicians have an incentive to promote the interests of business. Supporting policies that inspire business confidence and encourage investment correspond to politicians' own career needs to promote their constituents' well-being and take credit for new services. The way in which the economic power of business structures the incentives of politicians gives business a distinct political advantage, which we refer to as **the structural power of business**. We refer to it as "structural" because the bias toward business is built into the political system as a result of its control over the means of production. It exists before the first vote is cast, the first campaign contribution is made, or the first lobbyist contacts a member of Congress. The structural power of business is concerned not with the relative strengths of the players on the field—business may enjoy an advantage there, too!—but with how the game is set up so that one team always has home-field advantage.

But the home team doesn't always win. Although the structural power of business gives it a special political advantage, that does not guarantee political success. As the political scientist Neil J. Mitchell explains, business must engage in policy struggles that involve "a shifting set of adversaries, and volatile public preferences."[24]

There are several reasons why business interests may be thwarted. First, business is not always able to present a united political front. Companies often compete with each other and have conflicting interests depending on their region and industry, whether they produce for local or international markets, whether they are capital or labor intensive, and so on. Business groupings have had conflicting positions on public policies from the time slaveholders and manufacturers fought over the tariff in the 1800s to more contemporary struggles over trade policy between domestic producers and export-oriented firms. Internal conflicts weaken business and empower opposition groups in policy debates.

Second, democratic procedures require policy makers to respond to many pressures and interests beyond those of business. Popular movements from below have won significant victories over business, despite the latter's threat that reform would undermine business confidence. Elected officials cannot simply dismiss popular bills that business opposes. When the public is organized and mobilized, politicians are required to recalculate the risks of conceding to business and instead support alternative groups and policies. Politicians redefine their self-interest under these circumstances and oppose business. While the political burden of proof is much greater for popular movements than it is for business interests, public opinion cannot wholly be ignored.[25]

Popular movements have periodically achieved significant political victories over business, especially during economic crises like the Great Depression of the 1930s, when Social Security and Minimum Wage laws were passed over business's opposition. More recently, business was defeated during President George W. Bush's presidential tenure following corporate scandals involving the issuance of fraudulent financial statements, insider trading, and stock analysts' misleading recommendations. Public outrage forced Congress to pass legislation (the Sarbanes-Oxley Act of 2002) providing for tougher regulation of accounting and securities trading, despite stiff lobbying by business against the bill. Similarly, public anger over bailing out irresponsible banks in the recent financial crisis led to passage of the Dodd-Frank Wall Street Reform and Consumer Protection Act in 2010. Dodd-Frank increased regulatory oversight of the financial industry and was passed despite fierce lobbying against it by the banks.

Politics matters. If, as the political scientist Neil J. Mitchell argues, the "House" or the home team always won, then citizens would think the game is fixed and not view its results as legitimate. Instead, citizens play with gusto because business does not always win. The fix is not in. Policy stretches and bends in response to the pressures exerted on it. Even though business derives an enormous advantage from its structural power, political struggle matters. Whether business wins depends on such contingent factors as whether politicians regard business's threat to disinvest as credible, whether opposition groups are mobilized and organized, and whether business is united enough to translate the structural power it enjoys into coordinated support for specific policies. None of these can be taken for granted.

This book examines the complex relationship between democratic politics and the undemocratic private government of capitalism. The politics of power is affected by the capitalist organization of the economy, and the capitalist organization of the economy is affected, in turn, by the democratic political system. Although the structural power of business gives it a political advantage no other group enjoys, democratic pressure is capable of mitigating it. *The Politics of Power* describes both sides of this complicated coin. In the following sections, we review the structure of corporate capitalism, who owns America's private government, the occupational structure of the American economy, and the distinctive form of corporate capitalism that prevails in the United States.

THE CORPORATE AND COMPETITIVE SECTORS OF THE ECONOMY

Suppose it was learned that a small group controlled vast economic resources in the United States. Imagine that in a country with a population of over 300 million people, a small group of several thousand Americans—unrepresentative, not democratically chosen, and not even known to most people—made economic decisions that profoundly affected the quality of life for all Americans. Imagine, moreover, that they based their decisions not on what the country needed but on what would be most profitable for themselves and the companies they directed. While they owned multiple mansions, other Americans were homeless; while they ate sumptuous meals at expensive restaurants, other Americans ate in soup kitchens; and while they purchased luxury cars and private jets, other Americans put off medical care they needed because they could not afford it.

This small group at the top of the economic pyramid not only was fabulously wealthy but also wielded enormous political influence. They spent lavishly in support of favored candidates; some dispensed with the middleman entirely and became politicians themselves. They hired high-priced lobbyists and lawyers to represent their interests, and they funded think tanks and owned media outlets that promoted their views.

A troubling question is whether such an economic system could be considered fair or just, and whether such a political system could be regarded as democratic if it tolerated, indeed promoted, the existence of such a small group. And yet everything that has been described is fact, not fiction. A convenient shorthand label for the system in which a small group controls the U.S. economy and, consequently, possesses immense political power is **corporate capitalism**.

Corporate capitalism includes the country's largest mining and manufacturing companies, investment banks, financial-services firms, retail chains, utilities, high-tech businesses, media conglomerates, and corporate law firms. The giant companies listed in the Fortune 500 (a list of the country's 500 largest corporations, compiled annually by *Fortune Magazine*) represent the core of corporate capitalism. Figure 2.1 lists the top 20 U.S. companies.

Large corporations tend to be capital intensive, highly productive, diversified, and global in their reach. The largest is ExxonMobil, with revenues of $453 billion in 2011, a little less than the GDP of Sweden. Total revenues of the 10 largest American companies would make them collectively the seventh-largest economy in the world, just behind the United Kingdom, and account for about one-seventh of the total American GDP.[26]

Alongside the corporate sector is the **competitive sector**, which includes more than 5 million small businesses (not including the more than 20 million "nonemployer firms" that refer to the self-employed). These small firms range from convenience stores to car-repair shops to locally owned restaurants. Two-thirds of them—more than 4 million businesses—employed less than 10 people and collectively earned revenues of $2 trillion in 2007. Their sales are dwarfed by those of the fewer than 1,000 firms with more than 10,000 employees, which racked up over $10 trillion in sales.[27] Competitive-sector businesses are not only smaller in terms of profits, sales, assets, and employees than large corporations; they also sell in more local markets and are more labor intensive.

Small firms in the competitive sector of the economy are dependent on the corporate sector and exist in its orbit. They are like planets that revolve around and are sustained by the heat and light of the corporate sun. For example, they rely on the corporate sector for orders, act as suppliers to large corporations, provide retail-sales outlets for corporate products, and furnish services to corporations. When large corporations cut back, small firms feel the effects first. They act as shock absorbers for the economy. They are the first firms to fail when recessions occur because they lack the resources to survive them.

According to the economist Eric Schultz, small may be beautiful but power and profits go to those with size.[28] Large corporations can take advantage of their size to buy in volume so they pay less for goods; receive lower interest rates when they borrow money because they are regarded as better credit risks; spread the costs of advertising over a larger volume of sales to capture market share; and, finally, subsidize political activity to obtain favorable policies.

Despite new competitors elbowing their way into formerly closed markets, markets have become more concentrated. That is, fewer firms account for a larger percentage of all industry sales. Part of this is the result of corporate

FIGURE 2.1

TOP 20 FORTUNE 500 COMPANIES, 2012

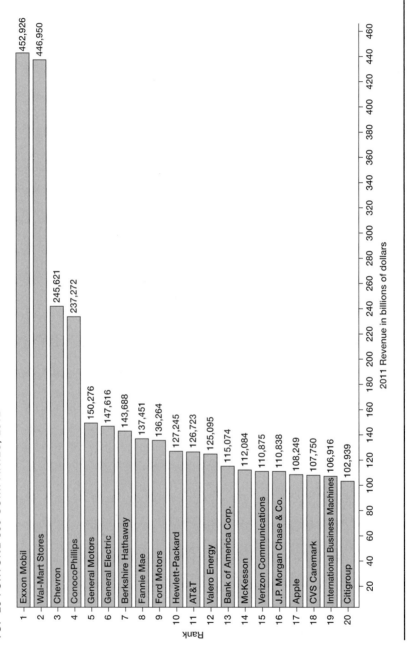

SOURCE: CNN Money, "Fortune 500," http://money.cnn.com/magazines/fortune/fortune500/2012/full_list/(accessed October 18, 2012).

mergers and acquisitions, in which larger corporations absorb smaller ones. Mobil and Exxon merged to become the world's largest industrial corporation, and telephone companies merged to produce nationwide empires. Part of this is also due simply to the advantages of size that we alluded to previously. As Figure 2.2 makes clear, the number and percentage of U.S. manufacturing industries in which four companies account for at least 50 percent of shipped value have increased dramatically since 1947.

FIGURE 2.2

NUMBER AND PERCENTAGE OF U.S. MANUFACTURING INDUSTRIES IN WHICH LARGEST FOUR COMPANIES ACCOUNTED FOR AT LEAST 50 PERCENT OF SHIPMENT VALUE IN THEIR INDUSTRIES, 1947–2007

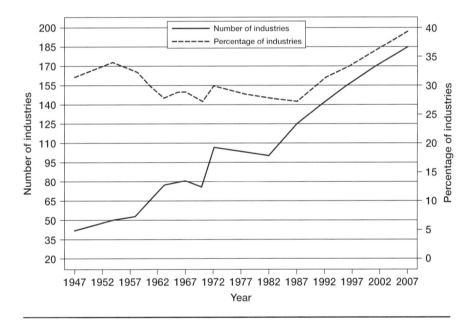

NOTES: The Census Bureau added new industries (i.e., Standard Industrial Classification [SIC] codes) each year since 1947; in that year there were 134; in 1967, 281; and by 1992, 458. Beginning in 1997, the SIC system was replaced by the North American Industrial Classification System (NAICS) and since this time the number of industries leveled off at approximately 472 (in 1997 and 2002, 473; and 2007, 471).

SOURCES: John Bellamy Foster, Robert W. McChesney, and R. Jamil Jonna, "Monopoly and Competition in Twenty-First Century Capitalism," *Monthly Review*, 62 no. 1 (April 2011) and "Shipments Share of 4, 8, 20, & 50 Largest Companies in Each SIC: 1992–1947," Census of Manufactures; and "Economic Census," 1997, 2002, and 2007, American FactFinder (U.S. Census Bureau, 2011), http://census.gov/epcd/www/concentration.html.

The rise in concentration measured by the four largest companies capturing a larger proportion of all sales in their industry is also evident in general-merchandise retailing, where Walmart continues to capture market share; in food and beverage stores; in computers and software; and in finance.[29] Since the early 1970s, the share of assets controlled by the five largest banking institutions in the U.S. has tripled to 54 percent (2012) from 17 percent. The recent financial crisis increased concentration in the industry, as large banks acquired failed banks. Before the crisis, policy makers were worried that some banks posed a systemic danger because they were too big to fail. Now, after a series of mergers and acquisitions, these banks are even bigger.

When production becomes concentrated, control becomes centralized in fewer hands. The concentration of economic power poses a threat to democracy because it tends to promote the concentration of political power. The business professor Jeffrey E. Garton warns that corporate concentration has produced a "growing imbalance between public and private power in our society."[30] Corporate giants, especially in the financial sector, are regarded as "too big to fail" and as "systemically important"—to the extent that there is an implicit promise that the government will bail them out should they falter. This privileged position gives them extraordinary clout and enables them to take greater risks at the expense of the American taxpayer.

WHO OWNS AMERICA'S PRIVATE GOVERNMENT?

Ownership and control of the giant corporations that comprise America's private government are determined through stock ownership. People can own a share of corporate assets by purchasing the corporation's stock. Stockholders are entitled to a share of the firm's profits in proportion to the amount of stock they own. They also get to elect the corporation's board of directors, which chooses the firm's management and reviews its performance and decisions. The number of votes that investors cast depends on the amount of stock they hold. The question of who owns America's private government can thus be rephrased as, how is corporate-stock ownership distributed among Americans?

Some argue that a shareholder democracy exists since anyone can purchase stock in publicly owned corporations. As one Wall Street executive explained, "In our system of free enterprise, the capitalist system, industry is owned by the American public."[31] But the idea that the economy is guided by a shareholder democracy is as implausible as the notion that it is ruled by a consumer democracy. According to Table 2.1, about half of all American households do not own any stock in any form, either directly, as shareholders, or indirectly, through mutual funds or retirement plans. That is, they don't get to cast any votes over corporate policy since they don't own any shares of stock. This makes a mockery of the concept of shareholder democracy.

Moreover, shareholding is highly skewed among the remaining half of American households who do own stock. In 2007, the latest year for which data is available, the wealthiest 1 percent of all American households held 38 percent of all U.S. stocks, and the wealthiest 10 percent held 80 percent of all stock shares. In contrast, the bottom four quintiles of American households— 80 percent of American households—reported owning less than 10 percent of all stock. The answer to the question of who owns America's private government is thus quite simple: shareholding is concentrated among the wealthiest American households and the richest among even that select group. So much for the notion of shareholder democracy.

TABLE 2.1

CONCENTRATION OF STOCK OWNERSHIP BY WEALTH CLASS, 2007

Wealth Class	Percent of Households Owning Stock Worth More Than:			Percent of Stock Owned		
	Zero	$4,999	$9,999	Shares	Cumulative	Cumulative– 2001
Top 1 percent	92.6	89.1	88.4	38.3	38.3	33.5
Next 4 percent	92.2	90.7	89.5	30.8	69.1	62.3
Next 5 percent	86.8	85.0	81.4	12.1	81.2	76.9
Next 10 percent	82.1	77.1	71.2	9.9	91.1	89.3
Second quintile	65.4	54.3	47.1	6.4	97.5	97.1
Third quintile	47.7	28.9	22.1	1.9	99.4	99.3
Fourth quintile	30.3	12.3	8.7	0.5	99.9	99.8
Bottom quintile	16.3	3.5	2.0	0.1	100.0	100.0
All	49.1	36.3	31.6	100.0		

NOTE: Includes direct ownership of stock shares and indirect ownership through mutual funds, trusts, IRAs, Keogh plans, 401(k) plans, and other retirement accounts. All figures are in 2007 dollars.

SOURCE: Edward N. Wolf, "Recent Trends in Household Wealth in the United States: Rising Debt and the Middle-class Squeeze—an Update to 2007," Levi Institute of Bard College, working paper no. 589 (March 2010).

Aside from the unequal distribution of stock ownership that disenfranchises half of all American households and reserves almost all the votes over corporate policy to a small sliver of the wealthiest Americans, most elections to corporate boards of directors are not even contested. As in the former Soviet Union, under communism, shareholders often have the option to vote for only one slate of candidates for the board of directors.

Finally, in Chapter 1 we suggested that one way to evaluate the quality of democracy is by the extent to which political representatives reflect the social diversity of society. When we apply this standard to the corporate elite, the men and women on the boards of directors of Fortune 500 companies, the results are dismaying. Those who oversee corporate capitalism are with few exceptions white and male. More than three-quarters of all seats on Fortune 500 boards were held by white males. Nonwhite males occupied 7 percent of all seats, white women 12 percent, and nonwhite women just 3 percent.[32] The picture is even worse when we turn our attention away from corporate boardrooms to the Fortune 500 chief executives who actually make policy and run those companies. In 2011, women accounted for just 4 percent of Fortune 500 CEOs, and only two of them were nonwhite. The percentage of nonwhite males who ran Fortune 500 companies was also just 4 percent. Over 90 percent of Fortune 500 CEOs were white males. The corporate world performs worse than the political world when it comes to the democratic

Indra Nooyi, the CEO of PepsiCo, is one of the few nonwhite women to head a major corporation.

standard that rulers should roughly reflect the demographic characteristics of those they rule.

CAPITALIST CLASS COHESION

Capitalist economies are in constant motion. The engine of change is competition among firms for markets and profits. But corporate capitalism is also characterized by cooperation and coordination among firms. In 1935, E. E. Schattschneider noted, "Businessmen collectively constitute the most class-conscious group in American society. As a class they are the most highly organized, more easily mobilized, have more facilities for communication, are more like-minded, and are more accustomed to stand together in defense of their privileges than any other group."[33]

Capital is linked through a dense organizational network. One mechanism is exclusive social clubs, such as the Links and Century clubs in New York, the California Club in Los Angeles, and the Pacific Union Club in San Francisco. Social clubs promote capitalist class cohesion by creating information and friendship networks among the elite. The exclusive social club is the culmination of a process of elite socialization that begins in prep school, is reinforced at prestigious private colleges, is strengthened at selective law and business schools, and is polished at corporate headquarters.[34] Along with elite social clubs, networking occurs in organizations such as the World Economic Forum, a group that hosts an annual forum at the posh Alpine resort of Davos, Switzerland. The forum provides an opportunity for not only American but also world business and political leaders to socialize and exchange opinions.

Peak business associations are another source of capitalist class cohesion. At the very top is the Business Roundtable, which seeks to develop common positions on public issues among CEOs of the largest corporations in the United States, from Intel in the technology industry to International Paper in manufacturing. In 2012, the Roundtable membership included CEOs from 202 corporations that, collectively, had $7.3 trillion in annual revenues, employed 16 million workers worldwide, and accounted for a third of the total value of the U.S. stock market. The Roundtable does not employ lobbyists. Instead, chief executives convey the Roundtable's position on key public issues to legislators and policy makers directly in one-on-one exchanges.

At a broader, less elite level, thousands of large and small firms belong to the U.S. Chamber of Commerce and the National Association of Manufacturers.

These peak associations seek to represent the collective interests of business across industries. At the level of specific industries, countless trade associations represent the interests of firms in the sector, from the relatively inconsequential Fresh Garlic Association to the powerful American Banking Association.

A third source of capitalist class cohesion is corporate interlocks, in which a member of one corporate board of directors also serves on the board of another corporation. Interlocks facilitate communication between firms. According to the sociologist Michael Useem, interlocks promote "the flow of information throughout the [corporate] network about the practices and concerns of most large companies."[35] Directors who sit on multiple corporate boards comprise what Useem characterizes as the "inner circle" of capital. Their perspective goes beyond the interests of any particular firm or industry to encompass the interests of corporate capitalism as a whole.

Relations within corporate capitalism are characterized by both conflict and cooperation. No single organization enforces discipline and unity among the firms that comprise corporate capitalism. Yet social clubs, peak business organizations, and corporate interlocks form an infrastructure that promotes a broad, class-wide understanding, if not agreement on specific policies. Some issues provoke conflict within the business community. Some issues mobilize certain sectors while others remain indifferent. And on some issues, especially challenges to managerial authority posed by unions and government regulation, the business community often stands armed and united. While the coherence of the business community depends on the specific issue, the political scientists Kay Lehman Schlozman and John Tierney report that "[c]ooperation within the business community is far more commonplace than conflict." They find that members of the business community are more likely to identify other business interests as political allies than as antagonists.[36]

THE CHANGING STRUCTURE OF EMPLOYMENT

Below the top level of corporate executives that comprise the capitalist class is a workforce that is shaped by the changing needs of capital. An industrial occupational order based on manual, blue-collar factory workers has been largely replaced by a postindustrial order in which professionals, service employees, and white-collar office workers predominate.

Industry first began to overtake agriculture as the basis of employment after the Civil War. Workers employed in manufacturing increased from just 2.5 million in 1870 to over 11 million by 1920. Hand tools were replaced by machines, workshops were replaced by factories, artisans were replaced by unskilled manual workers, and craft goods were replaced by standardized products. Foreign immigrants and native farmers took jobs as industrial workers in factories, converting villages into towns and towns into cities. Pittsburgh grew up around steel, Akron around rubber, and Detroit around cars. Flint was transformed from a sleepy town of 13,000 in 1900 into a bustling city of 150,000 by 1929. Sixty thousand industrial workers toiled within its city limits, many of them in GM factories.[37]

The industrial workforce, in turn, laid the foundations for a new occupational order based on white-collar workers that would supersede it. Productivity growth in industry required firms to hire salespeople and market researchers to create new outlets for its prodigious output. The application of science to industry (i.e., using technology to improve productivity) required firms to hire technical experts to develop new products and improve existing methods. The need to improve labor productivity required firms to hire engineers to design the labor process and supervisors to manage it. The increase in the size of business required it to hire office workers and managers to coordinate the flow of work within the firm. Industrialization also required a larger public sector in the form of teachers to educate the labor force and social workers and police to manage the conflicts it generated. When increasing numbers of women entered the labor force, new jobs in service industries, such as restaurants, cleaning, child care, and elder care were created to substitute for the functions women previously did at home. In brief, the growth of a postindustrial, white-collar, service-sector workforce did not occur independently of the grimy world of industrial production but developed in response to the changes and demands it provoked. In 1950, manufacturing jobs accounted for almost 60 percent of the labor market. But the white-collar and service-sector occupations that industry required were poised to overtake it. By 2000, manufacturing accounted for less than a quarter of the labor market, while white-collar and service-sector jobs were three-quarters and agriculture a mere 1 percent of the workforce.

The white-collar and service sectors are so large and diverse today that it is much more helpful to analyze the contemporary labor market in terms of skill levels than the traditional blue- and white-collar divide. According to the economists David Auter and Daron Acegmolu, the American labor market can be divided into three segments. At the top are managerial and professional jobs that are well compensated, offer good fringe benefits, and require a college or postgraduate education. Jobs in this segment, which includes doctors, lawyers, engineers, and business executives have grown in number to about 40 percent of the labor market. Below this group are jobs that require a bit

WHAT DO YOU THINK?

What Criteria Should Determine How Much People Should Be Paid?

It is often claimed that economic inequalities within capitalism are justified. Inequality is a great way to motivate people, because those who work harder and are better at competing in the market receive greater rewards. Inequality reflects people's unequal contributions to social welfare. According to this line of reasoning, those who contribute more deserve to be given greater rewards. Critics of this view counter that capitalism does not distribute rewards based on merit. For example, poets, firefighters—and professors!—have far lower incomes than stockbrokers. But poets, firefighters, and professors— as well as office workers, engineers, and nurses' aides—do not necessarily work less or contribute less to society than stockbrokers. Where do you stand in this debate? How do patterns of economic inequality in the United States strengthen or weaken your argument?

less skill, such as white-collar teachers and office managers as well as blue-collar manufacturing and construction workers. Workers in this segment have relatively well-paying and secure jobs that would place them in the middle class. They comprise another 20 percent of the labor force. At the bottom of the labor market are low-skill, low-paying jobs that offer little security, such as hospital orderlies, security guards, and home health aides. Low-skill jobs account for the remaining 40 percent of the labor market. Acegmolu and Auter found that over the last fifty years the top and bottom tiers of the labor market have surged in growth, while the middle level has languished. The labor market is bifurcating: good and bad jobs are both growing at the expense of those in the middle. [38]

The bifurcation of the labor market contributes to inequality. This would not be so painful to accept if workers moved out of the bottom of the labor market to join the middle or top tiers, or their children succeeded in doing so. But instead of experiencing more social mobility, Americans are experiencing less of it. Economists find that where you begin in the pecking order increasingly determines where you end up. Affluent, well-educated parents are increasingly able to transmit their economic status to their children, while children from poor and poorly educated families are more likely to end up like their parents. Nor are Americans more likely to move up and achieve the American Dream than citizens in other countries. The United States is in the middle of the pack of Western countries when it comes to class mobility from one generation to the next. After reviewing different American social-mobility studies, three political scientists concluded, "Rags-to-riches—and riches-to-rags—however noteworthy, are exceptional, and, over time, most people stay quite close to the economic stratum in which they started out."[39]

AMERICAN CORPORATE CAPITALISM

Corporate capitalism comes in many flavors. Large corporations play a dominant role in all Western capitalist democracies. But fewer corporations account for a larger share of total economic activity in Sweden than in the U.S., and markets are less dominated by a few firms in Germany than they are in America. The capitalist class is more formally knit together and disciplined in corporatist countries such as Austria and Norway, while Canada and Spain are similar to the U.S. in the extent to which upper-class coordination is more informal and less bureaucratic. And some countries have a more postindustrial occupational structure than the U.S., with a larger percentage of workers in Canada engaged in white-collar jobs, while in Germany a larger percentage is engaged in industry. In the following paragraphs we describe what is distinctively American about American corporate capitalism, what gives American corporate capitalism its distinctive flavor.

Western capitalist democracies draw the line between states and markets at different places. At one end of the continuum, states are small and markets are relatively free and unregulated. At the other end, states are large and interventionist; they regulate private business more intrusively and redistribute market outcomes more aggressively. The United States is much closer to the market pole than to the other end of the spectrum.

Despite all the complaints about "big government" in the U.S., the American state is actually quite small and unobtrusive compared to other Western capitalist democracies. Government at all levels in the U.S.—state, local, and federal—employs just 15 percent of the labor force, while public-sector employment in other rich democracies is typically 25 to 30 percent. The American state not only employs fewer people; it also collects less in taxes and spends less as a proportion of the economy. As we will see in Chapter 9, the U.S. collects a lower proportion of its GDP in the form of taxes than any other advanced industrialized country and spends less as a percentage of GDP than any other affluent democracy except for Australia, Ireland, Japan, and Switzerland. The relatively tiny size of the American public sector, in terms of employees, revenues, and expenditures, is reflected in the less-generous benefits and fewer public services Americans receive from it. For example, in many other rich democracies, the government either provides child-care services directly or offers families more generous subsidies to obtain it. (The welfare state is covered in more depth in Chapter 10.)

In addition, the regulatory impact of the U.S. government is actually quite light compared to other affluent democracies. That is, the U.S. boasts some of the freest markets in the world. A standard measure used to compare the thickness of a country's regulatory environment is the World Bank's "ease of doing business" index. This takes into account the cost, time, and number of procedures it takes to start a new business. The U.S. was ranked fourth out of 23 affluent democracies by the World Bank in terms of posing the fewest bureaucratic obstacles to new entrepreneurs.[40] Similarly, government regulation of the workplace is unusually thin in the United States. In many European countries, managers are required to negotiate with workers' councils in their shops, companies must follow a tedious and lengthy process before laying off workers, and employee representatives are entitled to seats on the corporate board of directors. Employers in the U.S. do not have to adopt any of these practices because there are no laws requiring them. They do not have to negotiate with their employees or let them participate in setting corporate strategy, and they can fire any worker for any reason, except discrimination, without having to justify their decision legally. "By most international standards," one study concluded, "American employers are . . . confronted with fewer direct regulations of employment conditions than employers in other countries."[41] American employers are remarkably unencumbered by regulations that protect workers from the unilateral power of management.

Another distinctive characteristic of American corporate capitalism is the weakness of its labor unions. In 2012, only 11.3 percent of the workforce belonged to unions. In the private-sector workforce, the results were even more dismal: just over one in twenty workers belonged to a union. (The decline of unions is covered in greater detail in Chapter 5.) Among affluent Western countries, only France has a lower proportion of unionized workers.

The low rate of unionization wouldn't be such an issue if it wasn't so meaningful in the U.S. In the U.S., only union members are protected by collective-bargaining agreements that limit the power of management over its workforce. By contrast, in Europe collective-bargaining coverage often extends beyond union members to include non-union workers, too. For example, although France is the only country that ranks lower than the U.S. in union membership, over 90 percent of its workers are covered by negotiated workplace contracts. American workers have the worst of both worlds: a smaller proportion of workers who are unionized and an even smaller proportion of workers relative to Europe who enjoy the protection of union-negotiated contracts. With few rules governing the workplace, and few workers belonging to unions or covered by workplace contracts, the gap between the power of management and the power of workers is greater in the U.S. than it is elsewhere. According to Seymour Martin Lipset and Gary Marks, "When one compares the United States with other western democracies, the picture that emerges . . . is one of continued lower-class weakness. . . . No other western democracy approximates America in this regard."[42]

Finally, the small state, reluctance to interfere with markets, and the weakness of unions all contribute to higher levels of inequality than are found in other Western countries. As we alluded to in Chapter 1, the "one-percenters" in first class have seen their wealth increase substantially, while those with third-class tickets have seen the value of their holdings plummet over the last 30 years. The decline has been particularly acute for the "99 percent" because their most valuable asset is their home. The pricking of the housing bubble in the recent recession sent housing values tumbling. This decimated the net worth of the many Americans whose homes account for much more of their total net worth than is the case for the mega-rich. A much larger proportion of the one-percenters' wealth, instead, takes the form of financial assets, such as stocks, bank deposits, and the value of private businesses they may own, not the value of their homes. These financial assets weathered the recession much better than real-estate values. Consequently, the drop in housing prices over the course of the recent recession made the gap between the super-rich and everyone else even greater than it was before.

In 1980, according to one study by the Organization for Economic Cooperation and Development (OECD), a research group comprised of the richest democracies, the U.S. held the dubious distinction of having the most income inequality of any Western country. Over the next 30 years, income inequality increased throughout the West, with the exception of France and Belgium, where it was unchanged. Countries that could previously boast of having low inequality, such as Germany, Denmark, and Sweden, had more growth in income inequality than anyone between 1980 and 2010. But the U.S., which had the most income inequality to start with, was right on their heels. While Germany, Denmark, and Sweden were catching up with the middle of the pack, the U.S. was pulling away from it in the income-inequality sweepstakes (see Figure 2.3).[43]

FIGURE 2.3

GINI COEFFICIENTS OF INCOME INEQUALITY, MID 1980s AND LATE 2000s

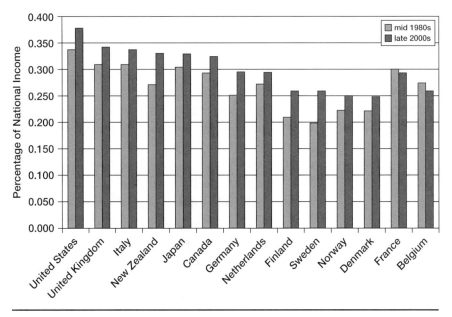

SOURCE: OECD States Extracts, "Income distribution—Inequality: Income distribution—Inequality—Country tables," http://stats.oecd.org/Index.aspx?QueryId=26068 (accessed October 18, 2012).

The greater extent of inequality in the U.S. than in other Western societies is particularly evident when one looks at the gap between the 1 percent and everyone else and not simply at the disparity between the top- and bottom-10-percent income earners. According to Figure 2.4, in the 1970s the national income captured by the top 1 percent in the U.S. was within the range of Western European countries. About 8 percent of the national income was captured by the top 1 percent in the U.S. in the 1970s. Germany, Switzerland, Canada, and France all had a higher share of income going to the richest of the rich. A generation later, things look much different. The U.S. is now the leader of the pack with regard to both the level and the rate of increase of this group's income. The top 1 percent now receive 16 percent of all income in the U.S., double the percentage from thirty years' prior. In contrast, France, Germany, the Netherlands, Sweden, and Switzerland have all experienced little or no increase in the share going to this select group. The U.S. wins the gold medal in the affluent-democracies category for income inequality. Hands down.[44]

FIGURE 2.4

THE TOP 1 PERCENT'S SHARE OF NATIONAL INCOME (EXCLUDING CAPITAL GAINS), MID- '70s VS. CIRCA 2000

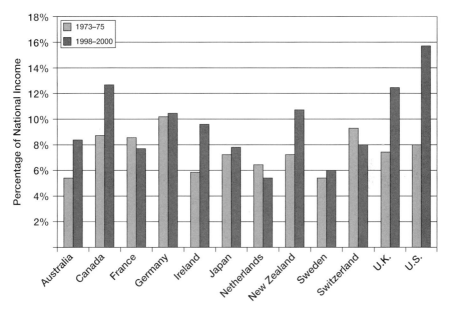

NOTES: The first bar for each nation is the top 1 percent's average share of national income (excluding capital gains) in 1973–75 (except for Ireland, for which data are unavailable until 1976; the first bar for Ireland averages the years 1976–79). The second bar for each nation is the top 1 percent's average share in 1998–2000 (except, for reasons of data availability, France and Germany (1996–98), the Netherlands (1997–99), and Switzerland (1994–96).

SOURCE: Andrew Leigh, "How Closely Do Top Income Shares Track Other Measures of Inequality? *The Economic Journal* 117 (November 2007); F589-F603. Data available at http://people.anu.edu.au/andrew.leigh/pdf/ToplncomesPanel.xls. (The figure uses leigh's data on the top 1 percent excluding capital gains, adjusted for consistency across nations.)

FROM: Jacob S. Hacker and Paul Pierson, *Winner-Take-All Politics: How Washington Made the Rich Richer and Turned Its Back on the Middle Class* (New York: Simon & Schuster, 2010) 39.

Thus, American corporate capitalism has many distinctive features: markets are freer and less likely to be regulated by the state; the state is smaller and less likely to alter market outcomes; labor is weaker and less able to protect the interests of workers; and incomes are more unequal, creating more inequality than in any other Western country.

CONCLUSION

Capitalism does not simply distribute money and wealth unequally. It also distributes economic power unequally. A small elite of corporate executives and large shareholders own and control the means of production, have power over the working lives of their employees, and make decisions that have far-reaching consequences for the entire society. Capitalists decide whether to invest, where to invest, and what to invest in based on what will yield the greatest profit, not the greatest good. Moreover, their economic wealth and power give them an advantage politically that no other group can claim. They enjoy a "structural advantage" based on the fact that the welfare of the community depends on business prosperity.

At the same time, the interests of business and society may conflict. There is thus both harmony and conflict between business firms and other groups. When conflicts occur, the results depend on a host of factors, including how unified capitalists are and the extent of popular opposition that they encounter. Mobilization from below can mitigate and counteract the power of business.

Below the group at the top of the economic pyramid is a workforce divided between professional, technical, and educated employees who are relatively well compensated, and poorly paid service-sector workers. Corporate capitalism takes a distinctive form in the U.S., where it is characterized by freer markets, a smaller state, weaker unions, and more inequality.

CHAPTER SUMMARY

Introduction
There is a fundamental tension between the equality and democratic procedures of the political sphere and the inequality and undemocratic character of a market-based or capitalist system of production. Capitalism has been a remarkably productive, dynamic, innovative economic system that has defeated its adversaries, including centralized, planned economies. It has been so successful that few rivals to it remain.

The Dilemmas of Markets
While market systems have been extraordinarily productive, they also have harmful features and effects. Capitalism promotes higher and higher

levels of production and consumption that place strain on the ecosystem; the lack of coordination between supply, demand, and investment leads to volatile business cycles that are disruptive and wasteful; externalities or harmful spillovers are not charged against private profits but against taxpayers and individuals; and the rights of private property give capitalists unilateral authority over work and their workers.

The System of Corporate Capitalism
Capitalism can be considered a system of private government. A small and undemocratically chosen group owns a disproportionate part of the American economy. It controls a range of vitally important economic decisions that affect the fundamental welfare of the society, including whether to invest productive resources (capital), where to invest, what to invest in, and how production is organized.

The Structural Advantage of Business
Business firms enjoy a unique political advantage because the entire society is dependent on them to invest and provide jobs, products, and services. Consequently, policy makers are anxious to support pro-business policies in order to give businesses the confidence to invest and create jobs. This creates an uneven playing field, which we refer to as the structural advantage of business. But the special political advantage business enjoys does not mean it always wins politically. Political struggle still matters. Sometimes, when public opinion is focused and opponents are organized and mobilized, the power of democracy can overcome the power of business.

The Corporate and Competitive Sectors of the Economy
American business is composed of corporate and competitive sectors. Firms in the corporate sector produce for global markets and are capital intensive, highly diversified, and extraordinarily productive. The few firms in this sector account for the majority of revenue and sales in the economy. They are serviced by small firms in the competitive sector of the economy who rely on the corporate sector for orders. Competitive-sector firms are much smaller in terms of revenues and assets. They also tend to be more labor intensive and produce for more local markets.

Who Owns America's Private Government?

The ownership of corporate stock in the United States is highly concentrated. As a result, a small minority of Americans control a vastly disproportionate share of economic resources in the United States. Not only is economic power concentrated among a few Americans, but this elite group is unrepresentative of the American public. Corporate executives and corporate board members are overwhelmingly white males; women and people of color are grossly underrepresented among them.

Capitalist Class Cohesion

The capitalist upper class is knit together by shared experiences that include attending the best colleges and professional schools, informal social ties at the same social clubs, joining the same business organizations, and membership on each other's corporate boards of directors.

The Changing Structure of Employment

The American labor market has gone through three transitions, from a predominantly agricultural to an industrial and now to a postindustrial workforce. More than three-quarters of Americans are engaged in some form of white-collar or service-sector work. This postindustrial workforce can be separated into well-paid, high-skill work; medium-skilled white-collar and manufacturing jobs that provide a middle-class standard of living; and low-skill, low-wage work that offers little job security and no fringe benefits, such as health insurance and pensions. The top and bottom tiers of the labor market are growing much faster than the middle. The labor market is bifurcating, contributing to inequality.

American Corporate Capitalism

Corporate capitalism comes in many varieties. The American type is distinctive in four interrelated ways: the state is less intrusive and less willing to regulate the market; the state is smaller and less willing to disturb market outcomes; unions are weaker and less able to counteract the political and economic power of business; and inequality is greater than in any Western country.

Critical Thinking Questions

1. Do the benefits of capitalism outweigh its disadvantages? Are its drawbacks avoidable?

2. How can the structural advantage of business be minimized?

3. What are some of the advantages and disadvantages of the distinctive form of American corporate capitalism?

4. What factors do you think contributed to the distinctive form that corporate capitalism takes in the U.S.?

5. Since it is rational for Americans to identify their interests with business and equally rational for them to regard their interests as opposed to business, what determines how Americans resolve this dilemma?

Suggested Readings

Robert Kuttner, *Everything for Sale: The Virtues and Limits of Markets*. New York: Knopf, 1997.

Charles E. Lindblom, *Politics and Markets: The World's Political-Economic Systems*. New York: Basic Books, 1977.

John McMillan, *Reinventing the Bazaar: A Natural History of Markets*. New York: W. W. Norton, 2002.

Jonas Pontusson, *Inequality and Prosperity: Social Europe and Liberal America*. Ithaca: Cornell University Press, 2005.

Richard Richardson and Kate Pickett, *The Spirit Level: Why Greater Equality Makes Societies Stronger*. New York: Bloomsbury Press, 2009.

Wolfgang Streek, "The Crisis of Democratic Capitalism," *New Left Review* 71, September-October 2011, 5–29.

THE HISTORY OF AMERICAN POLITICAL ECONOMY

INTRODUCTION

In Chapter 2 we described how capitalism creates a structural advantage for business in the struggle for political power. The corporate elite own and control the means of production, giving them the power to manage the workforce, organize production, and decide how accrued profits are invested and distributed. These decisions are made in corporate boardrooms by business executives and not in legislative chambers by elected public officials. Yet politicians have an abiding interest in these decisions because their political careers depend on inducing corporations to invest, create jobs, and grow the economy. Politicians can then take credit with voters for the prosperity that results and avoid the wrath that voters express when business fails to invest and unemployment ensues. Consequently, even before groups take the field to compete in the struggle over policy, policy makers have an incentive to satisfy the needs of business.

This chapter examines the development of the relationship between the American state and corporate capitalism. By *state*, we mean the totality of public institutions that form the government of a country. The core of the state in the U.S. is the executive, which includes the president, the office of the president, and the executive branch or bureaucracy along with the military. But the state also includes Congress, the courts, and, in a federal system such as ours, state and local governments.

Capitalism is often described as a system in which production for private profit is organized and coordinated through markets that are free of political direction. But the free market has always been a fiction. As we mentioned in the previous chapter, markets cannot exist without a government to maintain order, enforce contracts, create currency, and provide a host of other public goods. Markets require a protective, facilitating political order to function.

Even in the United States, where the government's role in the economy has been less extensive than elsewhere, the government has been deeply implicated in the economy from the very start. Soon after the founding of the United States, following ratification of the Constitution in the late eighteenth century, state and local governments developed a commercial code and legal framework to bring order and stability to economic activity, created a common currency to facilitate trade and exchange, employed a military and police to secure property and markets, financed the building of roads and bridges to promote production and trade, and provided rudimentary social services to those in need. As capitalism matured, the different forms of government assistance increased.

The relationship between the state and market-based production for private profit (or capitalism) is especially complicated in countries, such as the United States, where capitalist production exists alongside democratic political institutions. A tension may exist between capitalism, an economic system based on profits for the few, and democracy, a political system based on democratic rights for the many.

The way in which this tension between capitalism and democracy is managed at any given time depends on the outcome of political struggles. Farmers and industrialists, workers and employers, men and women, whites and minorities, the South and the North have all tried to impose their vision of the proper balance between capitalism and democracy. But the politics of power extends beyond the issue of whether markets or politics should determine who gets what in society. It also includes what institutions should be responsible, what policies they should follow, and who should benefit. The politics of power includes struggles not only over how much government is needed but also over what it should do, which branches and agencies should do it, and which interests they should serve.

Although the result of these political conflicts is uncertain, some groups have prevailed more often than others. Over the course of American history, business has been unusually successful in these struggles. It has limited the reach of government, influenced the distribution of power among the state's various branches and agencies, and shaped the policies they implement.

But under popular pressure, state policy has sometimes diverged from business interests. At different junctures, farmers, workers, environmentalists, and other groups have emerged to challenge business successfully and required the government to adopt policies that regulate markets for the public interest and produce more equitable results. Indeed, one can discern periodic swings throughout American history in which the power of business has ebbed and flowed, and the government has supported and limited the play of markets. Since the 1930s, as we describe in more detail in this chapter, there have been three major swings of the pendulum, the latest of which began in 2008 in response to the deepest and fastest economic decline in 70 years.

The pendulum first swung in favor of a more expansive role for government during the 1930s, in response to the Great Depression. President Franklin Delano Roosevelt's **New Deal** created the outlines of the modern welfare state to cope with the distress. This was followed by the government's enormous success in managing and coordinating the transition to a wartime economy during World War II. Prosperity followed in the 1950s and 1960s as the standard of living increased for many Americans. But the formula for success that the government followed was exhausted by the 1970s, which saw unemployment and inflation take their toll on living standards.

Economic decline created an opening for the Republican Party's political success that began with Ronald Reagan's presidency in the 1980s. Under Republican Party dominance, the pendulum swung in the opposite direction. Government was condemned as the problem, not the solution. Markets needed to be freed from unnecessary government regulations, and taxes needed to be cut. Corporate managers needed to be given more autonomy to respond to a fast-changing and global marketplace. Groups seeking to restrict market forces in order to defend the environment, help the less affluent, protect consumers, and safeguard the interests of workers were thrown on the defensive. But faith in the self-correcting and beneficent nature of the market dissipated in the first decade of the twenty-first century when the worst economic crisis since the Great Depression hit, leaving a tidal wave of home foreclosures, massive unemployment, and innumerable bank failures in its wake.

The deep recession that began in 2008 initiated another swing of the pendulum. The government responded aggressively to the economic crisis. Under President George W. Bush, the government bailed out distressed banks. When the Democrats took both houses of Congress and the presidency in the 2008 elections, they passed a $787 billion stimulus bill to rouse demand and spur spending. The government also stepped in to guarantee loans to assure panicked creditors, arrange marriages between sick and healthy banks to stabilize the banking system, and make loans available when firms could not get credit from normal sources. As a result of its efforts to cope with the recession, the federal government was now a major stockholder in the biggest banks, guaranteed half the mortgages in the country, controlled one of the biggest insurance companies in the world, and in the course of bailing out the auto industry became the major stockholder in General Motors.

Instead of earning gratitude for bailing out the banks and trying to stimulate commerce, government policy elicited a strong backlash from the corporate elite. Once banks recovered, they turned on the government doctors who had saved them. They took exception to government efforts to limit executive pay, tried to weaken financial regulations designed to prevent another banking crisis, and resented being condemned as rapacious and irresponsible when they felt they deserved appreciation for doing what Goldman Sach's chief executive, Lloyd Blankfein, described as "God's Work."

The corporate elite also struck back through the Republican Party, which was unified in opposition to President Obama's initiatives. The 2009 stimulus package and Obama's health care plan passed without a single Republican vote in the House. The Tea Party (profiled in Chapter 5) emerged to stiffen the spine of wavering Republicans. When Republicans became the majority in the House of Representatives after the 2010 midterm elections, economic policy was held hostage by obstruction and dysfunction. The Republicans even initially refused to extend the debt limit, which threatened a catastrophic default on our debt. Why would anyone in the future lend money to the government to finance its activities if the U.S. didn't stand behind its promise to pay its creditors?

The pendulum, which had been moving back toward more government, was stuck. Democrats called for more government programs to stimulate the economy, reduce unemployment, and help those in need. Republicans claimed that such efforts only added to the federal deficit. Business would lead the recovery and create jobs, they argued, if only the government would lower tax rates and reduce regulations. With the parties at nearly equal strength, no policy paradigm could prevail. The contest between state and market was stuck in neutral.

In this chapter, we study the state's changing relationship to the economy. In each instance, economic crisis and political change initiated a new policy paradigm that realigned the relationship between government and the economy and created different winners and losers. We detail this relationship from the early days of the Republic, in which government prepared the ground for capitalist production, to the present, in which government collects the debris after capitalism fails.

COMPETITIVE CAPITALISM

The first expansionary phase in American economic history, starting in the 1840s, was based on a revolution in transportation. New roadways, canals, and railroads allowed farmers in the Ohio and Mississippi valleys to ship their products more quickly to seaboard cities like New York, Baltimore, and Philadelphia. Shipping midwestern grain to New York by wagon took almost two months; by canal, it took three weeks; by rail, it took just seven days.[1] Regional and even national markets in labor and commodities soon developed as a result of increasingly efficient transportation. In addition, railroad construction required massive inputs of labor and material, which also propelled the entire economy forward.

But the revolution in transportation would not have had the impact it did without a powerful helping hand from government. Almost a century ago, one historian wrote that, despite popular images of the United States as "the land of private enterprise *par excellence*; the place where 'State interference' has played the smallest part, and individual enterprise has been given the largest scope, it is a fact that this country was one of the first to exhibit the modern tendency to extend the activity of the State into industry."[2] The mistaken impression of minimal state interference in the economy persists because people often look for the state in the wrong place. *State governments*, far more than the federal government, were involved in shaping the contours of the pre–Civil War political economy.[3]

Nowhere was the influence of state governments more apparent than in their contribution to railroad development. For example, a number of state governments built and operated railroads themselves or invested heavily in privately owned railroads. State and local governments financed almost 30 percent of the more than $1 billion invested in railroads before the Civil War. In addition, state governments regulated railroads through charters they issued to private railroad companies, through appointments to railroad commissions, and by setting railroad rates.

During this classic era of **competitive capitalism**, when small firms competed in local markets, the federal government's role was quite limited. The political scientist Stephen Skowronek found that "[t]he national government throughout the nineteenth century routinely provided promotional and support services for the state governments and left the substantive tasks of governing to these regional units."[4] The national government's jurisdiction in economic matters was limited basically to trade, banking and monetary policy, managing public lands, collecting taxes, and maintaining order.

The activities pursued by state and national government in the early nineteenth century were essential to creating a framework within which business could grow. They challenge the common belief that before the twentieth century government did little to influence the economy. But the economic role governments played in the early nineteenth century paled in comparison to the range and level of activity that governments pursued later in that century, as they tried to respond to the challenges posed by industrialization, the rise of corporate capitalism, and economic instability.

The first wave of economic expansion, which was initiated by the transportation revolution, ended in 1873. Prices fell 25 percent throughout the last quarter of the nineteenth century as fierce competition drove entrepreneurs to introduce new, efficient production methods in an attempt to cut costs and prices. The downturn initiated a wave of business consolidations and acquisitions, creating large corporations that could dominate their markets. Citizens were at the mercy of these corporations, forced to accept the wages they offered and the prices they charged. The labor historian Melvin Dubofsky quotes a Pennsylvania coal miner who lamented, "The working people of this country . . . find monopolies as strong as government itself. They find capital as rigid as absolute monarchy. They find their so-called independence a myth."[5]

These grievances soon found expression in organized political movements. In the 1870s, farmers mobilized through the Farmers Alliance and the Grange, which promoted farmer cooperatives, to put pressure on state legislatures and on Congress to demand fairer rates from the railroads. Workers also mobilized in what became known as the Great Uprising of 1877. Railway workers from Baltimore to San Francisco struck to protest wage cuts. Local governments were either sympathetic to the workers' demands or overwhelmed by their protests, which led the federal government to dispatch troops to crush the first national strike in U.S. history. At the same time that workers manned picket lines, farmers in the South and the West joined the Populist Party. The Populists challenged both major political parties and criticized their ties to banks and large corporations.

All of these disparate movements opposed the growth of large corporations able to dominate their markets at the expense of farmers, workers, and consumers. They shared a belief in equality; a sense that labor, not capital, created wealth; a fear that big business and their Wall Street financiers had captured political power; and an optimism that the majority could tame the corrupting influence of capital.

Although these broad-based social movements failed to capture government from the capitalists they believed had usurped it, they did leave a legacy.

First, these movements left a local heritage of radicalism, which later generations could draw on. For example, in the 1900s the Socialist Party garnered
remarkable support from farmers in the Southwest because it could draw on
an earlier tradition of populism in the region.[6] Second, the political program of
these groups became the basis for later reforms of the Progressive period, which
sought to restrain corporate capitalism.[7] Finally, these movements created an
alternative to the dominant culture of competitive individualism—one based
on the dignity of labor, the benefits of a rough equality, the value of solidarity,
and the virtues of self-sufficiency.[8]

THE RISE OF CORPORATE CAPITALISM

By 1900, small firms that existed in competitive markets were steadily being
driven out of business or were capitulating by combining with larger firms.
"American industry is not free," Princeton professor and future president
Woodrow Wilson wrote in 1913, because "the man with only a little capital is
finding it harder to get into the field, more and more impossible to compete
with the big fellow. Why? Because the laws of this country do not prevent the
strong from crushing the weak."[9] The result was a wave of corporate mergers
and greater industrial concentration. By 1904, a total of 318 corporations held
40 percent of all U.S. manufacturing assets. The House of Morgan alone held
341 directorships in 112 corporations with a net worth totaling $22 billion,
more than twice the assessed value of all property in the southern conglomera-
tion of states that had once comprised the Confederacy.

What is called the Progressive era, from 1900 to 1916, marked a profound
change in the American political economy. The rise of trusts—large corporations that had the raw power to dominate their markets and exploit consumers,
farmers, and employees—generated popular demands for government action.
In the past, state governments had intervened in the economy to *promote*
business. Now citizens demanded that the federal government intervene to
regulate it. President Theodore Roosevelt articulated the view of many citizens
when he argued that if "this irresponsible outside power is to be controlled
in the interest of the general public, it can be controlled in only one way—by
giving adequate power of control . . . to the National Government."[10] Under
popular pressure, the federal government assumed increased responsibility for
regulating business activity, but in a distinctively American way that avoided
"big" government and retained a great deal of freedom for corporations.[11]
Rather than closely scrutinize corporate behavior as many demanded, the federal government would simply prohibit corporations from engaging in what

was described as "unreasonable restraint of trade," such as price fixing. Hence, firms would continue to enjoy a free hand, and government's role would be limited to preventing unfair business practices.[12]

Government intervention in the economy substantially increased during World War I (1917–19) because of the pressing need to mobilize all available resources. The federal government formed tripartite committees, composed of representatives from business, labor, and the government, to develop policy that would coordinate production for the war effort. Although highly successful, the tripartite committees were disbanded at business's insistence when the war ended. In the ensuing prosperity of the 1920s, national income rose throughout the decade. But it rose faster for those at the top of the income scale than it did for those at the bottom. Despite the boom, a majority of families did not have sufficient income to reach "the American standard," a modestly defined measure of minimum comfort, and almost one-quarter of all families lived in severe poverty.[13]

The Roaring Twenties ended on October 21, 1929, when the stock market crashed. The Dow Jones Industrial Average, a barometer of the entire market, lost half its value in just two weeks. The "era of good feelings" was replaced first by gloom and then by despair. Unemployment rose steadily, from 4 million in January 1930 to 6 million by November and then to 8 million by the following January. Employers increased the distress by cutting wages. Each line of defense against poverty—first, family savings; next, private charities; and finally, state- and local-government relief programs—was overwhelmed by the demands for help placed upon it. Meanwhile, President Herbert Hoover, a Republican, stubbornly remained faithful to the prevailing economic orthodoxy, which claimed that the government should not engage in spending to lift the economy out of depression.

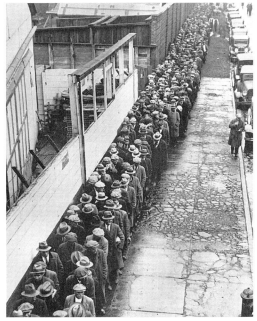

A long line of jobless men in New York City waiting for a free dinner during the Great Depression.

The depth and persistence of the Depression undermined people's faith in capitalism, in capitalists, and in the government. Bread lines, soup kitchens, and unemployment in the millions led people to demand large-scale change. Farmers struck, refusing to bring their crops to market because prices had dropped below production costs. Workers in the great manufacturing centers began to organize into unions. General strikes closed down San Francisco and Minneapolis. Rubber workers in Akron, Ohio, and autoworkers in Flint, Michigan, held sit-down strikes and occupied factories until their demands for union recognition were met. A group of unions broke away from the conservative American Federation of Labor (AFL) to organize unskilled workers in mass-production industries into a new, more militant labor federation called the Congress of Industrial Organizations (CIO). By the end of the thirties, unions affiliated with the CIO boasted over 3.6 million members.

A NEW DEAL

From one end of the country to the other, from farms to factories, people demanded change. In 1932, a new electoral coalition of working people, Catholics, Jews, and southerners elected the Democratic candidate, Franklin Delano Roosevelt, president. In dramatic contrast to a dithering President Hoover, Roosevelt boldly promised a New Deal. He proposed that the government devise measures to end the Depression, provide relief, and manage the economy to restore growth. Roosevelt was not hostile to capitalism but believed that greater management by the federal government was required to save it. But as the Depression was superseded by a new emergency—World War II—a subtle but significant shift in prevailing economic ideas occurred. The Roosevelt administration's priorities shifted from promoting growth through greater state intervention to promoting growth through greater private consumption.

This new economic paradigm, in which consumption drove the economy, was based on ideas first developed by the British economist John Maynard Keynes. Keynes claimed that the major cause of the Depression was inadequate consumer demand. The economy was caught in a vicious circle in which mass unemployment reduced the demand for goods. As inventories piled up for lack of consumers to purchase them, firms laid off even more workers. To break the destructive cycle, government would have to step into the breach. By running a deficit in the federal budget—spending more than it collected in taxes—government would increase the amount of money in circulation and thereby increase demand. Once people had money to spend again, business would react to the new consumer demand by rehiring workers and increasing production.

With workers back on the job earning and spending wages, demand would grow and the economic recovery would become self-sustaining. Thus, Keynes argued, deficit spending by the government in times of slack demand was the key to transforming vicious circles of stagnation into virtuous circles of growth.

Corporations frightened by the potential radicalism of the New Deal found Roosevelt's new emphasis on increasing consumption preferable to earlier, more ambitious New Deal proposals. Budget deficits required no change in the distribution of economic power between government and business, whereas the initial proposals had involved more-sweeping structural reforms such as government planning. According to the historian Alan Brinkley, New Dealers in President Roosevelt's inner circle now spoke less about redistributing economic power and more about increasing mass purchasing power.[14]

In many ways, the Depression and World War II emergencies represented a missed opportunity to regulate private economic power.[15] Further structural changes were considered but eventually lost out in favor of the less threatening solution to use government to stimulate demand. That these more-radical proposals were discarded in no way minimizes the substantial changes that took place. For example, the outlines of the welfare state were forged during the New Deal, offering citizens some protection against the swings of the business cycle. Unemployment insurance and Social Security created at least a minimal safety net where none existed previously. The labor market also came in for a degree of regulation as child labor was outlawed and a minimum-wage law was passed. Labor unions grew from 3 million members in 1929 to 14 million by 1945, offering workers some protection against the unilateral power of management. The federal government also grew. Federal expenditures that were just 3 percent of the gross domestic product (GDP) in 1929 were 10 percent of GDP a decade later. The number of federal employees almost doubled in the same ten-year period. The growth of the welfare state, unions, and the federal government was consolidated after World War II. Their larger size and power were recognized as part of the postwar landscape and regarded as legitimate by both Democrats and Republicans until the 1980s.

Significant as these changes were, when set against comparable developments that occurred in Europe they appear trifling. Although the federal government emerged from World War II owning 40 percent of all capital assets in the United States, there was no vigorous push to nationalize such basic industries as telecommunications, airlines, utilities, railways, and steel as occurred in many European countries. In addition, the government applied the most conservative form of **Keynesianism** possible. For example, Keynes believed that full employment was essential to increasing aggregate—total—demand.

Consistent with this belief, President Harry Truman (who replaced President Roosevelt when the latter died in office) submitted the Full Employment Act to Congress in 1945, just two weeks after the end of World War II. However, conservatives in Congress proceeded to dilute the bill beyond recognition, even removing the term *Full* from what was now simply called the Employment Act.[16] Keynes also believed that some kind of redistribution of income from the top to the bottom was required. He identified as one of the "outstanding faults of the [capitalist] economic society in which we live . . . its arbitrary and inequitable distribution of wealth."[17] But Keynes's prescription to redistribute wealth was rejected in America. Welfare-state spending was lower and less redistributive in the United States than in Europe. Finally, the conservative form Keynesianism took in the United States was evident in the way it ran deficits. Both Democratic and Republican administrations chose to pursue deficit spending through cutting taxes rather than increasing expenditures.[18] Demand would be stimulated through increasing private consumption as opposed to promoting public goods. And even when the government did prop up demand through spending, it did so disproportionately through increasing military as opposed to welfare-state outlays.

In brief, a conservative form of Keynesianism became the new economic orthodoxy following the war, accepted not only by Democrats but eventually by Republicans as well. The American version of Keynesianism included only a symbolic commitment to full employment; economic stimulation through military spending, not redistribution; and deficit spending through tax cuts, not public investment. When recast in this form, even business, which was initially hostile to Keynesianism, came to appreciate its benefits. Although the Democratic Party was the first to embrace Keynesianism, by the 1970s even President Richard Nixon, a Republican, could declare, "We are all Keynesians now."[19]

THE RISE AND FALL OF THE GOLDEN AGE, 1945–1980

Many feared that the economy would slide back into recession once the artificial stimulus of World War II was removed. Instead, the United States experienced the most prosperous 25 years in its history, often dubbed the **golden age** of capitalism. Median family income almost doubled between 1950 and 1970. As the historian Jack Metzgar recalls in his memoir of the period, the affluence of the postwar years was "new, and surprising—like a first kiss."[20] Urban working families moved out of tenements and acquired new homes in the suburbs. Televisions, cars, washing machines, and telephones—beyond the reach of most families in 1940—were now owned by a majority of families just 20 years later.

The success of the U.S. economy can be attributed to an unusual coincidence of national and international factors that distinguish this period from what came before—and after. First, pent-up consumer demand fueled the postwar economy. Production for the war effort restricted the supply of consumer goods at the same time that it put people to work and money in their pockets. The combination of disposable income and pent-up demand led Americans to spend freely once wartime controls were lifted.

Second, the huge demand for consumer goods led businesses to expand capacity and invest in new plants and equipment. Third, labor relations simmered down following the 1946 strike wave, the largest in American history. Employers now resentfully acknowledged unions as a fact of life they could not avoid. Fourth, big government contributed to the new affluence. Government spending climbed steadily from $47.1 billion in 1950, or 21 percent of GDP, to $236.1 billion by 1970, or almost 27 percent of GDP. Big government was not a drag on economic growth during the golden age of capitalism but, rather, was essential to it.

Finally, the postwar economy profited from the emergence of U.S. global dominance. American firms were busy not only satisfying the voracious appetite of American consumers but also supplying war-torn Europe with food and clothes as well as equipment and other supplies to rebuild its devastated economies. Moreover, American firms had the world market to themselves. The only potential competitors, in Europe and Japan, were heavily damaged from World War II and needed to devote their scarce resources to wartime recovery.

By mid-century, the terms of the informal national bargain that had been struck between business and government were clear. Strategic decisions governing the American economy—how much to invest, where to invest, what to invest in, how to organize the work—would be made by corporate capital. Government would not intrude on corporate decision making or engage in economic planning that might interfere with business's right to manage. Instead, by smoothing out the business cycle, educating workers, stimulating consumption, funding research, and protecting corporate markets and investments abroad, government would create a political and economic environment that would encourage corporate investment and job creation.[21]

Over the course of the 1970s, however, prosperity waned as the economy began to experience **stagflation**, an unprecedented situation in which rising unemployment and inflation occurred simultaneously. In the past, unemployment and inflation moved in opposite directions. Now they both rose together.

The average rate of unemployment was 6.2 percent in the 1970s, compared to just 4.8 percent in the 1960s. Similarly, the average rate of inflation was much higher than in the preceding decade. The exceptional conditions that so clearly favored American firms in the golden age crumbled. For example, European and Japanese industry, which were in ruins following World War II, had been rebuilt and could now compete with American manufacturers in world markets.

Symptomatic of America's economic decline was slower productivity growth, which squeezed profits. Managers tried to restore productivity growth and relieve the profit squeeze by coercing employees to work harder for less money. Business threatened to close plants if unions did not agree to wage and work-rule concessions in collective bargaining. Meanwhile, business engaged in old-fashioned union busting to reassert managerial control and speed up work. In 1978, United Auto Workers president Douglas Fraser bitterly charged, "I believe leaders of the business community, with few exceptions, have chosen to wage a one-sided class war in this country—a war against working people, the unemployed, the poor, the minorities, the very young and the very old, even many in the middle class of our society. The leaders of industry, commerce, and finance in the U.S. have broken and discarded the fragile, unwritten contract previously existing during a period of growth and progress."[22]

Conservative Keynesianism collapsed in the 1970s, defeated by unemployment, inflation, lower productivity growth, and rising trade deficits. The end of growth undermined confidence in the Democratic Party and discredited its formula of conservative Keynesianism. A new economic paradigm we label "market fundamentalism," articulated by a resurgent Republican Party, would soon replace Keynesian orthodoxy.

THE RISE AND FALL OF MARKET FUNDAMENTALISM, 1980–2008

In 1980, American voters, battered by stagflation, turned to the Republican Party and elected Ronald Reagan as president. Reagan was at the forefront of a new majority coalition that articulated a new economic philosophy of market fundamentalism. In the previous era, government intervention was regarded as useful in reducing inequality, policing corporate behavior, and stabilizing the business cycle; but now the burden of proof had shifted. Free markets now were regarded as appropriate and beneficial, and government oversight of them was perceived as inefficient and illegitimate. Even Bill Clinton, the only Democrat elected president during this period, declared approvingly in his 1996 State of the Union address to the country, "The era of big government is over."

Market fundamentalism held that markets are rational, self-correcting, and beneficial. That is, prices set by markets reflect the actual value of what goods and assets are worth (rational); the business cycle has been tamed and government regulation is unnecessary (self-correcting); and the results of leaving markets alone to work their magic are good for society (beneficial).

Two policy changes mark the shift away from the preceding period of conservative Keynesianism. First, prosperity would no longer depend on the welfare of workers whose wages propelled aggregate demand. Now, according to the new theory of supply-side economics, prosperity would depend on the welfare of the affluent, whose savings supplied the capital for investment.

Supply-side economics argued that the economy suffered from insufficient investment capital, not insufficient demand. To boost the supply of investment capital, Republicans proposed to cut taxes—most of all for the rich. Those who needed tax relief the least received the most, on the premise they were more likely to save and contribute to the stock of capital needed for investment.

Supply-side economists forecast that the powerful growth resulting from tax cuts would increase tax revenue despite the cut in tax rates. Campaigning against Reagan in the Republican primaries in 1980, George H. W. Bush dismissed this theory as "voodoo economics." But he joined Reagan's administration as his vice president to pass one of the largest tax cuts in American history. One of his sons, George W. Bush, became president in 2000 and passed tax cuts that surpassed even those of President Reagan. The Bush tax cuts reduced government revenues and contributed to the deficit. Further, the rich received the most benefits from the Bush tax cuts, which in addition to reducing tax rates also eliminated the estate tax.

Republicans promoted tax cuts because they had political, as well as economic, advantages. They saw tax breaks as a way to reward voters and bind them to the party, just as Democrats before them had used spending programs to pay off their supporters. Balanced budgets "were for chumps."[23] The Democratic Party's strategy of bidding for votes with spending would be countered by the new Republican practice of bidding for votes by offering new tax breaks.

In addition to serving as a crass payoff to voters, tax cuts were intended to impose fiscal restraint on the government. Some Republicans dismissed the supply-side faith that cutting tax rates would increase net revenues. In contrast, they saw economic virtue in cutting tax rates precisely because it would create pressure to reduce revenues. Less tax revenues would force governments to cut spending or else be criticized as fiscally irresponsible for the ensuing deficits.

Whether lower taxes led to lower spending or to deficits, the goal was the same, as one supply-sider revealed: to reduce "the size and scale of government by draining its lifeblood," by starving government of the funds it needed.[24]

The second policy shift, alongside tax cuts, identified with market fundamentalism was **deregulation.** Republicans argued that regulations such as environmental standards and consumer protection needed to be rolled back if business was going to compete in a fast-moving, global marketplace. Deregulation would restore business's right to manage without being hampered by expensive, burdensome rules. Republicans pursued deregulaton by cutting agency budgets to reduce their effectiveness. For example, from 2001 to 2007, when the Republicans controlled the House of Representatives and the presidency, funding for the Environmental Protection Agency (EPA) declined by $1.3 billion, or 15 percent of its budget. As a result, the EPA could not do enough inspections to ensure that environmental standards were followed or to develop new rules to keep pace with new pollutants.

Republican presidents also promoted deregulation by increasing White House oversight of new rules that agencies proposed. Rules had to pass cost-benefit-analysis stress tests administered by the White House before being approved. The White House also developed procedures designed to frustrate new regulations by permitting industry at any point along the rulemaking process to question the data agencies used in support of the regulations. Finally, deregulation proceeded through appointments in which the foxes were invited to guard the chickens—that is, people who were opposed to the mission of regulatory agencies were appointed to direct them.

The shift away from conservative Keynesianism to the new paradigm of market fundamentalism had three significant outcomes. First, it created large budget deficits because the government spent more than it received in taxes. During the period of conservative Keynesianism, the national debt as a percentage of the GDP had declined steadily, from about 90 percent of GDP in 1950 to about 33 percent when President Jimmy Carter left office in 1980. Following that period, the federal deficit as a proportion of GDP nearly doubled to about 63 percent when President George W. Bush left office in 2009. Much of the deficit during this period was due not to increased federal outlays, which remained fairly steady as a percentage of GDP since 1980, but to a decline in revenues resulting from tax cuts.

Second, market fundamentalism contributed to growing inequality, as revealed in Table 3.1. From 1950 to 1980, during the golden age, the middle quintiles (each quintile equals one-fifth) fared better than those either at the top or at the bottom. The bottom two quintiles, composed of the poorest households, lost some ground; they received 15.7 percent of all income in 1950 and 14.6 percent 30 years later. The next two quintiles, however, fared better; both saw their share of household

WHAT DO YOU THINK?

Which Poses the Greater Danger: Market Failure or Political Failure?

Some people believe that society benefits when governments intervene in the economy, as occurred under the Democrats and their policies of conservative Keynesianism; others believe that society suffers when the government intervenes and that we are better off following the Republican model of market fundamentalism. Those in the former group believe that government intervention is necessary to protect society from market failure. Left alone, the market leads to too much inequality and too much neglect of the public good. The latter group believes that government intervention leads to political failure. Left alone, politicans will spend recklessly to attract voters and invest in projects with the biggest political, not economic, payoffs. Does government intervention yield better results for citizens than free markets? What criteria should be used to evaluate whether more government intervention is preferable to more market freedom?

income rise. The middle and second-to-top quintiles saw their share of income rise by 0.8 percent and 2.8 percent, respectively. The biggest losers were the highest income earners, those in the top fifth of households. Their share of income declined from 46.1 percent of all income in 1950 to 43.7 percent in 1980. The steepest losses within this group were among the top 5 percent of households, whose share of income declined dramatically, from 21.4 to 15.8 percent.

TABLE 3.1

HOUSEHOLD SHARES OF AGGREGATE INCOME, 1950-2006

Year	Bottom Quintile	Second Quintile	Third Quintile	Fourth Quintile	Top Quintile	Top 5%
1950	4.8	10.9	16.1	22.1	46.1	21.4
1980	4.3	10.3	16.9	24.9	43.7	15.8
2006	3.4	8.6	14.5	22.9	50.5	22.3

SOURCE: For 1980 and 2006 figures, see U.S. Census Bureau, Current Population Survey, "Annual Social and Economic Supplements," Table H-2, at www.census.gov/hhes/www/income/histinc/h02AR.html (accessed April 16, 2010). For 1950 figures, see Paul Ryscarage, *Income Inventory in America: An Analysis of Trends* (New York: Sharpe, 1998), Table 6.6, 154.

But then a stunningly different pattern emerges under market fundamentalism promoted by Republicans. The share of income received by the bottom 40 percent of households dropped from 14.6 percent to 12 percent—more than twice the decline that this group experienced from 1950 to 1980. The middle quintile also saw its share of income fall, from 16.9 percent to 14 percent, as did households in the second-to-top quintile, whose share fell from 24.9 to 22.9 percent. The only group whose share of income grew was the top 20 percent, which by itself now earned more than half of all household income—more than the combined income of the bottom four-fifths of all American households— and within this select group, income had become more concentrated among the richest 5 percent of all American households. The biggest losers under the Democratic Party program of conservative Keynesianism had become the biggest winners under the Republican policy of market fundamentalism.

Finally, market fundamentalism coincided with a profound shift in the basis of the economy, from industry to finance. Deindustrialization and the contraction of core industries, such as autos, steel, machine tools, and electrical goods, accelerated dramatically in the last quarter of the twentieth century. Industrial capital, which produced something, was eclipsed by financial capital, which produced nothing. In 1980, not one bank or company active in financial services was included in the top 100 firms of the Fortune 500. Instead, it was populated by auto (GM), oil (Mobil), steel (US Steel), paper (Weyerhauser), and chemical (DuPont) companies, which owned real assets and produced material wealth. By contrast, in 2007, before the financial crisis hit, financial-services companies that produced intangible assets and paper wealth comprised one-fifth of all the firms in the top 20 of the Fortune 500, and another 5 were among the largest 50 firms in the U.S. The financial sector's share of total U.S. corporate profits was 10 percent on average from the 1950s to the 1980s. It then doubled, to 22 percent, in the 1990s and then rose by half again, to 34 percent on average, during 2000–05—more than twice the share of profits as energy, the next-largest sector. Pay in the financial sector also rose dramatically. From 1948 to 1982, average compensation in the financial sector ranged between 99 and 108 percent of the average for workers in all domestic private industries. But beginning in 1983, pay per worker in the financial sector shot upward to 181 percent of the average compensation per worker in the United States by 2007. Whereas the financial industry once accounted for just 3 percent of all wages and salaries in the 1950s, its take had doubled to 7 percent by 2007.[25] As if to announce the financial sector's new economic dominance, eight major-league baseball stadiums are currently named for banks or insurance companies.

The financialization of the economy has been corrosive in many ways. Banks that are too big to fail are considered so indispensable that politicians are reluctant to challenge their policy preferences. Consequently, the financial sector has been able to wield extraordinary influence over the government, affecting policies that create new sources of profits for banks but also increase risk, debt, and instability throughout the economy.

The financial dominance of banks has also had a disproportionate effect on the way people behave economically. Debt is valued over savings, and the virtues of consumerism have replaced those of thrift. During the golden age, the ratio of debt to household disposable income increased only modestly, from 55 percent in 1960 to 65 percent by the 1980s. But in the ensuing period, debt more than doubled, to 133 percent of household disposable income by 2007. Low interest rates and easy access to borrowed money that banks offered through credit cards and home loans enticed families to live beyond their means. Consumption as a share of GDP rose from 62 percent in the 1960s to 73 percent by 2008. As consumption increased, the savings rate dropped from 12 percent of household income to less than zero by 2005.[26] All of this debt-fueled consumption then contributed to the rising balance of trade deficits, as Americans used the money they borrowed from banks to buy goods produced in China.

THE FINANCIAL CRISIS

The recession struck with a ferocity and speed that few had anticipated. Between 2007 and 2010 about $12 trillion of wealth evaporated as housing prices collapsed and the stock market tumbled. The collapse of the housing market in 2007 precipitated the calamity. Housing prices had been escalating, driven by low interest rates set by the Federal Reserve Board (the Fed) and easy lending practiced by banks. The Fed kept the interest rate it charged banks so low that for 31 consecutive months, from 2001 through 2003, it was negative after adjusting for inflation. Money was essentially free to banks that were anxious to give out loans that generated fees and interest. Consequently, the banks loosened their lending standards in order to make more loans. Lenders required little documentation and provided NINJA (no income, no job, no assets) loans to people who would not ordinarily have qualified for them. Subprime lending to less creditworthy customers jumped from $145 billion in 2001 to $625 billion in 2005, more than 20 percent of total home loans.[27]

Banks then bundled these loans together and sold them as securities, or negotiable assets, to get new money and make even more loans. Other banks and investors bought these securities because they had been given AAA ratings by companies that vouched for them as safe investments. And bank regulators were unconcerned about the amount of debt banks took on to provide more loans because they trusted banks to assess their own risk. Everyone made money: people who bought homes would flip them six months later for a profit; banks received interest and fees on mortgage loans to homeowners; and investment firms made fees by selling securities of mortgages that had been bundled together.

As the housing market boomed, however, it became a speculative bubble, driven by new waves of investors hoping to cash in on rising housing prices, creating more demand and ever higher prices. But then the music stopped. Investors who provided the seed money for housing loans to banks became skeptical of the housing values underlying the mortgage securities they bought. When the money that kept this confidence scheme afloat dried up, housing prices began to fall. In Fort Myers, Florida, the median price of a home that had been as high as $322,000 in December 2005 fell to an astonishing $106,900 by January 2008. Subprime homeowners who had borrowed on easy lending terms offered by banks could not pay their debt, which was now greater than their homes were worth. Others, who had bought homes in hopes of flipping them at a profit, were now stuck with property that would not sell, and they, too, could not afford their loans. As more homes were put up for sale, prices fell. New homes that had been constructed during the boom stood empty and were joined by an inventory of foreclosed homes, which depressed prices even more. Just as rising demand for houses had pushed home prices higher, which attracted more investors who drove prices even higher, so did the increasing supply of unsold homes now drive prices lower, creating its own momentum in the other direction.

Housing defaults cascaded all the way through the system. Banks that had become highly leveraged with debt in order to provide mortgages now found themselves with loans they could not recover. Nor did they have enough assets to cover their losses. The investment bank Lehman Brothers, for example, had $700 billion in various investments at the time of its bankruptcy in 2007, but its shareholder equity was only $23 billion. All the rest of its investments were supported with borrowed money. Other banks also sustained heavy losses; they had borrowed money to buy mortgage securities that had lost much of their value and could not find investors for the securities they held and intended to sell.

With banks collapsing, the wheels of commerce ground to a halt. As quick as they were to lend money in good times, banks were now reluctant to lend it when conditions worsened. Banks hoarded capital and would not extend credit. Without access to credit, firms could not pay suppliers, meet payrolls, or purchase goods. The crisis in housing now threatened to take down the entire economy. To restore confidence and credit, the government stepped in to bail out the banks. It took stock in failing banks, such as Citigroup and Bank of America, which were deemed too big to fail; this step injected them with the money they needed to keep operating. The government also passed a $787 billion stimulus bill to ward off recession, guaranteed loans to restore confidence, and oversaw the reorganization and partial nationalization of the auto industry. The policy of letting markets rule required government to step into the breach to save the economy.

THE DEADLOCK OF DEMOCRACY

In the 1980s, market fundamentalists silenced their critics by asserting that "there is no alternative" (what came to be known as TINA) if the mistakes of the previous period under Democratic rule were to be avoided. TINA was a powerful bludgeon that Republicans used to intimidate liberals who demanded more regulation to protect the public and more spending to spur demand.

But with the economy caught in a downward spiral, TINA was now invoked by President Obama and Democrats who wanted to expand government's role in the economy, not reduce it—by those who wanted to regulate markets, not extend them. Advocates of government claimed there was no alternative if the costly blunders of market fundamentalism under the Republicans were to be reversed. TINA—the true sorcerer's stone in politics, giving power to whoever can wield it—had switched sides.

The recession and financial crisis discredited market fundamentalism, revealing its flawed premises. Markets do not behave rationally but are subject to what Keynes referred to as "animal spirits." Markets are vulnerable to unwarranted outbreaks of confidence that lead to speculative bubbles and to crises of confidence in which credit dries up. Nor are markets self-correcting. In the midst of the housing bubble, the former chair of the Federal Reserve Bank Alan Greenspan informed Congress there was nothing to worry about: "Market pricing and counterparty surveillance can be expected to do most of the job of sustaining safety and soundness."[28] But Greenspan, as he later admitted, was wrong. The temptation for banks to take outsize risks was too great to resist, especially because compensation for bank executives was tied to profits. It became apparent that government regulation was necessary to ensure banks acted in ways that were in the public's interest, as well as their own. Finally, leaving decisions to the market does not always lead to the best results for society. It contributes to instability and inequality. Economic volatility creates insecurity and weakens people's ability to plan for the future, while inequality undermines social cohesion and corrupts democracy.

In the midst of the recession, the government displayed a new aggressiveness. The Bush and Obama administrations rescued failing banks by injecting money into them on very favorable terms. New regulations were imposed on banks to prevent another meltdown, and new agencies were created to protect consumers from predatory financial practices. But the two main tools the government relied on to stimulate the economy and put people back to work were fiscal and monetary policy. (Both are covered in much greater detail in Chapter 9.)

Fiscal policy involves using the federal budget, specifically tax revenues and spending, to influence the economy. The Obama administration tried to give the economy a boost by cutting taxes and increasing spending. Both strategies were part of Obama's $787 billion stimulus bill in 2009. But the stimulus was too small to have much effect on an economy measured at $14 trillion GDP. In addition, federal policies were mitigated by state- and local-government policies that moved in the opposite direction. They increased taxes and reduced spending to cope with their own budget crises. Consequently, the U.S. economy's fiscal stimulus was one of the smallest of any Western country. Even though the dosage was too small to bring the fever down very much, further shots of fiscal stimulus were precluded by Republican opposition.

Fiscal policy was applied timidly. The patient showed only limited signs of improvement. At the same time, another team of doctors was working on the patient using a different approach. The Federal Reserve Bank (the Fed) applied monetary policy, which involved adjusting the money supply to affect interest rates. While fiscal policy was applied tentatively, monetary policy was employed aggressively. First, the Fed brought down short-term interest rates to near zero, as low as they can go, to encourage lending. Wanting to do more, the Fed purchased about $2 trillion in government bonds, mortgage-based assets, and other securities in three different rounds of what is called quantitative easing. This pumped new money into the economy to reduce long-term interest rates, which apply to housing and other crucial markets. The treatments did not restore the patient to health, but the disease was arrested.

Unemployment remains lamentably high. But the U.S., which was the epicenter of the financial crisis, has performed better and has had more GDP growth than almost all of its peers. It has avoided the staggering unemployment that afflicts Italy and Spain; the dispiriting lack of growth that bedevils France and Britain; and its banks are in better shape than those in Germany.

The Eurozone economy, comprised of 17 of the countries in the European Union that use the euro as their currency, did not see any growth in 2012 and is now smaller than it was five years ago. In contrast, the U.S. economy was expected to grow by about 2 percent in 2012 and is 2.9 percent bigger than it was five years ago, before the financial crisis hit. Employment is the one area in which the U.S. has not responded as effectively as Europe to the recession. Although the U.S. had more growth, it also had higher rates of unemployment than many European countries. But this was only because European governments were more aggressive in subsidizing wages to keep workers at their jobs and in financing public works to put them back to work. In other words, the one way in which the U.S. response to the recession was less impressive than Europe's was the result of too little government, not too much.[29]

Despite the comparatively successful response to the recession, the activism of the Obama administration spurred a backlash. Subsidized by corporate money, the Tea Party emerged to condemn growing deficits. Its enthusiasm radicalized and energized the Republican Party, which triumphed in the 2010 midterm elections. Republicans became the new majority in the House, winning a stunning 65 seats from Democrats, and an additional 5 seats in the Senate. A freshman class of Tea Party–supported Republicans came to Washington determined to change its extravagant ways. First, they threatened to shut down the government. They refused to pass continuing resolutions to keep the government funded unless the Obama administration agreed to $100 billion in budget cuts. Then they threatened the U.S. with default on its debt. They refused to increase the debt limit unless the president agreed to entitlement reform, which meant cutting Medicare, Medicaid, and Social Security. The president indicated he would reform entitlements, but only if the Republicans agreed to increase taxes. The deficit, Obama argued, had to be attacked from both sides: by increasing taxes as well as reducing spending. Negotiations between the administration and congressional leaders were at an impasse. The August 2, 2011 deadline when loans were due was fast approaching. If the government defaulted, it would not have enough money on hand to pay Social Security benefits or the salaries of troops in the field, or to keep federal offices and institutions open. Interest rates would skyrocket. Just three days before the looming deadline, negotiators announced an agreement. Republicans in Congress blinked and agreed to vote to increase the debt ceiling, permitting the government to borrow additional money to pay its creditors and finance its activities. In return for their cooperation, a supercommittee composed of Senate and House leaders from both parties would be empowered to devise a plan to reduce the deficit by $1.5 trillion and report back in ten weeks.

A group of protestors stands behind Congressional Budget Office Director Douglas Elmendorf at a 2011 hearing on the national debt. The hearing came in the wake of the ceiling crisis that almost led to a government shutdown.

Markets were stunned by the dysfunction that almost brought the country to default. Standard & Poor's downgraded America's credit rating from AAA to AA+ for the first time in history. Americans also gave its political leaders failing grades. Obama's approval rating dropped to 44 percent. But the public saved its greatest contempt and scorn for Congress, whose approval rating dropped to 9 percent, an all-time low.

Negotiators had built in a poison pill to give the supercommittee an incentive to reach a settlement. If it did not succeed, then automatic cuts in defense and domestic programs would ensue; only Social Security and Medicaid would be exempt from these cuts, called sequestration, which would begin to take effect on January 2, 2013. But there was little chance that fear of sequestration would produce a settlement when the more dire threat of default had failed to do so earlier. Moreover, it was unlikely that Democrats and Republicans on the supercommittee would be able to reach an agreement in ten weeks when congressional leaders had failed to do so in the seven months of negotiations leading up to the debt-ceiling deadline. As many had anticipated, negotiations in the supercommittee failed. But now members of Congress balked when they were faced with the threat of large cuts to defense and domestic programs they had created themselves! They were reluctant to accept the pain they had built into the process back in July.

Dysfunction, partisanship, and gridlock were evident not only in the maneuvering over default but in the fact that Congress had not sent a budget for the president to sign since April 2009. The government, instead, had been kept running from one continuing resolution to the next.[30]

The drama of economic policy—reducing deficits, cutting spending, and raising taxes—became even more intense following Obama's reelection in 2012. The country was headed for the fiscal cliff. Bush-era tax cuts for all citizens were set to expire on January 1, 2013, at virtually the same time sequestration—the automatic cuts to defense and domestic programs—were scheduled to take effect. The double-whammy of higher taxes and less government spending threatened to tip the economy into another recession. Negotiations between President Obama and Republican Speaker of the House John Boehner collapsed. President Obama wanted to deliver on his campaign pledge to retain the Bush tax cuts for all but the richest Americans. But Boehner rejected the offer under pressure from Republicans in the House who opposed raising taxes on anyone—even though failure to reach a deal would raise taxes on everyone. With the deadline approaching and no deal in sight, scorn and ridicule rained down on Congress. The noted sex therapist Ruth Westheimer even tried to embarrass congressional negotiators by suggesting that people who could not compromise were probably bad lovers. Finally, a deal was hammered out that passed the Senate with bipartisan support. Those who earned less than $400,000 would continue to be taxed at current Bush-era rates, while those earning more would now be subject to higher tax rates on income, capital gains, and dividends. The bill also delayed the sequester for two months and included a one-year extension of unemployment insurance, and a five-year extension of tax credits for college tuition, child care, and for low-income workers. In total, the bill was the largest and most progressive tax increase in decades, with the tax burden falling predominantly on the wealthy.

But it still was not certain that the Senate bill could pass the more conservative House, where Republicans had a majority. Finally, on New Year's Day, the House passed the bill, with a minority of House Republicans joining almost all the House Democrats in supporting it. The vote on the measure revealed geographic and political fissures within the Republican Party. Almost all the House Republicans who voted for the bill were from outside the South. These G.O.P. representatives were frightened that they would be held responsible by general-election voters for taking the country over the cliff and into recession if the bill failed. Republicans who voted against the measure were from safe districts in the South. They were more worried about surviving a Tea Party challenge in the Republican primary than about winning in November. They could more easily suffer criticism about sending the economy into recession than they could withstand accusations from conservatives of voting to raise taxes.

Averting the fiscal cliff involved retaining Bush era tax cuts for all but the wealthy and delaying for two months the first installment of $1.2 trillion in sequestration cuts to defense and domestic programs over the next nine years. As the March 1, 2013 deadline loomed for the first set of cuts, Obama proposed offsetting some of them with new revenue by closing tax loopholes. He feared that cutting spending when the economy was still fragile might induce another recession. Republicans refused, claiming that Obama already got his additional tax revenue when tax rates for the wealthy increased back in January. Unable to agree, indiscriminant, across-the-board sequestration cuts to defense and domestic programs that few thought were likely when they were first proposed, and that fewer thought were good policy now that they were imminent, commenced. Congress swallowed what was initially designed to be a poison pill.

As Obama took office for a second term, economic policy lurched from one deadline-induced crisis to another. First the country had to suffer the drama of the fiscal cliff in January, 2013. Two months later, Democrats and Republicans were at odds over sequestration, with more fights over raising the debt limit and approving the budget looming in the future.

Economic policy is paralyzed by the deadlock of democracy, which is magnified by divided government (in which one party holds the presidency and the other party one or both branches of Congress). In the past, one party was dominant politically and able to assert its economic paradigm. During the golden age of capitalism from 1945–1980, the Democrats were powerful enough to impose their program of conservative Keynesianism. Similarly, between 1980 and 2008, the Republicans predominantly held sway and were able to enact their model of market fundamentalism. But today, the balance between the parties is exquisitely even. The last few election cycles have resulted in frequent shifts in power from one party to the next, or yielded divided government. Neither the Democrats nor the Republicans can impose their economic model. The infuriating deadlock and embarrassing dysfunction of the last few years will end only when one of the parties is able to gain a decisive and enduring political advantage.

CONCLUSION

The American political economy—the balance struck between state and markets, between public and private power—has been the result of unremitting conflict. Conflict has occurred not only over how much the government should intervene in the market, but also over which government institutions should be responsible for intervening, what policies they should adopt, and who should benefit from them. Promotion of industry by state governments in the nineteenth century was replaced by regulation of industry by the federal government at the beginning of the twentieth century.

The Great Depression of the 1930s initiated a shift not only in political power but also in the balance between states and markets. Democrats replaced Republicans as the ruling party and more actively tried to manage capitalism in response to its failure. They created the modern welfare state to establish a safety net for citizens who fell out of the market, used government budgets to stabilize production, and engaged in more regulation to protect the public interest. But the Democratic formula was exhausted by the 1970s, leading to both inflation and unemployment. The Democratic Party lost power, and its economic model was replaced with a new paradigm calling for less government intervention. Republicans, with the exception of the Clinton interlude, captured the presidency and used gains in Congress to redraw the boundary between states and markets. They initiated tax cuts to limit government by starving it of the funds it needs and removed regulations on business to restore managerial authority.

Just as the Democrats lost power when their economic model failed, so the Republicans lost power as their economic paradigm failed in the financial meltdown and recession that began in 2008. Democrats proceeded to use the instruments of government to pull capitalism back from the brink. They proposed new regulations to rein in Wall Street, ran budget deficits to stimulate production, and brought more government control to the health-care market. But this elicited a backlash from conservatives and corporations. They mobilized to check what they perceived as the unwarranted expansion of government. Restoring capitalist vitality, they argued, required less government, not more. Balance between the Democrats and Republicans, each representing these alternate approaches, has resulted in deadlock and dysfunction.

CHAPTER SUMMARY

Introduction
American history has been replete with conflict over how much government should intervene in markets and private firms, what parts of the government should be responsible for economic policy, and what policies they should follow. Business has often been successful in these struggles,

but their outcomes are always open and contingent, dependent on the political capacity of contending groups.

Competitive Capitalism

State governments, more than the federal government, were extraordinarily active in promoting capitalist development in the early days of the republic. But small firms producing for competitive markets soon gave way to large firms able to dictate prices and wages. Workers and consumers increasingly looked to the federal government for protection from the market power of large corporations.

The Rise of Corporate Capitalism

By the 1880s, large corporations dominated industrial production. Their economic power precipitated protests that forced their allies in the Republican Party to accept some regulation of corporate practices. But the public lost faith in both the Republican Party and large corporations when those organizations failed to respond adequately to the Great Depression.

A New Deal

President Roosevelt and the Democratic Party took power in 1933 amid the Great Depression and introduced a new model of economic policy based on more government intervention. Roosevelt's New Deal included the welfare state, more regulation of business, and a plan to stimulate the economy through increasing demand by putting people to work, supporting unions, and promoting deficit spending.

The Rise and Fall of the Golden Age, 1945–1980

The Democrats retained power following World War II and continued using the state to support capitalist production by smoothing out the business cycle, expanding the welfare state, educating workers, funding research, and protecting markets abroad. But the policies Democrats followed were conservative to the extent that they did not redistribute income to those who needed it most, that government outlays increased more for the military than for the welfare state, and that there was little effort to change the balance of public and private power through either nationalization or planning as occurred in Europe. Democrats and their formula of conservative Keynesianism were discredited in the downturn of the 1970s.

The Rise and Fall of Market Fundamentalism, 1980–2008

Republicans were emboldened by political success in the 1980s and proposed a new economic model, based on tax cuts and deregulation, that was designed to roll back the frontier of government. Market fundamentalism led to economic growth but also contributed to larger deficits, more inequality, and a shift in the balance between industrial and financial capital. Market fundamentalism lost credibility when the housing market collapsed in 2007, leading to bank failures and the deepest recession since the 1930s.

The Financial Crisis

The drop in the housing market precipitated a financial crisis because banks were awash in bad debts. Lending ceased as bankers tried to conserve capital, choking off credit that the economy needed. Government rescued the banks with bailouts to revive credit. Belief in the recuperative power of the market gave way to faith in the restorative power of the government.

The Deadlock of Democracy

Democrats returned to power and used government aggressively to rescue the banks and restore economic growth. It intervened in the economy—investing in auto companies, as well as setting executive pay—in ways that would have been unimaginable under the previous regime. But it is still unclear whether this new government activism will simply repair a broken financial system without changing which groups it serves; that is, whether more government intervention will redirect the economy from meeting the needs of the one percent to meeting the needs of the 99 percent.

Critical Thinking Questions

1. Was the New Deal a success?

2. What factors contributed to American prosperity during the golden age of capitalism and eventually led to its demise in the 1970s?

3. Have Republicans been better economic managers than Democrats?

4. Can anything be done to tame the business cycle and prevent bubbles from arising and bursting with such calamitous force as occurred during the recent recession?

5. What do you think the government should have done in response to the recent recession?

6. What standards would you use to assess whether American policy makers were more successful in responding to the recent recession than their counterparts in Europe?

Suggested Readings

American Social History Project, *Who Built America?* Vols. I and II, 3rd ed. New York: St. Martin's, 2008.

Harry Braverman, *Labor and Monopoly Capitalism.* New York: Monthly Review Press, 1975.

Alan Brinkley, *The End of Reform: New Deal Liberalism in Recession and War.* New York: Knopf, 1995.

Robert Draper, *Do Not Ask What Good We Do: Inside the U.S. House of Representatives.* New York: Free Press, 2012.

Elizabeth Sanders, *The Roots of Reform: Farmers, Workers and the American State, 1896–1917.* Chicago: University of Chicago Press, 1999.

Mark Zandi, *Financial Shock: Global Panic and Government Bailouts—How We Got There and What Must Be Done to Fix It.* Saddle River, NJ: FT Press, 2009.

PART II

POLITICAL PARTICIPATION

I t is easy to imagine how democracy would work in small-scale societies. Citizens would gather in a public space, such as a town hall, to decide issues among themselves. Direct democracy, in which people engage in face-to-face discussion and decision making, would occur. Under these circumstances, democracy would be vibrant. But what happens when one moves from a small-scale society to a large one of over 300 million citizens, such as the United States in the twenty-first century? A democracy in which all citizens participate directly in decision making is simply not possible.

Moreover, the United States is not only a large society but also a diverse one. It is not easy to identify a single group that represents "the people," who can make decisions for the common good when society is driven by deep racial, economic, and gender inequalities. The people are divided into groups that have unequal access to resources and power.

Some democratic theorists have retreated in the face of this dilemma and proposed that we create some sort of procedural democracy, with rules for choosing, by election, among competing political leaders. This is the optimal approach, according to the economist Joseph Schumpeter. In his influential account, he criticized what he called the classical conception of democracy, in which citizens participate in politics by reflecting on which policies are most desirable and choosing representatives to implement those policies. He proposed a new way to think about democracy, based on the claim that political elites are more competent than ordinary citizens to make policy decisions. Democracy, he contended, should be thought of as a market, like those where goods and services are bought and sold. Just as consumers choose among competing products, Schumpeter suggests, voters should be considered political consumers who choose among competing elites.[1]

We reject Schumpeter's weakened version of democracy and stress the importance of active citizenship and robust political participation. In our view, democracy should not be reserved simply for election day, when citizens choose among the candidates offered to them. Democracy should be broader and fuller. Part II takes up the challenge of extending democracy beyond the limits of procedural democracy, which Schumpeter argued was the best we could achieve in a large, diverse society.

Chapter 4 focuses on political parties and elections, the major—although not only—arena in which citizens participate in politics. The chapter highlights the importance of the two-party system in the United States as well as the influence of large campaign contributions by private corporate and affluent donors. The chapter analyzes reasons for low voter turnout, changes in the social and ideological composition of the two major parties' bases, the issue of political polarization, and the outcome of the 2012 elections; it also compares the U.S. party system to those of other countries. Chapter 5 looks at other mechanisms of political participation, notably interest groups and social movements, both of which require a higher level of political engagement and commitment than voting. They also tend to be more pointed and targeted forms of political action than voting. When change through the ballot box appears unlikely, groups look for other alternatives. But these alternative forms of political participation also supplement each other. Voting, interest-group activity, and social-movement participation are not mutually exclusive forms of political participation.

These chapters make clear that the most privileged members of society tend to be the most politically active. They have more time, money, and organizational resources to devote to political participation than other groups. Consequently, politicians tend to be more responsive to their demands. But political inequality is not a foregone conclusion. Citizens in the United States enjoy political rights that permit them to organize and develop their political voices to influence policy makers. This is especially true when large numbers of them are mobilized at the polls, in interest groups, and through social movements to make their demands heard: when they go beyond the bounds of procedural democracy to the richer and fuller terms of direct democracy.

4

POLITICAL PARTIES AND ELECTIONS

INTRODUCTION

The Founders of the American constitutional order who gathered in Philadelphia at the Constitutional Convention in 1787 designed what they proudly (and rightly) regarded as a new political system. They did not construct a democratic system—nor did they aim to. Since democracy meant the rule of the many—that is, the majority—they feared that it would inevitably produce rule by the poor, who formed the majority of people in their own or in any then-conceivable society. If the poor were provided with total political power through the ballot box, it was assumed they would use it to appropriate the wealth and property of the affluent—a result that the Founders regarded as tyranny. Indeed, they judged that one of the flaws of the Articles of Confederation, the political arrangements prevailing in the first years after independence, was an excess of democracy.

The framers sought to create a system whose priority was maximizing **liberty**. They feared that a democratic system of direct and universal participation would maximize **equality**, which at the extreme they equated with tyranny. Their answer was a **representative system**—that is, one in which citizens elected delegates who in turn elected political officeholders.[1] Thus, the new system was designed to be neither a democracy, where the people ruled directly, nor a monarchy or aristocracy, where high political offices were inherited. Instead, the framers described the government they designed in Philadelphia as a **republic**. This was a hybrid form of government, a system in which the people participated—but only indirectly, by electing representatives who directed the government and were accountable to the people.[2]

Quite soon, however, in the young life of the republic, strong pressures to increase popular power produced important formal and informal changes that deepened the democratic features of American politics. Political parties and elections quickly emerged as a key institutional arena that expanded democracy by creating the opportunity for organized popular participation. Another important arena—social movements and interest groups—will be examined in Chapter 5.

During the founding period, popular participation was extremely limited. For example, suffrage was at first generally limited to white males over 21 years of age who owned property and met religious requirements. Two major changes that deepened democracy were a broadening of the electorate (such as through the abolition in many states of a property qualification for voting) and an increase in the number of political leaders chosen by direct election. Both changes made political parties and elections a more important part of the political system.

However, the expansion of democratic elements was limited by institutional safeguards, such as the constitutional provisions for lifetime tenure of federal judges and six-year terms for senators. Democratic elements were further limited by the growing power of money to shape electoral outcomes and political decisions. In particular, as capitalism developed during the nineteenth and twentieth centuries, wealth became increasingly concentrated at the top and was used to check popular power.

The ability of affluent individuals and business firms to translate their wealth into political power has not grown continuously. There have been periodic challenges to this trend, as well as partial reverses throughout American history, including at the national level during the New Deal, the 1960s and 1970s, and to some extent under the presidency of Barack Obama. It should also be recalled that the American political system consists not only of the federal government but also of state governments, as well as county and municipal governments, school boards, and other elected bodies. The politics of power occurs in all these jurisdictions, with widely varying outcomes.

What is the importance of popular participation in the present era and to what extent does participation, as organized through political parties and elections, offset the power of money? This is the central question analyzed in this chapter. The question is especially important given our concern with the relation between democracy and capitalism. Since political parties and elections facilitate popular participation in the American political system, assessing their performance has important implications for the quality of American democracy.

In their authoritative study of political participation and representation, political scientists Kay Lehman Schlozman, Sidney Verba, and Henry E. Brady identify the pattern that will be explored in this chapter: "[I]nequalities of political voice are deeply embedded in American politics. Although public issues and citizen concerns may come and go, the affluent and well educated are consistently overrepresented."[3] Another way of expressing this point is that parties and elections often contribute to maintaining the dominance of the structural power of business described in Chapters 2 and 3. The present chapter describes how and why parties and elections play this role. Lurking in the background are these questions: Must it be so? What possibilities are there for broadening political participation and thereby deepening the democratic character of American politics?

POLITICAL PARTIES AND AMERICAN DEMOCRACY

The importance of political parties for democratic practice cannot be overstated. According to the political scientist E. E. Schattschneider, "The political parties created modern democracy and modern democracy is unthinkable save in terms of the parties."[4] Political parties are the only organized means of transmitting the will of the majority to the government in a regularized, institutional fashion. (As Chapter 5 describes, social movements may do so in a less organized and sporadic fashion.) But although parties and elections provide citizens with a powerful tool to enrich democracy, in *practice* American parties and elections usually fall short of their potential.

Parties are the heart of any democratic system because they enable citizens with common purposes to join together in an attempt to influence government to adopt their agenda. Political parties are above all organizations committed to winning elections on the basis of their programmatic goals, but they also educate and mobilize voters, and recruit and nominate candidates for office. Their core activities include advocating policies that mobilize popular support, choosing candidates that champion these policies, linking like-minded voters to these candidates, seeking to elect their candidates to public office, and holding accountable the leaders they have elected.

Given the central importance of political parties to the functioning of democracy, it might seem surprising that the Constitution made no provision for them. The reason, according to the historian Richard Hofstadter, is that "the creators of the first American party system on both sides, Federalists and Republicans, were men who looked upon parties as sores on the body politic."[5] The Founders "hoped to create not a system of party government under a constitution, but rather a constitutional government that would check and control parties."[6]

Ironically, however, even while condemning parties in theory, the Founders helped create them in practice. Parties emerged quickly in Congress as legislators formed stable opposing alliances in response to pressing issues of the day. When legislators appealed to the people to settle party divisions brewing in Congress, the result boosted popular participation. At the same time, a partisan press emerged, party officials began to campaign for office, and Fourth of July celebrations turned into partisan rallies. Party in government gave birth to party in the electorate.[7] Thus, from the start parties proved to be a democratizing force in the United States. They expanded political participation, mobilized eligible voters, and shattered a system of politics in which only the socially privileged and wealthy could participate.[8] By the time of Andrew Jackson's presidency (1828–36), the historian Michael Schudson writes, "the rule of gentlemen was replaced by the rule of majorities."[9] In 1824, less than 30 percent of eligible voters turned out to vote for president; by the time parties were fully established in 1840—less than two decades later—turnout had increased to 78 percent.

As the nineteenth century proceeded, parties developed solid organizational bases and mass followings.[10] Thanks to parties' success in mobilizing voters, the United States can be considered the first popular government in the modern world. It should be stressed, however, that voting rights were restricted to white men. Women, Native Americans, blacks, and other non-whites—a large majority of the population—were deprived of voting rights. The United States did not even approach universal suffrage until the passage of voting-rights legislation in the 1960s finally enabled southern blacks to exercise the franchise. Further, as we shall see, the struggle to achieve full and equal voting rights is never over. By various means, some questionable yet legal, others downright illegal, many Americans have never effectively possessed the franchise. Moreover, a recent campaign by affluent, conservative, and Republican groups, reviewed later in the chapter, has sought to deter minority and low-income citizens from voting.

ORIGINS OF THE TWO-PARTY SYSTEM

Americans tend to think of the two-party system as natural and inevitable. Yet in most democracies, three or four political parties each garner a significant share of the vote and thereby widen the options for citizens. The two-party system is a product of many factors. First is the **single-member-district plurality system** of voting. Most elections in the United States are governed by winner-take-all rules in single-member districts, meaning that whichever one of the candidates competing in a given district gets the most votes wins. Since there are no rewards for parties and candidates that lose, even if they just miss getting a majority, most citizens regard voting for candidates from small parties as wasting their ballot. Instead, voters usually confine their choice to a candidate from one of the two major parties. And this pattern tends to get further locked in through time by socialization, since young people often adopt their parents' party identification.

The major alternative to the single-member-district plurality system is **proportional representation (PR)**, whereby legislative seats are allotted to parties based on the percentages of the vote they receive in multimember districts. This system is used to elect the legislature in most democracies around the world. In elections held according to PR, parties that receive a significant share of the vote in a district elect one or more representatives to the legislature. Further, since voters need not fear wasting their ballots by voting for candidates who stand little chance of coming in first, they are more apt to vote for third parties. PR thus tends to promote multiparty systems.

Second, the winner-take-all procedure used to elect the U.S. president further strengthens the two-party system. Parties have a strong incentive to form broad **coalitions** in order to improve their chances of winning the ultimate prize, the most powerful office in government. The Republican Party's failure to be sufficiently inclusive partially explains its 2012 electoral setback.

A third factor promoting the two-party system is a strong media bias. The media devotes most coverage to candidates from the two major parties and ignores others. Since the media only considers candidates from the two major parties as serious contenders, voters come to view them as such; polls then reflect this opinion, and the media follows the polls by confining coverage even more to the major parties' candidates.

Finally, the Democratic and Republican parties form a tacit cartel to marginalize America's many splinter parties. For example, the nationally televised presidential debates, organized with heavy input from the Democratic and Republican parties, are usually limited to the two parties' candidates.

Although third parties find it hard to break the two-party mold, it has been done. The Republican Party emerged in the 1850s as a third party and successfully replaced the Whigs. (The party's relatively unknown standard-bearer in 1860—Abraham Lincoln—became one of the most revered presidents in American history.) While third parties generally fail to achieve national prominence, many have successfully contested state and local elections. One example was Minnesota's Farmer-Labor Party, whose best-known leader was Hubert Humphrey—a long-time senator, vice president, and unsuccessful Democratic presidential candidate in 1968. (The Farmer-Labor Party often allied itself with the Democrats.)

Although countless third parties are on the ballot in virtually every election, the two major parties tend to monopolize voter choice. However, third-party candidates do occasionally affect presidential-election outcomes. In 1992, the maverick conservative Ross Perot won 19 percent of the **popular vote**, probably enabling Bill Clinton to defeat the incumbent president, George H. W. Bush. In 2000, if the votes cast for the Green Party candidate, Ralph Nader, in Florida had gone to the Democratic candidate, Al Gore, Gore would have won Florida and the presidency.

What difference does it make that the United States has a two-party system? Political scientists agree that multiparty systems generally encourage parties to highlight their separate identities and appeal to distinctive segments of the electorate. There is less incentive to form a broad alliance, since a party obtaining less than a majority is still able to elect candidates. As a general rule, two-party systems foster moderation, stability, and predictability—that is, centrism. When an exception to this pattern occurs—for example, when the Republican Party veered away from the center toward the extreme right in recent decades—it requires a particular explanation. Later in the chapter, we analyze this exceptional development.

PARTY ORGANIZATION AND REALIGNMENTS SINCE 1896

The typical pattern in the two-party system in the United States has been for there to be alternating, extended periods of control by one or the other party. As noted, the two-party system tends to encourage broad coalitions of diverse and sometimes conflicting groups. For example, for many years the Democratic Party included both northern blacks, who supported integration, and white southerners, who opposed it. Similarly, for years the Republican Party included voters who were moderately conservative on economic issues and socially liberal, along with a group further to the right on both counts. In general, parties that do not offer a big tent to welcome diverse groups are doomed to defeat. Most of the time, American political parties try to contain conflicts by blurring their positions and resisting new demands. The result is that demands accumulate, pressure in the system mounts, and popular dissatisfaction grows as the party system fails to reflect changes occurring in the broader society.

At first, citizens seek answers outside the party system, in the form of support for social movements. Eventually, however, the minority party may capitalize on this dissatisfaction by championing the issues not adequately represented in the existing party system. If it captures a majority and replaces the governing party, political scientists refer to the tidal shift as a **critical** or **realigning election**. Such elections, which shake up the established order and usher in a new era of stability, are relatively rare.[11] Critical or realigning elections are characterized by unusually high turnout and more intense ideological conflict between the parties. If the winning party can consolidate its dominance by repeated electoral victories, it may reshape the ideological and policy agenda for years to come.

The 2008 and 2012 presidential elections may have produced the most recent political realignment, following a period, beginning in the 1980s, when the Republican Party was dominant. Under Barack Obama's presidency, the Democratic Party has reshuffled the demographic and ideological deck in a way that may enable it to exercise durable political dominance. We examine this issue below.

1896: The Beginning of Republican Dominance

The American party system has undergone enormous changes since its formation over two centuries ago. We survey here the reversals of fortune between the Democratic and Republican parties since the late nineteenth century, often considered the period when American political parties were strongest. According to the political scientist Stephen Skowronek, at this turbulent point in the nation's history parties lent "order, predictability and continuity to governmental activity."[12] Parties were powerful and well-staffed organizational structures that reached deep down into the grass roots, communicated to voters through a partisan popular press, and controlled the nomination of candidates and the platforms on which they ran.[13] Turnout was high, and because low-income and affluent citizens voted at about the same rate, there was less class bias in turnout than today. Furthermore, both parties competed to recruit the millions of immigrants pouring into the United States. By so doing, the parties played a key role in integrating the new arrivals into American society.

Political parties of this period were far from flawless. They mostly depended on patronage and spoils to motivate activists and voters. Urban **political machines** competed for the votes of workers and immigrants by offering them municipal jobs and gifts, such as a holiday turkey. This mode of integrating them into the political system insulated businesses from democratic challenge.[14] Thus, high working-class turnout did not guarantee that economic elites would be challenged.[15]

Party decline set in following the critical election of 1896, when the probusiness Republican Party took over. It realigned the electorate by astutely championing industrialization, which was on the rise at the time, against the Democratic Party's more backward-looking defense of rural America. The Republican platform appealed not only to business interests but also to the rapidly expanding ranks of the industrial working class.

Soon after the critical election of 1896, turnout in presidential elections plummeted: from 79 percent in 1896 to 49 percent in 1924. The falloff in turnout was particularly great among members of the working class and eth-nic and racial minorities. Three factors explain why. First, party competition declined dramatically following the 1896 election. Both the South and the North became one-party regions. The Democrats enjoyed a political monopoly in the South, where the party became the vehicle for the defense of white racism, while the Republicans dominated the North. Without meaningful competition, voters lost interest.

Second, following the 1896 election, business groups and middle-class reformers made vigorous and effective efforts to weaken parties. They dis-liked the expense and corruption of urban political machines. Moreover, they feared that incorporating working-class immigrants into the party sys-tem might encourage a radical turn. Under the banner of ending political corruption and cleaning up government, reformers sponsored measures to weaken political parties by ending their control of patronage. Instead of being doled out to party loyalists, civil-service positions would now be awarded according to merit, as determined by competitive exams. Another reform involved holding local elections on a nonpartisan basis, which weakened the parties' grip on urban governments. The system by which parties controlling urban governments awarded public-works contracts to their cronies was replaced by a system of competitive bidding. While these reforms were desirable, they fostered a kind of antiseptic politics that favored the status quo and weakened parties' ability to mobilize the broad mass of the electorate.

Finally, turnout was depressed in the South by racial barriers to voting. After the Civil War, Southern states had relied on fraud and violence to keep blacks from the polls. They now institutionalized racial—as well as class—exclusion through such devices as poll taxes (requiring citizens to pay a hefty fee to vote), literacy tests, and tests of "good character." Three-quarters of all citizens in the South—especially blacks and poor, uneducated whites—lost the right to vote through these stratagems. Turnout in the South in presidential elections declined from 57 percent in 1896 to 19 percent by 1924.[16]

Northern elites pursued a similar goal of shrinking the electorate, although by less violent and openly racist methods. Complicated voter-registration systems and residency requirements discouraged voting by making it difficult to register to vote. Although the formal right to vote remained, new procedural obstacles prevented millions of citizens from exercising that right.[17]

The process of party decline lasted for decades. Party organizations decayed as their major functions were hived off. The political scientist Andrea Louise Campbell points out:

A series of technological, institutional, legal, and cultural shifts diminished [parties'] once central function as the organizers and inclusive mobilizers of American elections. They ceded control over nominations and were pushed aside by new candidate-centered campaigns. Technological advances allowed candidates to speak directly to the people, and the parties lost their monopoly on electoral contestation in the United States.[18]

The rise of presidential primaries in many states since the 1970s further weakened party organizations. While the reform was adopted to permit greater rank-and-file participation in the choice of the party's presidential candidate, it enabled small but well-organized groups to exert a powerful influence over the party's candidates and platforms. It also weakened the ability of party leaders to act strategically to maximize the party's electoral prospects.

Two developments—candidate-centered campaigning and the emergence of fundraising organizations that operate independently of the parties and throw their weight behind particular candidates—warrant special emphasis. Candidates nowadays often raise their own money through computer-generated direct mail, the Internet, and fund-raisers with affluent supporters. They organize their own campaigns by hiring polling organizations and political consultants. They reach voters through television advertising, the Internet, and their own campaign workers. The emergence of organizations known as **political action committees** (**PACs**) and **super PACs**, which are vehicles for raising and spending funds in support of candidates and issues, further reduces the importance of political parties. (We discuss these organizations later in the chapter.)

The New Deal Coalition

Republican dominance lasted until the critical election of 1932. When the Republican Party failed to end the Great Depression, voters abandoned the Republican President, Herbert Hoover, and chose the Democratic standard-bearer, Franklin Delano Roosevelt. His election ushered in decades of Democratic Party control and involved a fundamental shift in the relations between government and the economy and society. The New Deal coalition that Roosevelt forged by winning four consecutive presidential elections (1932–44) included blacks, who received some (albeit an unequal share) of the benefits from New Deal programs that targeted the poor and unemployed; southerners, whose Democratic sympathies dated back to the Civil War; immigrant Jewish and Catholic workers from southern and eastern Europe, who supported

WHAT DO YOU THINK?

Are Political Parties Weapons of the Weak against the Strong?

Robert Michels, an Italian sociologist, famously declared that political parties are weapons of the weak against the strong. By this he meant that because parties enable the weak (who are numerous) to act collectively, they are able to check the power of the strong (who are few). In what ways have American political parties enabled the weaker members of American society to check the power of the strong and privileged? What factors have limited the way that parties have redistributed political power? What reforms might make parties more effective weapons of the weak against the strong?

Roosevelt's policies to end the Depression; Irish supporters of big-city political machines; industrial workers, organized in labor unions newly created in sectors of mass production; and a handful of financiers and corporate executives who believed that the New Deal's sponsorship of activist government could help end the Depression. The coalition involved a tense partnership between the Democratic Party's southern, white, segregationist wing, which was passionately hostile to federal policies that would benefit blacks and undermine the South's feudal structure, and a Northern, liberal wing based in large urban areas with millions of first- and second-generation working-class immigrants.

The New Deal involved a fundamental shift in the politics of power, as described in Chapter 3, greatly expanding government's role. From an agency primarily charged with maintaining law and order—which often meant preventing threats to private property—government began to be seen as a mechanism for actively promoting economic stability and growth, as well as the social welfare of the broad mass of citizens. Thanks to the popularity of New Deal programs like Social Security, the New Deal coalition maintained control of the federal government for decades.

The New Deal represented both an idealistic vision of a kinder, more inclusive capitalism, and a diverse coalition of groups that supported the Democratic Party for the benefits they received from the federal government. While Roosevelt and his successors designed programs that distributed benefits to broad segments of the population, southern white Democrats in Congress ensured that programs were designed to withhold benefits from millions of southern blacks, who lived and worked in a state of semi-bondage.[19]

As the civil rights movement gained momentum in the 1960s, the Democratic Party leadership became less successful in holding together the southern and northern wings of the party. The coalition frayed when President Lyndon Johnson relied on northern Democrats and moderate Republicans to pass legislation that outlawed racial discrimination in voting. Native southern whites' identification with the Democratic Party dropped from 74 percent in 1956 to half that level by 1984.[20] Beginning in 1968, the South became a Republican bastion in presidential elections, and in the following years southerners started voting for Republican candidates for state and local offices.[21] By 1994, for the first time in the twentieth century, Republicans comprised a majority of the southern delegation to both the Senate and the House and of the region's governors. This realignment of the once solidly Democratic South, which continues today, helped revive Republican Party fortunes and enabled it for a time to become the dominant party.[22]

Several additional factors hastened Democratic decline beginning in the 1960s. First, the emergence of new issues created intraparty political and cultural conflict. The Vietnam War divided the Democratic Party, as some members of the New Deal coalition supported Lyndon Johnson's prosecution of the war while other, formerly pro-Democratic, groups, such as students and liberal Democrats, were fiercely opposed.

Feminism, gay rights, and abortion further split the New Deal coalition. Working-class voters were economically liberal but socially conservative. They supported federal regulation of markets and welfare-state programs but opposed policies defending gay and abortion rights. Conversely, wealthier, more educated, and more recent Democratic supporters were economically conservative but socially liberal. Reconciling the two wings of the party was a difficult balancing act.

The New Deal coalition was further wounded by the decline of labor unions. Union members are more reliable Democratic Party voters than their nonunion counterparts, and labor unions traditionally provided solid financial assistance and organizational support to Democratic candidates. Union membership as a proportion of the workforce has declined steadily from its peak of 33 percent in 1953 to under 12 percent today. (This issue is analyzed in Chapter 5.)

Following its great achievements in the 1930s and 1940s, the New Deal eventually became a victim of policy failure. The New Deal policy of conservative Keynesianism described in Chapter 3 offered economic growth with relatively little redistribution, and fiscal fine-tuning as a substitute for structural economic change. While this formula was initially successful, its inadequacy became apparent in the 1970s, when economic growth faltered and both inflation and unemployment accelerated. Conservative Keynesianism could no longer deliver the economic growth that the New Deal coalition needed to reward its various constituents. Nor did the Democrats develop a new economic formula around which to revive the faltering coalition. Although Johnson's Great Society program, involving an expansion of the social safety net and business regulation, was designed to revitalize the New Deal, it provoked a fierce backlash from conservative business groups, who counterattacked to defend their interests.

The Reagan Coalition

When the Democratic-led New Deal coalition faltered, the Republican Party seized the opportunity to spearhead a conservative revolution. It achieved a breakthrough in the critical election of 1980, when the Republican challenger, Ronald Reagan, replaced the Democratic incumbent, Jimmy Carter. The point of departure for the party's transformation came even earlier, with its nomination of the highly conservative Senator Barry Goldwater from Arizona for president in 1964. The choice signaled that power had shifted from the Eastern Establishment of moderate conservatives to far-right conservatives from the South and the West, who were militantly anti-government, anti-taxes, anti-union, and anti-Communist. The Sun Belt (the cluster of states stretching from the Southeast through the deep South to the Southwest) nourished a new brand of conservative Republicanism because it was the home of many defense industries and military bases; because the federal government owned large tracts of western land and was perceived as intrusive; and also because the region became a favored destination for many conservative, white, middle-class migrants from the Northeast and Midwest.[23]

Although Goldwater lost the 1964 election by the largest margin in American history, his conservative allies and agenda eventually triumphed. After years of tenacious efforts by well-funded conservative think tanks and grassroots groups, the outer fringe of the Republican Party succeeded in nominating the deeply conservative Ronald Reagan in 1980. As one historian noted, "If there had been no Barry Goldwater, there would have been no Ronald Reagan."[24] One might add that if there had been no Ronald Reagan, there would have been no George H. W. Bush, who was elected when Reagan's two terms of office ended in 1988. Bush extended policies initiated by Reagan, including deregulation of the economy and environment, tax cuts skewed toward the rich, and conservative social policies. Bush pursued harder-right policies than Reagan ever dreamed of trying, largely because the Republican Party became increasingly united around the conservative agenda forged by right-wing religious groups and a conservative and well-financed corporate lobby.

After developing a policy orientation distinct from—in most respects opposite to—the New Deal, the Republican Party dominated the political landscape until 2008. Five factors help explain why. First, white men became solidly pro-Republican as Republican candidates stoked their fears that the Democratic Party was dismantling racial and gender hierarchies. Second, the party developed an enthusiastic base among religious fundamentalists by championing conservative cultural values to prevent what it claimed was moral decay threatening American society. Third, the business community grew more united in supporting the Republican Party thanks to the tax and other benefits it received from Republican policies. Fourth, the party benefited from population growth in the suburbs and the Sun Belt, areas "sympathetic to Republican appeals of self-reliance and less government" and where there was little union presence.[25] Fifth, the Republican Party was rebranded by a network of highly conservative organizations. The political scientists Jacob Hacker and Paul Pierson describe the shift in the Republican party as follows: "The past few decades have witnessed the gradual replacement of an older generation of political moderates and fiscal conservatives with a new generation of hard-line conservatives and radical tax cutters."[26] The Republican revival was the product of brilliant strategy and patient organizational effort by ideological extremists. The description "*ideological extremists*" is not ours. It comes from the moderate Republican Christine Todd Whitman, former governor of New Jersey, whom George W. Bush appointed to be Environmental Protection Agency administrator and who chaired Bush's 2004 reelection campaign in New Jersey.[27]

2008 as a Possible Electoral Realignment?

When Barack Obama was elected in 2008, political scientists questioned whether his victory might involve another realignment in American politics. The answer depended on whether the Democratic coalition could reshape the federal government's role and retain the loyalty of groups forming a majority of the population. The passage of Obama's signature piece of reform, the Affordable Care Act (popularly known as Obamacare) and Obama's reelection in 2012, which involved a partial restructuring of the two parties' electorates, lend weight to this possibility, one that we consider below.

Whether or not the 2008 election produced an electoral realignment, it did represent a break with some enduring patterns in American politics. For starters, until 2008 every one of America's 43 presidents was white. Obama, an African American whose father was Kenyan and whose mother was white, alluded to this fact in his victory speech on election night: "If there is anyone out there who still doubts that America is a place where all things are possible, who still wonders if the dream of our Founders is alive in our time, who still questions the power of our democracy, tonight is your answer." Obama's defeated rival, John McCain, highlighted the same point in his gracious concession speech that night: "This is a historic election, and I recognize the significance it has for African Americans and the special pride that must be theirs tonight. We both realize that we have come a long way from the injustices that once stained our nation's reputation."[28]

Beyond this, the 2008 election suggested that the Democratic Party might be benefiting from political and demographic trends in American society. While the eruption of the Tea Party after the 2008 presidential election helped produce an immediate reversal of party fortunes, leading the Republicans to gain control of the House of Representatives in the 2010 elections, the Democratic Party's ideological positions are closer to those of mainstream society. The *New York Times* columnist Charles M. Blow found in early 2012 that majorities of Americans believe that Democrats are more "attuned to issues that affect them."[29] He also identified a socially liberal trend that could further boost Democratic Party fortunes. He observed, "We are slowly becoming less religious, more diverse and increasingly open-minded. That is completely at odds with today's Republican Party." The 2012 election corroborated Blow's analysis—and then some.

THE 2012 PRESIDENTIAL ELECTION

Given the anemic state of the U.S. economy during Barack Obama's first presidential term, victory in the 2012 election might have been assured for Republican candidate Mitt Romney. While incumbent presidents running for reelection usually begin with an edge over challengers, this advantage is erased during bleak economic times. And bleak was certainly an accurate description of the American economy in 2012, as economic growth continued to be feeble and the unemployment rate still exceeded 8 percent, as it had for most of Obama's first term. When voters are asked if the economy is heading in the right direction, the answers typically provide an excellent indication of whether they plan to support the incumbent or the challenger. In 2012, a majority of Americans gave a pessimistic response. As the *New York Times* columnist Nicholas D. Kristof noted, "In Europe, in similar circumstances [in 2011–12], one government after another lost reelection."[30]

The Romney campaign, moreover, seemed supremely confident. Romney himself was apparently so sure of victory that he did not prepare a concession speech to deliver if he lost. When Karl Rove, one of George W. Bush's top advisers, appeared on Fox News TV on election night and was informed that Fox had called Ohio for Obama, he angrily challenged the Fox number crunchers. (The outcome in Ohio was so important because no Republican had ever won the presidency without winning Ohio.)

In fact, it was Rove who was mistaken. Obama did win Ohio. He won the nationwide popular vote by a comfortable 52 to 47 percent, and the Electoral College tally by the lopsided margin of 332 to 206. He won all nine **swing** (also known as **battleground**) **states** except for North Carolina. (These are evenly divided states often decided by very close margins.)

The Democrats' victory extended well beyond the presidential race. Instead of losing control of the Senate, as seemed likely when the campaign season began, the Democrats increased their majority by two. The number of Democrats elected to the House of Representatives also increased, by eight.

Obama's reelection was no fluke. Some of the factors we review are specific to the 2012 election; others suggest that an electoral realignment has been occurring since 2008 to the benefit of the Democratic Party. We focus in this chapter on the presidential race; Chapter 7 analyzes the results of the 2012 congressional elections.

The Economy

While there is no denying how badly the economy performed in 2012, and indeed throughout Obama's first term, polls found that most voters did not blame Obama but his predecessor, George W. Bush, for the poor economic situation. An exit poll reported on the *PBS News Hour* on November 7, 2012, found that 52 percent of respondents judged that George W. Bush was to blame for the current economic problems; only 38 percent held Obama responsible.

Further, the persistence of economic difficulties was partially offset by a steady, if slight, decline in the unemployment rate in the years before 2012, along with net job creation for 32 consecutive months prior to the election. A preelection poll found that more Americans judged that the Democrats would do "a better job of keeping the country prosperous."[31]

Obama's, and the Democratic Party's, electoral advantage was the product of deeper and more durable factors than the current state of the economy. The political scientists Andrew Gelman and Avi Feller found that the Democratic Party has a structural electoral advantage involving a historically durable link between economic cleavages in the U.S. and voters' party preferences. They cite public-opinion-poll data stretching back decades documenting that

FIGURE 4.1

DISTRIBUTION OF ELECTORAL VOTES IN THE 2012 ELECTION

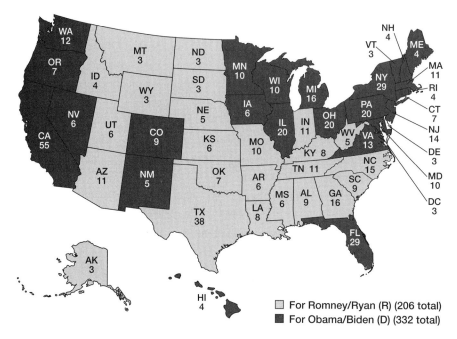

For Romney/Ryan (R) (206 total)
For Obama/Biden (D) (332 total)

substantial majorities of low-income voters, who constitute a sizeable proportion of the electorate, consistently support the Democratic Party. A CBS exit poll after the 2012 election found that voters with total family income under $50,000—a group comprising 41 percent of the population—favored Obama by a hefty 60 to 40 percent. Affluent voters, a much smaller group, generally favor the Republican Party, but they do so by a smaller margin. Gelman and Feller observe:

> Remarkably, this same pattern has occurred in every presidential contest over the past twenty years. Lower-income voters consistently support the Democratic candidate in nearly every state. Upper-income voters, on the other hand, are more mixed in their political views. . . . In other words, contrary to what you have heard, there's only a strong red America–blue America split toward the top of the income distribution. Toward the bottom, the electoral map is a sea of blue. . . . Our research on opinion poll data from earlier elections finds that lower-income Americans tend to vote based on economic issues, while richer voters consider social issues as well as economics in their voting decisions.[32]

Demography

The Obama and Romney electorates were a study in contrasts. And, as with the economic cleavage just reviewed, many other significant groups in American society displayed pro-Democratic preferences.

Exit polls enable us to identify the two candidates' coalitions in broad brush strokes. Obama had strong support from women, youth (those under age 45 and especially under age 30), and those with low and moderate income (under $100,000). Reverse the signs and you have the Romney electorate, which was predominantly composed of men (especially white men), older voters, and the affluent. One key to Obama's victory is that all three of the pro-Obama demographic groups just identified (women, youth, and those with low to moderate income) were significantly larger than the opposite three pro-Romney groups (men, older voters, and the affluent).

Obama's victory becomes more understandable when one engages in more fine-grained analysis.[33] Consider, for example, differences among subgroups in a large demographic group such as women. Although a majority of women voted for Obama, by 55 to 44 percent, this overall finding fails to reveal an important difference between the partisan preferences of married and unmarried women. In fact, married women favored Romney by 53 to 46 percent. However, unmarried women voted for Obama by a whopping 62 to 35 percent. Their lopsided support produced the pro-Obama gender gap. Thus, given the very different preferences of married and unmarried women, it may actually be misleading to speak of a gender gap at all.

Obama's victory also resulted from especially strong support from other demographic groups, particularly racial and ethnic minorities. Whereas whites favored Romney by 59 to 39 percent, nonwhites were vastly more likely to support Obama: African Americans by 93 to 6 percent, Asian Americans by 73 to 26 percent, and Hispanics by 71 to 27 percent.

Americans' religious practices and partisan preferences are closely correlated. Whereas Americans who attend religious services at least weekly favored Romney by 59 to 39 percent, those who never attend religious services voted for Obama 62 to 34 percent.

There are systematic differences in the political preferences of Americans who live in cities, towns, suburbs, and rural areas. Obama enjoyed a 69 to 29 percent edge among Americans living in medium-sized and large cities and a narrow edge among Americans living in small cities (50,000–500,000 inhabitants). Those living in the suburbs split their vote evenly, while a majority of those living in smaller towns (10,000–50,000 inhabitants) supported Romney.

TABLE 4.1

VOTING PREFERENCES FOR VARIOUS GROUPS

Category	B. Obama	M. Romney	% of Total Electorate
Male	45	52	47
Female	55	44	53
Age			
18–29	60	37	19
30–44	52	45	27
45–64	47	51	38
65 or over	44	56	16
Race/Ethnicity			
White	39	59	72
Black	93	6	13
Hispanic/Latino	71	27	10
Asian	73	26	3
Currently Married			
Yes	42	56	60
No	62	35	40
Gay/Lesbian/Bisexual			
Yes	76	22	5
No	49	49	95
Population of Area			
over 500,000	69	29	11
50,000–500,000	58	40	21
Suburbs	48	50	47
10,000–50,000	42	56	8
Rural	37	61	14
Education—Last Grade of School Completed			
No high school diploma	64	35	3
High school graduate	51	48	21
Some college/assoc. degree	49	48	29
College graduate	47	51	29
Postgraduate study	55	42	18
Family Income			
Under $30,000	63	35	20
$30,000–$40,999	57	42	21
$50,000–$49,999	46	52	31
$100,000–$199,999	44	54	21
$200,000–$249,999	47	52	3
$250,000 or more	42	55	4
Religious Observance—Attend Religious Services			
Weekly	39	59	42
Occasionally	55	43	40
Never	62	34	17

Category	B. Obama	M. Romney	% of Total Electorate
Religion			
Protestant	37	62	29
Catholic	50	48	25
Mormon	21	78	2
Other Christian	50	49	23
Jewish	69	30	2
None	70	26	12
Immigration			
Offered a chance to apply for legal status	61	37	65
Deported to the country they came from	24	73	28

SOURCE: CBS News, Election 2012, Exit Poll Results, at www.cbsnews.com/election-results-2012/exit.shtml?tag=contextMain;contentBody.

Rural residents supported Romney by 61 to 37 percent. Unfortunately for him, the U.S. is highly urbanized. There are also regional differences in partisan preferences, often stretching back decades and more. The Deep South was solidly pro-Romney; New England and most coastal states strongly favored Obama.

A close election can be decided by small groups if they vote in a cohesive way. Consider the issue of sexual orientation. Whereas equal numbers of straight Americans supported Romney and Obama, the far smaller group of self-identified gay, lesbian, and transgender voters split 76 to 22 percent for Obama. From this perspective, their overwhelming support provided Obama's margin of victory.

The statistics above provide a snapshot of Obama's 2012 victory. However, the electorate is not static: it is constantly changing. Analyzing the dynamics of demographic groups—their changing size in the electorate, as well as their partisan preferences—helps explain Obama's victory and apparently points toward a bright future for the Democratic Party.

The demographics of the 2008 and 2012 elections, as well as ideological divisions between the two parties, suggest that a possible electoral realignment has occurred in favor of the Democratic Party. Although we examine the factors favoring the Democrats, we urge caution: many developments might alter the trend. Regarding demography, while the groups supporting the GOP are shrinking in size, the groups supporting the Democratic Party are growing from one election to the next. To illustrate, Hispanics are the fastest growing minority group in the country. Between 2000 and 2012, they accounted for half of all U.S. population growth, and they now constitute one sixth of the population.[34] In the past, Hispanics were divided in their political loyalties. However, 71 percent of Hispanic voters chose Obama in 2012—an even higher proportion than had voted for him in 2008. An important reason was the Republican Party's harsh position regarding immigration. Although it was popular among the GOP's core conservative base, it repelled most Hispanics, as well as Asian-Americans.

The Republican Party's future prospects will hinge on how effectively it adapts to the increasingly diverse racial and ethnic composition of American society. If it remains committed to a fortress mentality, as in 2012, the Democrats will continue to reap the electoral rewards. The defensive posture was illustrated by the radio talk-show host Rush Limbaugh, who lamented the day after the election, "I went to bed last night thinking we've lost our country." In a more dispassionate vein, the headline of a post-election article in the *New York Times* identified the danger for Republicans: "As Electorate Changes, Fresh Worry for G.O.P." The reporter Robert Shear observed, "The demographic changes in the American electorate have come with striking speed and have left many Republicans . . . concerned about their future. The Republicans' Southern strategy, of appealing mostly to white voters, appears to have run into a demographic wall."[35]

Candidate Characteristics and Ideology

In 2012, as in 2008, demography was closely linked to ideology. The Democrats were popular among newly rising groups because of the party's message, while the Republican Party appeared to be the party of yesterday. True, Romney pivoted during the campaign from the Republicans' hard-right platform and what he described during a primary debate as his own "severely conservative" position on these issues. Indeed, his dramatic shift in the first TV debate in early October caught Obama napping and provoked a sharp if brief reversal in the campaign's trajectory. (See Figure 4.2.) One report pointed out, "Romney—who crammed for [the debate for] weeks while Obama reportedly skipped practices—behaved as if he knew that a good 90 minutes in front of 67.2 million viewers could erase a summer of floundering."[36]

However, Romney's bounce did not last. One probable reason is that Americans judged that Romney was out of touch with ordinary Americans. Polls showed that large majorities of Americans found Obama more personally appealing than Romney. One reason was the success of the Obama campaign's

FIGURE 4.2

THE DENVER DIFFERENCE

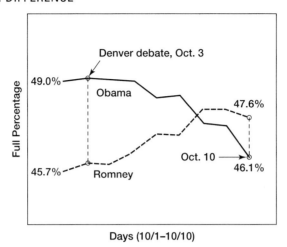

Days (10/1–10/10)

From Oct. 2 to Oct. 10, Obama lost 4.8 points in national polls, dropping from a 3.3-point lead to a 1.5-point deficit.

SOURCE: Real Clear Politics.

barrage of negative ads about Romney. They portrayed him as a venture capitalist who grew rich by buying up bankrupt firms at bargain-basement prices, firing their American employees, and outsourcing production. (Romney reinforced this image when he declared, in an unguarded moment, that he enjoyed being able to fire people.)

Romney's personal fortune of $250 million and his lavish lifestyle placed him in a different world from most Americans. He underscored this difference through some of his casual remarks during the campaign. In an attempt to relate to Michigan autoworkers, he mentioned that his wife drove a couple of Cadillacs. Seeking to demonstrate that he shared the values of working-class men, he told an interviewer that he was friends with owners of several NASCAR racing teams.

The most damaging evidence of Romney's disconnect with mainstream America came from a secretly recorded video (that quickly went viral) of his remarks at a fundraising event in Florida. In this informal and private setting, Romney referred to 47 percent of Americans as people who saw themselves as victims, did not pay taxes, and relied on government assistance. Democrats immediately replied that this group of "dependents" included Social Security recipients who had paid taxes during their working lives, low-income employees who paid payroll and sales taxes, disabled veterans receiving government benefits, and students on college loans. In an editorial entitled "Mitt Romney, Class Warrior," The New York Times tartly remarked, "The shame is not that those people [the poor] don't pay income taxes. The shame is how many poor people there are when the top 1 percent can amass fortunes fed by tax breaks and can donate tens of millions of dollars to political candidates who keep it that way."[37]

The contrast in the two candidates' ability to connect with most Americans was highlighted by an exit poll reported on MSNBC TV the day after the election that asked voters which candidate "cares about people like me." Eighty-one percent of respondents chose Obama, while 18 percent favored Romney.

Perhaps a greater problem than Romney's public persona was the product that he was selling. As a New York Times editorial after the election commented, "For a party that has built itself up on explicit and implied appeals to xenophobia, cultural resentment and income-redistribution for the rich, ideological purity is not a long-term strategy for success."[38] The two candidates agreed on one thing: that they represented different visions for America. Unfortunately for Romney, a majority of Americans supported the Democratic Party's vision. Polls found that majorities of voters favored the Democratic Party's position on most questions, including tax policy, immigration, and social issues.

One reason that the Republican Party has adopted positions out of tune with mainstream America is the Tea Party's influence. Although Tea Party activists are a minority of the party's electorate, they turned out in high numbers in Republican primaries in 2012. In order to gain the nomination, Romney adopted hard-right positions during the primary campaign. For example, he urged that the government should make conditions so harsh for undocumented immigrants that they would "self-deport." He also took highly conservative positions on tax policy and social issues.

After Romney gained the nomination, he quickly moderated his former ideological stance. The shift had been anticipated months earlier by Eric Fehrnstrom, a campaign aide who predicted that Romney would pivot back toward the center after obtaining the nomination: "You hit a reset button for the fall campaign. Everything changes. It's almost like an Etch-A-Sketch. You can kind of shake it up and we start all over again."[39] While the comment proved remarkably accurate, it highlighted Romney's long-standing reputation for changing positions to suit his audience. (Obama referred to the pattern as "Romnesia.")

The Obama Campaign Organization

Obama's victory owed much to the fact that his campaign organization ran circles around Romney's. Thanks to the long and bruising Republican primary competition, Obama—who did not face a primary challenge for his nomination—had a substantial head start in organizing his campaign. The Democratic Party began preparing for the presidential contest years before 2012. The Romney forces could not begin organizing his campaign until he was assured of the nomination, only months before the general election.

Aside from timing, Obama benefited from a campaign organization so effective that political scientists have described it as revolutionary. Three innovative elements can be identified. First, the organization engaged in intensive micro-targeting of voters in the key battleground states. Thanks to high-speed super-computers, sophisticated software, data mining, and commercially available databases, the campaign used consumer-research-marketing techniques to gather hundreds of data points on individuals' consumption tastes, TV and online viewing preferences, and friendship networks. The campaign mined this information to customize online ads, to direct campaign workers to households and neighborhoods where personal contact could make a difference, and to organize get-out-the-vote efforts.

Second, the Obama campaign gained a key advantage through its extensive use of the new social media. Both campaigns invested heavily in media advertising: by one estimate, advertising by political parties and super PACs in the 2012 campaign season reached $5 billion for elections at all levels: federal, state, and local.[40] However, the Obama campaign achieved a decisive advantage by supplementing television advertising with an intense focus on social media, including YouTube, Facebook, and Twitter. The *New York Times* columnist Richard Parker observed, "Demographics helped Obama beat [Romney]. But so did the changing landscape of media consumption. The very groups—young women, Hispanics, African Americans, Asian-Americans—that made the [electoral] difference are among the fastest adapters of social and mobile media."[41] Parker reports that the president of one market-research firm characterized the two candidates' campaign organization as follows: "Obama is an Apple, while Romney is a Dell." Obama's social-media campaign left Romney's in the dust. The campaign used social media to persuade, fundraise, and encourage early voting and turnout on election day. Obama attracted twice as many Facebook likes; twice as many YouTube likes, comments and views; and over 20 times as many tweets as Romney.

The third element was Obama's superior ground game. In most swing states, which received the greatest amount of attention from the two candidates' campaign organizations, the Democrats had far more campaign offices, as well as more volunteer and paid campaign workers. For example, in Florida, the largest swing state, the Democrats had 104 field offices to the Republicans' 47.[42]

The synergy among the three elements just identified produced a formidable electoral machine. The Obama campaign relied heavily on data mining and micro-targeting to shape its ground game. Campaign workers were given precise instructions from campaign headquarters about whom to contact and what customized message to deliver. According to the *New York Times* reporter Jim Rutenberg, in a dispatch before the election, "[U]ltimately, if Mr. Obama does win, it could come down to the huge room of technicians and data crunchers in a corporate office here [in Obama's Chicago campaign headquarters] . . . as they dispatch information to volunteers knocking on doors hundreds of miles away."[43] Armed with these resources, the campaign was well equipped to persuade independents, engage in online fundraising, use social media to encourage supporters to contact their friends, and focus efforts on ensuring that the committed would turn out to vote.

PARTIES AND VOTER TURNOUT

If, as Schattschneider claimed, political parties are the measure of democracy's health, American democracy urgently needs a visit to the ER. Measured by their ability to mobilize voters, American political parties are suffering from a case of severe political anemia. Although turnout increased in recent presidential contests, compared to other countries' party systems the American system still lacks vitality. One study found that the United States ranked fourth lowest in turnout among more than 34 democratic countries.[44]

Many factors contribute to low turnout in the United States. First, casting a ballot is difficult. One must register in advance of an election—and information about how and when to register may be scarce. For those who do register, turnout is very high: 80 percent in the 2004 election.[45] An analysis of the 2008 elections—a year of record turnout—reported, "Four million to five million voters did not cast a ballot in the 2008 presidential elections because they encountered registration problems or failed to receive absentee ballots."[46]

The problem does not end with registration. The report just cited notes that an additional two to four million registered voters were discouraged from voting in 2008 by long lines or voter-identification requirements. (We discuss this issue later in this section.)

Turnout is further reduced because 13 states permanently deprive convicted felons of the right to vote, and many other states deprive them of voting rights while they are in prison or until they have completed parole and probation. Since the United States has among the highest proportions of incarcerated citizens in the world, the impact of this restriction is significant.

Many voters are deterred from voting by the electoral system.[47] We noted earlier that most congressional elections in the United States are organized according to the winner-take-all plurality system in single-member districts. If districts are considered safe because one party enjoys a clear advantage and the outcome is predictable, there is little incentive to vote.

A similar situation prevails in presidential elections thanks to the **Electoral College**, the system established by the Constitution whereby the president is elected not by citizens directly but by a majority vote of Electoral College delegates. In the first decades of the United States, delegates from a given state were elected by members of that state's legislature. During the nineteenth century, popular pressure led to the present system of direct or popular election of delegates. This system discourages turnout because of the **unit rule**, which specifies that the entire slate of delegates in a given state must cast their votes for the presidential candidate who receives the most votes in that state. This winner-take-all feature at the state level means that a presidential candidate who receives a bare plurality or majority of the popular vote in a state still obtains 100 percent of the state's votes in the Electoral College. The unit rule is not a constitutional requirement, but it prevails in 48 states. (The exceptions are Maine and Nebraska.) The unit rule lowers voter turnout because most states are considered "safe" for one party or the other. This pattern has given rise to the terms "red states" (which reliably vote Republican) and "blue states" (where Democrats enjoy a comfortable majority).

Most states are solidly and stably red or blue in presidential elections, and the two blocs of states elect about equal numbers of delegates to the Electoral College. The result is that presidential races are usually decided in a handful of battleground, or swing, states: those that are highly competitive and that swing back and forth between the two parties from one election to the next. The swing states with the most electoral votes are Florida, Ohio, and Virginia. Others include Colorado, Nevada, New Hampshire, and Iowa. In these states, undecided voters—independents and switch voters (who lack firm partisan loyalty and stable support for one party or the other)—decide the elections. Understandably, the candidates and their campaign organizations devote the vast bulk of their resources to this tiny minority of voters.

The 2012 presidential election corroborated this pattern. The *New York Times* reporter Adam Liptak observed that during the campaign, "Just three states—Florida, Ohio and Virginia—have accounted for almost two-thirds of the recent campaign appearances of the presidential candidates and their running mates. The three are home to [only] an eighth of the nation's population."[48] The remainder of presidential campaigning was concentrated in seven other swing states. (It should be noted that candidates also make time to visit cash-rich states like New York and California, where they hold private fundraisers to woo wealthy donors.) The bulk of TV advertising is also concentrated in swing states. For example, in 2012, campaign ads ran 97,000 times on Iowa TV stations and 115,000 times in Ohio—nearly triple the number in 2008. While presidential campaigns—and candidates—devote the lion's share of their efforts to wooing undecided voters in swing states, these voters may account for only a small number of votes in each state. But they may determine the electoral outcome in that state—and the nation.[49]

In most countries, elections are held on Sunday, or Election Day is declared a national holiday. Yet another barrier to casting a ballot in the United States is that elections are held on Tuesday, a working day when many citizens, especially lower-income voters on hourly wages, pay a price for going to the polls. (This is compounded when long lines mean that it will take hours to vote.) This was why, according to an Obama campaign official who spoke shortly before the 2012 election, "We made a strategic decision very early on that getting out our supporters—and the right type of supporters—to the polls before Election Day was a big priority for us. . . ." Early voting was a good way to ensure that supporters' votes would be banked.[50] The attempt succeeded. According to an MSNBC newscast on October 27, 2012, whereas just 10 percent of total votes cast in the 2008 presidential election came from early voters, early voters cast one-third of all votes in 2012.

Nonvoting is not randomly distributed. According to the political scientist Walter Dean Burnham, there is a hole in the American electorate where working-class, less educated, and low-income Americans should be.[51] Figure 4.3 documents the sharp disparity in voting turnout between more and less affluent citizens. The wealthiest fifth of the population votes at nearly double the rate of the lowest-income fifth. This difference is far greater than in other Western nations.[52]

Important as unequal turnout is among various income groups, Figure 4.3 demonstrates that they pale in comparison with economic inequalities regarding other forms of political participation. According to the political scientist Stephen Wayne, "Those who are most disadvantaged, who have the least education, and who need a change in conditions the most actually participate

FIGURE 4.3

POLITICAL PARTICIPATION OF VARIOUS INCOME GROUPS (BY SES QUINTILES, 1990)

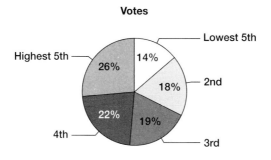

Votes

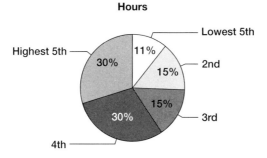

Hours

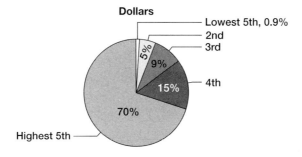

Dollars

SOURCE: Citizen Participation Study (1990); Kay Lehman Schlozman, Sidney Verta, and Henry E. Brady, *The Unheavenly Chorus: Unequal Political Voice and the Broken Promise of American Democracy* (Princeton, NJ: Princeton University Press, 2012), p. 15.

NOTE: Inputs are percentage of votes, percentage of hours given to politics, and percentage of dollars give to politics.

the least. Those who are the most advantaged, who benefit from existing conditions and presumably from public policy as it stands, vote [and participate in other ways] more often."[53] For example, the richest fifth of Americans devote nearly triple the amount of time to participating in political activity than do the poorest fifth. By far the most extreme form of class inequality regarding political participation, however, involves political contributions. Figure 4.3 documents that the richest fifth accounts for 70 percent of all political contributions; the remaining 80 percent of the population accounts for 30 percent of political contributions.

As one rises toward the top of the class pyramid, inequalities increase even more sharply. A study of the 2010 election cycle found that whereas only one in 10,000 Americans contributed at least $10,000 to political campaigns, these $10,000-plus contributions represented one fourth of all political contributions from individuals to parties, campaigns, PACs, and independent expenditure groups.[54]

Two other issues that bear on turnout are the conduct of elections and the tabulation of votes. The first issue is whether there is fraud and corruption involved in counting ballots. Although dishonest methods were common a century ago—bribing voters, stuffing ballot boxes, and so on—such practices are not a thing of the past. For example, following the 2004 presidential elections, the journalist David Corn enumerated several fraudulent practices that contributed to George W. Bush's victory in the key state of Ohio: "odd voting patterns, suspicious election day activity, voter suppression [described below], 'spoiled' ballots and the susceptibility of e-voting machines to errors or, worse, hacking. . . . Was there an organized GOP effort to tamp down the vote in Kerry strongholds? Probably."[55] Many electronic voting machines used in Ohio and elsewhere were produced by Diebold, a firm that Corn notes is "headed by a GOP fundraiser." Nor was Ohio the only state where there were suspicions of rigged voting machines. In Florida, many Kerry voters reported that their touch-screen voting machines indicated they had voted for Bush.

A tactic designed to reduce turnout, known as **voter suppression**, involves preventing opponents from voting by creating legal or informal barriers to voting.[56] While justified on the grounds that they prevent fraud, the real goal of these barriers is to deter certain groups of citizens from voting. Voter-suppression practices include restricting voter-registration campaigns, limiting early and absentee voting, reducing the hours when polls are open, challenging the credentials of those attempting to vote, purging voter rolls, and intimidating citizens by conducting immigrant sweeps around election time. In the current period, voter-suppression efforts have targeted ethnic minorities, youth, and those with lower education and income. Efforts to limit early voting damage Democrats more than Republicans, since the groups just named are generally pro-Democratic. The Republican Party has dealt with its meager support from these groups by trying to restrict turnout among them. Voter suppression compensates for Republicans' disadvantage stemming from the demographic shifts described above. Rather than adapt its position to appeal to these groups, the GOP's response has been to seek to deter them from voting.

Voter suppression commonly involves setting stiff eligibility requirements as a condition to register and/or to vote. State governments are authorized to establish voting eligibility, although the Constitution and federal laws impose some limits on their freedom. The most commonly used technique is to require citizens to produce a birth certificate or government-issued photo ID, such as a driver's license, passport, or state-issued ID. These documents may be difficult to obtain even when they are free (as is the case for state-issued IDs).

The voter-ID requirement primarily affects urban residents, poor citizens, blacks, youth, and immigrants because they are less likely to possess such documentation. For example, because fewer of these citizens own or drive cars, they are less likely to have a driver's license. (The same is true for the elderly, a group that is pro-Republican. In this respect, restrictive registration and voting regulations reduce Republican vote totals.) Other techniques for reducing turnout include eliminating same-day registration and restricting early voting and absentee voting. In Ohio, for example, the Republican governor ended the long-standing practice of allowing people to vote the weekend before Election Day. In Florida, the Republican governor eliminated half the early voting days, including the Sunday before Election Day, a day when, in past years, African American voters had often gone together to polling stations following church services. (A Florida newspaper reported that the author of the law reducing early voting was the general counsel of Florida's Republican Party.)[57] In another instance, the Republican-controlled government in Nebraska closed half the polling stations in Omaha before the 2012 elections. Nebraskans for Civic Reforms, a civil rights organization, reported that the closures were especially likely in minority neighborhoods.

There is a long history of government policies restricting voting eligibility. The most notorious involved literacy tests and poll taxes imposed by southern states after the Civil War to prevent black citizens from voting. After the passage of two federal voting-rights acts in the 1960s limited such racist measures, the right to vote appeared finally to be firmly established. Not so. In recent years, new forms of voter suppression have been adopted to restrict ballot access.

The voter-suppression campaign went into high gear after Republicans gained control of 28 of the 50 state legislatures following the 2010 elections. Before 2006, no state required citizens to produce a government-issued photo ID to vote, and only two states had adopted this requirement by 2010. Since then, over three quarters of all state legislatures, mostly Republican-controlled, have considered legislation tightening voting requirements. In 2011 alone, 16 states adopted 21 additional restrictions. One estimate is that the most rigid ID laws affect about 10 percent of eligible voters.[58]

Allegations of widespread voter fraud appear to be highly questionable. During George W. Bush's presidency, the Justice Department conducted a five-year investigation of voter fraud. The result? It failed to produce a single case of voter impersonation—that is, someone voting by fraudulently impersonating a legal voter. The investigation led to a grand total of 86 successful prosecutions for voter fraud—out of 300 million votes cast during national elections in those years. As the *New York Times* remarked in an editorial, "Voter identity fraud is all but nonexistent, but the assertion that it might exist is used as an excuse to reduce the political rights of minorities, the poor, students, older Americans and other groups that tend to vote Democratic."[59] (Older Americans, who are more likely to vote Republican, might be considered collateral damage of this campaign.)

Activists from the NAACP and unions protest against the implementation of stricter voting laws in New York in December 2011.

Michael Tarzai, the Republican Majority Leader in the Pennsylvania House, provided a graphic example of the partisan basis of the voter-suppression campaign after the Republican-controlled state legislature passed a strict voter-ID law. Mr. Tarzai told a meeting of the Pennsylvania Republican Committee in June 2012 that the law would "allow Governor Romney to win the State of Pennsylvania. . . . Done!" However, a state-court judge temporarily suspended the Pennsylvania voter-ID law for the 2012 election, on the grounds that state officials had not adequately prepared to implement the law. Legal challenges to block or suspend voter-ID laws have also succeeded in South Carolina, Texas, and Wisconsin.

It is uncertain how many voters were prevented from casting a ballot in the 2012 election. On the one hand, preventing even a small number of citizens from voting can decide a close election. And even if voter suppression does not change an election outcome, it constitutes an outrageous assault on democratic procedures. On the other hand, as the *New York Times* columnist Charles M. Blow suggests in the 2012 presidential election, "There may have been a backlash against voter suppression laws, bringing more minorities to the polls, not fewer. . . . Threaten to steal something, and its owner's grip grows tighter."[60]

MONEY AND ELECTIONS

Candidates need more than votes to succeed; they also need money—these days, vast amounts of it. The comment by Mark Hanna, the manager of the Republican presidential candidate William McKinley's successful campaign in 1896, remains as relevant today as it did over a century ago: "There are two things that are important in politics. The first is money, and I can't remember the second."[61] Nowadays, money pays for television advertising, pollsters, political consultants and campaign staff, research and advance work, travel costs, and overhead expenses. As discussed in Chapter 1, the vast increase in the amount and importance of political money is a major trend in American politics. The amounts raised in each presidential electoral cycle make previous outlays seem puny.

The United States is exceptional in the impact that private contributions have on electoral outcomes. Political campaigns in this country last longer, cost more, are less regulated, and are financed by a far higher proportion of private (as opposed to public) funds than in any other Western democracy. Scandals and public outcry over the purchase of political influence by large contributors have periodically resulted in the passage of reform legislation. But the power of money has time after time proven stronger than efforts to control it. In 1971, Congress passed the Federal Election Campaign Act (FECA) and amended it in 1974 to limit political contributions to candidates and parties, to control spending, and to require public disclosure of all campaign receipts and disbursements. It also prohibited businesses, unions, and other groups from contributing money directly to federal-election campaigns.

An indirect result was the creation of PACs and super PACs, organized for the purpose of evading campaign-finance limits. PACs can raise and spend unlimited money to promote issues, candidates, and parties. The two differ in that PACs raise money directly, while super PACs bundle money from other sources. Although PACs and super PACs are legally prohibited from coordinating their activities with a political party, this restriction is routinely ignored. These organizations are often directed by party strategists who have formally severed their links to the party. (For example, two former members of Obama's White House staff ran the major Democratic super PAC in 2012, Priorities USA.)

Presidential campaigns through 2008 were typically costly affairs despite campaign-finance laws that limited spending. However, a 5–4 decision of the Supreme Court in 2010 in a landmark case—*Citizens United v. Federal Elections Commission*—virtually gutted restrictions on campaign spending and opened the floodgates to unlimited political contributions by wealthy individuals, corporations, and (to a lesser extent) labor unions. The Supreme Court ruled that the First Amendment's prohibition of government restriction of free speech meant that most existing laws and regulations setting limits on campaign donations, and prohibiting corporations and labor unions from endorsing and spending funds to promote political candidates, violated the Constitution. One commentator accurately predicted at the time that the "ruling may make the hundreds of millions spent in past presidential and congressional elections look like a pittance."[62]

Thanks to the *Citizens United* ruling, individuals and corporations can now contribute unlimited amounts of money to PACs and super PACs. In turn, these organizations are authorized to funnel funds to candidates. The impact of the *Citizens United* decision was immediately evident in the 2010 congressional elections. It was further evident in the 2012 presidential and congressional elections, when about $6 billion was spent.

Perhaps even more important than the increased volume of funds pouring into political campaigns as a result of the *Citizens United* ruling is the highly skewed source of those funds. The *Citizens United* decision has made political candidates more dependent than ever on corporations and wealthy individuals, who provide the bulk of all political contributions. In 2012, for example, the top 100 individual contributors accounted for nearly three quarters of all funds raised by the super PACs.[63] The undisputed record-holders in the political-contribution competition in 2012 were the Koch brothers, discussed in Chapter 5, who pledged to spend $400 million to prevent Barack Obama's reelection. The next-most-generous Republican donors were the billionaire casino magnate Sheldon Adelson, who was reported to have spent $70 million to support Republicans in the 2012 electoral cycle, and the Texas homebuilder Bob Perry, who donated $9 million to the pro-Romney Restore Our Future super PAC.

The *Citizens United* ruling and subsequent Supreme Court decisions overturning state campaign-finance laws and regulations have further increased the chances that electoral outcomes will be decided by how much money a candidate raises rather than on the basis of one person, one vote.

The aim of campaign spending is to translate money into political power. Jerome Kohlberg, a founding partner of the Kohlberg, Kravis Roberts & Co. investment firm, noted that political "contributions are a small price for big corporations to pay to gain political influence. . . . [C]orporations give for one reason: self-interest. They can easily justify their expenditures because they get an outstanding return on their investment."[64] Justin Dart, a corporate leader, large political contributor, and fund-raiser, made the point beautifully when he observed that dialogue with politicians "is a fine thing, but with a little money they hear you better."[65]

From the viewpoint of wealthy donors and corporations, PACs and super PACs have one drawback: while the *Citizens United* ruling struck down most campaign-finance regulations, it upheld the public-disclosure requirement for contributions to PACs and super PACs. However, donors can circumvent this requirement by contributing to **501(c)(4)** organizations, named after the relevant provision of the federal tax code. The provision was designed to encourage tax-deductible private contributions to groups that promote public discussion of issues involving "social welfare." It became so attractive for the affluent because contributors to 501(c)(4) organizations can remain anonymous. While the precise meaning of social welfare can be debated, what is beyond debate is that this provision has been misused by affluent Americans to provide vast sums to political campaigns that, because they are tax-deductible, are partly made at taxpayer expense. Further, 501(c)(4) organizations can contribute funds to super PACs, which in turn can spend unlimited funds to support candidates. The bulk of 501(c)(4) spending supports Republican candidates and conservative positions.

The *New York Times* business reporter Joe Nocera observed, "What's truly different about this [2012 presidential] election [is] the rise of the 'super PACs' and 501(c)(4)s, which are essentially a form of campaign moneylaundering, allowing wealthy people to contribute millions toward supposedly 'independent' spending on campaign advertising, polling and other expensive campaign goodies."[66]

Does substantial spending, especially when it exceeds spending by one's opponent, guarantee victory? Usually—but not always. The 2012 presidential election provides a fine illustration that lavish spending does not always guarantee success. According to the Center for Responsive Politics, super PACs raised about $660 million during the 2012 electoral cycle. The Republican strategist Karl Rove's two super PACs accounted for nearly half the total raised by all super PACs. Yet their political investments garnered a meager return. Seven of nine candidates that one of Rove's super PACs backed were defeated. Only seven of the nineteen backed by Rove's other super PAC were elected.[67] Sheldon Adelson's record was also dismal: of the nine congressional candidates he backed in 2012, only two were elected.[68]

However, the 2012 election was exceptional. In most elections, the candidate spending the most wins. In the 2004 congressional elections, for example, 96 percent of the House races and 91 percent of the Senate races were won by the better-financed candidates.[69] Further, the need for ample funds begins long before an election. Because a large war chest is usually required to mount an effective primary campaign, the only viable candidates are almost always those who have personal fortunes and/or are supported by organized groups and donors with deep pockets.

The influence of money on political campaigns is most evident in presidential and congressional elections. But political money also influences contests for municipal, county, and state offices. Further, political money has increasingly poured in from outside the locality or state in which a contest is held, undermining local autonomy.[70] For example, the New York Times columnist and healthy-food advocate Mark Bittman reported that in the 2012 elections, outside corporate spending helped defeat many state and local referenda backed by the healthy-food movement.[71]

The fact that those with great wealth provide the bulk of campaign contributions means that political finance marches in lockstep with economic inequalities in the United States, and, in turn, these inequalities perpetuate the disproportionate political power wielded by the wealthy. According to a report sponsored by the American Political Science Association (APSA), the scholarly organization of American political scientists, "The direct impact of rising economic inequality may be most directly apparent in campaign contributions. As wealth and income have become more concentrated and the flow of money into elections has grown, wealthy individuals and families have opportunities for political clout not open to those of more modest means."[72] Increased economic inequality and increased political spending go hand in hand; the increase in one contributes to the increase in the other. Instead of acting as an engine of democracy, political parties yield to the pressure exerted by political money to sustain the structural power of business. While modest challenges to this pattern may occur, as the Obama presidency illustrates, the challenges are at the margins. For example, after his re-election, President Obama gained congressional approval to increase income tax rates for Americans with annual incomes over $400,000. While this was enough to mobilize the wealthy against him, it was hardly an all-out assault on economic inequality.

We have focused until now on the institutional mechanisms that organize citizens' electoral choices. We next analyze the topic of polarization in American politics. The link between this topic and the role of money in politics may not be evident: the country may seem deeply divided for reasons having little to do with the recent vast increase in political spending. In fact, however, the two are closely linked.

POLARIZATION AND AMERICAN POLITICS

There has always been considerable polarization in the United States—that is, divisions regarding partisan preferences, social identities, and ideological orientations. However, a distinctive feature of the recent period is that *partisan* polarization has become more closely linked than in the past to *social* differentiation and *ideological* polarization. In an analysis of poll data on voters' social identity, Charles Blow observes, "The Republican-Democratic divide is increasingly becoming an all-white/multicultural divide, a male/female divide, and a more religious/less religious divide. . . ."[73] Figure 4.4 illustrates this trend. More than in most previous periods in American history, ideological choices are closely linked to party preferences. The political scientists Earl and Merle Black claim that "[f]or American voters who call themselves Democrats or Republicans, the social and cultural differences between the two national parties are infinitely greater in the first decade of the twenty-first century than they were in the past."[74] Further, because voters also tend to sort themselves out geographically, the two parties' social bases reinforce their distinctive regional bases of support.

Not only do the majority of states display stable partisan preferences for long periods—the red state/blue state phenomenon—but the red states are becoming more red and the blue states more blue. Figure 4.5 documents the decreasing number of states in which the partisan distribution of the vote is close to the national vote distribution.

FIGURE 4.4

CHANGES IN PARTIES' SOCIAL BASE

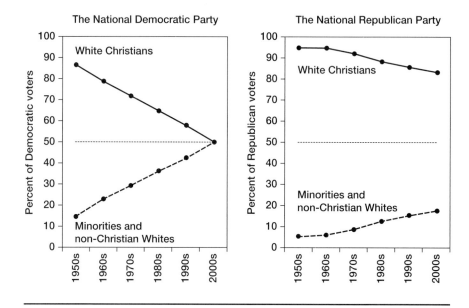

SOURCE: Earl Black and Merle Black, *Divided America: The Ferocious Power Struggle in American Politics* (New York: Simon & Schuster, 2007), 257.

Detailed historical analysis is needed to explain why most states and regions have developed relatively stable patterns of one-party dominance. Just as parties are becoming more polarized on the basis of issues, so are geographic areas becoming increasingly defined by the party affiliation of their residents.

Consider the South, a key to explaining Republican dominance from the 1980s through 2008. Unlike most regions, which were generally competitive until recently, the South has been a solidly one-party region since the Civil War. It switched from being securely under Democratic Party control to being a pro-Republican region for three reasons. The first is race. The divorce between the South and the Democratic Party began in 1964, when President Lyndon Baines Johnson (LBJ) sponsored the Civil Rights Act, followed by the Voting Rights Act of 1965. Most white southerners, the vast majority of southern voters in that era of racial repression, fiercely opposed racial integration and voting rights for African Americans. During the bitter congressional fight to pass the Civil Rights Act, LBJ ruefully predicted

FIGURE 4.5

GEOGRAPHIC POLARIZATION

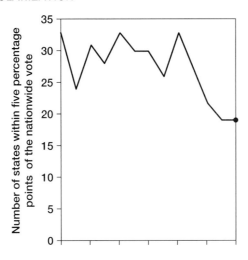

SOURCE: Adam Liptak, "Revanishing Battleground," *New York Times*, November 4, 2012.

the consequence: "We may win this legislation, but we're going to lose the South for a generation."[75] Second, the South is the most religiously observant region in the country, the home of many Protestant evangelicals. Ever since Ronald Reagan's election in 1980, the Republican Party has been highly successful in courting this group. Third, southern voters were quite conservative on economic issues. Southerners had an additional incentive to switch party preference when Ronald Reagan championed conservative economic values in the 1980s.

The political scientist Morris Fiorina has questioned whether there is actually more intense partisan polarization among the electorate today.[76] He claims that the source of political polarization in the United States is not the general electorate. Indeed, he cites public-opinion data documenting a *decline* in polarization among rank-and-file citizens on significant issues. For example, there has been increased public acceptance of a woman's right to choose abortion and of gays having the right to teach in public schools and marry.

Fiorina does not deny that a change has occurred. But he claims that what has changed is that ideological positions align more closely today with partisan preferences. Thus, one can more accurately predict people's stands on issues by knowing which party they favor. (Similarly, recall Figure 4.5 above, which documents a trend toward one-party dominance in most states.) According to Fiorina, the closer fit these days between party and ideology has occurred because party leaders have sponsored an ideological sorting process. In the 1950s and 1960s, both parties were broad tents in which a moderate (that is, centrist) faction coexisted with a more extreme faction—more liberal for the Democratic Party, more conservative for the Republican Party. The defection of the South to the Republican Party tipped the party toward the conservative side of the spectrum and left the Democratic Party more liberal.

David Leonhardt, an economics journalist for the *New York Times*, supports Fiorina's claim:

> Americans of different races are no more polarized in their political views than they were 25 years ago. Men and women are no more polarized either. The same goes for people of different education levels, different income groups and different levels of religiosity. The one big exception . . . is political party. Self-described Democrats and self-described Republicans hold beliefs that contrast far more sharply than a generation ago on a wide range of issues, including environmental policy, the safety net and immigration.

Leonhardt does not believe that ideological polarization has increased. What has changed is that Americans "have increasingly sorted themselves into two ideologically cohesive political parties."[77]

The process of partisan and ideological self-sorting is not symmetrical—that is, both parties have not moved equally far from the ideological center. Instead, the Republican Party has moved much further right than the Democratic Party has moved left. As we described earlier in the chapter, since the late 1970s power has shifted within the Republican Party to a coalition of hard-right conservative groups, including cultural conservatives and free-market economic conservatives.[78]

The puzzle thus becomes: why did the Republican Party move so far? And once it did, how could it score frequent electoral and policy successes until 2008? We suggest that for an answer to both questions, follow the money! As discussed above, the politically active do not represent the entire citizenry. Wealthy citizens are more likely to vote in primaries and general elections, and they usually support more conservative policies than the general electorate. Moreover, turnout in primary elections in particular is very low, and the primary electorate is even more unrepresentative of the country than the general electorate. It is more ideological, more educated, and more

WHAT DO YOU THINK?

Is America Polarized?

Political scientists disagree about the extent and character of polarization in American politics. Some political scientists claim that rank-and-file Americans have moved away from centrist or moderate political views and adopted more sharply edged positions on economic and social issues. Other political scientists suggest that polarization has occurred not because Americans are more ideologically extremist but because party coalitions are becoming more differentiated—that is, like-minded voters are gravitating to the same party. As a result, although the distribution of opinions in the electorate has not changed, party coalitions have become more polarized. Summarize the opposing positions and the evidence in favor of each one. Which view—or yet another one—do you think better explains the extent and character of polarization in American politics? Why?

affluent than that in regular elections. Thus, hard-core conservative activists, allied with well-financed pro-business lobbies, think tanks, and grassroots movements, have placed their candidates on the ballot by winning primary elections. The result is to make the general election much more intensely partisan.

AMERICAN PARTIES AND ELECTIONS IN COMPARATIVE PERSPECTIVE

The American party system and electoral process are outliers among the world's democracies. To begin with, the U.S. is nearly the only country with a two-party system. Virtually all other democracies have multiparty systems. When it comes to political finance, the U.S. is also unique among industrialized democracies. In no other democratic country does money talk so loud. Elsewhere, the government finances the bulk of party and candidate expenditures. Further, the entire scale of political finance is far more modest than in the U. S.

What difference do these features of the system of political finance make? Three can be identified. First, the role of private finance is much smaller in other countries. Where the government provides the bulk of political funds, and there are strict limits on private contributions, the system of parties and elections is more insulated from the private sector. In particular, this means that economic inequalities elsewhere have a smaller influence on the electoral process. Second, because public subsidies to parties are of similar size, parties compete on a relatively equal footing. Third, since fewer funds are spent on parties and elections, there is less professionalization of the electoral process. The single largest expense of American parties involves television advertising. Most countries prohibit political ads on television. Instead, the government requires television broadcasters to allot free time to all parties to present their case.

Taken together, these differences vastly reduce the influence of private money in elections elsewhere and make party competition abroad more fair and inclusive. The immense role of private money in the U.S. makes the electoral playing field highly unequal, especially since wealthy Americans and corporate interests account for the lion's share of private contributions.

The most important way that private money makes its influence felt in the U.S. is not to tip the advantage to one party or the other (although the Republican Party, as the more pro-business party, often has the advantage in this respect). The most important impact is to shape the ideological orientation of the entire party system to sustain the capitalist system and the structural power of business. This helps explain why programs promoting social solidarity like public health insurance and public housing were created elsewhere before they arrived in the U.S., and are more extensive there. (We discuss these features of the American political economy in Chapter 10.)

CONCLUSION

The fundamental idea of democracy is that citizens should have equal ability to influence political outcomes. Political participation, parties, and elections are the key mechanisms by which citizens' preferences are expressed and citizens' influence over political decisions and policies is exerted. This chapter thus provides an important test of the health of American democracy.

Using this yardstick to measure the extent and character of American democracy suggests that the political system falls woefully short. This chapter has documented how parties and elections tend to reinforce rather than offset economic inequality. In the *Citizens United* case described earlier in the chapter, the Supreme Court held that political spending could not be limited because doing so limited free speech. Applying this logic, it is clear that the wealthy—both individuals and corporations—speak far more freely than the vast majority of Americans. This chapter has documented how the political power of money has sharply increased in recent decades.

The report of the APSA Task Force on Inequality and American Democracy, referred to earlier, described the typical pattern in the U.S. as follows:

Today . . . the voices of American citizens are raised and heard unequally. The privileged participate more than others and are increasingly well organized to press their demands on government. Public officials, in turn, are much more responsive to the privileged than to average citizens and the less affluent. The voices of citizens with lower or moderate incomes are lost on the ears of inattentive government officials, while the advantaged roar with a clarity and consistency that policymakers readily hear and routinely follow. [The result is a] growing concentration of the country's wealth, income, and political influence in the hands of the few. . . . We find that our governing institutions are much more responsive to the privileged and well-organized narrow interests than to other Americans.[79]

This chapter has explored why political parties and elections in the U.S. fail to meet the democratic test in important respects. Reasons involve the organization of political parties, finance, and elections—that is, the core mechanisms of political participation. We have highlighted the increased importance since the 1980s of ideology, polarization, and political money. These changes have produced more starkly divided parties. Although the parties offer voters more clear-cut choices, the result has been to poison the political air and promote political stalemate, especially when the Republican Party has moved so far to the right. This situation is what motivated Thomas Mann and Norman Ornstein to call their pessimistic account of congressional gridlock *It's Even Worse Than You Think*.[80]

The chapter has demonstrated that political participation in the United States is slanted toward the wealthy in terms of voter turnout, campaign contributions, and political activism. As a classic study of participation by the political scientists Sidney Verba, Kay Lehman Schlozman, and Henry E. Brady points out, "Over and over, our data showed that participatory input is tilted in the direction of the more advantaged groups in society—especially in terms of economic and education position, but in terms of race and ethnicity as well."[81] Republican dominance for much of the period since the 1980s was a product of this situation.

Yet while the democratic deck may be stacked, the dealer does not always win. Periodically in American history, progressive candidates were elected to Congress despite the opposition of powerful corporate interests. Some distinguished examples in the late twentieth and early twenty-first century include

Paul Wellstone, Dennis Kucinich, Bernard Sanders, and Barney Frank. Barack Obama's election and reelection also suggest that popular majorities can at least partially offset the power of money. Beyond the electoral arena, social movements (described in the next chapter) have arisen over and over to challenge inequality and propose ways to democratize the political and economic spheres. In the 1930s, the newly mobilized labor movement played a key role in FDR's sponsorship of New Deal reforms. In the 1960s and 1970s, the civil rights movement pressured presidents Kennedy and Johnson to propose a "War on Poverty" and "Great Society." Many progressive successes have occurred at state and local levels. The efforts of these movements and leaders, however imperfect and incomplete, demonstrate that despite unequal resources, progressive movements sometimes win. Unlike dictatorial regimes, which actively repress political participation, democratic regimes allow citizens to participate in the choice of leaders and to influence the laws that govern them. Although political participation often strengthens privilege and inequality, it can also counteract advantages of class, race, and gender.

When the convention that drafted the Constitution concluded its work in 1787, the revered elder statesman Benjamin Franklin was asked to evaluate the result. He is famously recorded as replying, "A republic if you can keep it."[82] Political parties and elections potentially enable citizens to keep—and deepen—the United States' republican and democratic forms of government. However, for this to occur citizens must mobilize to challenge the power of money and the tendency for inequalities in political participation to parallel economic inequalities. The politics of power turns on these central issues.

CHAPTER SUMMARY

Introduction
This chapter analyzes the impact of political parties, elections, and political contributions on American democracy. The general claim is that, while the arena of parties and elections can potentially offset economic and social inequalities, this rarely occurs. The chapter seeks to understand how the system of parties and elections enables economic inequalities to be translated into political power.

Political Parties and American Democracy
Political parties are key elements in a democracy. They structure electoral and policy choices, nominate candidates for office, and connect

citizens to government. Although they play a fundamental role in the American political system, parties are not identified in the Constitution, and the Founders thought parties were divisive and undesirable. Yet parties developed early in the country's history and, by the 1830s, became a permanent fixture in American politics. One of their key roles was to transform politics from an elite to a popular activity by mobilizing citizens to turn out to vote. (At the same time, the electorate remained restricted to white males for many years.)

Origins of the Two-Party System

A key—and unusual—feature of the American political-party system is that only two major parties dominate most elections. This section analyzes why. A key factor includes the unusual procedures that govern elections, especially the single-member-district, plurality, winner-take-all system, in which the one candidate who receives the plurality of votes in a district wins the seat. This system is compared with the more common system of proportional representation (PR), in which many candidates are elected from a given district and seats are allotted according to the proportion of votes cast for each party. The PR system promotes a greater number of parties and a wider range of ideological options.

Party Organization and Realignments Since 1896

In America's party system, parties have rarely presented sharply differing programs. Periodically, however, when a critical election occurs, there has been a shift from one broad partisan coalition to another. For much of the nineteenth century, parties were highly influential in integrating newly arrived immigrants and mobilizing citizens to turn out in elections. Progressive reforms in the early twentieth century considerably weakened parties, and there was a corresponding decline in voting turnout. Parties were further undermined by the advent of radio, television, public-opinion polling, and professional consultants. These developments sidelined parties in favor of candidate-centered campaign organizations. The rise of presidential primaries in many states since the 1970s further weakened party organizations.

The 2012 Presidential Election

Barack Obama's reelection was the result of several factors. He was more personally popular and inspired more trust than his Republican opponent, Mitt Romney. By consolidating the Democratic Party's appeal to ascending demographic groups in American society, Obama's victory may have further contributed to a possible electoral realignment that began with his election in 2008. The Democratic Party electorate included these demographically ascending groups—notably, nonwhite minorities—as well as youth, low-income voters, and women, especially unmarried women. The Obama victory was also due to the Democratic Party's superior campaign organization, which integrated a pioneering use of data mining, micro-targeting, and new social media with an extensive ground game to assure its victory in traditionally blue states as well as most battleground states.

Parties and Voters Turnout

Turnout in the United States is unusually low compared to that in other industrialized democracies. Several factors explain this situation. First, there is widespread popular cynicism and suspicion of political elites. This is especially true among younger voters, who turn out to vote in smaller proportions. Further barriers to voting are caused by difficulties in registering and in voting on Tuesdays, which are workdays for most Americans. Recent voter-suppression campaigns sponsored by conservative organizations further depress voting levels throughout the electorate and are especially likely to affect lower-income, less educated, and working-class Americans. One result of unequal rates of turnout is the promotion policies that favor the interests of affluent Americans and businesses.

Money and Elections

Political parties and candidates require large sums of money to wage nomination campaigns and compete in the general election. Campaign contributions reflect the structural power of business, in that the bulk of political money is provided by affluent citizens, business firms, and organized interests. Although campaign-finance laws somewhat limit the influence of large donors, wealthy individuals and business interests continue to have an enormous influence on elections by providing the bulk of campaign contributions. This tendency has been increased by the 2010 Supreme Court *Citizens United* decision, which eliminated a prohibition on corporate endorsements of candidates and direct contributions to their campaigns.

Polarization and American Politics

Today there is a strong tendency for various forms of polarization—partisan, social, and ideological—to coincide. The result is an intensely conflictual political climate. Political scientists are divided about whether polarization is primarily a product of a chasm between citizens of different outlooks or a result of party leaders, think tanks, and PACs who have moved both parties, particularly the Republican Party, toward the ideological extremes.

American Parties and Elections in Comparative Perspective

America's two-party system and campaign finance regulations are outliers among the world's democracies. The two-party system was analyzed in an earlier section of this chapter, *The Origins of the Two-Party System*. Regarding political finance, the U.S. is distinctive in three ways. First, the amount of private contributions financing candidates, parties, and campaigns is far greater in the U.S. than elsewhere. The result is to increase the influence of affluent donors, who provide the vast proportion of political contributions. Second, since these funds are mostly provided to the two major parties, the result is to lock in the two-party system. Third, the system of private political finance increases the importance of television advertising, polling, and professional campaign consultants and organizations. Overall, the cumulative impact of these factors is to shape the ideological orientation of the party system toward sustaining the capitalist system and the structural power of business.

Conclusion

The chapter concludes that the system of parties, elections, and campaign finance generally serves to reinforce the structural power of business in the American political system rather than to offset the power of money. Nonetheless, there have been significant exceptions to this trend at the local, state, and national level.

Critical Thinking Questions

1. What are the advantages and drawbacks of electing representatives by the single-member-district plurality system as opposed to proportional representation (PR)? Which system is preferable, and why?

2. Do you agree with the Supreme Court's *Citizens United* ruling that struck down legislation and regulations limiting the amount of money that corporations and unions could spend to support candidates and parties?

The Court held that spending limits violate their First Amendment right to free expression. Do you agree? Why or why not?

3. What are two factors that explain why Barack Obama was reelected president in 2012? Which of the two factors you cited is most important, and why?

4. Is it fair to say elections are bought and sold? Why or why not?

5. Analyze a historical example of when popular participation has offset the power of money. What factors (social, economic, strategic, or other) have enabled this to occur?

6. Is demography destiny? Does the relative size of various socioeconomic and demographic groups determine electoral outcomes? Why or why not?

Suggested Readings

Larry M. Bartels, *Unequal Democracy: The Political Economy of the Gilded Age.* New York: Russell Sage Foundation; Princeton, NJ: Princeton University Press, 2008.

Earl Black and Merle Black, *Divided America: The Ferocious Power Struggle in American Politics.* New York: Simon & Schuster, 2007.

Walter Dean Burnham, *Critical Elections and the Mainsprings of American Politics.* New York: W. W. Norton, 1970.

E. J. Dionne, Jr., *Our Divided Political Heart: The Battle for the American Idea in an Age of Discontent.* New York: Bloomsbury, 2012.

Morris Fiorina, with Samuel J. Abrams and Jeremy C. Pope, *Culture War? The Myth of Polarized America.* New York: Pearson Longman, 2006.

Andrew Gelman, David Park, Boris Shor, Joseph Bafumi, and Jeronimo Cortina, *Red States, Blue States, Rich States, Poor States.* Princeton, NJ: Princeton University Press, 2008.

Jacob S. Hacker and Paul Pierson, *Off Center: The Republican Revolution and the Erosion of American Democracy.* New Haven, CT: Yale University Press, 2006.

Jacob S. Hacker and Paul Pierson, *Winner-Take-All Politics: How Washington Made the Rich Richer—and Turned Its Back on the Middle Class.* New York: Simon & Schuster, 2010.

Zoltan L. Hajnal and Taeku Lee, *Why Americans Don't Join the Party: Race, Immigration, and the Failure (of Political Parties) to Engage the Electorate.* Princeton: Princeton, NJ: Princeton University Press, 2011.

Marc J. Hetherington and Jonathan D. Weiler, *Authoritarianism & Polarization in American Politics*. New York: Cambridge University Press, 2009.

Geoffrey Kabaservice, *Rule and Ruin: The Downfall of Moderation and the Destruction of the Republican Party, from Eisenhower to the Tea Party*. New York: Oxford University Press, 2012.

Jan E. Leighley, ed., *The Oxford Handbook of American Elections and Political Behavior*. New York: Oxford University Press, 2010.

L. Sandy Maisel and Jeffrey M. Berry, eds., *The Oxford Handbook of American Political Parties and Interest Groups*. New York: Oxford University Press, 2010.

Thomas E. Mann and Norman J. Ornstein, *It's Even Worse Than It Looks: How the American Constitutional System Collided with the New Politics of Extremism*. New York: Basic Books, 2012.

Andrew S. McFarland, *Boycotts and Dixie Chicks: Creative Participation at Home and Abroad*. Boulder, CO: Paradigm Publishers, 2011.

Pietro S. Nivola and David W. Brady, eds., *Red and Blue Nation? Characteristics and Causes of America's Polarized Politics*. Vol. 1. Washington, D.C.: Brookings Institution Press, 2006.

Paul Pierson and Theda Skocpol, eds., *The Transformation of American Politics: Activist Government and the Rise of Conservatism*. Princeton, NJ: Princeton University Press, 2007.

Frances Fox Piven and Richard Cloward, *Why Americans Don't Vote*. New York: Pantheon, 1988.

Robert D. Putnam, *Bowling Alone: The Collapse and Revival of American Community*. New York: Simon & Schuster, 2000.

Kay Lehman Schlozman, Sidney Verba, and Henry E. Brady, *The Unheavenly Chorus: Unequal Political Voice and the Broken Promise of American Democracy*. Princeton, NJ: Princeton University Press, 2012.

Theda Skocpol and Vanessa Williamson, *The Tea Party and the Remaking of American Conservatism*. New York: Oxford University Press, 2012.

Gerald Sussman, *Global Electioneering: Campaign Consulting, Communications, and Corporate Financing*. Lanham, MD: Rowman & Littlefield, 2005.

Sidney Verba, Kay Lehman Schlozman, and Henry E. Brady, *Voice and Equality: Civic Voluntarism in American Politics*. Cambridge, MA: Harvard University Press, 1995.

INTEREST GROUPS AND SOCIAL MOVEMENTS

INTRODUCTION

Spring 2012 was the warmest ever recorded in the U.S. Bill McKibben, an environmentalist, reports that it "crushed the old record by so much that it represented the largest temperature departure from average of any season on record." May 2012 was the warmest ever recorded in the Northern Hemisphere, and June broke or tied 3,215 high-temperature records across the United States. Summer offered no relief, as shimmering heat, withering drought, and terrifying wildfires gripped the nation.[1]

The temperature is rising. Increasing carbon dioxide emissions are heating the planet, creating what is known as global warming, which threatens to disrupt normal weather patterns and melt the polar ice caps. Both changes would have catastrophic consequences. The former portends destructive hurricanes, droughts, tornados and typhoons, while the latter augurs rising ocean levels that threaten to inundate coastal land and cities. In addition, global warming endangers food production and water availability, heightening the risk of international conflict.

But global warming has not only raised the earth's heat; it has also raised the political temperature in the U.S. Environmentalists warn that we must check global warming before it is too late. They are opposed by some conservatives, who dismiss global warming as a problem because efforts to solve it, they warn, would require "command and control laws and regulations imposed from Washington." According to the conservative Environmental Policy Analysis Network, political reforms to prevent global warming would trample "on traditional values by limiting individual liberty, unconstitutionally expanding the reach of government, hindering free markets, and harming our national prosperity."[2] Nowhere was this more evident than in some conservatives' efforts to deny and obfuscate the science behind global warming. According to two analysts, global-warming science has been the target of a "well-funded, highly complex, relatively coordinated 'denial machine' that includes conservative think tanks, corporate donors, front groups, and right-wing pundits and media."[3]

Oil and coal companies, such as ExxonMobil and Peabody Coal, as well their trade associations, including the American Petroleum Institute and the Western Fuels Association, were among the first to engage in climate-change denial. They tried to disparage the science behind global warming because of the threat it posed to their interests once it was recognized that burning fossil fuels was a major contributor to greenhouse-gas emissions. But oil and coal companies were not alone in trying to dismiss global warming as the product of "junk science." They were joined by automobile manufacturers, forestry companies, and the U.S. Chamber of Commerce. But none have been more zealous in promoting climate-change denial than the brothers David and Charles Koch, whose combined fortunes are exceeded only by Microsoft founder Bill Gates and the famed investor Warren Buffett. They own virtually all of Koch Industries, the second-largest private company in the U.S., with significant oil holdings. While Gates and Buffett have left their fortunes to charity, the Koch brothers invest in promoting right-wing causes, including trying to debunk global warming, which has earned them the dubious label "kingpins of climate science denial."[4]

Much of the corporate money from the Koch brothers and other sources goes to supporting front groups—to give climate-change denial an aura of popular support—and to conservative think tanks, such as the George C. Marshall Institute and the Heritage Foundation, that reward their paymasters by manufacturing uncertainty about climate science. These think tanks finance their own experts to dispute the scientific consensus that global warming is occurring, host conferences where these contrarian views are presented, and disseminate their findings to media outlets by producing press releases, opinion pieces for newspapers, and videos. The most notorious of these groups is the Heartland Institute. In 2012 leaked documents from the institute revealed that it was preparing a climate-change-denial curriculum for public schools because "principals and teachers are heavily biased toward the alarmist perspective."[5] But then it gave its own corporate benefactors cause for alarm when it put up digital billboards on the Eisenhower Expressway in Chicago claiming that global-warming advocates were equivalent to mass murderers. This was so outrageous and embarrassing that some of Heartland's corporate donors subsequently withdrew their support.[6]

Prostituted science produced by these think tanks is then widely distributed through conservative media, such as the talk-radio hosts Rush Limbaugh and Sean Hannity, Fox News, and the editorial pages of the *Wall Street Journal*. Finally, these views are picked up by Republican politicians, like former Oklahoma Senator James Inhofe, who labeled global warming "the greatest hoax ever perpetrated on the American people."[7]

We discuss interest groups, such as climate-change deniers, and social movements, such as environmentalism, together in this chapter because they are forms of political participation that are complementary to voting and elections, covered in the previous chapter. Citizens join interest groups and participate in social movements to express their demands to decision makers. These different forms of political participation—voting, joining an interest group, and social-movement activity—are not neatly sealed off from one another. Rather, political actors devise strategies that they judge are appropriate given the resources they have and the opportunities available to them. Depending upon the circumstances, activists may mobilize voters, lobby officials, and organize demonstrations simultaneously, anticipating that each form of political participation will supplement and support the others. For example, every year on Earth Day, environmental groups stage rallies, remind supporters to register to vote, and encourage them to contact members of Congress. Political actors not only engage in different forms of political participation simultaneously but also pursue different forms of participation sequentially. For instance, the civil rights movement shifted strategies from marches and protests to voter registration and mobilization as the rewards of the former declined and opportunities for the latter increased. One form of political participation paved the way to another. And finally, activists sometimes pursue one form of political participation at the expense of others. For example, as voter turnout declined through the last half of the twentieth century, interest-group formation and activity increased. In other words, as citizens lost confidence in the electoral process, they pursued their political interests through other means.

Like water trying to escape through the weakest part of a dam, political actors are always looking for the weakest point in the wall of power. They may engage in different forms of political participation simultaneously, or they may concentrate exclusively on mobilizing voters, lobbying officials, or organizing protests. But the appropriate mix of strategies used by political actors depends upon the circumstances they confront. Consider the difference between the mass demonstrations that marked opposition to the Vietnam War in the 1960s and the relative absence of such protests by opponents of the Iraq War forty years later. Antiwar activists participated in mass demonstrations against the Vietnam War because electoral politics was a dead end for them. There was no alternative to direct action because both the Democratic and Republican parties supported the war. Forty years later, peace activists faced different circumstances. By 2004 many Democrats had come out against the Iraq War. Opponents of the war could eschew direct action because electoral alternatives not open to Vietnam War protestors were available to them.[8] The sequence in which different forms of political participation appear, and whether they supplement or substitute one another, depends upon the resources political actors can mobilize and the opportunities they have to deploy them.

Interest groups are organizations that political actors form to influence public policy. Groups seek to influence what bills are proposed, what provisions they contain, and how legislators vote on them. They also try to affect administrative rulings by federal agencies, executive and judicial appointments, and the awarding of government contracts. Examples of interest groups include well-known organizations like the National Rifle Association and Mothers Against Drunk Driving, as well as more obscure ones like the Dollar Coin Alliance and Americans for George. While the former wants to replace dollar bills with a coin and save Americans the trouble of having their soiled dollar bills rejected by vending machines, the latter wants to retain the venerable dollar bill, vowing to save Americans from the indignity of having their pockets and purses weighed down with heavy coins. Interest groups such as these connect individuals with government. They are a means for citizens to express their demands and preferences to public officials. Indeed, a variety of interest groups is found in every contemporary democracy, and it is difficult to imagine any democracy without them.[9]

Although interest groups share many properties with political parties and social movements, they can be distinguished from both. Like political parties, they raise money, mobilize voters, and campaign for candidates; but they do not nominate candidates to run for office. Like social movements, interest groups draw together people who share common interests with the intent of influencing policy makers; but they tend to be more formally structured, more durable, and less disruptive in their tactics.

Social movements, such as the civil rights and antiwar movements of the 1960s, engage in unconventional and more confrontational forms of political activism. Social movements are distinguished from interest groups in that they are less formally organized, less hierarchical, and less bureaucratic. Joining a social movement is also a more demanding form of political participation than belonging to an interest group or voting because the risks of social-movement activism are so much greater. Consequently, social-movements tend to attract people with intense feelings about an issue who are more committed and willing to assume the greater risks that social-movement participation entails.

The 2011 social movement Occupy Wall Street (OWS), which emerged to protest growing income inequality and corporate influence on government, reflects many of these qualities. The movement began in New York in September 2011, when a group of activists took over Zuccotti Park, a small plaza near Wall Street, in the heart of New York's financial district. For a month the protestors camped out in the park to protest the disproportionate wealth and power of the richest one percent at the expense of the remaining 99 percent. The movement then spread throughout the country, to Chicago, Los Angeles, and Washington, D.C., and even internationally, to Berlin, London, and Mumbai. While each Occupy movement had its own local flavor, they all shared qualities that characterize social movements. They lacked bureaucratic hierarchy, central coordination, and formal organization. They demanded a high level of commitment from their supporters, who left their homes to set up tents, soup kitchens, and aid stations in the parks and other public spaces they occupied. And protestors engaged in activities that disrupted normal routines to draw attention to their demands. While Occupy Wall Street had an ephemeral half-life, it did succeed in changing the political agenda. Demands to reduce federal deficits that Tea Party activists advocated were now replaced by calls to reduce inequality that scruffy occupiers articulated.

Occupy Wall Street protestors march in downtown New York City in October 2012.

Social movements are often identified with groups that have liberal, progressive agendas, such as Occupy Wall Street. But conservatives have also formed social movements to influence public policy. Participation in social movements is not the monopoly of any one ideological group but can be found across the political spectrum.

This chapter begins with a discussion of how the interest-group universe has changed to include a greater number and variety of groups than in the past. Today there are interest groups to cover all the policy bases—even, as noted earlier, groups that want policy makers to replace the dollar bill and those who want them to retain it! In 2010 there were more than 11,000 registered lobbyists—more than 20 for each member of Congress—involved in a $3.5 billion business. But that does not mean all these lobbyists and the interest groups they represent are equally powerful or successful. Groups that serve corporate interests—such as policy offices representing individual firms, trade associations representing specific industries, and peak associations representing businesses across industries—remain the most influential, largely due to the extensive resources at their command. We then proceed to show that interest-group formation cannot be taken for granted. Activists have to offer incentives to recruit members. We then turn to a discussion of public opinion and the role interest groups play in shaping it.

The second half of the chapter is devoted to social movements. Social movements, as we discussed earlier, are not as hierarchical or formally organized as political parties or interest groups, tend to be more ideological and contentious, and move participation up to a more active and demanding level than other forms of political participation. We then provide an extended case study of the American labor movement as an example of a social movement. More recently, new social movements have emerged that are not based on economic issues, like those that united workers or farmers. Social movements today are frequently based on shared racial, sexual, or ethnic identities; shared values; or quality-of-life issues. Consequently, we provide smaller, capsule accounts of the women's movement, the Tea Party movement, and the environmental movement to capture the emergence of these new forms of social movements alongside their older, more work-based counterparts.

INTEREST GROUPS

In Chapter 4 we saw that voters and political parties have changed much since the 1960s. So, too, have citizens and interest groups. Membership is more passive at the same time interest groups are more active. Since 1970, interest groups have proliferated, and more groups are raising more demands than ever before. Twice as many organizations were listed in the 2006 *Washington Representatives* directory as were included in the 1981 version.[10] But as new interest groups have emerged, it has become evident that they are operating differently from those that preceded them. They are more centralized and less participatory, more professional and less voluntary, more specialized and less inclusive. Their professionalization means that interest groups make fewer demands on their members. But their proliferation means they make greater demands on government.

Before the interest-group explosion in the 1970s, the vast majority of interest groups seeking to influence policy represented business: individual firms like General Motors and General Electric, trade associations like the Association of American Railroads and the Electronic Industries Alliance, or peak organizations like the National Association of Manufacturers and the U.S. Chamber of Commerce. These organizations exerted influence through "subgovernments" that dominated policy in specific issue arenas. Subgovernments, sometimes known as iron triangles, were traditionally composed of three actors whose interests overlapped and were mutually supportive: interest groups that had a stake in an issue, congressional subcommittees that had jurisdiction over the area, and federal agencies that had responsibility for it. All three actors benefited from the relationship and consequently cooperated to their mutual satisfaction. One of the most formidable subgovernments was in the realm of national defense, where all participants had an interest in increasing defense expenditures. For defense contractors, more spending meant more contracts and profits; for members of the House Armed Services Committee, more defense spending meant more money they could direct to their districts; and for the Pentagon, more outlays meant more sophisticated weaponry and more career opportunities. Subgovernments were exclusive, discouraging intervention from outsiders; stable, encouraging familiarity and agreement among participants; and insular, protecting their shared interests at the expense of the public interest.[11]

While subgovernments can still be found in areas that involve "low visibility, noncontroversial routine policy making," they are not as prominent or widespread as they once were.[12] New participants forced their way into the game, and their goals often conflicted with those of the established players. Beginning in the 1960s, groups that were previously underrepresented, such as environmental activists and civil rights advocates, emerged to alter the geometry of iron triangles. Their presence shattered the insular and collusive world of subgovernments. Issues that had been the interest of a few were now the concern of many. As the policy community grew and included more players, it now included more dissident views, thus breaking up the closed, incestuous relationships that had defined policymaking in the past.

The emergence of these new interest groups was an outgrowth of the civil rights, environmental, consumer, and feminist social movements of the 1960s. As these movements matured, they experienced a shift that the civil rights leader Bayard Rustin called moving from "protest to politics."[13] Their focus changed from marching on Washington to lobbying it, from condemning politicians to endorsing them, and from engaging in spontaneous actions to building permanent organizations. These public-interest groups became formidable fixtures in Washington, able to provide some countervailing power to business elites.

The shift from protest to politics that saw the energy of the 1960s social movements expressed in the interest-group explosion of the 1970s and 1980s was a sign of their success as much as their exhaustion. Groups that previously had been excluded because they were either dismissed or unorganized, such as feminists, minorities, consumers, and environmentalists, were now testifying before deferential members of Congress and offering their expert judgment to appreciative federal agencies. Outsiders had finally achieved their goal of becoming insiders.

But the interest-group explosion was not only the result of movements from below successfully elbowing their way in. Government expanded the range of its activities, and new interest groups emerged around the affected policy areas. The state's footprint in terms of what it sought to encourage, regulate, monitor, and prohibit grew (and continues to grow). Government used to be concerned only with core activities, such as security and welfare, but its scope has widened considerably to include such issues as obesity, species extinction, doping in sports, and the use of cell phones while driving. With each new policy initiative by government, a new group of stakeholders has emerged anxious to influence it. Just as interest-group influence may lead government to extend its policy reach into new areas, new policy domains also create new interest groups.

Finally, institutional changes in Congress that made it more accessible and inviting to outside influence also contributed to increased levels of interest-group formation and activity. As the realms of federal policy expanded, congressional procedures became more democratic, providing interest groups with more opportunities to press their demands. Congressional hearings were opened to the public, and subcommittees became more numerous and assertive. The new accessibility of Congress encouraged groups to organize and take advantage of the opportunities that were now available.

DAVID AND GOLIATH

Despite the addition of new groups articulating voices that were previously unorganized and unheard, business remains the largest, most organized, best-funded interest group of all. The emergence and success of the new kids on the block generated a countermobilization from business to defend its turf. It was like the awakening of a sleeping giant; business began responding to the challenge these new groups posed to them in the form of new environmental, consumer-protection, and fair-employment legislation. Businesses and industries that previously did not have a presence in Washington now created corporate government-affairs offices to represent their interests. Whereas about 200 businesses had their own lobbying shops in Washington before 1970, over 2,000 had opened Washington offices ten year later. Those that were already established now invested more in their existing political operations. New organizations to promote corporate policies, such as the Business Roundtable, were formed, while old ones, like the National Federation of Small Business, grew dramatically, from just a few hundred members at the beginning of the 1970s to over 6,000 by the decade's end.[14]

Although the interest-group universe may now be more crowded and diverse, business interests still predominate within it,[15] comprising more than half of active interest groups. In contrast, there is a dearth of organizations that represent the disadvantaged, and except for the presence of unions "*there are no occupational associations at all* to organize those who labor at low-skill jobs."[16]

FIGURE 5.1

INTEREST GROUPS BY TYPE

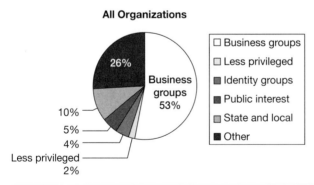

SOURCE: Washington Representatives Study; Kay Lehman Schlozman, Sidney Verba, and Henry E. Brady, *The Unheavenly Chorus: Unequal Political Voice and the Broken Promise of American Democracy* (Princeton, NJ: Princeton University Press, 2012) p. 439.

Businesses not only put more players on the field; they also enjoy a size advantage when they compete. Business groups have more resources—more money, staff members, and social connections—to devote to influencing policymakers. While businesses comprised a little more than half the total number of interest groups in 2001, they accounted for almost three-quarters of all lobbying expenditures.[17] From his perch as Director of the Securities and Exchange Commission (SEC) from 1993 to 2001, Arthur Levitt was astonished at the imbalance between business groups who actively lobbied his agency and the unorganized public whose voice was rarely heard. Levitt described how "groups representing Wall Street firms, mutual fund companies, accounting firms, or corporate managers would quickly set about to defeat even minor threats. Individual investors, with no organized labor or trade association to represent their views in Washington, never knew what hit them."[18] An example of the imbalance of views that agencies receive involved Levitt's own SEC after his departure. The SEC held 34 meetings in 2011 through 2012 to solicit opinions on changes to the Volker Rule, which mandates that banks should not make speculative bets that taxpayers would be liable for if the banks failed. Only one of those meetings was with a consumer-advocate organization; all others were with big banks and their representatives. After hearing from these lobbyists, the SEC issued a 530-page rule that was bloated with so many exemptions that even corporate lobbyists complained about the complexity they had succeeded in creating.[19] The contrast between the number of meetings that banking representatives had with federal agencies charged with writing rules to implement the Dodd–Frank Wall Street Reform and Consumer Protection Act and the number of such meetings consumer representatives had is captured in Figure 5.2.

Take the case of Google as an example of corporate influence in Washington. Before 2005, but after Google's public stock offering had transformed the little search engine that could into a market behemoth, the company still did not have a Washington office. But as Google grew, it became a political target. It found itself locked in political combat with telephone companies over net neutrality—that is, whether the phone companies could control what went over their network. It was also the target of antitrust investigations by the Department of Justice, and of lawsuits by citizens concerned about privacy. In response, Google opened a Washington office in 2005 and hired one lobbyist.[20] From humble beginnings, the company's Washington presence has grown dramatically. In the first few years, its lobbying expenses increased steadily by almost $1 million per year, totaling over $5 million in 2010. But then Google's investment in lobbying rose dramatically, to $9 million in the first six months of 2012 alone—more than Apple, Facebook, Amazon, and Microsoft combined![21]

FIGURE 5.2

NUMBER OF DODD–FRANK-RELATED MEETINGS WITH SELECT FEDERAL AGENCIES

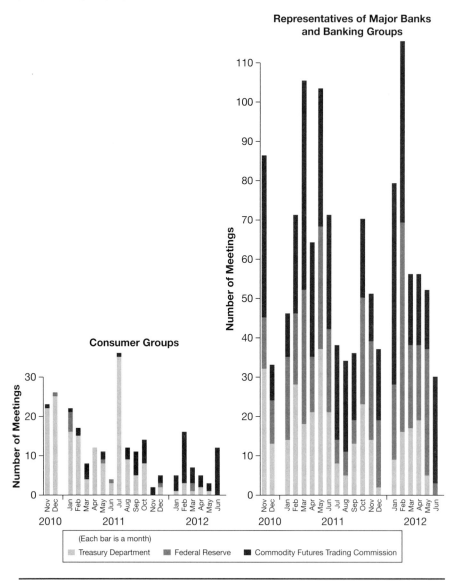

SOURCES: Center for Responsive Politics; Davis Polk; the Sunlight Foundation; "Deconstructing Dodd–Frank," the *New York Times*, December, 11, 2012, www.nytimes.com/interactive/2012/12/11/business/Deconstructing-Dodd-Frank.html (accessed February 5, 2013).

Google's lobbying efforts have come a long way from its one-man shop. Its Washington staff has grown so large that Google has had to move out of its original office in the nation's capital in 2008 to accommodate it. In 2012, Google took the lead in launching a new trade association called the Internet Association, along with some of Silicon Valley's biggest Internet firms, including Facebook, Amazon, and Yahoo. When the head of Google's Washington office retired in 2012, it hired Susan Molinari, a former member of Congress, to run it. Google also hired 12 outside lobbying firms, including such heavy hitters as the Akin Group, which is led by Molinari's husband, Bill Paxon, another former member of Congress, and the Gephardt Group, led by Richard Gephardt, the former House Majority Leader. And Google ensures that its lobbyists will encounter a friendly reception regardless of which party is in power by dividing donations from its political-action committee between Democrats and Republicans. Google's corporate mantra, "Don't Be Evil," has become "See No Evil" when it comes to choosing its political allies.

Google is a relatively new player in Washington, but its lobbying efforts are fast approaching those of other corporations its size. Even so, these expenditures by an individual company pale in comparison to what trade groups spend to influence policy. No group spends more on lobbying the government than the pharmaceutical industry. The drug lobby has more registered lobbyists than there are members of Congress. In addition, many of its lobbyists are either former members of Congress or former congressional staff members, so that when they go to work they are often lobbying their former colleagues. Lobbying firms are anxious to hire former staffers and members of Congress because they bring expertise and access. For example, in response to President Obama's 2009 proposal to increase health-care coverage for Americans and restrict insurers from "cherry-picking" clients, the largest insurers, hospitals, and medical groups hired more than 350 former members of Congress and staff people to lobby their former colleagues. The largest health-care-industry lobbying group, Pharmaceutical Research and Manufacturers of America (PhRMA), alone employed 137 former government officials among its 165 lobbyists to lobby Congress with regard to Obama's health-care bill.[22] Jack Abramoff, a lobbyist convicted for bribery, explained how he would approach congressional staff people with promises of work once they were done working on the Hill, and that once he did so, "We owned them. And what does that mean? Every request from our office, every request from our clients, everything that we want, they're gonna do. And not only that, they're gonna think of things we can't think of to do."[23] One critic of the practice complained, "Hiring a well-connected staffer can run a firm something like $300,000 to $600,000 a year, and for a member of Congress, it's anywhere from $1 million to $3 million. The only businesses that can really afford that are those that are very wealthy, but clearly these companies are getting their money's worth."[24]

More money is devoted to lobbying than ever before. Spending by registered lobbyists more than doubled in the last ten years, from $1.56 billion in 1999 to $3.49 billion in 2009. And this figure is only the tip of the iceberg, as it does not include money spent on nonregulated lobbying activities, such as survey research, donations to think tanks, media buys, and coalition building. Lobbying is more expensive today, in part because it is more sophisticated and multifaceted. It involves more than simply donating money to members of Congress, taking them to dinner, or providing them with reliable facts and convincing analyses of legislation. All of these strategies for exerting influence remain essential but are increasingly regarded as insufficient. Contemporary lobbying now extends in all directions to include providing reporters and editors with information, forging alliances with and even creating grassroots groups, and contributing money to sympathetic research and policy organizations that can pose as credible sources. Interest groups are now as active in trying to shape public opinion and frame how issues are perceived as they are in trying to influence what policy makers should do about them. They lobby the public in addition to policy makers. For example, in 2008 the oil industry "embarked on a multiyear, multimedia, multimillion dollar campaign" to try and explain itself to a public that was angry at high gas prices. This included newspaper ads, news conferences, and an interactive exhibit that included video games designed to show the efforts oil companies were making to produce cheaper and cleaner oil and gas. The American Petroleum Institute president explained, "We decided that if we didn't do something to help people understand our industry, we'd be on the losing end as far as the eye can see."[25] Success at grassroots strategies that shape the political agenda paves the way for success in how Washington policy makers react to it. A consequence of **all-directional lobbying** that pursues insider and outsider strategies simultaneously is to ratchet up its cost. As lobbying becomes more extensive, it becomes more expensive. It now costs more to play competitively, thus giving an advantage to those groups, such as business, that have the resources to do so.[26]

In addition to their resource advantage in interest-group competition, business leaders have social connections with policy makers that members of other groups do not have. They also have a structural advantage based upon their control of the means of production that is not available to other groups. The result is a privileged position for business that is seen as so natural that business is often not regarded as a special interest at all.[27] But just because business is bigger, stronger, and faster than other groups does not mean it always wins. One analysis found that what matters most in interest-group combat is not who is bigger and stronger but who is defending the status quo; those who defend the status quo are more likely to prevail over those who want to change it, regardless of each side's relative resources. But, as this analysis acknowledges, the status quo is the result of past struggles that reflected the relative resources of groups involved in the conflict.[28]

The size advantage of business is also canceled out when different firms and industries—some representing importers and others exporters, some representing producers and others distributers—are arrayed against one another. For example, in the struggle over President Obama's health-care bill, the U.S. Chamber of Commerce opposed a mandate on employers to provide health insurance, but Walmart and the temporary-employment agency Kelly Services supported it. A similar rupture occurred in response to President Obama's climate-change bill, designed to limit greenhouse-gas emissions. Major oil companies opposed the bill, while natural-gas producers supported it. Utilities with access to hydroelectric or nuclear power were in favor of it, and coal-dependent utilities lobbied against it. A once monolithic industry was divided in its approach to climate-change legislation because of the differential impact it would have on energy producers.[29]

Moreover, even when business interests are unified, they may not execute their political strategy well. Sometimes they adopt the wrong game plan and find themselves outmaneuvered in the struggle over policy by more agile and creative opponents. And sometimes business has to play in the hostile court of public opinion, which neutralizes its advantages. For example, even though lobbyists opposing financial reform outnumbered proreform lobbyists by more than 11 to 1, the Dodd–Frank Wall Street Reform and Consumer Protection Act still passed and was signed into law in 2010.[30] Policy makers did not want to be perceived by the public as coddling Wall Street investment firms responsible for the recent financial meltdown and consequently were less inclined to accede to their demands.

According to Pepper D. Culpepper, the more salient the issue, the less the interest-group advantages of business—access to decision makers, legislative and media deference to managerial expertise, strong lobbying capacities, and the structural bias—matter. Business influence is greatest when it operates in the shadows, when the public is indifferent. When issues become salient and voters pay attention, the incentives of policy makers shift. The special advantages business enjoys lose their grip because politicians now have to cater to voters to be reelected.[31] Thus, while organized business interests may be bigger, stronger, and faster, the spotlight of sustained public attention—the power of democracy—is sometimes sufficient to overcome their many advantages.[32]

THE CHANGING QUALITY OF MEMBERSHIP

In 1831 a young French aristocrat came to the United States to examine how the new democracy worked. He spent two years touring what were then the 26 states of the Republic and came away impressed with Americans as "a nation of joiners." In his brilliant account, *Democracy in America*, Alexis de Tocqueville wrote, "Americans of all ages, all conditions, and all dispositions constantly form associations. They have not only commercial and manufacturing companies, in which all take part, but associations of a thousand other kinds, religious, moral, serious, futile, general or restricted, enormous or diminutive."[33]

Tocqueville left readers with the impression that forming organizations is easy and natural. People with common interests simply get together to pursue their shared goals. But forming an organization is not so straightforward. Someone has to invest time, provide leadership, and commit resources to make it happen. Time, leadership, and resources may not exist and certainly are not evenly distributed among groups. For this reason, organizations of poor people, who lack time, resources, and leadership skills, are very rare while those of higher-status groups are more common. In addition, organizations face the **free-rider problem**. That is, if people acted rationally, they would not contribute to a group if they could still receive its benefits without paying for them. Instead, they would free ride, letting others go to meetings and pay dues to, say, the Sierra Club and then just sitting back and enjoying the benefits of clean air and water that environmentalists worked for. Of course, if everyone behaved like this, the Sierra Club would not exist.

But the Sierra Club does exist. And it exists partly because groups offer a variety of incentives that entice people to join them. Some groups, for instance, offer material incentives to recruit members. Members receive some tangible reward for joining. For example, AARP, which represents the interests of the elderly and is the second-largest membership organization in the United States after the Catholic Church, recruits members by offering medical insurance and travel discounts to those who join.

Other groups depend upon purposive incentives, rather than material benefits, to recruit members. Such organizations give people an opportunity to express their common values and realize their common goals. Membership in these organizations—such as the National Right to Life Committee (NRLC), which opposes abortion rights, and the National Abortion and Reproductive Rights Action League (NARAL), which supports them—is an expression of one's values.[34]

Much of the interest-group surge in the 1970s involved groups that recruited on the basis of purposive as opposed to material incentives. This focus has given contemporary interest-group political activity a more ideological, partisan, and aggressive character. Political conflict becomes harsher and less compromising when people are organized on the basis of their convictions.

Another striking shift among interest groups has been a change in the quality and class character of their memberships. Traditional mass-membership organizations, such as the National Association for the Advancement of Colored People (NAACP), had state and local chapters and required members to pay dues. Members engaged in politics by participating in the life of their organization, developing civic values and organizational skills in the process. And these organizations reached down to include workers and promote their civic and political engagement. But such organizations now face increased competition from more professionally managed advocacy organizations, such as the Children's Defense Fund or MoveOn.org, that do not have dues-paying members or local chapters. These types of organizations are funded by foundations, direct mail, or Internet fund-raising appeals as opposed to membership dues.[35] Traditional membership organizations have declined and been replaced by professionally managed interest groups, to the extent that they now comprise less than one-eighth of the organizations active in Washington today.[36]

The emergence of these new professionalized organizations has increased existing class inequalities. Wealthy and well-educated citizens have always been disproportionately represented through interest groups, but this is particularly true of these new professionalized advocacy organizations. A higher proportion of their supporters is drawn from the middle and upper classes than was true of more traditional mass-membership organizations. As a result, the predominance of these new professionalized advocacy groups amplifies the voice of the well-off and well educated, who find their minimal demands congenial, while the voice of the lower classes has been muted as the traditional mass-membership organizations have declined.[37] Thus, the impact of these new organizations on the quality of American democracy has been somewhat paradoxical. The proliferation of these centralized, professional advocacy groups has brought new voices into the political arena but has exacerbated class-based inequalities in terms of who is speaking. They have increased the number of views expressed in the political process without broadening the base of who expresses them.[38]

E-MEDIA, INTEREST GROUPS, AND POLITICAL PARTICIPATION

The rise of new professional advocacy organizations has been given added impetus by the emergence of the Internet. The Internet has been conducive to their growth because these types of organizations require only weak ties between supporters and organizers that can be managed online at low cost. According to the political scientist Mark S. Bonchek, "[E]lectronic forms of communication reduce communication, coordination and information costs, facilitating group formation, group efficiency, membership recruitment, and member retention."[39] A website that may cost only $100 to create can be used by political organizers to recruit members, appeal for contributions, inform supporters, coordinate their activity, and mobilize them for action. With the touch of a button on a phone or keyboard, supporters can send public officials a message through e-mail links that interest groups provide. Furthermore, software packages are available that permit interest groups to sign up their supporters for e-mail alerts, follow who responds, and track how many e-mail appeals are received by each targeted official. Thus, the Internet has increased the reach of interest groups at the same time it has reduced their costs. The bureaucracy that membership organizations once found necessary to carry out basic functions of recruitment and coordination is less necessary because these tasks can now be done more quickly and cheaply through computer-mediated communication.

No group reflects the brave new world of interest groups in the Internet era more than MoveOn.org. In 1998, the spouses Wes Boyd and Joan Blades formed MoveOn.org in their basement using a standard Internet account. They e-mailed friends, requesting them to visit their website and sign a petition that urged Congress to "move on" and censure President Clinton for his sexual escapades as opposed to impeaching him. They also suggested that friends forward their appeal to people they knew. Within a short period, the site accumulated 500,000 signatures. The website also solicited money for candidates running against pro-impeachment incumbents in Congress. The appeal broke records for online political fund-raising, hauling in $13 million by the end of 1999. From humble beginnings, MoveOn.org has become a formidable advocacy group for liberal causes and a major fund-raiser for progressive Democratic candidates. It continues to use electronic media to communicate with and mobilize supporters.

Like previous technological breakthroughs such as radio and television, the Internet has had a transformative effect on politics. Because it is so effective at reducing the organizational costs of recruiting and coordinating supporters, the Internet facilitates collective action. **Political entrepreneurs** can now mobilize a virtual community for political action at very low cost, leading to more activity by more groups. E-media, which include the Internet, chat rooms, websites, blogging, e-mail, and other electronic forms of communication, broaden the range of interests represented, making collective action accessible to those who lack financial and institutional resources.

E-media also quicken the pace of politics, accelerating the process of recruiting and mobilizing supporters. New groups can form and deploy rapidly using

WHAT DO YOU THINK?

Social Media and Social Movements

The significance of social media was evident in the recent Arab Spring movement, when people used Facebook and Twitter to organize and challenge Arab dictators in Libya, Egypt, Tunisia, Yemen, and elsewhere. Is social media a game changer? Some people argue that it lowers the cost of organizing and is hard for the authorities to control. Others argue that social media produces only a light commitment among those in its web, that its effects are more fleeting and less substantial than the bureaucratic structures it functionally replaces. What do you think?

electronic media. Furthermore, the Internet makes the interest-group universe less stable. Just as easily as new groups form, so can they dissolve. Internet-based groups travel light. The virtual community that is built around an issue requires little commitment and is easily dispersed once that issue is exhausted.[40] Finally, e-media permit people to communicate more directly with one another, independently of leaders and formal organizations. Collective action no longer requires bureaucratic structures to organize and coordinate activity, which can now be done through e-mail, chat rooms, and a website. E-media alter not only the way in which interest groups mobilize but also their internal structures.

But even as the Internet makes it more convenient to contact public officials, donate to a campaign, or join a group, the same select group of affluent, educated people who are politically engaged off-line are more likely to be active online. Kay Lehman Schlozman, Sidney Verba, and Henry E. Brady found that the advantages the Internet offers for political participation are used the most by those who are the most advantaged. The Internet has not dismantled inequalities in political participation so much as it has reflected them.[41]

INTEREST GROUPS AND PUBLIC OPINION

Interest groups are as concerned with trying to influence public opinion as they are with trying to sway policy makers. They cultivate popular support because it is easier to convince politicians they should support interest groups' policy suggestions when voters favor them. For example, as we alluded to earlier, climate-change deniers have tried to influence public opinion by going so far as to develop public-school curriculums that cast doubt on global warming.

One of the ways interest groups try to influence public opinion is by funding think tanks—private, not-for-profit organizations that investigate public-policy issues. Think tanks, such as the Heartland Institute and the George C. Marshall Institute, as we mentioned previously, have been especially active in promoting climate-change denial. These think tanks try to shape public preferences by developing arguments and producing evidence that make a particular course of action more attractive. They fund research, host conferences, and advocate through the media. All of this takes money. Staff needs to be hired, rent needs to be paid, and programs need to be funded.

Big business seriously began to subsidize think tanks in the 1970s in response to what it perceived as a liberal bias in the media and among intellectuals. It was losing the battle for the hearts and minds of the public to environmentalists and consumer activists who blamed corporations for pollution and unsafe products. The impetus for business to engage the public was sketched out in a memorandum that Lewis F. Powell, Jr., then a corporate lawyer, sent to the director of the U.S. Chamber of Commerce in 1971. Powell argued that the free-enterprise system was under ideological attack and that business had responded so far with apathy, appeasement, and ineptitude. It needed instead to meet the ideological challenge head-on and subsidize scholars and speakers who would defend capitalist values, pressure college administrators to create opportunities for such advocates to speak on campus and offer courses, monitor textbooks and television to root out insidious criticism of free enterprise, use its skills in advertising to promote the benefits of free enterprise, and bring strategic cases to court. Two months after Powell sent this memo he was appointed a Justice to the Supreme Court by President Richard Nixon.

Powell's memo struck a chord. The development of an intellectual conservative infrastructure took off. Funding for the previously unimportant American Enterprise Institute increased ten-fold over the course of the 1970s, based mainly on corporate donations. Funding from the beer magnate Joseph Coors was critical in 1973 to the creation of the Heritage Foundation, whose mission is to "formulate and promote conservative public policies based on the principles of free enterprise, limited government, individual freedom, traditional American values, and a strong national defense." The Heritage Foundation could soon boast that it received funding from 87 percent of the Fortune 500 companies. Other important conservative think tanks that were created or greatly expanded during this time included the Cato Institute, the Hudson Institute, and the Manhattan Institute.[42] Having conducted a careful investigation of the impact these think tanks have had on the media and the media have had on the public, the political scientist Mark A. Smith argues that business's power to shape public opinion has grown significantly. He writes, "As think tanks grew in prominence and corporations directed their contributions toward overtly conservative ones . . . business added a new weapon to its arsenal."[43]

Ideology, like policy, is contested terrain. Groups struggle to shape the values that comprise the dominant culture: the consensus or "common sense" that people use to make sense of the world around them. But this common sense is not common at all. It has to be constructed. And groups devote much effort and come into conflict with each other in doing so. They try to influence the values we use to interpret the events happening around us because these ideas shape how we behave in response to them.

Both democracy and capitalism are core values in the U.S. They are widely shared beliefs among Americans, part of our common sense.[44] For example, Americans overwhelmingly support a political system based on popular consent, elections, freedom of speech and religion, and the rule of law. But the road to liberal democracy and tolerance has been a long and painful one. A civil war to defeat slavery, a Constitutional amendment to enfranchise women, and social movements to overcome discrimination against minorities were required before Americans were fully committed to the dignity and equal worth of each citizen.

Americans also believe in private property and less government intervention, and they are morally willing to accept higher levels of inequality than are citizens in other developed capitalist countries, such as those in Western Europe. According to Herbert McClosky and John Zaller, these core beliefs—democracy and capitalism—are not mutually reinforcing or consistent with each other but are in tension. The former implies equality among individuals while the latter legitimates inequality among them. Moreover, democracy and capitalism offer two different principles for how society should decide who gets what. While "capitalism holds that the free market is not only the most efficient but also the fairest mechanism for distributing goods and services," McClosky and Zaller write, "democracy upholds the rights of popular majorities to override market mechanisms when necessary to alleviate social and economic distress."[45]

As we have stressed throughout this book, much of the conflict in American politics is about managing the tension between capitalism and democracy. One of the ways Americans try to reconcile these divergent principles is by subscribing to the value of equal opportunity: that people should have the same chance to freely pursue their ambitions. Some interpret this to mean that capitalist values should prevail, that government should not intervene and tilt the playing field on which people compete. Government intervention creates *unequal* opportunity. Others argue the opposite. Equal opportunity *requires* government intervention in order to compensate for social inequalities. People can't compete fairly if they begin at different starting points. Government is necessary to level the playing field. The point is that broadly held values, such as equal opportunity, do not point ineluctably toward any particular policy. The concept of equal opportunity can justify minimal state intervention or maximal government interference. The fact that widely held values can be used to support various and even conflicting policies explains why interest groups devote so much effort and resources to shaping public opinion. Interest groups want to convince the public that the policies they prefer are consistent with the dominant culture.

While Americans share common values of democracy and capitalism, they do not all share them to the same extent. Some Americans give different weight to different values. For example, blacks and whites share basic values about capitalism and democracy. But blacks tend to view each through a distinctive history in which government has played a key role in promoting black demands, in resolving the gap between the ideal of equal opportunity and the reality of racial exclusion. The federal government ended slavery, proscribed segregation, and outlawed racial discrimination. Consequently, blacks tend to be more supportive of government intervention and more skeptical of the legitimacy of market outcomes than whites. In this sense they are our native social-democratic movement within American politics. Many blacks believe the only way to achieve the "American" end of equal opportunity, whereby people are judged on their merits and not by their color, are through "European" means: social regulation by the government.[46]

Young people also have their own distinctive twist on American values. They tend to be more liberal than their parents and grandparents. They are more tolerant of difference and more supportive of government intervention in the economy—hardly surprising given the devastating impact the recent slump has had on their job prospects. Polls indicate, for example, that young people are more supportive of gay marriage, more positive toward immigrants, and more approving of economic intervention than their elders. According to Andrew Kohut, president of the Pew Research Center, "We've got a generation of young people who are more socially liberal and more open to activist government."[47]

SOCIAL MOVEMENTS

On December 1, 1955, Rosa Parks, a 42-year-old grandmother, was on a bus headed home after a hard day's work at a store in downtown Montgomery, Alabama. All 36 seats on the bus were filled, with blacks by law seated in the back and whites in the front. When the bus stopped to pick up a white passenger, the driver asked the four black passengers seated just behind the last row of whites to move so the new white passenger could take his accustomed place in front of them. No one got up to offer a seat. The driver then insisted that the four blacks vacate their seats. Three of them complied and moved to stand in the back of the bus, but Parks remained seated. The driver warned that she was now illegally in the white section of the bus. She calmly replied that she had taken her seat in the back of the bus behind whites, just as the law required. The driver countered that the white section of the bus was where he said it was, and that he had the power to enforce local segregation laws. He notified Parks that she was under arrest, and stopped the bus until two Montgomery police officers arrived to take Parks to jail.

Parks's defiance precipitated the Montgomery bus boycott, in which blacks walked, carpooled, and took taxis to get to work, visit relatives, and shop. Initially, the boycott was to last just one day and its demands were timid, negotiating the etiquette of segregation that required blacks who sat behind the last row of whites to give up their seats when the white section filled up. But the boycott was so successful that it was extended. And as it stretched from weeks into months, the demands of the emboldened black community became more radical. The target was no longer the humiliating practice of having to give up seats to whites but the end to segregation on buses itself. A new organization, the Montgomery Improvement Association (MIA), was created to provide

Rosa Parks sitting in the front of a bus in Montgomery, Alabama after the Supreme Court ruled segregation illegal on the city's bus system in 1956.

leadership, coordinate activity, and raise money. And a new pastor who had arrived in Montgomery just a year earlier, the 25-year-old Reverend Martin Luther King, Jr., was chosen to lead the MIA.

The white community in Montgomery responded viciously, with bombings, mass arrests, and police harassment. But on November 15, 1956—almost a full year after Parks's arrest—the U.S. Supreme Court upheld a lower-court decision declaring state and local laws requiring segregation on buses unconstitutional. Segregation on city buses was now illegal, and blacks in Montgomery celebrated their victory by ending the boycott.[48]

The Montgomery bus boycott was one of the early struggles in the budding civil rights movement. It is an example of a social movement; as we mentioned previously, social movements are not as hierarchical or formally organized as interest groups and political parties, tend to be more ideological and contentious, and move participation up to a more active and demanding level than other forms of political expression. Social movements share certain qualities, which we highlight below.[49]

Social movements rarely begin with radical demands. Their original claims are usually limited and conciliatory, which leads supporters to expect that they will be granted. It is the denial of what are regarded as reasonable claims that escalates challenges and radicalizes groups. Such was the case with the Montgomery bus boycott. Only when the MIA's initial effort to negotiate the etiquette of segregation was rejected by whites did blacks challenge the principle of segregation.

Second, social movements arise in response to changes in the political environment that create new opportunities groups can exploit. For example, new openings for political participation may arise as a result of the dimming repressive power of the state, or allies may emerge who can provide groups with new resources that permit them to mount challenges that would not otherwise have been possible.[50] In the case of the Montgomery bus boycott, conflict over racial policy between the federal and state governments gave hope to activists. The federal government had just outlawed school segregation in *Brown v. Board of Education,* signaling to activists that it would not support Alabama's segregation laws. The Supreme Court decision legitimized civil rights demands and emboldened activists to challenge state laws.

Third, social movements empower their followers and give them a sense of moral legitimacy—that their demands are justified and right. They replace feelings of resignation and deference with hope and self-confidence, and they offer a new way of interpreting events in place of the self-serving explanations that the dominant culture offers.[51] King gave voice to this alternative culture when he addressed the Montgomery black community on the eve of the bus boycott. Imploring his listeners to have faith in themselves and their collective power, he assured them, "If we are wrong—the Supreme Court of this nation is wrong. If we are wrong—God Almighty is wrong. If we are wrong—Jesus of Nazareth was merely a utopian dreamer and never came down to earth! If we are wrong—justice is a lie."[52]

Fourth, social movements require organizations that can develop and disseminate an alternative culture. Most social movements are built on organizations that cultivate identities, raise resources, and coordinate activities. Harry Boyte referred to such organizations as **free spaces**, in which an oppositional culture could be elaborated, insulated from the disapproval and reproach of the dominant culture. The black church offered such a haven for the Montgomery bus boycott by providing a physical space that was autonomous from white control, where meetings could be held and an affirming message of hope and moral worth could be articulated. It was an expression of the black community that served as the base of operations for the bus boycott.

Finally, social movements flourish when they are able to enlarge the scope of conflict and mobilize people who were previously bystanders.[53] They do so because protest and disruption are the strategies of people who lack more conventional political resources. Enlarging the scope of conflict draws new groups

WHAT DO YOU THINK?

Is the Shift from Protest to Politics a Sign of Failure or Success for Social Movements?

As groups make the transition from outsider to insider, some argue they are selling out, losing their radical edge, in exchange for approval and respect from the very groups they once opposed. They are giving up the threatening pose from which they drew their power. It is precisely their noncompliance that gives them power, requiring policy makers to grant them concessions to maintain order. Others argue that the transition from protest to politics is part of a maturation process for social movements. Social movements burn out if they can't make this transition to finally achieve the concessions they want through conventional political bargaining. Far from indicating capitulation, political bargaining is necessary to achieve the payoffs groups seek. Otherwise, supporters become discouraged and exhausted by the risks and demands of mobilization. Which of these views do you find more persuasive?

into the struggle to circumvent an unfavorable balance of power. For example, the MIA used tactics designed to dramatize the issue for the press and television to reach a broader audience beyond Montgomery, and the association replaced its initial, modest demands with a sweeping challenge to segregation, thereby drawing in national civil rights groups as allies.

In the next section we offer an extended case study of the labor movement followed by shorter, capsule accounts of the women's, Tea Party, and environmental movements. Just as the interest-group universe has become larger and more complicated as traditional economic groups have been joined by other types, the same is true of social movements. Older social movements, based around work and occupation, have been joined by new social movements organized around people's identities, moral values, and quality-of-life concerns. Following our discussion of the labor movement, we feature two groups on the left, the women's and environmental movements, and one on the right—the Tea Party—to exemplify these new social movements.

The Labor Movement

The modern American labor movement began with a punch. In 1935, at the American Federation of Labor (AFL) convention in Atlantic City, New Jersey, John L. Lewis, president of the United Mine Workers of America (UMWA), beseeched delegates to launch an aggressive organizing campaign among industrial workers. The time was ripe, he argued, as workers everywhere were on the march, looking to the AFL for leadership and direction. Textile workers in the South, longshoremen in the West, and autoworkers in the North had gone on strike and stopped production. Moreover, new political opportunities had opened up with President Roosevelt's election and his promise of a New Deal to millions of toiling workers and the unemployed. But the AFL, which organized skilled workers such as carpenters and machinists, was reluctant to welcome into its ranks unskilled workers in the burgeoning mass-production industries—auto, steel, rubber, electrical appliances, and textiles. Lewis could abide the AFL's dithering no longer. As the convention came to a close, Lewis's patience gave out. After an exchange of words with the powerful AFL traditionalist William B. Hutcheson, president of the United Brotherhood of Carpenters (UBC), Lewis jumped to his feet, leaped over a row of chairs, struck the UBC president with his fist, and sent him sprawling against a table. Afterward, journalists reported, "Lewis casually adjusted his tie and collar, relit his cigar, and sauntered through the crowded aisles."[54] Two weeks later, he led six affiliated unions out of the AFL to form a rival federation called the Congress of Industrial Organizations (CIO). The modern American labor movement was born.

When the Depression began, workers initially looked to their employers for help, and many placed their faith in company unions that their firms sponsored. But such hopes were quickly disappointed, and workers began to form their own unions. They believed that only a legally binding **collective-bargaining** agreement negotiated by an independent union could protect them from managerial favoritism and arbitrariness. Employers resisted these efforts fiercely. In response, workers occupied factories, fought with police, engaged in mass picketing, and staged industry-wide strikes in support of their demand for union recognition.

Responding to the groundswell of militancy and protest, Congress wrested jurisdiction over labor policy away from conservative and unsympathetic courts that were insulated from ripening public opinion. In 1935, Congress passed the National Labor Relations Act (NLRA), guaranteeing workers the right to form unions. Union membership surged. By 1941, the new CIO included 3 million members, while AFL unions displayed even greater growth, adding 4 million to their membership rolls. The labor movement could also point to achievements in the arena of social policy. Roosevelt's New Deal included the passage of Social Security, unemployment compensation, and minimum-wage laws that provided workers some security and protection from the vagaries of the market. Finally, labor was now regarded as a formidable political force. Unions devoted more resources to political activity once it became apparent that success in organizing and collective bargaining depended on the rules governing them. Unions not only increased their level of political activity but also directed more of it through the Democratic Party. This gave labor influence within the new governing coalition as the Democrats rose to become the majority party.

Economically and politically, then, the rise of the CIO and growth of the AFL in the 1930s transformed the politics of power. Greater industrial democracy, in the form of unions to check the unilateral power of management, was fused with greater political democracy, in the form of more working-class influence. New relations of power were evident on the shop floor, where workers in many industries now had rights codified in collective-bargaining agreements, and on the floor of Congress, where workers were now able to achieve legislative victories through their alliance with the Democrats.[55]

In the 1940s, unions consolidated many of the gains they had made during the previous decade. With firms hiring as many workers as they could find to fill wartime orders, union membership reached its peak in 1945, at 35 percent of the workforce. J. B. S. Hardman, a labor journalist, described the new era as one in which "American labor unions have become a social power in the nation."[56]

At the end of the war, employers wanted to roll back the gains labor had made in the preceding years. Workers were intent on protecting their standard of living. The result was the largest strike wave in American history, as hundreds of thousands of meat-packers, autoworkers, and steelworkers walked off their jobs. Not only did the unions survive this massive strike wave, but many new contracts included significant wage increases. But the strike wave also provoked a political backlash in the form of new antilabor legislation. In the 1946 elections, Republicans won majorities in both the House and the Senate and proceeded to pass the Taft-Hartley Act, which contained various provisions designed to constrain union organizing and strikes.

For the next 20 years, through the 1950s and 1960s, many managers reluctantly accepted unions as legitimate bargaining agents for their workers. In 1955, the AFL and CIO merged to become the AFL-CIO, thus uniting the two wings of the labor movement. Unions permitted workers in the postwar era to enjoy higher wages, more security, and greater political influence. Workers' lives as citizens and employees improved. But the foundation for such improvements was fragile. Union membership was increasing in absolute numbers but declining as a percentage of the workforce. The signifiance of regions (e.g., the South) and occupations (e.g., service-sector work) where unions were weak was growing while areas and industries where unions were strong were declining. Moreover, American business was facing more market pressure. As competition increased due to deregulation, globalization, and the growth of the nonunion sector, managerial attitudes toward unions hardened. To restore profits, management began to take back the slack they believed existed in labor relations; they demanded lower wages, cuts in benefits, fewer work rules, and less job protection. In many cases, demands for such concessions were a pretext for trying to eliminate unions altogether. In 1978 United Auto Workers President Douglas Fraser charged business with waging "a one-sided class war in this country" and complained that "the leaders of industry, commerce and finance in the U.S. have broken and discarded the fragile, unwritten contract previously existing during a period of growth and progress."[57] According to the sociologist Chris Rhomberg, unions wanted to reach a deal at the collective-bargaining table, while employers wanted to eliminate unions and get rid of the table altogether.[58]

The new employer offensive forced the unions to retreat. Unions signed concessionary contracts that rolled back gains they had achieved in previous negotiations.[59] Labor's retreat was also apparent in the decline of strikes. The U.S. averaged 289 work stoppages per year involving 1,000 or more workers over the course of the 1970s. By the 1990s, the average number of work stoppages had fallen to 35. [60] In 2010 there were just ten. Work stoppages became less frequent because unions did not believe they could win them anymore. Strikes failed to stop production because employers hired replacement workers and court injunctions rendered picket lines ineffective. *Fortune*, a business journal, reported, "Managers are discovering that strikes can be broken, that the cost of breaking them is often lower than the cost of taking them, and that strike-breaking doesn't have to be a dirty word."[61] For unions that still dared to call their members out on strike, success was no longer measured by their ability to prevent concessions but by the more humble criterion of avoiding elimination.

Finally, labor's decline was evident in its waning membership. Today, among all Western democracies only France has a lower proportion of its workforce that belongs to unions than the U.S.[62] From a peak of 35 percent in 1945, the percentage of unionized American workers plummeted to only 11.3 percent in 2012, the lowest rate in 70 years. And even this grim statistic overstates the degree of unionization in the United States. If one looks only at private-sector workers, the unionization rate in 2011 was just 6.6 percent. The last time private-sector-union density was so low was more than a century ago, in 1910. The drop in membership can be attributed to three factors. First, changes in labor law made it harder to organize. As a resurgent Republican Party pulled American politics to the right, labor law increasingly was interpreted in a way that made it more difficult to organize new members. Second, employers have become more antagonistic to unions. Whereas days lost due to work stoppages were previously the result of workers going on strike to pressure employers, they are increasingly likely to arise from employers locking out their workers to pressure them into concessions. Lockouts, such as those in professional basketball, hockey, and football, in which the owners told their players not to show up for work unless they were willing to agree to new terms, were used in a record number of less publicized disputes to put workers on the defensive.[63] Finally, union membership fell as a result of a sharp drop in manufacturing jobs due to plant closings and pressure from imports.

And now even unions' last redoubt, in the public sector, is in danger of slipping away. In 2010 and 2011, Republican legislatures and governors in Wisconsin, Ohio, and Idaho passed laws stripping public employees of bargaining rights, while other states have privatized jobs that previously were performed by public employees.[64] Union density in the public sector fell from 37 percent in 2011 to 35.9 percent in 2012.

Labor today is depleted and disarmed. The labor historian Nick Salvatore describes the union movement today as "weaker and more defensive than at any time since the early twentieth century."[65] But there is still movement in the labor movement. In retreat, it has looked to new strategies to stem its decline. First, unions recognize that traditional strikes at the point of production are no longer effective, and so they are conducting corporate campaigns outside of it. **Corporate campaigns** try to raise the stakes for business by informing authorities of regulatory violations that employers have committed, publicizing unsavory corporate conduct, or pressuring banks to withdraw lines of credit to recalcitrant firms.[66] For example, unions have bankrolled efforts to embarrass and harass Walmart in order to soften the company's anti-union policies.

In addition, unions are now more willing to appeal to allies, such as community groups, students, and religious leaders, for support. Unions that were previously skeptical of outsiders and avoided issues beyond immediate workplace concerns are now more likely to participate in coalitions with such groups and support their demands. Unions, for example, actively supported the Occupy Wall Street movement. They donated money, lobbied mayors not to remove the protesters, and provided in-kind assistance in the form of blankets, medical care, tents, and meals to the protesters occupying city parks throughout the country.[67]

Socially and politically, unions can also see signs of renewal. The number of people who report in surveys that they would like to belong to a union has gone up 25 percent since 1984; over half of all respondents now indicate they would like to join one.[68] And union households continue to be a dependable, distinctive, and substantial voting bloc. In 2012, they comprised about 18 percent of all voters and 58 percent of them voted for Barack Obama. Moreover, union membership increases turnout, especially among groups, such as minorities and low-income whites, that historically have low turnout rates. Finally, union

WHAT DO YOU THINK?

Was the New Deal a Victory or Defeat for Workers?

Some view the New Deal as a lost opportunity in which an insurgent labor movement was channeled into support for unions and the Democratic Party. More radical change that challenged the structure of American capitalism was compromised in favor of cosmetic bureaucratic reforms that, in the end, strengthened it. Others argue that workers achieved remarkable gains during the New Deal. Stable unions were created, and the modern American welfare state was established. Should the New Deal be condemned for pacifying insurgent workers and guiding their demands into mere bureaucratic reforms, or should it be celebrated as a victory that improved working-class lives?

households tend not only to vote more but to vote for Democrats. Peter L. Francia found that "the union household vote for Democrats . . . has been consistently higher than it has been for those in non-union households in every election since 1952," even after one controls for standard influences on voting behavior, such as race, income, ideology, gender, and education.[69] The pulse is weak within the labor movement. But the heart is still beating.

The Women's Movement

Historians often separate the women's movement into three waves of activism. The first wave, which began in 1848, owed a large debt to the antislavery movement, in which many women participated. They saw parallels between the oppression of slaves and that of women, and their participation in the abolitionist movement gave women an opportunity to develop leadership and organizational skills that they could then apply to their own movement.

Following the Civil War, when the Reconstruction Congress passed a constitutional amendment giving blacks the right to vote, it pointedly failed to do the same for women. Consequently, an independent women's movement developed whose goal was female **suffrage**. By the 1890s, groups such as female temperance workers, social reformers who worked with women in immigrant slums, and middle-class women involved in charitable volunteer work began to coalesce around the demand for female suffrage because it could help them advance their diverse interests. The National American Woman Suffrage Association organized and concentrated the considerable power of these diverse groups into a movement that successfully pressured Congress to pass the Nineteenth Amendment, which enfranchised women in 1920.

The second wave of feminist activism began in the 1960s. Like the first wave, in which the emergence of women's activism was connected closely to the antislavery movement, women's liberation in the second wave was closely tied to the civil rights movement. Parallels were again drawn between discrimination against women and bias against blacks, and women gained organizing and leadership skills through their participation in the struggle for black equality. But female activists realized that they needed to act independently because their own grievances often were dismissed as trivial in comparison to those of blacks, and because they were sometimes victims of sexism within the civil rights movement.

Second-wave feminism moved along two fronts. The first was to win political equality for women, which led to the creation of the National Organization of Women (NOW). Founded in 1966 as a civil rights organization for women, NOW's mission was to lobby and litigate on behalf of equal rights for women.

It enjoyed many successes, such as outlawing pay and employment discrimination on the basis of sex. It also lobbied for the Equal Rights Amendment to the Constitution, which passed Congress but fell three states short of the two-thirds required for ratification. In 1975 *Time* magazine awarded its "Person of the Year" award to American women in celebration of the feminist movement's many achievements.

But legal, formal change was not sufficient. Many female activists opened another front in the war against sexism, claiming that the personal was political. Laws needed to be changed, but so did people's attitudes. Accordingly, some women joined consciousness-raising groups in which experiences were shared and patriarchal values challenged. These groups provided the free space in which women developed the confidence and ideological clarity to become political activists. Part of revealing the personal as political involved challenging female stereotypes and gender roles. For example, activists protested the Miss America pageant as a sexist objectification of women, and women began to demand that men do their fair share of the housework and child care. Feminists argued that women's liberation began at home.

Feminism flourished during the second wave and was expressed in many tendencies and groups. It included liberal feminists, who defined women's liberation in terms of formal legal equality for women; socialist feminists, who perceived women's subordination as part of a larger system of racial and class inequality; and radical feminists, who defined male domination as the root of the problem. Despite the ultimate failure of the Equal Rights Amendment, the second wave could point to many successes, such as making discrimination against women illegal, getting women admitted to such male bastions as the military academies, obtaining equal funding for women's collegiate and public high school sports, and raising awareness about socially constructed gender roles.

Third-wave feminism marked a generational change as much as it did a change in goals and strategy for the women's movement. It emerged in the 1990s among young women who, some argue, grew up taking the achievements of second-wave feminism for granted. Third-wave feminists tend to be less invested in issues of equality than in exploring their own identities and promoting individual empowerment for women. Women should be free to pursue their lives unhindered either by traditional stereotypes about women or by feminist demands that women reject such stereotypes. Third-wave feminists want to move beyond those who would put women on a pedestal and those who would portray them only as victims.[70]

The generational conflict between second- and third-wave feminism was displayed vividly during the 2008 election season. Gloria Steinem, who cofounded

Ms. magazine in the 1960s, dismissed post-feminist claims from a younger generation that discrimination against women was a thing of the past and argued that feminists should support Hillary Clinton in the 2008 Democratic primary because "she'll be a great president and because she's a woman." Second-wave feminists made support for Mrs. Clinton in the 2008 Democratic primaries "a feminist litmus test," supporting her candidacy on the basis of her gender.[71] But younger, third-wave feminists disagreed, arguing that feminism "meant greater choice, not just in one's life choices, but for president as well." They rejected appeals for Mrs. Clinton from older, second-wave feminists based on identity politics, arguing that feminism was about judging men and women on their merits. Second-wave feminists were chastised for "lamenting the fact that the twenty-something daughters of boomer women are for Obama, [instead of] applauding the fact that these women, whom we have raised to think for themselves, are doing just that."[72]

The Tea Party Movement

President Obama had not been president for more than a few months before protesters dressed like Paul Revere, wearing three-cornered hats and breeches, began appearing at rallies and meetings to oppose his policies. They called themselves the Tea Party. Their name and quaint Revolutionary-era clothes were meant to evoke the rebellious founding of the country, when colonists dumped tea into Boston Harbor to protest onerous British taxes. Now, following the 2008 elections, with Democrats in control of Congress and the presidency, contemporary Tea Party members saw America threatened by a new tyrannical power determined to impose unjust taxes like those the colonists had suffered under the British.

The Tea Party movement contributed to the massive Republican victory in the 2010 midterm elections. But more important was the role it played in seizing the national agenda. Despite record levels of unemployment in 2009, the Tea Party shifted the focus of government from creating jobs to reducing the deficit. This conformed to broader Tea Party goals that included reducing spending, lowering tax rates, eliminating regulations, curbing immigration, and promoting family values.

The Tea Party is composed of more than 1,000 groups nationwide, some large enough to require a gymnasium to hold meetings while others could fit in a locker room. It is an authentic grassroots movement, in which engaged citizens organized to create local, self-governing organizations. While all Tea Party organizations are socially and economically conservative, they give priority to different goals depending upon their location: those in the South stress defending family values, those in the West emphasize curbing immigration, while those in the North highlight reducing deficits. Regardless of their regional base, all Tea Party members express a profound cultural and economic pessimism. They see the country diverging from the values on which it was founded and coming under the control of opponents whom they view as the enemy. Immigrants use schools and services they do not pay for; welfare chiselers fleece hard-working taxpayers; a pervasive government limits personal freedom; and a morally blind state violates timeless truths about gender roles and marriage.

The Tea Party movement resembles other populist movements that preceded it. Populist movements tend to divide the world into opposing forces: the people and the elites, the producers and the parasites, the virtuous and the immoral. Before World War II, populism had a left-wing impulse. The "elites" were corporate owners of industry, the "parasites" were bankers, and the "immoral" were the decadent rich, while the "people" referred to ordinary workers and their families, the "producers" to those who farmed the land and toiled in factories, and the "virtuous" to those who earned their keep through hard work. But after World War II, populism took a right turn. The rhetoric remained the same but the terms were given new meanings. The elites were

Tea party supporters protest outside the Utah State Capitol on April 15 (Tax Day), 2010, to decry the nation's high taxes and programs that they claim are loading debt on citizens.

no longer the captains of industry but arrogant politicians; the parasites were no longer financiers but pointy-headed intellectuals; and the immoral were no longer the idle rich but deadbeats on welfare. Such rhetoric infused earlier conservative populist movements, such as the anticommunist crusades of the 1950s, former Alabama Governor George Wallace's presidential campaigns in the 1960s, President Richard Nixon's promotion of the "silent majority" in the 1970s, and the Reagan insurgency within the Republican Party in the 1980s. The Tea Party simply inherited and appropriated these familiar themes from conservative populist movements that preceded it.[73]

The Tea Party movement draws its supporters and activists from a narrow slice of the American public. Typical Tea Party enthusiasts are whiter, wealthier, more educated, and more religious than their fellow Americans. But their most salient characteristic is their age and ideology. On average, Tea Party supporters are considerably older than the average citizen and hold more extreme conservative views than even typical Republicans.[74] These factors have contributed to an incipient generational conflict behind their sense of grievance. Tea Party supporters resent paying taxes for a younger generation that requires more government services; that does not look like them, as it is more Hispanic, black, and Asian; and that does not share their conservative social values. The Tea Party gives voice to a "gray" verses "brown" divide, in which older, white, conservative Americans "resent and fear" the political consequences of a nation "transformed by rising young cohorts with different experiences, values and social characteristics." President Obama and his young and nonwhite supporters embody these Tea Party fears about what the future holds and where the country is headed.[75]

Like other social movements, the Tea Party evokes a strong sense of community in its members. Supporters are willing to devote time and money to the movement and derive a sense of fellowship and purpose from it. And, like other social movements, the Tea Party is not structured hierarchically. Local groups operate independently and fiercely guard their autonomy. The political scientists Theda Skocpol and Vanessa Williams describe the Tea Party as a "disunited field of jostling organizations."[76] Conservative media outlets, especially Fox News, have played an important role in cuing and coordinating disparate Tea Party groups, providing a substitute for the bureaucratic structures that perform these functions in more traditional organizations. But conservative media have done more than that. They actually helped create the movement they covered. Throughout 2009 and 2010, Fox News indicated where Tea Party rallies were being held and encouraged participation by having conservative television personalities attend them. It thus helped create events that other news outlets felt obliged to cover, generating a sense of legitimacy and significance for the Tea Party. It also kept the Tea Party on message by feeding it critical stories of alleged Democratic Party malfeasance. Charges that Barack Obama was born outside the United States and thus ineligible to be president and claims that his health-care law included "death panels" circulated among conservative news media and became widely accepted among Tea Party members.

Finally, the Tea Party was assisted by a well-funded infrastructure of preexisting conservative policy organizations. Washington-based groups like FreedomWorks and Americans for Prosperity, that ardently oppose taxes, regulations, and government spending, trained activists and provided funds for local Tea Party groups to attend rallies. Most important, they provided essential programming, such as speakers and training literature, to local groups that were challenged to schedule interesting and informative activities to fill regular meetings. The relation of these Washington-based advocacy groups to the Tea Party is one of mutual convenience. Corporate-funded conservative policy shops get the aura of authentic popular support, in exchange for which Tea Party organizations receive funding and logistical help.

The Tea Party made the shift from protest to politics quickly, moving rapidly from mass rallies in Washington, D.C., to electoral politics. But it did so not as an arm of the Republican Party but as a force determined to remake the GOP in its own conservative image. It fielded primary challengers to Republicans who were regarded as insufficiently conservative, and it put Republicans who received Tea Party support on notice that they would be scrutinized for backsliding. Once the euphoria of victory in 2010 subsided, Tea Party activists began to take over Republican Party organizations at the precinct and local levels, much as evangelical Christians had done in the 1990s.

The Tea Party's emergence has been both a blessing and curse for the Republican Party. On the one hand, the Tea Party energized the Republican base. The Tea Party provided the momentum that drove the GOP to victory in the 2010 midterm elections. But Tea Party support has not come without its price for Republicans. In some states, Tea Party–favored conservatives ran against and defeated more moderate Republicans in the primaries. But those Tea Party–backed candidates were then beaten in the general election because voters regarded them as so right-wing that they were outside the mainstream. For example, Tea Party–backed Richard Mourdock defeated incumbent Senator Richard Lugar in the Indiana Republican primary in 2012. Lugar was a moderate Republican and would have been heavily favored in the general election to hold the seat he had occupied for 36 years. But Republicans ended up losing the Senate seat when voters in Indiana rejected Mourdock as too conservative even for them. He was defeated in November by his Democratic opponent, Joe Donnelly. Hoosier state voters were willing to cast their ballot for Mitt Romney for president, making Indiana the only Midwestern state that went Republican in the 2012 presidential race, but Mourdock's Tea Party brand of conservatism was too far out of the mainstream even for them. Tea Party support was the "embrace that kills" in Indiana in 2012, costing the Republicans a Senate seat they should have won. Whether the Tea Party will vanish because its success in transforming the Republican Party makes it unnecessary, or whether the Tea Party will become a fringe movement because Republicans find its zealous conservatism to be an electoral liability, is an open question at this point.

The Environmental Movement

The history of the environmental movement, like that of the women's movement, can be divided into waves of activism. The first wave appeared during the Progressive era at the beginning of the twentieth century. The early environmental movement included conservationists, who wanted the country's natural resources to be managed efficiently by the government, and preservationists, who wanted to retain the land in its natural state. The former believed that the country's natural resources should be managed with an eye to the future and that resources in the public domain should serve public rather than private interests. The latter felt that nature should be left unspoiled to preserve its scenic beauty and provide unique spiritual and recreational opportunities. Both groups found their champion in President Theodore Roosevelt, who enlarged the national-forest system from 41 to 109 million acres, established five national parks, and created the first wildlife refuges.

Urban elites, middle-class women, and rod-and-gun enthusiasts composed the narrow base of the early environmental movement. Urban elites identified with environmentalism because they perceived it as a way to preserve their culture of refinement and aristocratic pretension against industrial blight and consumerism. Middle-class women were attracted to environmentalism as an extension of their domestic duties. Pollution and filth threatened the health of their families and the attractiveness of their homes. And sportsmen joined the fray to preserve wilderness areas for hunting game and birds. They formed organizations such as the Sierra Club to demand that the public domain, "the commons," be managed in the public interest, something that could be done only by government. Hence, a by-product of the early environmental movement was to expand the scope of government, especially the executive branch, to include responsibility for the environment.

When the environmental movement reemerged after World War II, it had a different focus and constituency. While one group of critics protested the environmental dangers of radioactive fallout from nuclear tests, another objected to the use of toxic pesticides by farmers. Their critiques shifted the movement's attention away from conservation and preservation to **ecology**, to an appreciation of the fragility and interconnectedness of nature. Toxic pesticides and radioactive isotopes could be carried through the air and the food chain to poison people and animals. This new ecological perspective broadened the movement's goals beyond simply preserving wilderness areas and using resources efficiently to ensure clean air, pure water, and safe food. It also broadened the base of the movement beyond elites to newly affluent middle-class people who were concerned about the damage being done to nature and its potential for deadly repercussions.

The next wave of environmental activism occurred in the late 1960s as the environmental movement drew energy from the emergence of the New Left, which opposed the Vietnam War. The "Give Peace a Chance!" slogan of Vietnam War protesters became the "Give Earth a Chance!" chant of environmentalists. Just as New Left protesters engaged in acts of guerrilla theater to dramatize their grievances, so did environmentalists engage in ecosabotage, such as disabling construction equipment that was used to cut down forests. And just as the New Left held teach-ins to inform the public and challenge the dominant culture, so did environmentalists. In April 1970, the first Earth Day teach-ins were held across the country in colleges, schools, and parks; 20 million people reportedly participated in discussions about the environment that day.[77] The environmental movement became more provocative and radical as it absorbed New Left activists and their critiques of consumerism and corporate power as well as their demands for authenticity and fundamental change. A movement that had previously been known for blocking legislation through genteel lobbying was now known for blocking logging roads through direct action.

The environmental movement had grown, especially among the middle class, during a period of postwar affluence. But beginning in the 1970s, affluence was replaced by recession and unemployment. Environmentalism was no longer perceived as an outcome of economic growth, but as a threat to it. Environmentalists were increasingly ridiculed as elitists who were interested more in protecting spotted owls than in preserving people's jobs. More ominously, the Republicans who took power with Reagan's election in 1980 were concerned less with reducing the carbon footprint of industry than with reducing the regulatory footprint of government.

As economic and political conditions became more challenging, the environmental movement became more politically and strategically diverse.

The ecological perspective introduced earlier now defined the movement, especially in the fight against global warming. It found expression in such developments as deep ecology, which held that people were part of nature's order and not the other way around. The movement also began to address issues of environmental justice, looking at environmental issues through the prism of racial and class inequality. This perspective was expressed by grassroots activists in working-class and minority neighborhoods who protested the placement of toxic-waste dumps in their communities.

While some elements of the environmental movement became more radical in theory and practice, the old, mainline environmentalist organizations such as the National Wildlife Federation, Sierra Club, and Audubon Society became more pragmatic. They continued to lobby for green policies, but now they also performed important oversight of existing environmental legislation. This required them to develop scientific and legal expertise so they could propose their own solutions to environmental problems and challenge polluters and administrative agencies in court. Environmental reform through the political system was now being pursued in a more professional and sophisticated manner. Indeed, one study found that environmental-advocacy groups in Washington were similar to other Washington-based interest groups in terms of their organization and activities, although the environmental groups were more litigious. Environmental groups were more likely to turn to federal courts to make their case.[78]

The environmental movement currently has a fundamentalist and a pragmatic wing. Fundamentalist deep-ecology theorists and Earth First! activists vie with pragmatists who want to lobby Washington and work with industry to help it become greener. Fundamentalists regard environmental pragmatists as "risk averse, . . . overly analytical, humorless, . . . [and] technocratic," while pragmatists dismiss environmental fundamentalists as irrelevant, silly, and immature.[79] The issue for contemporary environmentalism is whether its fundamentalist and pragmatic wings will augment or detract from each other—that is, whether the movement's political and strategic diversity will make it stronger or weaker.

CONCLUSION

In contrast to people living in authoritarian regimes, American citizens can participate in politics and influence the laws that govern them. They can vote, join interest groups, participate in social movements, contribute money to political campaigns, and write letters to their representatives. In principle, anyone can use these means of political expression. But some citizens are in a better position to take advantage of these opportunities than others. Political participation may be open, but it is not free. It is greatly facilitated by class-related factors such as time, money, education, civic skills, self-confidence, and contacts with broader social networks. The uneven distribution of these politically relevant resources leads to uneven levels of political participation.

Inequalities in political participation lead to inequalities in outcomes. Policy makers respond to demands that are expressed. What they hear influences what they do. Consequently, which issues are considered and what is done about them reflect the interests of those who have the resources to make their views heard.

But inequalities in political participation are not inevitable, nor are the inequalities in outcomes that result from them. Citizens can develop their political voices and by doing so change the policies that govern them. Davids can emerge to slay Goliaths. The previous chapter showed how citizens can use elections to select leaders who will take the country in a different direction. This chapter has shown how citizens can also use interest groups and social movements to influence policy. Joining interest groups and participating in social movements are alternative and supplemental means of political expression to the ballot box. The quality of democracy and the output of government would be poorer without their contributions.

CHAPTER SUMMARY

Introduction
Political participation can take various forms, from voting and contributing money to election campaigns to joining an interest group or participating in a social movement. Citizens participate in different forms of political activity depending on their level of commitment, the resources available to them, and the opportunities and constraints they encounter in using them.

Interest Groups
More interest groups are more active on more issues than in the past. Interest-group activity increased in response to procedural changes in Congress that increased its accessibility to lobbyists, new policy initiatives by government that created new stakeholders, and the institutionalization of social movements from the 1960s.

David and Goliath

Despite the addition of new players, interest groups representing business have more resources to influence policy makers than do other groups. Yet being bigger, faster, and stronger does not guarantee that business always prevails. Groups representing business may oppose each other, may adopt the wrong political strategy, or sometimes may find public opinion arrayed against them.

The Changing Quality of Membership

More interest groups today rely on purposive, as opposed to material, incentives to attract members. And more contemporary interest groups are centralized, professional advocacy groups as opposed to mass-membership organizations. These new professional advocacy groups tend to attract wealthier supporters and do not provide their members the same civic lessons as more traditional mass-membership organizations.

E-Media, Interest Groups, and Political Participation

E-media have reduced the cost of recruiting interest-group members and coordinating and mobilizing their activities. Although start-up costs for web-based advocacy groups are low, so is their members' commitment.

Interest Groups and Public Opinion

Interest-group conflict occurs over ideas as much as policies. Interest groups try to provide interpretations of the dominant culture that legitimize the policies they want to promote. While many Americans believe in basic values of democracy and capitalism, they may apply those values differently. Groups develop different political values depending upon their different experiences.

Social Movements

Social movements arise when changes in relations of power permit previously passive groups to mount a challenge. Social movements articulate an alternative culture that legitimizes their demands and tend to attract ideologically committed supporters who are willing to engage in more-demanding forms of political participation.

Critical Thinking Questions

1. Which form of political expression—voting, interest-group activity, or social movements—do you believe has been most effective in the United States?

2. Business interests enjoy many advantages in interest-group competition, yet they do not always win. What conditions are most conducive to defeating business interests in policy debates?

3. Has the rise of the Internet and the decline of membership-based organizations been healthy for American democracy?

4. What, if anything, can and should be done to equalize the political participation of disadvantaged and wealthier citizens?

Suggested Readings

Jo Freeman, *We Will Be Heard: Women's Struggles for Political Power in the United States.* New York: Rowman and Littlefield, 2008.

Kay Lehman Schlozman, Sidney Verba, and Henry E. Brady, *The Unheavenly Chorus: Unequal Political Voice and the Broken Promise of American Democracy.* Princeton: Princeton University Press, 2012.

Theda Skocpol, *Diminished Democracy: From Membership to Management in American Civic Life.* Norman: University of Oklahoma Press, 2003.

Thomas R. Wheelock, *Preserving the Nation: The Conservation and Environmental Movements, 1870–2000.* Wheeling, IL: Harlan Davidson, 2007.

Robert Zieger and Gilbert Gall, *American Workers, American Unions*, 3rd ed. Baltimore: Johns Hopkins University Press, 2002.

PART III

POLITICAL INSTITUTIONS

As we saw in Chapter 1, the Constitution lays out the architecture of government. By *architecture*, we mean the design of political institutions—notably, the three branches of the federal government: the executive, legislature, and judiciary. The Constitution also specifies how political authority is distributed among these different institutions as well as between the federal and state governments. With over 88,000 governmental units of all types nationwide—from familiar state legislatures to obscure special district authorities—the design is complicated. Much overlap and jurisdictional conflict occur among different government bodies. The design of the American political system is quite distinctive because of the degree to which the Constitution disperses authority widely among a variety of political institutions. Authority is divided in two ways. First, the United States is a federal system, which means that authority is divided between national and state governments. This is commonly described as the division of powers. The Tenth Amendment to the Constitution specifies that all powers not expressly delegated to the national government by the Constitution are reserved to the states. For much of American history, state governments exercised the bulk of governmental power. In comparison, the national or federal government was lean and mean, primarily engaged in enforcing laws, arbitrating conflicts, issuing currency, and defending the country.

Today, considerable power has gravitated to the federal level, although state governments continue to formulate, implement, and finance programs in vitally important domains like education, transportation, and property rights. Although the Constitution created a federal system with power distributed between national and state governments, one cannot neatly distinguish which level of government is responsible for which function. Sometimes there is a nearly complete separation of functions: the national government alone decides whether to commit troops abroad; state governments are primarily responsible for regulating marriage and divorce. But the typical situation is more complicated because federal and state governments are operating in the same policy areas. Political scientist Morton Grodzins challenged what he called the layer cake image of federalism, in which the national and state governments are neatly separated from each other and perform different tasks. He suggested that despite this common impression, American federalism in fact resembles a marble cake, in which governmental functions are interwoven and shared among the different levels of government.[1]

The Constitution fragments governing authority in a second way. Political power is divided not only vertically between different levels of government but also horizontally between different branches of government. Rather than uniting power within a single powerful agency, as in what political scientists call the "Westminster model" of British parliamentary government (Westminster Palace is the home of the British parliament), power is divided among the legislative, executive, and judicial branches of the federal government. The term *separation of powers* is often used to describe this dispersion of power among the different branches of government (see Chapter 1). But like the layer cake image of federalism, the concept of the separation of powers can be misleading if taken to mean that each branch of government has exclusive authority in certain domains. In fact, the opposite is the case. A better term to describe how power is distributed within the federal government would be *shared* or *overlapping powers*, as opposed to separation of powers. For example, both the Congress and the president share power in the realm of foreign policy. The president can make treaties with foreign governments, but these must be ratified by a two-thirds vote in the Senate. The president can command the military, but Congress appropriates the necessary funds for military operations. Similarly, all three branches share power when it comes to legislation. Congress can pass a law, but the president is authorized to approve or veto it. Congress can then override a presidential veto with a two-thirds vote in both the Senate and the House. Finally, the Supreme Court can nullify the law by finding it unconstitutional. But Congress can override the decision by amending the Constitution. Suggesting that the three branches share responsibility and power with regard to many governmental functions does not mean that they possess equal power. Although the balance of power among the three branches has varied through time, it is generally agreed that the executive, directed by the president, has become the preeminent branch nowadays.

The architecture of shared or overlapping powers creates the famed system of checks and balances, according to which each branch of government has the power to check the actions of the other branches and must depend on their cooperation to achieve its goals. Again, we do not mean to imply by checks and balances that the three branches have equal power, only that government is designed in such a way that many policies and activities require the tacit or explicit support of all three institutions. Unlike a parliamentary system, where the executive and legislative branches are fused, the system of divided, yet shared, powers ensures that each branch possesses autonomous power.

The process of policy formulation, especially when it involves legislation, must run a difficult gauntlet in a political system where each branch of government can check the others and success depends on the cooperation of all of them. Chances of completing this obstacle course are made even smaller by having each elected branch of government represent different constituencies. The president is elected nationally, senators are elected from each state, and members of the House of Representatives are elected from districts within states. In effect, our constitutional design requires legislation to win three different types of majorities—nationally, by state, and by district. That is, shared powers require groups to build overlapping, simultaneous majorities at the level of the presidency, the Senate, and the House. Legislation must run the equivalent of a triathlon (neglecting the courts for the moment), a series of three different athletic events requiring three different kinds of skills: running, cycling, and swimming—but with one important difference. In a triathlon, a contestant can lose one event but still be declared the winner so long as he or she has the highest combined score at the end of the contest. This would be insufficient under our system of government. The Constitution requires contestants to win all three events *outright*. Groups that desire political change must win at every step of the process, but those groups that want to defend the status quo have to win just once to block a bill. Legislation must pass the House, be approved by the Senate, and then be accepted by the president (excluding the difficult task of overriding a presidential veto), or it will fall short of passage. The first two years of Barack Obama's first term as president provide a perfect illustration of the conservative bias of these institutional arrangements. Despite Obama having been elected by a solid majority and enjoying large Democratic majorities in both houses of Congress, he encountered immense obstacles in attempting to persuade Congress to pass several of his signature reforms.

The design of government in the Constitution, with its system of shared powers among independent institutions representing different constituencies, thus has highly conservative implications. This bias is no accident: it was intended by the Founders who created it. On the one hand, the designers of the Constitution embarked on a remarkable political experiment in 1787.

They proposed to create the first republic in which political authority would be located in the hands of the people instead of a king. The architects of the Constitution were intent on protecting the government against tyranny, which they had just fought a revolution to defeat. On the other hand, the Founders were frightened by the audacity of their own democratic inclinations. They believed that democracy, if left to its own devices, posed a threat to the natural hierarchy in society. Political scientist Robert Dahl observes that the Founders were "alarmed by the prospect that democracy, political equality, and even political liberty itself would endanger the rights of property owners to preserve their property and use it as they please."[2] They thus devised checks and balances as a way to protect the unequal social order without taking away any of the majority's democratic rights. Checks and balances, they believed, would protect the rich by requiring workers and farmers to build concurrent majorities at every level of government. Majorities would have to be built in the House of Representatives by districts based on population, in the Senate according to states, and in the presidency across the entire country. The Founders anticipated that the result would be deadlock and government paralysis, for majorities would find it difficult to win at every level required of them.

The Founders sought to create a government powerful enough to promote market-based economic development but not so powerful that it could be used as an instrument of popular forces to restrict the rights of property. They brilliantly achieved this task of constitutional engineering. When public power is unable to rule because it is gripped by deadlock, private power rules in its place.

The next three chapters, covering the presidency, Congress, and the courts, respectively, examine the institutional structure of government and how power is distributed within and among the three branches. The structure of government, the relationships among the different institutions of government, and the formal and informal rules that govern how they work internally have important consequences for policy. In other words, institutions count. Policy is not simply a reflection of economic and social forces; rather, these social forces are refracted through institutions whose rules and relationships affect the outcome of their struggle. Some groups win and some groups lose, depending on the structure of government. But the structure of government, the relationship among institutions, and their formal and informal rules are not set in stone and are themselves subject to political conflict. The Constitution may have created the architecture of government more than two hundred years ago, but the design is constantly being remodeled. The executive branch does not look like it did 50 years ago, nor is its relationship to

Congress the same as it was 50 years ago. Groups struggle over not only who will occupy the government but also what it will look like. The institutional form of government changes as a result of political conflict. Political institutions—through their relationships to each other and their internal procedures—reflect the larger distribution of power in society at the same time they help to shape it. The focal point of the federal government, and therefore the place we begin our study of political institutions, is the presidency.

THE PRESIDENCY

INTRODUCTION

The 2000 American presidential election was a reminder both that every vote counts and that votes don't always count as much as we think. Election night on November 7, 2000, extended over 36 days before the citizens knew the results. The election depended on returns from Florida, where the Republican candidate, George W. Bush, and the Democratic candidate, Al Gore, were tied in an apparent dead heat. At first, the television networks called Florida for Gore. A few hours later they reversed themselves and called the state for Bush, and then they corrected themselves once again and acknowledged the state was too close to call. At that point, Bush enjoyed a slim margin of a few hundred votes out of the five million that had been cast statewide. With attention riveted on Florida, charges of massive voting irregularities and disputed ballots in the state emerged to cast suspicion on the results. Gore sued to have Florida's disputed ballots counted manually. Bush tried to prevent the recount. The legal case eventually landed in the Supreme Court, which, in a controversial decision, ruled 5–4 to stop a recount of ballots that was already underway. With Bush ahead by 537 votes in the state's official tally, the Court's decision led to awarding Florida's 25 Electoral College votes to Bush, giving him the majority in the Electoral College required to become president.

While every vote counted in Florida, they apparently did not have the same meaning nationwide, where Gore received 550,000 more total votes than Bush. When George W. Bush took his oath of office on January 20, 2001, as the 43rd president of the United States, he was the fourth president to be inaugurated who had received fewer votes than his opponent.

Presidents are not chosen by popular vote but by a majority in the Electoral College, which is presently 270 votes. The Constitution specifies that states have as many votes in the Electoral College as they have senators and representatives in Congress. (Citizens of Washington, D.C., also elect delegates to the Electoral College and are granted three Electoral College votes.) In the rare case when no candidate clears this threshold, either because of a tie or because some votes go to a third-party candidate, the House of Representatives selects the president by majority vote.

In practice, all states, except Maine and Nebraska, cast their votes in the Electoral College as a unit for the candidate who received the most votes in the state, regardless of how narrow the margin. Consequently, the Electoral College vote for president often diverges significantly from the popular vote. It can even turn winners of the nationwide popular vote into losers in the Electoral College—as happened in 2000 to Al Gore. This **unit rule** permits candidates who win a state narrowly to still receive all of that state's Electoral College votes. For example, even though Bush won Florida by .00001 percent of the vote, he received 100 percent of its Electoral College votes. In 2012, Barack Obama benefited from the unit rule when he won all of the Electoral College votes from Florida, even though he carried the state by less than 1 percent of the popular vote.

The method by which Americans select a president through the Electoral College reflects the Founders' distrust of democracy even as they sought to create one. The Electoral College was perceived as a way to check and redirect the will of the people. It embodied both the promise and perversity of a new American democracy: a government that renounced monarchy and enfranchised citizens at the same time it undermined the power of the vote and distorted its effect.

This chapter examines the presidency and the opportunities and obstacles that face those who occupy the office. It begins with a historical overview, examining how the presidency has grown in stature to become the most powerful office in the government. It then describes the different roles presidents play in using that power: conducting foreign policy, supervising the executive branch, directing the economy, and managing conflict. Next, it examines the different sources of power wielded by presidents as they try to succeed in those roles. But presidents are often thwarted and face powerful constraints, which we also take up. Finally, we assess why some presidents are more effective than others and the circumstances that contribute to their success.

THE HISTORICAL PRESIDENCY

In the debates over the writing of the Constitution in Philadelphia, Alexander Hamilton defended the office of the president as one that would give "energy" to the government. He believed that a strong executive was necessary to provide leadership and decisiveness to a government that could otherwise drift and be stalemated in a system of checks and balances. According to the political scientist Stephen Skowronek, the "energy" that Hamilton sought to invest in the office has made the president a powerful source of political change. Regardless of whether they are liberals or conservatives, Democrats or Republicans, all presidents, Skowronek argues, routinely "disrupt systems [and] reshape political landscapes."[1] They put the wheels of government in motion to transform society.

Today the presidency has become the energy center of the government, just as Hamilton envisioned it. But even as presidents set the government's agenda, there is no guarantee that it will be enacted. The system of checks and balances among the different branches of government constitutes a powerful brake on presidential initiatives. Presidential power must be constructed; it cannot be taken for granted. Some presidents are transformative, able to translate their agenda into policy. Many are ultimately frustrated by the obstacles they encounter, despite the awesome powers of their office.

Before the Civil War, most presidents exercised relatively few powers because the responsibilities of the national government were quite limited. According to one scholar, chief executives in the nineteenth century were "chief of very little and executive of even less."[2] Bold innovators like Andrew Jackson and Abraham Lincoln were isolated exceptions, not the rule. In 1885, a young Princeton professor published an influential study of American politics entitled *Congressional Government*. The book conveyed the wisdom of its time—that Congress was the foremost policy-making institution and that presidents were powerful only to the extent that they could **veto** bills passed by it. Twenty-three years later, however, the scholar changed his mind and, in *Constitutional Government in the United States*, developed a far more expansive view of the presidency. Soon after, by his actions as president, Woodrow Wilson—the former Princeton professor—contributed even more directly to the creation of a powerful presidency.[3]

Throughout the nineteenth and early twentieth centuries, there were swings between strong and weak presidents, and between presidential and congressional supremacy. But as giant corporations developed in the twentieth century, the federal government grew in size and power, and the presidency as an institution expanded with it. First, the regulatory role of the federal government increased because corporations outgrew the narrow boundaries of mere states. Firms found it difficult to conduct business on a national scale when each state had its own commercial laws. Firms sought relief from the variety of state regulations in federal law that applied nationally and would be enforced by the executive branch. Second, the federal government became responsible for economic management in response to the Great Depression of the 1930s. Business, labor, and consumers expected political leaders in Washington to manage the boom-and-bust swings of the business cycle. Third, the federal government also took on new social responsibilities in the 1930s. It created a welfare state that distributed resources to the elderly, poor, and disabled who could not provide for themselves. Finally, the federal government grew in response to the new, global character of American capitalism. The U.S. projected diplomatic and military power to ensure open markets for American goods and investment. As the focal point of the federal government, the president was positioned to take advantage of its new regulatory, economic, social, and global responsibilities. The federal government, the presidency, and corporate capitalism all grew together in a mutually supportive relationship.

The New Deal in the 1930s, World War II in the 1940s, and the ensuing Cold War in the 1950s, supersized the presidency and executive branch. Power tilted decisively toward the executive branch and toward the president at its core. Joseph Cooper observes, "The New Deal and World War II preeminently established the president as the single most powerful figure in both the legislative and administrative processes of government, as well as the elected official charged, in the eyes of the public, with primary responsibility for initiating and securing policies in the public interest."[4] Another scholar writes that the president was increasingly looked upon as "the preeminent source of moral leadership, legislative guidance, and public policy."[5]

Presidents encouraged such expectations and performed a variety of roles to meet them. The presidential scholar Clinton Rossiter identified ten presidential "hats" or roles: chief of state, chief executive, commander in chief of the armed forces, chief diplomat, chief legislator, chief of the party, voice of the people, protector of the peace, manager of prosperity, and world leader.[6] The political scientist Thomas E. Cronin proposed four spheres or subpresidencies: domestic policy, economic management, symbolic or moral leadership, and foreign policy.[7] Aaron Wildavsky, a specialist in public policy, distinguished just two presidencies, one for foreign affairs and the other for domestic affairs.[8] While these ways of classifying what presidents do is helpful, we believe presidential activity can most usefully be divided into these four roles: conducting foreign policy, supervising the federal bureaucracy, directing the economy, and managing conflict. We review each of them below.

ROLES OF THE PRESIDENT

Conducting Foreign Policy

Presidents are supposed to keep Americans safe. They are granted immense powers and wide latitude in using them to ensure national security. Their powers and use of them have increased in tandem with the rise of the United States as a superpower and in response to domestic security threats.

The Constitution balances the president's war powers as commander in chief of the armed forces with Congress's power to declare war and appropriate funds for military expenditures. But presidents have broadly interpreted their powers as commander in chief to avoid the checks and balances the Founders intended. For example, President James K. Polk provoked war with Mexico in 1846 when he sent American troops into disputed land between Texas and Mexico. When Mexican forces fired on American soldiers, Polk quickly extracted a declaration of war from Congress. Polk's provocative action brought an angry response from a young Illinois congressman: "Allow the president to invade a neighboring nation, whenever he shall deem it necessary to repel an invasion . . . and you allow him to make war at his pleasure. Study to see if you can fix any limit on his power in this respect."[9]

The words of the worried legislator, Abraham Lincoln, proved prescient. Lincoln himself used war as a pretext to expand presidential powers substantially during his time in office. He directed southern ports to be blockaded without congressional authorization at the start of the Civil War, expanded the armed forces beyond their congressionally prescribed size, and spent money for purposes not approved by Congress.

Contemporary presidents, like their predecessors, have often dispatched troops first and sought congressional approval later—if they bothered to seek approval at all. In 1983, President Reagan ordered U.S. armed forces to invade the tiny Caribbean nation of Grenada and overthrow its government without seeking authorization from Congress. After Saddam Hussein of Iraq invaded Kuwait in 1991, President George H. W. Bush sent 200,000 troops to neighboring Saudi Arabia to protect its oil fields without seeking congressional approval. When he later did so, two political scientists observed Congress "had little choice except to grant the president the authority he requested." They commented, "As most legislators were doubtless aware, withholding such approval would mean that the United States stood in real danger of incurring a serious diplomatic and military defeat in the Middle East. This was an outcome for which few legislators were willing to take responsibility."[10] President Obama also bypassed congressional approval when he authorized the use of American ordnance and warplanes to help bring down the Qaddafi regime in Libya in 2011. His administration claimed

President Barack Obama greets U.S. troops at a mess hall at Bagram Air Field in Afghanistan in March 2010.

that military actions in Libya did not meet the definition of war, or even hostilities, because they "did not involve sustained fighting . . . nor do they involve the presence of U.S. ground troops, U.S. casualties or a serious threat thereof."[11]

But no president was more aggressive in interpreting his authority as commander in chief to justify expanding presidential powers than George W. Bush. He asserted an exclusive presidential power to declare preventive war, deny U.S. citizens their civil liberties, abduct suspects and deport them to countries where they would be tortured, and permit the use of torture in interrogating prisoners.

Presidents try to ensure national security not only through expansive use of their authority as commander in chief but also in their role as diplomat in chief. Presidents have the authority to negotiate treaties and receive ambassadors from foreign countries (which implies the right to recognize or refuse to recognize the government of a particular country). They also appoint ambassadors to foreign countries and representatives to international organizations, such as the United Nations.

Supervising the Federal Bureaucracy

The president is at the core of a federal bureaucracy that is supposed to implement the law. But as the political scientist Gary Orfield wisely suggests, passing a law "means very little until the resources of the executive bureaucracies are committed to its implementation."[12] Presidential commitment matters because legislation is often vague and leaves bureaucrats with a great deal of discretion in translating it into actual, applied policy. For example, when Congress created the Federal Trade Commission (FTC) in 1914 to prevent "unfair methods of competition . . . and unfair or deceptive acts or practices in or affecting commerce," it did not define exactly what constituted unfair competition or deceptive commercial practices. The FTC had to determine what these terms meant. It did so by issuing rules that clarified what the law meant in practice and how it should be applied to specific cases. Rule making by executive agencies is, thus, a form of policy making in which federal agencies don't simply implement the law but use their discretion to fill in the fine print. But fine print can have large consequences for those affected by it. For example, the Wall Street Reform and Consumer Protection Act of 2010, which was intended to bring about financial regulatory reform, required different federal agencies to issue over 385 new rules clarifying what the law meant in practice. This gave the agencies charged with writing such rules tremendous power to determine who the ultimate winners and losers would be *after* Congress passed the reform law. Their decisions could cost banks or consumers tens of millions of dollars depending on what rules they devised. It also subjected agencies to tremendous political pressure. With so much at stake, agencies charged with issuing rules interpreting the Wall Street reform bill became the target of presidential, congressional, and interest-group pressure.

To the extent that anyone directs the vast federal bureaucracy, it is the chief executive—that is, the president. However, presidents have a hard time getting the different parts of the executive branch to cooperate and respond to their leadership. The federal bureaucracy employs about three million people, who work for a dispersed and haphazardly organized array of bureaus, agencies, commissions, and executive departments. The key institution through which presidents seek to impose their will is the **Executive Office of the President (EOP)**. This collection of specialized agencies with about 2,500 staff members includes the White House Office (the president's personal staff and closest advisers), National Security Council, National Economic Council, Council of Economic Advisors, and Office of the Vice President. The largest unit in the EOP is the Office of Management and Budget (OMB), which prepares the president's budget.[13]

The EOP provides presidents with expertise and performs management tasks on their behalf. It is the first in a series of concentric circles surrounding the presidency (see Figure 6.1). Members of the EOP, especially the White House staff, are passionately loyal to the president and often worked on the president's

FIGURE 6.1

EXECUTIVE BRANCH

Executive Office of the President (EOP)
includes
Council of Economic Advisors
National Economic Council
National Security Council
Office of Management and Budget

Cabinet Departments
Agriculture
Commerce
Defense
Education
Energy
Health and Human Services
Homeland Security
Housing and Urban Development
Interior
Justice
Labor
State
Transportation
Treasury
Veterans Affairs

Independent Regulatory Commissions
includes
Federal Reserve Board
National Labor Relations Board

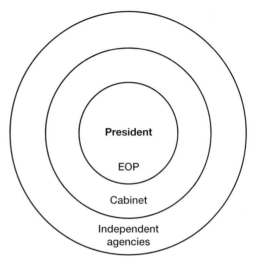

election campaign before moving to their posts in the White House inner circle. According to one estimate, 80 percent of the White House staff under President George W. Bush had served in his campaign organization.[14] When President Obama took office in 2009, the *New York Times* noted, "The Obama White House is now populated with as many Chicagoans as it previously housed Texans."[15] President Obama's closest advisors on his White House staff—David Axelrod, David Plouffe, Valerie Jarrett, and Peter Rouse—were either part of his entourage from Chicago who had worked with him when he was a lowly Illinois state senator or were veterans of his 2008 campaign.[16]

Until recently, the office of vice president warranted only passing mention in a survey of the presidency. The vice president's main job was to represent the United States at funerals of foreign dignitaries and to do little but wait without complaint for the president to die in office. However, the office of vice president became more important when President Bill Clinton gave Vice President Al Gore authority to supervise important policy sectors, including technological development and climate change. The office became even more significant under President George W. Bush, who delegated power over energy, foreign, and security policy to his vice president, Dick Cheney. President Obama has defined the role of the vice president in much less ambitious terms. Vice President Joe Biden's main role has been to use his contacts as a former senator to promote the administration's agenda in Congress.

The next ring out from the Executive Office of the President is the "permanent government," consisting of the 15 departments in the executive branch, including the Department of Defense, State Department, Department of Commerce, and Treasury Department. Departments are umbrella organizations containing most of the agencies and bureaus that comprise the federal bureaucracy. For example, the Department of Commerce includes over two dozen diverse offices and agencies, including the Bureau of the Census, the Patent and Trademark Office, and the National Oceanic and Atmospheric Administration. When George W. Bush created the Department of Homeland Security in 2003, he simply filled it with agencies, such as the Immigration and Naturalization Service (Justice), the Customs Service (Treasury), and the Lawrence Livermore National Laboratory (Defense), that were pulled from other departments.

The president appoints a secretary to lead each department, and the 15 department secretaries (along with a few other officials, including the vice president and, under President Obama, the small-business administrator) compose the president's **cabinet**. The cabinet rarely plays an important role in presidential decision making. Presidents come to office promising to consult frequently with their cabinet, but few ever do so. In fact, presidents rarely meet with their full cabinet at all. One report claimed that President Obama had not had even a phone conversation with some of the members of his cabinet in their first two years on the job. The classic story about presidents' relations with their cabinet involves Lincoln's announcement following a vote of his cabinet: "Eight votes for and one against [the president's]; the nays have it."

While each administration comes to Washington promising to bring new people with it, they somehow all seem to arrive from the same revolving corporate door. Department secretaries who are members of the president's cabinet are drawn overwhelmingly from the ranks of Washington insiders and the corporate elite, with financiers and corporate lawyers predominating. While the cabinet has become more diverse, women and minority cabinet secretaries often have the same corporate connections and pedigrees as their male, white predecessors.

The third ring out from the president, after the EOP and the departments, consists of the **independent regulatory commissions (IRCs)**, such as the National Labor Relations Board, the Federal Trade Commission, and the Federal Reserve Board. These agencies enjoy more autonomy from presidential control than other parts of the executive branch. Presidents appoint commissioners to direct these agencies, subject to confirmation by Congress; but unlike secretaries of departments, these appointees serve for a fixed term and cannot be fired by the president. The terms of IRC appointees often straddle administrations, and newly elected presidents must wait for commissioners' terms to expire before replacing them.

As this description of the federal bureaucracy makes clear, the federal government is not organized hierarchically but rather in concentric circles that surround the president. The federal bureaucracy is like a solar system, with some agencies orbiting closer to the presidential sun than others. But federal departments and their agencies are also under the gravitational pull of other suns in the galaxy that threaten to draw them away from presidents' directions. The system of shared powers endows Congress with influence over federal agencies and exerts a pull on them that competes with the president's force. Federal agencies depend on Congress for appropriations, and Congress provides their legislative mandate— their job description. Congress also performs oversight to ensure they comply with their mandate. They can summon federal officials to testify before congressional committees. Finally, an increasing number of presidential appointments to the executive branch require Senate approval, and senators are now more likely to use procedural rules and filibusters to block or delay presidential nominees. When George W. Bush was president, Democrats in the Senate approved 75 percent of his appointees to federal agencies. But Senate Republicans have raised obstruction to a whole new level under President Obama to prevent him from appointing agency heads who share his values. During the 112th Congress (2011–13), only 57 percent of Obama's civilian nominees were confirmed. Senate Republicans were opposed not to a particular candidate but to *any* candidate that Obama nominated. They held appointees hostage in exchange for policy concessions from the administration, such as when they vowed to block any appointment to head the newly created Consumer Financial Protection Agency until the agency's powers were reduced.[17]

Not only do presidents have to compete with Congress for influence over federal agencies, but bureaucrats have their own sources of power to defy presidential direction. Most political appointees directed to lead agencies are unfamiliar with their procedures and lack expertise. They are often dependent on the information that bureaucrats possess and have to become advocates of the agency to obtain it.

Consequently, presidents often complain that their appointees abandon them and "go native." Instead of acting as the president's agent, ensuring that the agency complies with the president's program, the appointee is "turned" and becomes a double agent, representing the agency's interests to the president.[18]

Finally, presidential command of the bureaucracy is challenged by interest groups that develop mutually supportive, friendly—sometimes called clientelistic—relations with federal agencies. Interest groups gravitate to federal agencies because they have legal authority to provide sanctions and rewards to them. Thus clients seek to "rent" the agency for their own benefit. In exchange for favorable rulings, clients offer political support to the agency when it appeals to Congress for appropriations, when it comes into conflict with other agencies over turf, or when it has to appeal to the administration for support.

Given the many challenges to their management of the executive branch, presidents often prefer to circumvent the bureaucracy altogether. As one White House staff person explained ruefully, "Everybody believes in democracy until he gets to the White House and then you begin to believe in dictatorship because it's so hard to get things done."[19] Presidents concentrate policy making inside the EOP, relying on staff assistants whom they know and trust and who are personally loyal to them. President Obama's administration followed his predecessors in preferring to run "its policy priorities out of the White House rather than through executive branch departments and agencies."[20] Obama appointed "czars" in the EOP, special advisors to supervise policy development and implementation in high-priority sectors because he did not have confidence in the responsiveness of federal agencies. Former Senator George Mitchell had the Mideast peace talks portfolio, operating parallel to the State Department; Carol Browner worked on energy and climate change, parallel to the Environmental Protection Agency; and Nancy-Ann DeParle worked on health reform, parallel to the Department of Health and Human Services. The political scientist G. Calvin Mackenzie explained that presidents make growing use of special advisors, such as policy czars, within the White House because "you get people who are really loyal and the president is their only constituency. Administrators in every kind of setting want that. They all try to have people who can cut through the administrative structures they inherit."[21]

Directing the Economy

According to Jacob S. Hacker and Paul Pierson, "the president is widely recognized as a manager of prosperity, the elected official with the greatest incentive and capacity to focus on the economy as a whole."[22] No office other than the presidency can present a coherent program and coordinate a fragmented government to promote economic growth. Economic management is an essential feature of presidential leadership, no less under a conservative like Ronald Reagan than under a "New Democrat" like Bill Clinton, a "compassionate conservative" like George W. Bush, or a "post-partisan" like Barack Obama. A major presidential goal is to promote a vibrant capitalist economy.

All presidents are consumed with making capitalism work. Unemployment is bad politics, causing voters to lose confidence in the president's leadership and policies. Economic stagnation reduces tax revenues that allow presidents to enact new programs that appeal to voters. Consequently, presidents are concerned with economic management, and much of the EOP, including the Office of Management and Budget, the National Economic Council, and the Council of Economic Advisors, is devoted to it. President Obama was so concerned with this aspect of his job that he directed the head of the White House National Economic Council to provide him with a daily economic briefing as a counterpart to the briefing he received from his National Security Advisor.

Outside the EOP a wide array of government agencies has major economic responsibilities. These agencies include the Treasury, State, Agriculture, Commerce, Labor, and Energy departments, as well as the Small Business Administration, Federal Reserve Bank, and independent regulatory commissions such as the Securities and Exchange Commission. Many of these agencies have multiple loyalties. Congress and the president compete for power over them, along with the industries that agencies regulate or have jurisdiction over. The Federal Reserve Bank is beholden to bankers; the Agriculture Department tailors its policies to favor agribusiness; and the Interior Department looks out for the interests of extractive industries. On the other hand, agencies whose mandate is to represent groups and interests at the periphery of corporate capitalism, such as the Labor and Education departments, have far less power and occupy a lower rank in the informal hierarchy of federal agencies.

Presidents are weaker in this policy arena than in the other three because their efforts to shape economic policy unilaterally are more constrained. Their success, particularly in this field, depends upon the cooperation of other actors, especially Congress and the regulatory agencies. Presidents can act unilaterally by appointing key economic officials and by vetoing legislation. But these assertions of power are not very effective. Vetoes don't get presidents the economic policies they want. They only prevent Congress from getting what it wants. And the most important economic appointment that presidents make is the chair of the Federal Reserve Board, which sets monetary policy.

But presidents are reluctant to appoint someone to this position who would not receive a favorable reception from the financial community.[23]

According to Jacob S. Hacker and Paul Pierson, the greatest resource presidents have to affect economic policy occurs through mobilizing their coalition partners—congressional allies, electoral blocs, and interest groups—to support their demands. Since economic policy requires the cooperation of Congress and regulatory agencies, presidents have to depend on coalition partners that can apply pressure throughout the political system. Presidents may take credit for getting their economic policies passed, but responsibility is broadly shared with political allies that make it possible.[24] Such was the case, for example, in 2012 when President Obama successfully appealed to his coalition partners, the interest groups and electoral blocs who reelected him, in negotiating higher taxes on the rich with Republicans.

Managing Conflict

Capitalist production generates dislocations, inequalities, and discontents that form the structural context for the fourth arena of presidential activity: managing the conflicts that arise from the collision of democratic politics and social inequalities. Thomas E. Cronin suggests that "calibration and management of conflict is the core of presidential leadership."[25] A major presidential concern is to prevent conflict from threatening political and economic stability.

Presidents often manage conflict by draping themselves in the flag and appealing to patriotic sentiments. Patriotism in the U.S. is a functional substitute for a state religion in which the president acts as the high priest. President George W. Bush made effective use of this strategy when he appeared at Ground Zero, where the World Trade Center had stood, following the 9/11 attack. He identified the presidency with unifying patriotic sentiments during a time of crisis.

Presidents also use the media to shape public opinion and maintain political stability. Almost one-third of the White House staff works on packaging the president for media consumption. Speechwriters, press secretaries, pollsters, and media consultants seek to portray presidents and their policies in a favorable light.[26] They try to present the president as actively engaged in solving problems and responding confidently to crises. For example, when President Obama was asked what lessons he had learned in office, he responded that messaging is just as important as governing. Getting the policy right is not enough, Obama explained. Presidents also "have to tell a story to the American people that gives them a sense of unity and purpose and optimism, especially during tough times."[27] Presidents have to be cheerleader in chief as well as commander in chief.

President Bush at Ground Zero in the week following the attack on the World Trade Center on September 11, 2001.

In telling a story, presidents spend so much time burnishing their image that governing has become indistinguishable from campaigning. During the Clinton presidency, political consultants participated more actively in policy discussions than under previous presidents. The presidential scholar George C. Edwards described the Clinton administration as "the ultimate example of the public presidency—a presidency based on a perpetual campaign to obtain the public's support and fed by public opinion polls, focus groups, and public relations memos."[28]

Politics determined policy to an even greater extent during the George W. Bush presidency. The *New York Times* columnist Thomas Friedman claimed that the Bush administration's policy toward Iraq was driven more by domestic political concerns in the United States than by the stated aim of bringing democracy to Iraq. Friedman wrote, "That is why, I bet, Karl Rove [President Bush's political advisor] had more sway over this war than Assistant Secretary of State for Near Eastern Affairs Bill Burns. Mr. Burns knew only what would play in the Middle East. Mr. Rove knew what would play in the Middle West."[29] President Obama has also blended campaigning with governing, appearing on informal, entertaining television shows, such as "Late Show with David Letterman" and "The View."

Today the public face of the presidency is highly managed and contrived. The administration chooses what news to reveal and when to reveal it. When asked why President Bush waited until September to begin beating the drums of war against Iraq, his chief of staff explained, "From a marketing point of view you don't introduce new products in August."[30] Of course, presidents sometimes wish their actions escaped the media spotlight, and they cannot always control the spin the media gives to a story. Scandals, missteps, political defeats, and accidents that cast the president in an unflattering light also attract reporters. But whether the media presents an administration in a complimentary or critical way is the president's game to win or lose.

Sometimes presidents find that appeals to patriotism and media gestures are not enough to maintain stability. In these moments presidents try to deflect conflict by creating blue-ribbon commissions to study difficult issues in order to defuse the controversy surrounding them. According to one skeptic, "These commissions study the situation and, in due course, issue a report, which after a flurry of publicity, is filed away, its recommendations unimplemented and forgotten."[31] President Bush disregarded the recommendations of the National Commission on Terrorist Acts Upon the United States, known as the "9/11 Commission," which investigated the terrorist attacks and offered suggestions on how to prevent them in the future, while President Obama ignored the advice of his National Commission on Fiscal Responsibility and Reform, known as "Simpson-Bowles," on how to bring the federal budget back into balance.

At other times, if the challenge to the existing order is sufficiently great and appears to be escalating, a president can try to reestablish control by providing benefits to aggrieved groups. In their historical analysis of social policy, Frances Fox Piven and Richard A. Cloward found that welfare funding increased "during the occasional outbreaks of civil disorder produced by mass unemployment" and then contracted when stability was restored. For example, one response by the federal government to labor unrest in the 1930s and to black militancy in the 1960s was to sponsor new social programs.[32]

Presidents, as well as state and local authorities, may also choose to respond to acute challenges to social stability by calling out the National Guard, mobilizing the armed forces, engaging federal marshals, and using the FBI to maintain political order. Following 9/11, for example, federal agents arrested approximately 1,200 foreign nationals, refused to release their names, detained them in secret locations, and held deportation hearings for many without allowing them access to an attorney. In addition, presidents have often cooperated with local authorities in using violence to break strikes by workers and to quell urban protests.

THE IMPERIAL PRESIDENT

Conducting foreign policy, supervising the federal bureaucracy, directing the economy, and managing conflict are demanding roles. Presidents need power to fulfill them. They must be like Gullivers resisting the efforts of Lilliputians to restrain them. While still an academic and not yet elected president, Woodrow Wilson appreciated that presidents had extended their power beyond what the Founders had intended in order to cope with the demands of the office: "His office is anything he has the sagacity and force to make it. . . . Let him once win the admiration and confidence of the country, and no other single force can withstand him, no combination of other forces will easily overpower him."[33]

The president derives power from different sources. In the Constitution, the powers of the president are enumerated in Article II. It has been referred to as "the most loosely drawn chapter of the Constitution."[34] It is far shorter and more general than Article I, which defines the powers of Congress. And its location in the Constitution—in second position, with Congress having pride of place—is richly symbolic.

The Constitution empowers the president to approve or veto legislation passed by Congress, act as commander in chief of the armed forces, faithfully execute the laws, pardon criminals, make treaties, call Congress into special session, appoint government officials, and recognize foreign governments. These are substantial prerogatives. But the formal powers enumerated in Article II do not begin to exhaust the actual powers that presidents exercise. Presidential power is based on both legal and political grounds. That is, the extent of presidential powers depends not only on the specific powers enumerated in the Constitution but also on such subtle grounds as the president's reputation among citizens and legislators. Presidential powers are based on the inescapable authority attached to the office and on fickle impressions of the president's competence and popularity.

Part of the president's power derives from the aura attached to the office. Presidents draw an annual salary of $400,000 and are provided with an additional account of nearly $200,000 for travel, entertaining, and other personal expenses. Presidents travel in a specially designed limousine, helicopter, and jetliner (Air Force One), and their families reside in the 123-room White House at the most exclusive address in the world—1600 Pennsylvania Avenue. A staff of about 100 attends to the first family's personal needs at a cost of over $8 million per year. To escape the buzz of Washington, presidents can repair to Camp David, a 180-acre retreat in the mountains of Maryland reserved for their use.

In addition, only presidents (along with their vice-presidents) can legitimately claim to represent the entire country, because they are the only officials selected through a nationwide election. Only presidents can embody the nation and cloak themselves in all the emotional and patriotic symbolism that this evokes. In the words of Woodrow Wilson, "He is the only national voice in affairs. . . . He is the representative of no constituency, but of the whole people."[35] Unlike parliamentary regimes, in which prime ministers direct the government and monarchs or other officials perform ceremonial duties as heads of state, the American system makes the president **head of government** and **head of state** simultaneously. Both roles are fused in the president's office. By combining real and symbolic power, the presidency serves as "the focus for the most intense and persistent emotions in the American polity," in the words of the presidential scholar James David Barber.[36]

Presidents also command media attention that permits them to shape public opinion and appeal directly to the people for support of presidential initiatives. The media is endlessly fascinated with the president, covering everything from the first family's choice of a puppy to far-reaching policy decisions. Media coverage reinforces the impression that the presidency is the essential institution at the center of political life. Presidents go to extraordinary lengths to dramatize their message—for example, by delivering speeches in carefully selected settings. President George W. Bush famously made a "Top Gun" landing on board the aircraft carrier *U.S.S. Abraham Lincoln*, where he declared victory prematurely in the Iraq War in 2003. President Obama drew attention to one of his administration's achievements by granting reporters an interview in the Situation Room in the White House on the first anniversary of the successful mission to kill Osama bin Laden. The extent of coverage devoted to presidents is as helpful in presenting a favorable image of the office as the deferential reporting they generally receive.

Access to the media, according to the political scientist Bruce Miroff, gives "the president . . . an unparalleled advantage in defining political reality for most Americans. . . . Press or partisan criticism may challenge a president . . . but the outline of reality that he has sketched is usually left intact."[37] A graphic illustration of Miroff's point is that for years after 9/11, seven out of ten citizens believed that Iraq's dictator, Saddam Hussein, was involved in the terrorist attack. Yet there was never credible evidence of such a connection. But many Americans believed it because President George W. Bush and members of his administration repeatedly claimed that such a link existed.

As we described earlier, presidential power is further bolstered by supervision of the federal bureaucracy, which interprets and implements federal laws. Presidents can influence federal agencies through their budget requests and powers of appointment. Presidents make over 3,000 appointments—more than chief executives of other countries get to make—permitting presidents to place political allies throughout the government. They can also issue **executive orders** requiring or authorizing federal agencies to take some action. Through January 2011, President Obama had issued 76 executive orders, from an order setting more-demanding ethics requirements for those who work in the White House to one barring the use of torture in interrogating terrorism suspects.

Obama used executive orders more aggressively after 2010 in order to bypass an obstructive Congress once Republicans took control of the House of Representatives. "We Can't Wait" became Obama's motto as he grew more determined to push the envelope in finding things his administration could do on its own. He issued executive orders to raise fuel-economy standards, reduce fees to refinance federally insured mortgages, and create work programs for veterans. Obama was more willing to use executive orders to circumvent Congress because the legacy he wanted to run on for reelection was at stake.

Presidents also have rewards they can dispense to obtain compliance with their policies. They can make skillful use of patronage, including the power to nominate federal judges and ambassadors, channel resources to the districts of cooperative members of Congress, and invite supporters to White House events. They also have sticks to punish opponents as well as carrots to reward allies. They can divert federal money that would have gone to the districts of wayward members of Congress, and deny opponents access to federal officials. Presidents are also party leaders and can appeal for support from the party faithful and officeholders. In return, presidents can make appearances on behalf of political allies, raise money for them, and support their pet projects.

Finally, presidents have benefited immensely from the rise of the United States as a global power. As the United States has become the dominant actor on the world stage, presidents are in a privileged position to write the script because they are uniquely situated to speak for the national interest. As the world gets smaller, as foreign-policy issues touch people's lives in more immediate and intimate ways, from war and threats of terrorism to economic globalization and climate change, presidents get bigger. The more foreign policy matters, the more presidents matter.

Writing in the 1960s, Richard E. Neustadt, the most influential scholar on the modern presidency, described the trajectory of presidential power as follows: "In instance after instance, the exceptional behavior of our earlier 'strong' Presidents has now been set by statute as a regular requirement."[38] Presidential powers once thought to be extraordinary have become routine.[39] Bold initiatives of one president to extend the powers of the office are accepted as a normal feature of presidential power by their successors. For example, one of Bush's innovations was to issue a record number of signing statements—more than all previous presidents combined! **Signing statements** are documents that provide the president's interpretation of the meaning of laws just passed. They direct administrative officials to disregard provisions that presidents believe infringe on their constitutional prerogatives as commander in chief or chief executive. A *New York Times* journalist observed that "Mr. Bush transformed signing statements from an obscure tool into a commonplace term."[40]

Even though Obama criticized Bush for issuing signing statements when he was running for president, he adopted the same practice once in office, albeit less frequently. For example, when Obama signed a budget bill in 2011, he issued a signing statement claiming a right to ignore dozens of its provisions. These included objections to statutes, such as barring the use of money to transfer prisoners from the Guantanamo, Cuba, naval base to the custody of foreign countries, that he felt impinged on his constitutional prerogatives to conduct foreign affairs. Obama said, "I have advised the Congress that I will not treat these provisions as limiting my constitutional authorities in the area of foreign relations."[41]

While Obama diverged from his predecessor's policies regarding detainees suspected of terrorism in some respects and followed them in others, he did not depart from President Bush in his claims of constitutional prerogatives. President Obama has even gone beyond President Bush's practices in some instances, such as claiming the right of the president to order targeted killings not only of foreigners but also of American citizens regarded as security threats.[42] Obama has picked up the weapons other presidents have forged and, as we have seen, developed new ones of his own. When Senate Republicans used procedural rules to block or delay the confirmation of nearly 200 presidential appointees, President Obama claimed the authority to issue recess appointments even though the Senate was technically in session, sometimes with only one senator present to maintain the appearance of conducting business.

Presidents command the most powerful military in the world, manage a vast bureaucracy, shape public opinion through the media attention they receive, provide party leadership and can appeal for party discipline, embody the national interest, and use carrots and sticks. If this were the whole story, the president would be a modern Leviathan, an all-powerful leader. Despite such vast powers, however, presidents are also constrained. Alongside the imperial presidency is an imperiled one.

THE IMPERILED PRESIDENCY

In *Gulliver's Travels*, Jonathan Swift's satire on the modern human condition, Gulliver found himself not only towering above the Lilliputians but also, at times, tethered by them. Presidents, for all their awesome powers, may find themselves in a comparable position and unable to achieve their goals. This paradox was conveyed in a remark by President Harry Truman as he imagined what would happen when his newly elected successor, the World War II hero General Dwight D. Eisenhower, took office. Truman predicted, "He'll sit here and he'll say, 'Do this! Do that!' And nothing will happen. Poor Ike—it won't be a bit like the Army. He'll find it very frustrating."[43] Truman knew from bitter experience that presidents cannot exercise power simply by giving orders, as occurs in the military chain of command. Instead, presidential power often requires persuading other powerful officials that their own best interest lies in complying with what the president requests.

Throughout the 1970s, the presidency was a beleaguered institution. George Edwards captures this humble view of the presidency when he writes that the American political system "is too complicated, power too decentralized, and interests too diverse for one person, no matter how extraordinary, to dominate."[44] The power and majesty of the presidency were weakened by the debacle in Vietnam under President Lyndon Johnson and by President Richard Nixon's criminal involvement in Watergate. Both events temporarily removed the aura and veneration attached to the presidency. The end of the golden age of capitalism in the 1970s also weakened the presidency. The power and prestige of the president (as well as that of the entire government) flourish when corporate capitalism prospers, and the president's popular and professional standing falls when it stagnates, as it did in the 1970s.

In addition, beginning in the 1970s presidents frequently have been confronted by a resurgent Congress, often led by the opposing party. In the 1950s and 1960s, Congress was willing to follow the president's lead because it agreed with his policies. For example, during the Cold War, Congress often deferred to presidents because it shared their goal of containing communism. But when Congress and the president began to disagree over substantive issues of domestic and foreign policy, Congress sought to recover its lost prerogatives. Congress legislated limits on presidential powers in the War Powers Act of 1973 and created the Congressional Budget Office in 1974 to provide it with economic expertise to counter that available to the president.

The new assertiveness of Congress was also driven by the routine appearance of divided government, in which different parties control the legislative and executive branches. Democrats controlled Congress throughout much of the Republican presidencies of Richard Nixon, Ronald Reagan, and George H. W. Bush, whereas the Republicans controlled one or both houses of Congress through six of Bill Clinton's eight years in the White House, half of Barack Obama's first term, and the first half of his second term. Divided government gives Congress an incentive to challenge, not cooperate with, the president. This point is evident when one looks at how much more compliant Congress was in Barack Obama's first two years, when Democrats had majorities in both houses of Congress, than the years since, when he had to contend with a confrontational Republican majority in the House of Representatives and a larger group of GOP senators. Republicans used their congressional gains from the 2010 midterm elections to stymie President Obama's domestic agenda. They defeated Obama's economic-stimulus measure, the American Jobs Act, and blocked his appointments to fill vacancies in federal agencies.

Presidents have also been weakened by the recent proliferation of interest groups. According to Stephen Skowronek, the institutional universe that presidents face today has "gotten thicker all around." He asserts that "there are more organizations and authorities [for presidents] to contend with, and they are all more firmly entrenched and independent."[45]

WHAT DO YOU THINK?

Are Checks and Balances Alive and Well?

The president's power has generally increased as the size and power of the federal government has grown. Has the growth of presidential power invalidated checks and balances? What, if anything, can be done to reduce presidential powers? Or are we better off with strong presidents?

President Barack Obama talks with Speaker of the House John Boehner
(R-OH) in 2011.

Presidents often seek to circumvent them by building their own personal
coalitions. This entails appealing directly to the public for support instead of to
interest groups and members of Congress. While this may reduce the obligations presidents owe other political actors, it also means that interest groups
and members of Congress are less obliged to cooperate with the president.

In brief, there is no consistent trend in the amount of power that modern
presidents possess. Presidential power sometimes appears imperial and at other
times appears imperiled. If some modern presidents appeared weak and ineffective, such as Jimmy Carter (1977–81) and George H. W. Bush (1989–93),
others, such as Ronald Reagan (1981–89) and George W. Bush (2001–09),
deployed presidential power to the legal limit—and in some cases beyond. The
presidency is the strongest institution in American government, but presidents
also encounter powerful obstacles in the pursuit of their goals.

PRESIDENTIAL STYLES

How presidents construe their role and react to the opportunities and obstacles they face depends on the temperament, skills, and aptitudes they bring to office. John F. Kennedy was supremely confident to the point of arrogance, Lyndon Johnson was beset by profound insecurity, and Richard Nixon was suspicious by nature. Ronald Reagan had little patience for the details of policy but was brilliantly effective at communicating broad themes to the public. Jimmy Carter was just the opposite. He was absorbed by the details of policy but not effective at articulating a coherent narrative explaining them. George W. Bush delegated authority to trusted subordinates and tended to view issues in stark, moral terms, while Barack Obama has been more involved, analytical, and deliberate. He has often chosen a course of action only after a lengthy discussion among advisors with different views.[46] For example, Obama polled advisors about whether to raid Osama bin Laden's compound in Pakistan. Almost all of them hedged. Despite doubts among his advisors, Obama decided to give the raid his green light. But what stands out most about Obama is his ability to detach and compartmentalize. Consider, for example, that the night before Navy Seals left on their mission to kill Osama bin Laden, President Obama was cracking jokes at the White House Correspondents' Association dinner. The next day he played golf in the morning before sequestering himself in the West Wing of the White House in the afternoon to listen to reports about the Navy Seals' mission that would define, and possibly destroy, his presidency.[47] Table 6.1 presents the president's schedule on April 29, 2011, just three days before the fateful mission to raid Osama Bin Laden's hideout.

Presidential leadership depends on context as much as personality. Crisis and war permit presidents to overcome blockages that would normally compromise presidential power. The attacks of September 11, 2001, provide an illustration. Before 9/11, the Bush administration was floundering. Poll numbers were low and the economy was in recession. After 9/11, a presidency that had appeared small now loomed large. Approval ratings for President Bush soared. The system of checks and balances became seriously imbalanced. Congress meekly deferred to the president. Fears generated by the attacks were used to justify launching a preemptive war against Iraq, further consolidating power in the executive branch. Only the Supreme Court put up some belated resistance when it rejected some of President Bush's claims of power to deny terrorist suspects their rights. The Court reminded the administration that a "state of

TABLE 6.1

PRESIDENT'S SCHEDULE — APRIL 29, 2011

Previous	Friday, April 29, 2011 All Times ET
8:00 AM	The President meets with participants in the 1968 Memphis Sanitation Strike *Diplomatic Room* *Closed Press*
8:30 AM	The First Family departs the White House en route to Andrews Air Force Base *South Lawn* *Open Press*
8:45 AM	The First Family departs Andrews Air Force Base en route to Alabama *Andrews Air Force Base* *Travel Pool Coverage*
10:50 AM	The First Family arrives in Alabama *Local Event Time: 9:50 AM CDT* *Tuscaloosa Regional Airport* *Open Press*
11:10 AM	The President and the First Lady view the damage as well as meet with Governor Bentley, state and local officials and families affected by the storms *Local Event Time: 10:10 AM CDT* *Alabama* *Travel Pool Coverage*
12:45 PM	The First Family departs Alabama *Local Event Time: 11:45 AM CDT* *Tuscaloosa Regional Airport* *Open Press*
2:10 PM	The First Family arrives in Cape Canaveral, Florida *Cape Canaveral Skid Strip* *Open Press*
2:45 PM	The First Family tours the orbiter processing facility *Cape Canaveral, Florida, Orbiter Processing Facility* *Travel Pool Coverage*
3:30 PM	The First Family views the launch of the space shuttle Endeavour *Launch Control Center* *Travel Pool Coverage*
5:40 PM	Tha President arrives Miami, Florida *Miami International Airport* *Open Press*
6:55 PM	The President delivers the Miami Dade College commencement address *Florida, Miami, Miami Dade College* *Pooled TV, Open to Correspondents*
9:05 PM	The President departs Miami, Florida *Miami International Airport* *Open Press*
11:30 PM	The President arrives at the White House *South Lawn* *Open Press*

war is not a blank check for the president when it comes to the rights of the nation's citizens."[48]

Presidential effectiveness also depends on the circumstances in which presidents take office. Skowronek argues that presidents elected in the wake of a realignment, with the opposition in disarray, are in a favorable position to impose their will on the government. Effective presidents, Skowronek offers, come to power following electoral upheavals when "government has been most thoroughly discredited and when political resistance to the presidency is weakest."[49] Presidents who take office under conditions that permit them more freedom to maneuver are more likely to succeed. The personal factor can also weigh heavily. Some presidents are more skillful than others at playing the hand they have been dealt.

But the extent of presidential power depends most on what it is deployed to do. It is exercised most decisively and effectively when the president opposes some action. The Constitution permits the president to veto bills passed by Congress. Presidents do not require the cooperation of other political actors to make their veto effective. All they need is a pen that works. Nor do they have to fear that their veto will be overridden. It is very difficult for the House and the Senate to assemble the two-thirds majority in each chamber necessary to reverse a presidential veto.

But those who end up on historians' lists of great presidents make their mark not by vetoing bills and preventing change but by promoting it. Ironically, presidents find their power magnified and most effective when they thwart change and find their power diminished and most constrained when they try to foster it. The independence of Congress, the inflexibility of the federal bureaucracy, and the influence of special interests are daunting obstacles

WHAT DO YOU THINK?

Do the Best Reach the White House and How Can We Encourage Them to Try?

Critics often lament that the process of becoming president has grown so grueling and so daunting that it discourages many who are qualified from even trying. What qualities do you think we should look for in a president, and how can we better organize the process so that people with those qualities will seek the office?

to overcome. The hurdles are so high that after reviewing the record of the last 14 presidents, from Calvin Coolidge (1920) to George W. Bush (2008), one presidential scholar concluded, "Maybe about three were successful." (Only Franklin Roosevelt, Eisenhower, and Reagan made the grade.)[50] And yet, as we argued at the beginning of the chapter, presidents are agents of change in our political system, if only by default. No other office has the organizational coherence to pursue a concerted course of action across a range of policy fronts. That presidents may not succeed when they do so says less about their weakness and more about the power of the obstacles they have to overcome.

CONCLUSION

Political power is centralized in the executive branch, and in the executive branch it is concentrated in the Executive Office of the President. The presidency is at the apex of the government and is uniquely qualified to coordinate the different parts of the government. Presidents conduct foreign policy, supervise the executive branch, direct the economy, and manage conflict. Presidents enjoy an exalted position by virtue of the constitutional power vested in them and because, along with vice presidents, they are the only officials elected nationally.

At the same time, presidential power is highly contingent. Presidents must contend with countervailing pressures from an array of interest groups. Presidential success also requires obtaining the cooperation of the legislative and judicial branches, which are independent and may not be acquiescent. Finally, presidents have to contend with unruly federal agencies in the executive branch that resist presidential direction. In such circumstances, presidents tend to move policy making inside the EOP, where staff are more loyal and compliant, and to rely on techniques that bypass Congress and minimize bureaucratic obstruction.

Ironically, the power of presidents is most effective when it is least important to them (preventing change) and least effective when it is most important to them (creating change). Change is hard to achieve because the political and institutional obstacles presidents encounter are so great. Yet presidents are in the best position to provide energy and direction to government. Presidents may not always succeed at turning their proposals into policies, but it is their program that sets the agenda of government.

CHAPTER SUMMARY

Introduction

Presidents are not elected by a majority, or even a plurality, of voters but by a majority in the Electoral College. States are awarded votes in the Electoral College based upon the total number of congressional representatives and senators they have. Almost all states cast their votes in the Electoral College as a unit. Due to the unit rule, in which candidates who receive the most votes in a state receive all of that state's Electoral College votes, the popular vote and Electoral College results often diverge. The Founders created the Electoral College to select the president because they feared that direct election would make presidents too responsive and accountable to the will of the people.

The Historical Presidency

The Founders designed the presidency to provide energy to the executive branch. At the same time, fear of tyranny led them to construct a system of separated powers in which the executive would play a secondary role to Congress. For over a century, the presidency was a relatively weak institution, both because the federal government had limited power compared to state governments and because Congress was the more assertive branch of the federal government. Important events in the twentieth century, including the Great Depression, World War II, and the U.S.'s emergence as a world power, have contributed to the growth and power of the federal government and, especially, the president.

The Roles of the President

Presidents engage in a wide range of activity that can be divided into four roles. First, they are responsible for conducting foreign policy. Presidents represent the U.S. on the world stage. Second, presidents are responsible for supervising the executive branch. They must bring coherence to a large, fragmented federal bureaucracy that is responsive to divergent interests. Third, they are responsible for directing the economy. Their political career depends upon it. Finally, they must manage conflict, creating a sense of unity and domestic peace.

The Imperial President

In order to fulfill these roles successfully, presidents are endowed with an ample array of powers, including constitutionally granted powers in domestic and foreign affairs. They also have extensive informal powers, including the legitimacy they enjoy as the only official (along with the vice president) elected by the entire nation. Power also derives from their unique access to the media and their authority to direct the federal bureaucracy. They can also use sticks and carrots to threaten and reward potential opponents, and as leaders of their party they can appeal to officials who share their party affiliation. Finally, they enjoy additional power because the United States is the most powerful country in the world. As the power of the U.S. has grown, so has the power of the president.

Presidential Power Imperiled

Despite having enormous powers, presidents face many obstacles to the exercise of their leadership. Presidents must contend with an independent Congress and judiciary. In addition, presidents are confronted by an array of interest-group opponents and by federal bureaucrats who jealously defend their independence and turf.

Presidential Styles

Some presidents succeed more than others in overcoming the constraints they encounter. Some simply bring a better skill set to the job and face more congenial conditions in which they can wield power than others. Presidential power is most effective when presidents want to prevent change. But, ironically, this is also the expression of power that is least meaningful to them! Presidents become great by being transformative. But creating change requires the cooperation of other political institutions, creating opportunities for blockage and obstruction.

Critical Thinking Questions

1. President Obama complained that changing the orientation of the federal government is as difficult as changing the direction of an ocean liner. Why do presidents find it so hard to steer the ship when they are its captain?

2. Periodically, historians are polled to identify great presidents. Who do you consider the best and the worst president since World War II? Why? What criteria have you used in making your selection, and why are these criteria the most appropriate?

3. Would the U.S. be better off with weaker or stronger presidents?

4. Presidential power is at its peak when the country is at war or primed for it. Other political actors are reluctant to challenge the president for fear of undercutting the war effort and appearing unpatriotic. But it is precisely during such periods that we need checks and balances the most. What can be done to curb presidential power when the drums of war are beating and to prevent presidents from taking advantage of them?

Suggested Readings

Joel D. Aberbach and Mark A. Peterson, eds., *The Executive Branch.* New York: Oxford University Press, 2006.

Thomas E. Cronin, *On the Presidency: Teacher, Soldier, Shaman, Pol.* Boulder, CO: Paradigm Publishers, 2008.

Richard E. Neustadt, *Presidential Power and the Modern Presidents: The Politics of Leadership.* New York: Simon and Schuster, 1991.

Stephen Skowronek, *The Politics Presidents Make: Leadership from John Adams to George Bush.* Cambridge, MA: Harvard University Press, 1993.

Garry Wills, *Bomb Power: The Modern Presidency and the National Security State.* New York: Penguin Press, 2010.

7

THE CONGRESS

INTRODUCTION

Although Congress is just one of three branches that compose the federal government, Article I, Section 8, of the Constitution assigns it especially substantial responsibilities. These include the capacity to declare war; to build, support, and control the Army and Navy; to collect taxes, borrow money, and pay debt; to control immigration; to regulate commerce and set rules for overseas trade; to create courts inferior to the Supreme Court; to establish networks of post offices and roads; and, more generally, to "make all laws which shall be necessary and proper for carrying into execution the foregoing powers, and all other powers vested by this Constitution in the government of the United States, or any department or officer thereof." In addition, the House of Representatives was given the power to impeach—that is, bring charges against—members of the executive branch and the judiciary. The Senate then acts as a trial court for all impeachments, requiring a two-thirds majority of those voting in order to remove the person from office. Article II, Sections 2 and 3, further instruct the president to report to Congress on the **State of the Union** and to secure approval from the Senate for treaties negotiated with other countries and for appointments to high governmental positions, including justices of the Supreme Court.

By lodging these vast powers in Congress as the country's national representative body, the United States fulfilled the demand posed a century earlier by the political thinker John Locke, who had announced in his *Second Treatise of Government* that "the *first and fundamental positive* Law of all Commonwealths is the establishing of the Legislative Power. . . . This *Legislative* is not only *the supream power* of the Common-wealth, but sacred and unalterable."[1] In almost every other democracy, the national legislature, know as a parliament, lacks the kind of authority the American separation-of-powers system places in Congress.

In parliamentary systems, parliament may officially be sovereign, but in practice it is subordinate to the executive because the majority party forms the executive and largely dominates parliament. Thus, legislatures elsewhere largely confirm what the government of the day wishes to achieve, for not to do so can cause a government to fall, triggering new elections.

In 1885, 28 years before he became the president of the United States, Woodrow Wilson wrote an analysis of "the essential machinery of power" in America and concluded "that, unquestionably, the predominant and controlling force, the center and source of all motive and regulative power, is Congress."[2] As the representative body that is expected to bring into government the wishes of the people, members of the House and Senate are elected to represent districts and states and thus to transport the preferences of the people who live there to Washington. With senators and representatives exercising powers delegated to them by the people, Congress was designed to be the government's most popularly legitimate institution.

And yet there is a long tradition of popular doubt and distrust regarding Congress. Woodrow Wilson was suspicious of congressional power. He thought Congress was too unwieldy, too unpredictable, and too interested in patronage and spending to produce good government. Many Americans have shared such misgivings. Though most citizens tend to support their own members of the House and Senate, they consistently express less confidence in Congress than in the presidency or the Supreme Court. In February 2012, only 11 percent

WHAT DO YOU THINK?

The Importance of Congress

In *Leviathan*, a great seventeenth-century work of political theory, Thomas Hobbes placed the king at the center of his vision of a stable political order. In the *Second Treatise of Government*, another great seventeenth-century text, John Locke placed the legislature at the center of his vision of a good political system. The United States, of course, has no king; but it does have a large and capable executive branch that is headed by the president. The country also has the globe's most independent legislature, the result of its separation of powers. From today's perspective, which of these works, Hobbes's or Locke's, contrasts the role of the executive with the role of the legislature most compellingly? Can the two perspectives be reconciled and combined?

of Americans approved of the job that Congress was doing (a decline from the prior year, when about a quarter of Americans expressed approval). In the wake of a raft of recent scandals—including the 2005 resignation of the Republican California House member Randy ("Duke") Cunningham, who pleaded guilty to accepting $2.4 million in bribes; the 2009 conviction of the former Democratic Louisiana House member William Jennings ("Bill") Jefferson on eleven counts of bribery; the 2010 money-laundering conviction of the former Republican House Majority Leader Tom DeLay, or the 2011 censure of the New York Democratic House member Charles Rangel, who was found by the House Ethics Committee to have raised funds improperly and to have failed to sufficiently disclose his financial operations—a July 2011 report found that 46 percent of citizens polled thought Congress to be corrupt. Almost nine in ten believed that members of Congress are more interested in advancing their own careers than in helping the country.[3]

This chapter probes this puzzling and paradoxical situation. Congress is the most open and accessible of the three branches of the federal government. Its elected members have to stay alert to shifts in the public mood. Their jobs depend on it.[4] Congress thus is often responsive to pressures from less privileged groups because, according to Elizabeth Sanders, its members are "bound to local constituencies," making them "exquisitely sensitive to the economic pain and moral outrage of their electorates."[5] Although both the presidency and Congress are more responsive to groups that have wealth and power, they often are attuned to hear different voices. Congress, according to the Founders, was supposed to represent local constituencies, while the president, in Thomas Jefferson's words, was "the only national officer who commanded a view of the whole ground."[6] Some members of Congress, of course, develop national concerns and followings. Before he retired in 2012, for example, the Democratic House member Barney Frank had responsibilities as a member of the House Finance Committee that extended far beyond the interests of his Boston suburb; and as the first openly gay member of Congress, he often articulated concerns of that large national constituency. Yet even individual members of Congress whose positions induce them to take on broad national concerns can never stray far from the particular **preferences** and interests of their districts and their electorates.

Why, then, is the public so skeptical about Congress and the legislative process? Of course, gridlock that produces an inability to get things done is an important source of public skepticism. So, too, is anger about specific public policies. But reservations and suspicions about Congress, we argue, are also a reaction to the uneven patterns of influence and political representation that affect how congressional procedures operate and what they produce.

Many people perceive these practices to be unfair. As the political scientists John Hibbing and Elizabeth Theiss-Morse write, "[T]he people believe they see processes that are not just, processes that are not equitable. A minority—the extremists, the special interests—are seen as having more access and influence than 'the people.' Lobbyists are in and ordinary people are out, so there is a clear injustice present."[7] The public often lacks respect for Congress because it appears to be captured by special interests that generously contribute to congressional campaigns, employ vast numbers of well-funded lobbyists to influence legislation, and enjoy special access to congressional members. Because they are more likely to vote, contact their senator or representative, donate money, and belong to interest groups, those who command wealth and organization are best positioned to take advantage of access to Congress. Congress tends to hear these people and groups more clearly than other Americans because their money, their votes, and their access amplify their voices.

What happens inside Congress, however, is not simply the work of outside forces that bring their influence to bear in the form of lobbying, campaign contributions, and election results. Senators and representatives come to office with their own beliefs and ideological orientations. They are not blank pads on which outside interests simply inscribe their views. Public policy, moreover, is also a product of the structure, rules, and procedures of Congress. The most important aspect of congressional structure is its division into two parts, the Senate and the House of Representatives. Each chamber of Congress represents different kinds of constituencies. The Senate represents states, which have broad and varied populations. Each state elects two senators. The six-year terms for senators are staggered so that only one-third of all senators face election every two years. The House of Representatives, by contrast, represents districts within states based on the size of their population. These smaller constituences tend to be less diverse. Though the entire House must stand for election every two years and is thus exposed as a body to electoral swings, two-thirds of the Senate is not up for reelection and, at any given moment, is more insulated from its voters. Electoral forces thus wind their way through the Senate more slowly than they do through the House. With only 100 members—compared to the House, which has 435—the Senate is a more intimate chamber, providing more latitude for action by individual members. In addition, because senators represent large, diverse constituencies, they must moderate their politics. Senators have to reach out and satisfy broader electorates, and that tends to push them closer to the political center than House members. Each chamber, moreover, is governed by its own formal and informal rules that affect how it considers laws, certifies appointments, conducts investigations, and removes officials from office.

To probe why a powerful and open legislature based on elections and representation is often judged harshly, this chapter reviews the origins and history of Congress, discusses patterns of congressional influence and the nature of the legislative process, considers the relationship of the House and Senate to the wider society, and examines the powers of Congress within the political system.

THE ORIGIN OF TWO LEGISLATIVE CHAMBERS

James Madison put the matter bluntly to the delegates at the Constitutional Convention in Philadelphia in 1787. The problem confronting them was to devise a political formula that would guard against the "inconveniences of democracy" in a manner that was still "consistent with the democratic form of government."[8] The Founders, who believed in sovereignty by the people, also were concerned that democracy would threaten the social order. They perceived their task as one of "preserving the spirit and form of popular government" while avoiding what experience under the Articles of Confederation had taught them was its consequence: that the majority would use their democratic rights to pursue their economic interests through the government—what many Founders condemned as "the leveling spirit" that could threaten the stability of the social order.

To protect the government against what the Founders perceived as the excesses of democracy, they created the presidency (as we saw in Chapter 6). But they did not stop there. The Founders also sought to check too strong a popular voice in the government by creating a legislature with two separate chambers: a House of Representatives, whose members would be elected by popular vote; and a Senate, whose members would be chosen by the various state legislatures. Without a Senate with two members for each state, moreover, small states and slaveholding states might not have ratified the Constitution, for these states gained protection for their interests by securing this form of assured representation.

It was widely assumed at the convention, the political scientist Robert Dahl has written, that a popularly elected House of Representatives with small districts and frequent elections "would be the driving force in the system; that the people's representatives would be turbulent and insistent; that they would represent majorities and would be indifferent to the rights of [elite] minorities; that the people would be the winds driving the ship of state and their representatives would be the sails, swelling with every gust."[9] The Founders also believed that the will of the majority expressed in the House of Representatives needed to be modified and checked by a Senate.[10] The House might be filled by commoners, but the Senate was to be composed of society's natural aristocracy: its wealthy, educated, cultivated elites.[11] Senators were not to be elected directly but were to be appointed by state legislatures that were presumed to be more favorable to mercantile, financial, and business interests than to the electorate as a whole. The Founders sought to further ensure the autonomy of senators by permitting them to serve for a term three times longer than that of members of the directly elected House of Representatives. The independence, character, and virtue of senators, the Founders believed, would stand as a bulwark against what they feared would be the irresponsible democratic tendencies of representatives. The Senate, in the words of George Washington, would be "[t]he cooling saucer into which the hot coffee from the cup of the House should be poured."[12]

The most enduring protection against democratic excess that the Founders worked into the Senate's design was the way seats in that chamber were to be apportioned. Each state, regardless of whether it was large or small, populous or barely inhabited, was entitled to two members in the Senate, no more and no less. This deliberate malapportionment, whereby voters in less populated states have greater representation in the Senate than voters in more populated states, violates democratic principles of political equality. Today, the 570,000 people in Wyoming, our least populous state, receive the same two votes in the Senate as the 38 million people who live in California, our most populous state. When the Senate is measured by the one-person-one-vote standard, the political scientist Arend Lijphart found it was the most malapportioned legislative body in the world. Forty percent of all U.S. senators together represent just 10 percent of the population; more than 80 percent of all senators come from states that together account for just one-half

WHAT DO YOU THINK?

The Senate's Role

The United States Senate was fashioned to cool the heat of popular pressures and demands and to slow down the legislative process to make it more deliberative, based on reason rather than emotion. Some will argue that it operates all too well, thwarting the wishes of the people by overrepresenting small states and by having rules, including the filibuster, that give a minority of senators the ability to block legislative progress. Others believe this situation leads to better lawmaking and gives minorities a welcome capacity to resist majorities. Which of these arguments do you find most persuasive?

of all Americans.[13] If they joined together, these 40 senators, plus just one more, could block any new law and stymie any treaty or presidential appointment by conducting a **filibuster**, using the Senate's rules for unlimited debate that a super-majority of sixty is needed to end. Not only is unequal representation greater in the Senate, but its effects are more meaningful. In other countries with two separate legislative houses, the chamber not based on population—such as the House of Lords in Britain and the Senate in France and Canada—is always the weaker of the two. By contrast, the U.S. Senate is never less than equal in power to the House of Representatives, and it even possesses powers not granted to the House, such as approving presidential appointments and foreign treaties.[14]

The inequalities between large and small states reflected in the Senate are not innocent.[15] For example, states with large urban populations are disadvantaged compared to states with smaller, rural populations. In addition, because racial minorities are concentrated in the most populous states, such as California and New York, those populations are the least well represented in the Senate. By contrast, the votes of white citizens in demographically homogenous, small states like Wyoming and North Dakota are given more weight.[16]

CONGRESS: PAST AND PRESENT

Since the House and Senate are independent of each other, each chamber must agree with the other on most matters for action to be taken and laws enacted. Over the course of American history, the relative power and significance of each has varied. The House of Representatives reached the height of its powers in the early years of the twentieth century, appearing to confirm the Constitutional Convention's conception of the House as the driving force of the government. The House's power lay in its structure, which was highly centralized and concentrated in the Speaker, who led the majority party in the House. Joe Cannon, Speaker of the House from 1903 to 1911, was considered by many to be even more powerful than the president. The Speaker led his party's caucus, which adopted a formal legislative agenda that was then passed by disciplined party majorities.

The House of Representatives thrived during this period of party government. But the centralization of power in the Speaker and his ability to provide effective leadership to the majority party in the House came at the expense of individual representatives, who were reduced to near impotence. The House of Representatives as an institution may have been powerful, but individual members outside the leadership enjoyed little of its power. By 1910, the rank and file of the House had rebelled and stripped Cannon of much of his power. Ironically, the big winner from this revolution inside the House of Representatives was the president. Party unity imposed by the Speaker once brought representatives together; now it gave way to the tug of diverse local interests that pulled them apart. With power now decentralized and the majority party unable to act in a disciplined fashion in support of a common program, it was easier for the president to seize the initiative and exercise legislative authority. Once the era of party government came to an end in the House of Representatives, the president assumed legislative leadership by setting the agenda of issues to be considered, offering policy proposals, and rallying public opinion.

The Senate, likewise, changed dramatically in the early twentieth century. Until 1913 its membership was chosen by the legislatures of each state rather than by popular election. That year, upon ratification of the Seventeenth Amendment to the Constitution, which stipulated that "the Senate of the United States shall be composed of two Senators from each state, elected by the people thereof," the Senate became a more democratic body. The elections of 1914, 1916, and 1918—each one selecting a third of the Senate—replaced appointed senators with elected senators.

The significant shift in the balance of power from congressional to presidential leadership began during Woodrow Wilson's presidency (1913–21). This trend accelerated through the New Deal of President Franklin Delano Roosevelt (1933–45). Elected in 1932 during the Great Depression, Roosevelt presented an ambitious program to address the crisis of the Depression in his first 100 days. Congress largely followed his lead. When Congress occasionally balked at taking presidential direction, Roosevelt went over its head and appealed directly to the public through press conferences and radio "fireside chats."

Into the 1960s, Congress's role was mostly subordinate to the presidency in initiating policy proposals and setting the agenda of government. Congress was content to let the president provide leadership and even encroach on congressional powers because it largely agreed with his policies. Having left the broad design of policy to the president and the executive branch, the role of Congress, according to Samuel Huntington, was "largely . . . reduced to delay and amendment."[17]

But the uneasy consensus on domestic and foreign policy that had existed in previous decades began to collapse in the 1960s. Racial issues, which had been kept off the domestic agenda to create the appearance of a satisfied consensus, exploded in the streets of Birmingham, on the roads of Mississippi, and in the slums of Detroit, Newark, and Los Angeles. Concurrently, college campuses erupted in protest to the war in Vietnam, shattering the prior consensus about foreign policy. Disagreements between the presidency and Congress soon were reflected in institutional combat between the two branches. By the late 1960s and early 1970s, Congress was appropriating funds for domestic programs that President Richard Nixon refused to spend, and Nixon pursued a covert war in Cambodia despite congressional action proscribing it. Moreover, **divided government**, in which different parties control the presidency and one or both houses of Congress, became the norm (Table 7.1). When government is divided between the parties, congressional leaders have more incentive to pursue agendas independent of the president.

TABLE 7.1

PARTY CONTROL OF CONGRESS AND THE PRESIDENCY

Year	Congress	President	Senate (100)	House (435)
2012	113th	D	D-55*	R-234
2011	112th	D	D-51**	R-242
2009	111th	D	D-60***	D-256
2007	110th	R	D-51****	D-233
2005	109th	R	R-55	R-232
2003	108th	R	R-51	R-229
2001	107th	R	D-51*****	R-221
1999	106th	D	R-55	R-223
1997	105th	D	R-55	R-228
1995	104th	D	R-52	R-230
1993	103rd	D	D-57	D-258
1991	102nd	R	D-56	D-267
1989	101st	R	D-55	D-260
1987	100th	R	D-55	D-258
1985	99th	R	R-53	D-253
1983	98th	R	R-54	D-269
1981	97th	R	R-53	D-242
1979	96th	D	D-58	D-277
1977	95th	D	D-61	D-292
1975	94th	R	D-60	D-291
1973	93rd	R	D-56	D-242
1971	92nd	R	D-54	D-255
1969	91st	R	D-57	D-243
1967	90th	D	D-64	D-247
1965	89th	D	D-68	D-295
1963	88th	D	D-66	D-259
1961	87th	D	D-64	D-263

*Two Independents in the Senate, Angus King of Maine and Bernard Sanders of Vermont, caucused with the Democrats.
**Two Independents in the Senate, Joseph Lieberman of Connecticut and Bernard Sanders of Vermont, caucused with the Democrats.
***Three Independents caucused with the Democrats, including Arlen Specter (R-PA), who switched to Independent status effective May 2009.
****Independent Senator Bernard Sanders (VT) gave the Democratic party a one-seat majority.
*****There were 50 Ds and 50 Rs until Senator James Jeffords (R-VT) switched to Independent status effective June 6, 2001; he announced that he would caucus with the Democrats, giving the Democrats a one-seat advantage.

Reasserting itself in the 1970s, Congress began to reclaim the authority it had ceded to the president. Congress tried to restrict the president's encroachment on the legislature's war-making powers through the War Powers Resolution of 1973. It matched the president's budgetary powers by revamping its own budgetary procedures, challenging claims of presidential prerogatives, scrutinizing presidential appointments more carefully, and altering the president's legislative proposals. A series of internal reforms initiated by House Democrats in the 1970s vested power in party leaders in the House of Representatives. The Speaker of the House; the House Majority Leader, who assists the Speaker in setting strategy; and the Majority Whip, who lines up votes among the party's rank and file, were empowered to promote goals supported by the Democratic House caucus.[18] Other reforms were geared to make Congress more open. Previously, committee chairs had been free to act as petty tyrants who ruled independently of their party's leadership—even of the majority sentiment of their own party's members. That era's reforms also prohibited hearings closed to the public and increased the number of subcommittees, with the aim of making it easier for the public to influence lawmaking and to make members of Congress more equal in power to one another.

The shift in power to the party leadership that began under the Democrats accelerated when Republicans became the majority in 1994 for the first time in forty years. Republicans had drafted a "Contract with America," a ten-point legislative program aimed at lowering taxes and reducing the size of the federal government, which they pledged to enact if elected. The new Republican Speaker of the House, Newt Gingrich, claimed the election victory was a mandate to enact the Republican agenda, even though polls revealed that most voters had never even heard of it. After a hiatus of 85 years, going back to Speaker Joe Cannon, party government had returned to the House of Representatives.

But this moment of party government was brief. President Bill Clinton successfully portrayed the House Republicans and their leadership as extremists willing to hold the government hostage if he did not capitulate to their demands to dramatically cut the scale of federal spending. A government shutdown in late 1995, when Congress refused to pass a budget advocated by the president, turned the public against the Republican House leadership and broke the party's momentum. With House Republicans on the defensive, the legislative initiative passed to the president once again.

After the traumatic attacks on the World Trade Center and the Pentagon in September 2001, the nation and Congress looked to President

George W. Bush for strong leadership. His administration's international and domestic agenda—including wars in Afghanistan and Iraq, as well as the Patriot Act, which dramatically widened the federal government's ability to conduct intelligence gathering within the United States by listening to phone calls, reading e-mails, and looking into medical, financial, and library records—tolerated few compromises. Congress increasingly was eclipsed as a site of policy innovation and decision making. Moreover, after Congress passed laws that the president had reservations about but did not want to veto, President Bush frequently issued signing statements. As discussed in Chapter 6, these written pronouncements may accompany new statutes and in some cases order the executive branch to implement the statute according to the president's interpretation of the Constitution. The effect is to either ignore or undercut some, or even most, of the law's provisions.

The first decade of the twenty-first century primarily was a period of **unified government**. In May 2001, Senator Jim Jeffords of Vermont switched his party affiliation from Republican to Independent. His decision to join the Democratic Party caucus erased the Republican majority, but it was regained in the election of 2002 and held through 2006, when the Democratic Party secured control of both chambers. With the election of President Obama in 2008, unified government was again in place. Under unified government, the Obama White House entered into more robust collaborative relationships with the majority in Congress in crafting the details of key legislation, including the stimulus package and health-care reform.

The 2010 elections, however, brought a return to divided government, with the Republican Party regaining control of the House and the Democrats retaining control of the Senate. The inability of both parties to compromise in passing the 2011 budget nearly resulted in a shutdown of nonessential government services in April 2011. Only after weeks of negotiations did the parties reach agreement, and a shutdown was avoided. Tensions between the parties also came to a head in the summer of 2011, with the possibility that the public debt of the United States would exceed its statutory maximum. Failure to increase the debt limit would have resulted in the U.S. Treasury's being unable to borrow money to pay its bills. House Republicans refused to raise the debt limit unless spending cuts were ordered. Only after a package of cuts to both domestic and defense spending was agreed to did the Budget Control Act of 2011 become law, in August, setting the stage for further confrontation about fiscal issues.

WHAT DO YOU THINK?

Unified or Divided Government: Which Is Preferable?

Some argue that the country does best when the same political party controls Congress and the presidency, because that pattern facilitates getting a legislative program accomplished. Others contend that a split in party control is better because it forces moderation. Which pattern is likely to better serve the public interest?

CONGRESSIONAL CAREERS AND THE ELECTORAL CONNECTION

Senators and representatives have desirable jobs. They are treated with respect, they have a chance to influence policy, they meet interesting people, and their work is varied and stimulating. Their salary in 2012 was $174,000 (the Speaker of the House earned $223,000, and the majority and minority leaders in the House and Senate earned $193,400). Members of the House and Senate also receive generous pensions (if they last at least five years in office), inexpensive life insurance, tax breaks (if they own two homes), allowances for their offices, almost unlimited mailing privileges, nearly free medical care, free parking, frequent trips abroad at government expense, and a large staff. But such benefits and a much higher salary are available also to high-priced lawyers and corporate managers in the private sector who hold just the sort of jobs many people leave to run for Congress. What being a member of Congress provides that cannot be found in the private sector is the capacity to act directly in shaping public affairs. The job, though constrained by pressures from constituents and organized interests, offers politically informed persons the chance to act on their belief that they will serve the public well. This is immensely satisfying.[19] So, too, is the deference accorded to members of the House and Senate. "The most seductive part of it," a congressman from the Midwest acknowledged, "is the deference. My God, it's amazing how many people can never seem to be able to do enough for you, here or when you go home. . . . Maybe I could and maybe I couldn't make more money in private business, but I do know this: I'd never have my ego fed half so grandly."[20] Or, as former Senator Larry Pressler from South Dakota commented regarding his return to private life after 22 years in Congress, "I feel like Cinderella after the ball. Poof! . . . Overnight my staff dropped from more than 100 down to one. My personal assistants disappeared into thin air. . . . Christmas season is an eye opener. The traditional flood of holiday cards has dwindled to about one-fourth of the senatorial level.

And speaking of cards, I now hand out business cards. United States senators don't do business cards. Everyone knows who they are."[21]

Some members of Congress who retire complain that the job of representative is not as rewarding as it used to be because of increased partisanship and gridlock, but there is no lack of applicants to replace them. The House and Senate continue to be filled with professional politicians who view their job in Congress as their career. Even those members promising to leave after serving for a certain number of terms frequently find the office so enticing that they want to extend their stay. The political scientist David R. Mayhew argues that the behavior of representatives and senators follows from the objective of getting reelected. In pursuit of this goal, members of Congress try to generate favorable publicity and claim credit for benefits that they bring back to their district.[22] In this respect, no one in Congress has matched the late Senator Robert C. Byrd of West Virginia—the longest-serving member in the chamber's history—in the amount of federal projects, many of them bearing his name, he directed to his state. There is the Robert C. Byrd Courthouse in Charleston, the Robert C. Byrd National Aerospace Education Center in Bridgeport, and the Robert C. Byrd Locks and Dam at Gallipos Ferry, as well as health clinics, highways, bridges, and academic buildings that also bear the Byrd name and were paid for in whole or in part with federal money.

In the first presidential debate of 2008, the Republican candidate, Senator John McCain, strongly opposed such **earmarks** (the practice of inserting authorization for a specific project in a bill), referring to them as a "gateway drug . . . to out of control spending and corruption." Although not all members of Congress support the pork-barrel politics of earmarking, the Arizona Republican has been in the minority on this issue. When Senator McCain offered an amendment in 2009 that would have stripped an omnibus appropriations bill of some 9,000 earmarks, his proposal was defeated 63 to 32. Among his fellow Republicans voting with the majority was Senator Lindsey Graham of South Carolina, who told reporters, "I think I should have the ability as a United States Senator to direct money back to my state as long as it is transparent and it makes sense."[23] The house banned earmarks in 2010, and the senate followed suit in 2011, but some continue under different names.

The **electoral connection** between voters and Congress is not only based on what members do for their constituencies as a whole. It is also based on how members of Congress intervene in the various bureaucracies to solve individual constituents' problems with Social Security, passports, immigration, veterans' benefits, and other matters. More and more members of Congress, according to the political scientist Morris Fiorina, prefer "to be reelected as an errand boy than not be reelected at all."[24] One House member told Richard F. Fenno, Jr., who studied what representatives did back in their local districts, "This is a business, and like any other business you have to make time and motion studies" to determine what activities are most electorally rewarding.[25] Because the first order of business is to stay in business by getting elected, representatives develop what Fenno called a "home style," calculated to make members identify with voters in their district.

Of course, the most important job of a member of Congress is lawmaking. But before they can participate in passing legislation, they have to secure their relationship with their constituents, and that has come to require money . . . lots of money. The success of candidates for Congress depends in no small part on how effective they are at generating campaign funds. In 2012, the average cost of running a House race was nearly $1.8 million, and for a Senate race over $810 million (Table 7.2). In the hotly contested Massachusetts Senate

TABLE 7.2

MOST EXPENSIVE CONGRESSIONAL RACES, 2012 ELECTION

Senate

1	Massachusetts Senate	$75,455,498
2	Connecticut Senate	$65,734,337
3	Texas Senate	$56,129,666
4	Ohio Senate	$43,803,630
5	Pennsylvania Senate	$38,293,109
6	Missouri Senate	$37,374,430
7	Virginia Senate	$35,766,253
8	Wisconsin Senate	$34,634,331
9	Florida Senate	$30,660,356
10	Arizona Senate	$23,774,097

House

1	Missouri District 06	$25,098,137
2	Florida District 18	$24,214,733
3	Ohio District 08	$21,806,896
4	Connecticut District 05	$12,868,694
5	California District 33	$10,270,462
6	New York District 27	$8,715,835
7	Illinois District 08	$8,593,232
8	Virginia District 07	$8,579,224
9	Illinois District 10	$8,509,217
10	Texas District 33	$8,404,445

SOURCE: Center for Responsive Politics, "Most Expensive Races," Amount Raised, at www.opensecrets.org (accessed October 8, 2012); based on data released by the Federal Elections Commission on December 19, 2012.

race of that year, Republican Senator Scott Brown and his successful challenger, Elizabeth Warren, each spent over $35 million. Across the country, in 2012, the candidate who raised the most money won 95 percent of the time in the House, and 80 percent of the time in the Senate. The high cost of running is often prohibitive to new challengers, and it helps assure that many races remain uncompetitive. In 2010, 7 percent of House elections went uncontested, and 45 percent of incumbents won with more than a 30-point margin.

As Will Rogers quipped in 1931, "It takes a lot of money to even get beat nowadays."[26] In comparison, when Abraham Lincoln ran for Congress in 1846, he returned all but 75 cents of the $200 supporters had raised, reporting that "I did not need the money. I made the canvass on my own horse; my entertainment being at the houses of friends, cost me nothing; and my only outlay was seventy-five cents for a barrel of cider, which some farm-hands insisted I should treat them to."[27] Candidates today need to raise so much money not because they want to, but because they are afraid not to. Today, campaign fund-raising follows the same logic as an arms race: incumbents and challengers alike try to build up their arsenals and raise more money to prevent their opponent from gaining a financial advantage. Fear ratchets up the cost of campaigns to higher and higher levels. Most of these funds are spent for television advertisements designed to enhance name recognition and image rather than discuss substantive issues. "Half the money you spend in a campaign is wasted," admitted one old-time politician. The only problem is "you just don't know which half."[28]

The sheer cost of running for office has many consequences. The need to raise money gives donors privileged access to members of Congress. The list of congressional donors is very long, and it reflects local as well as national interests. The leading donor to the Senate Democratic Majority Leader Harry Reid's election coffer of over $25 million between 2007 and 2012 was a Las Vegas casino, a key industry in his home state of Nevada. The Senate's Republican Minority Leader,

WHAT DO YOU THINK?

Congressional Campaign Finance

Given how expensive congressional elections are, can you think of alternatives to the current system of financing campaigns that would make American democracy work better? Should there be restrictions on levels of spending? Should campaign financing come from public rather than private funds? Do campaign-finance regulations restrict or promote free speech?

Mitch McConnell of Kentucky, in turn raised $25.7 million between 2007 and 2012, including tens of thousands from his state's energy companies and legal firms. Money, though, often flows into a representative's or senator's campaign coffers from beyond the district or state he or she represents. Senators Reid and McConnell raised funds from health professionals, real-estate investors, and securities and investment firms from around the country. Three of Senator Reid's top five leading donors during the 2007–12 cycle were law firms, particularly law firms representing asbestos victims. Many of the top donors to Senator McConnell's coffers came from international banks. Interest groups contribute money to members of the House and Senate who sit on committees and subcommittees with jurisdiction over policy areas and issues that affect them. Most of these sources of funds are unknown to the average voter, and most of them help lobbyists gain access to Congress on behalf of issues that are of narrow concern to a particular group.

Congressional candidates are on the circuit continuously, asking for money, attending fund-raisers, and appealing to lobbyists. It usually does not matter whether a member of Congress has a safe seat and faces only token opposition or won by a narrow margin in the last election and can expect another close contest. Either way, the member will be out raising money relentlessly. Before he was selected as the Republican candidate for vice president in 2012, Wisconsin's Paul Ryan had raised $4,976,000 to secure reelection to the House.

Massachusetts senator Elizabeth Warren after winning the Democratic primary for Senate candidate in June 2012. Warren raised over $35 million in her successful campaign.

Money is particularly critical to making a race more competitive when an incumbent seeks reelection in a district where the challenger has a reasonably good chance to begin with. Incumbents have many advantages: voters have good reason to back them because they have experience at their jobs, and their seniority makes them more likely to influence legislation in ways that benefit their constituents. But there is a direct relationship between the amount of money challengers raise and their chances of meaningfully competing. Without sufficient funds, few challengers can escape obscurity and get known sufficiently to be recognized by voters.[29] The fund-raising advantage incumbents enjoy explains, in part, why such a large proportion of them win and why most congressional elections are not really competitive.[30] While members from competitive seats raise money to hold off capable rivals, those from safe seats build up war chests to discourage opponents. Most of the time, they succeed.

Elections are mechanisms designed to hold Congress accountable to the voters. In 1787, George Washington endorsed the two-year term for members of the House of Representatives, expecting its membership would turn over rapidly. Power, he wrote in a letter to his nephew Bushrod Washington in November 1787, "is entrusted for certain defined purposes, and for a certain limited period . . . and, whenever it is executed contrary to [the public] interest, or not agreeable to their wishes, their servants can and undoubtedly will be recalled." Washington's expectation has not been borne out. In the nineteenth century, congressional turnover was very high; in 1870, more than half of the representatives sent to the House were newly elected. But by 1900, new members comprised less than one-third; by 1940, less than one-quarter; and by 1988, less than one-tenth. Congress has become a career in which representatives and senators expect to serve long tenures. Even in relatively high-turnover congressional elections—like those of 2006 and 2008, in which the Democratic Party made significant gains, recapturing control of the House and Senate by gaining 31 seats in the House and 6 in the Senate in 2006 and netting a further 21 seats in the House and 8 in the Senate in 2008—only 23 incumbents lost their bid for reelection, including 4 who lost their primary battle. In 2010, when the Republicans regained control of the House for the first time since 2006, incumbents did not fare as well, with 58 incumbents failing to win their reelection bid. Still, although the percentage of incumbents reelected was less than in 2008 (when 94 percent of incumbents were reelected in the House), 85 percent of incumbents were reelected in the House in 2010 despite the fact that the 2010 House ousted more incumbents than any since 1948. Further, only 4 of the 25 senators seeking reelection lost their bid in 2010. In the 2012 election, over 90 percent of incumbents were reelected in both the House and Senate. In Figure 7.1, we can see the substantial job security members of Congress enjoy.

FIGURE 7.1

PERCENTAGE OF INCUMBENTS SEEKING REELECTION REELECTED TO CONGRESS

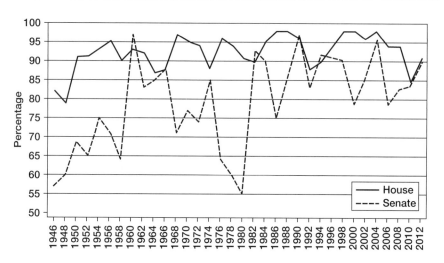

New blood is more likely to arrive in Congress by winning open seats in which the incumbent is not running than by defeating a sitting member seeking reelection. Incumbency is a powerful electoral asset because incumbents enjoy an enormous financial advantage over their opponents. In addition, incumbents have access to perquisites such as mailing privileges and staff with which to contact and serve voters back home, and they come from districts that have been carefully drawn to include voters already disposed to vote for members of their party.

When elections become mere rituals, turnout can decline, voters become cynical, and representatives feel less accountable. Senate elections tend to be more competitive because the incumbency advantage in the Senate is less powerful than in the House. Senate incumbents face more-experienced, better-financed opponents, and their statewide constituencies are large enough that one party does not dominate them so clearly, as is often true in smaller House districts.

MEMBERS OF CONGRESS

The ideal representative body mirrors the population as a whole. John Adams, the second president of the United States, once said that the legislature should be "an exact portrait in miniature, of the people at large."[31] No legislature in the world, of course, has the exact demographic profile of the citizens its members represent. Nor is perfect symmetry necessary for the interests of the population to be represented. But a disproportionately unrepresentative legislature is likely to leave many members of the population without representatives who even minimally comprehend their life situations and needs, while those who are overrepresented are likely to have their views taken into account as a matter of course.

It is emphatically *not* the case that just because someone comes from a certain social background, he or she will promote the interests of that group: former car dealers in Congress will not always promote the interests of car dealers, and wealthy members of Congress will not necessarily defend the interests of the rich. For example, Senator Jay Rockefeller of West Virginia comes from a very wealthy family, yet he has been among the leading advocates of social programs for the poor. Similarly, a white member of Congress can do a very good job representing a black-majority district, as Steve Cohen of Memphis, Tennessee, has been doing in the House since 2007; and a black member of Congress can do a good job representing a state where whites significantly outnumber blacks, as Barack Obama did for Illinois after his 2004 election to the Senate.

The effects of social background on congressional decision making are subtler than that. The social background of members of Congress is important because they bring assumptions to their work based on their life experiences. Those experiences mean that they are likely to be sensitive to, perhaps intuitively aware of, some issues more than others. Consequently, it matters whether the social backgrounds of members of Congress are roughly similar to those of the people they represent. It is certainly true that members of Congress, like all of us, are able to appreciate and understand issues outside their own limited experience. But they may have to make an extra effort not to gravitate naturally to the issues they are familiar with based on their life experiences. See Table 7.3 for a demographic breakdown of the 113th Congress.

It is ironic that Congress, our most democratic institution, is so demographically unrepresentative. Congress does not look like America. It contains a much higher proportion of white, male, educated, rich, and professional people than the population as a whole. Congress is less male and less white than it used to be, but the proportion of women and minorities in Congress still differs strikingly from that in the rest of the population. For example, blacks comprise 12 percent of the electorate. In the Congress that convened in 2013, they occupied 9 percent of the seats in the House, and one Senate seat (after South Carolina governor Nikki Haley appointed Representative Tim Scott to succeed the retiring Jim DeMint). Hispanics are 10 percent of the electorate, and they occupied 6 percent of the seats in the House and only 2 percent of all

TABLE 7.3

DEMOGRAPHIC COMPOSITION OF THE 113TH (2013–2014) CONGRESS*

	House	Senate
Gender**		
Male	352	79
Female	80	20
Race/Ethnicity		
White	348	95
Black	41	1
Hispanic	33	3
Asian	9	1
Native American	2	0
Religion***		
Christian	391	86
Jewish	22	10
Muslim	2	0
Buddhist	2	1
Hindu	1	0
Unspecified/Atheist	9	2
Age		
Born before 1980	428	99
Born after 1980	4	0

*These numbers represent the 435 voting members of the House and the 100 voting members of the Senate.

**Three members of Congress resigned their seats before the start of the 113th Congress. Also, Sen. Daniel Inouye, an Asian-American Senator from Hawaii, died shortly before the start of the 113th Congress. Successors have yet to be appointed or elected so these Congressman were omitted from the calculations.

*** Data for religious affiliation came from the Pew Research Center's Forum on Religion and Public Life, based on races called as of November 16, 2012. Congressman who have since resigned or who have since died were removed from the calculation.

Senate seats. Women make up 52 percent of all eligible voters, and they made up about 18 percent of the seats in the House and 20 percent in the Senate. Such imbalances have policy consequences. Female and minority representatives bring unique perspectives to Congress. Their underrepresentation means that the concerns of minorities and women are neglected.[32] Not only is Congress unrepresentative of the American people with respect to race, ethnicity, and gender, but a great gap exists in class position as well. The vast majority of members of Congress are lawyers, bankers, or business people. Very few people from working-class occupations are ever seated.[33]

Members of the Congressional Hispanic Caucus conduct a news conference on immigration reform in November 2012.

In circumstances marked by targeted fund-raising and campaign spending, as well as higher turnout among affluent voters (who have a greater ability to mobilize and command attention), it is harder for the less well represented to be heard. Recent research by the political scientist Larry Bartels compared the responsiveness of U.S. senators to the preferences of constituents who are wealthy, middle class, and poor. "In almost every instance," he concluded in a study of **roll call voting** in the House and Senate regarding government spending, abortion, civil rights, and the minimum wage, "senators appear to be considerably more responsive to the opinions of affluent constituents than to the opinions of middle-class constituents, while the opinions of constituents in the bottom third of the income distribution have *no* apparent statistical effect on their senators' roll calls."[34]

REALIGNMENT AND POLARIZATION

During the past four decades, two especially noteworthy changes in congressional membership have occurred. There has been a dramatic change to patterns of partisanship in the South, and a growing polarization has come to characterize the relationship between the Democratic and Republican parties. These developments are closely related.

The civil rights movement precipitated an electoral realignment in the South, which shifted its partisan sympathies from Democratic to Republican. In 1960, before the great civil rights struggles of that decade, the southern delegation included only six Republican members in the House and no Republican members in the Senate. Since then, Republicans have become dominant in southern congressional elections, and they now comprise a significant majority of the southern House and Senate delegations. In the 113th Congress, which began to serve in January 2013, 85 of the 116 southern House members were Republican, as were 18 of the 22 southern members of the Senate (Figure 7.2).

The result of this transformation in southern political representation has been a growing polarization between the two parties in Congress. Southern Democrats today are more liberal and more likely to vote with their party than were their Democratic forebears.[35] Southern Democrats have become national Democrats. By contrast, southern Republicans are among that party's most conservative members. The radical growth in their number has moved the Republican congressional party to the right. Southern Republicans "form an almost monolithic bloc" across a wide range of issues in Congress and score higher on conservative tests of ideological purity than do nonsouthern Republican legislators.[36]

FIGURE 7.2

PROPORTION OF SEATS HELD BY DEMOCRATS IN ELEVEN SOUTHERN STATES

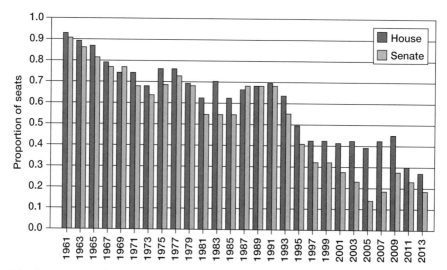

*Southern states include Alabama, Arkansas, Georgia, Kentucky, Louisiana, Mississippi, North Carolina, South Carolina, Tennessee, Texas, and Virginia.

With the replacement of most southern Democrats (the least partisan and least ideological group of legislators) by southern Republicans (the most partisan and most ideological group of legislators), the parties have grown increasingly divided and are characterized by an "incredible shrinking middle," as one senator referred to the decline of moderates in Congress.[37] Further, there has been a dramatic decline in the presence of Republicans in the Northeast. In 2013, there were no Republican members of the House from the New England states. In 1960, 27 out of 43 members of the House from New York State were Republicans. After the 2012 election, this number was 6 out of 27. The now dominant northern liberal wing of the Democratic Party has acted as a pole of attraction, pulling southern Democrats in the House to the left; at the same time, the southern conservative wing of the Republican Party has acted as a pole of attraction pulling the rest of the GOP to the right, a process that has been enhanced by the rise of the Tea Party's influence within the party.

The division between Republicans and Democrats has grown considerably. The average Democrat, who tends to represent urban areas populated with ethnic and racial minorities, has become more liberal on social and economic issues during this period. Meanwhile, the average Republican, who tends to represent more rural and suburban districts, has become more conservative. The political differences *within* the parties have declined, and the political differences *separating* the parties in Congress have grown. In both the House and the Senate, parties have become more cohesive and more polarized.

Two leading scholars of the ideological positions of members of Congress, Keith Poole and Howard Rosenthal, have tracked the degree of polarization in Congress over the course of the country's history. They have created a scoring system, known as NOMINATE, that places members of Congress in an ideological position based on their roll-call-voting pattern (Figure 7.3). The system puts the scores together by party, so it is possible to see how the parties diverge, over time, from the median ideological position (scored as zero) in a conservative (scored as positive) or liberal (scored as negative) direction, thus giving us a visual image of an increasing pattern of polarization in both the House and the Senate.

The regional and ideological circumstances in Congress thus are very different today from what they were even at the start of the Clinton administration in 1993. Then, southern members were still an important force in the Democratic Party, whereas today they constitute only about 16 percent of the party's members in the House and just 8 percent of its senators. For Republicans, southerners have become more dominant. Despite some losses in the two most recent elections, southern Republicans in 2013 made up

FIGURE 7.3

NOMINATE SCORES FOR HOUSE OF REPRESENTATIVES AND SENATE, 1947–2011

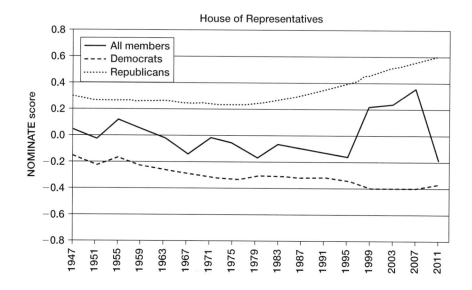

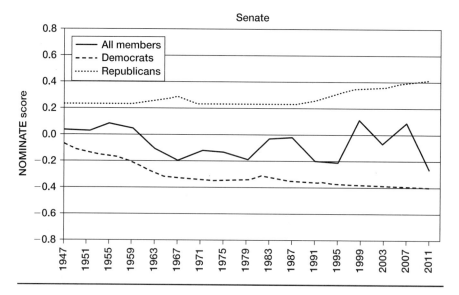

SOURCE: Poole and Rosenthal figures, available at http://voteview.comlpmediant.htm (accessed October 8, 2012). The figures for "All members" represent the NOMINATE score of the median member.

37 percent of the party's membership in the House and 41 percent in the Senate. As we have seen, these changes have ideological consequences. Presently, even the least liberal Democrats in Congress, the Blue Dog Coalition, are significantly less conservative than the bloc of more conservative Democrats that President Clinton had to deal with. And in the Republican Party, virtually all the moderates have disappeared.[38]

As a result of this mounting divergence between the parties, politics in Congress has become more divisive, and the impact of the political parties on congressional voting has increased. Partisan voting, in which a majority of Democrats vote against a majority of Republicans, is now more evident, as is the degree of party discipline.[39] A by-product of this partisan identification and conflict has been a greater centralization of power in the hands of party leaders. They control their party caucuses and the course of legislation by deciding whom they assign to committees, by rewarding the most loyal, by controlling access to the floor for legislation that committees advance, and by promoting roll-call behavior that either supports or opposes the president in as uniform a way as possible. All these levers of control have been enhanced by increasing ideological likeness within each party. When members of the majority party agree on policy, strengthening party leaders increases the chances that the majority's policy goals will prevail.[40]

Growing polarization also has an affinity with campaign contributions by issue-oriented groups. Since 1990, advocates of gun rights have contributed $29.3 million to congressional campaigns, of which $25.3 million has been directed into Republican coffers. By contrast, gun-control proponents have given $2 million, of which all but $100,000 has gone to Democrats. In the same period, of campaign donations to congressional candidates by individuals and groups relating to abortion policy alone, totaling $34.5 million since 1990, $21.8 million has gone to Democrats (98 percent on the pro-choice side) and $12.7 million to Republicans (95 percent on the pro-life side).[41]

THE LEGISLATIVE PROCESS

The legislative process begins with the submission of a bill to both the House and the Senate by a member or members of those chambers. Most bills are introduced without any expectation of success, often to appeal to particular groups of constituents. More than 6,000 pieces of legislation are introduced into Congress each year, and fewer than 400 actually have a chance of passage. Only members of the Senate and the House may submit bills. When legislators introduce a bill in Congress, they often are acting on behalf of constituents, interest groups, a federal agency, the president, or even their own personal convictions.

The quest for money, the social background, the patterns of electoral connection, and the ideological commitments of members of Congress all influence what they do when legislation navigates the labyrinth of formal and informal rules that govern congressional decision making. But the fate of legislation often is determined not only by these matters, or by the content of the legislation itself, but by how a bill moves through the legislative process, thus by the procedures and rules under which the Senate and House consider a bill. The route by which a proposed law seeks to get enacted shapes its prospects. For that reason, Representative John Dingell of Michigan reportedly said, "If you let me write the procedure and I let you write the substance, I'll [beat] you every time."[42]

Although each member of Congress has only one vote, some members are more powerful than others. Legislators have different amounts of power depending on which committee they sit on, whether they are a committee or subcommittee chair, whether they are a member of the majority party, and whether they are a party leader. The procedures and rules of the House and the Senate determine the powers invested in these positions and are never neutral. Some groups win and some groups lose, depending on how the rules distribute power within Congress.

The bills that have the greatest chance of success and that generally define the agenda of Congress are those submitted by legislators on behalf of the president. The Office of Management and Budget (OMB), together with the congressional liaison staff in the Executive Office, coordinates the executive's legislative efforts. The OMB acts as a clearinghouse, reviewing legislative requests from federal agencies and departments to ensure they conform to the president's program, while the legislative-affairs officers in the White House coordinate presidential lobbying of Congress.

Once a bill is introduced in the House and the Senate, it is sent to a committee for consideration. Most committees dealing with the substance of public policy mirror Cabinet agencies. Farm bills go to the House Agriculture Committee and the Senate Agriculture Committee, tax bills go to the House Ways and Means Committee and the Senate Finance Committee, and so on.[43] These referrals made by the House Speaker and Senate Majority Leader thus are generally routine. When issues cut across existing committee lines, Senate and House leaders have more discretion in referring bills to committee. This could affect the bill's chances of success because a legislative proposal might receive a warmer reception in one committee than in another.

Congress at work, Woodrow Wilson once said, is Congress in committees. Committees are legislative gatekeepers, "little legislatures," that perform the bulk of the legislative work in Congress. They collect information through hearings and investigations, they draft legislation in what are called markup sessions that go over the bill line by line to find the desired wording, and they report legislation to the floor of their respective chambers.[44] More than 90 percent of all bills submitted to Congress do not make it out of committee.

Once a bill leaves the committee, it is placed on the House and Senate calendars. In the House, the Rules Committee determines which bills will come to the House floor, when they will be scheduled, and under what conditions they will be debated. Such rules can put up obstacles or ease a bill's path to passage. Whereas the ratio of members on congressional committees from the majority party to those from the minority party ordinarily reflects the ratio in each chamber, the ratio on the Rules Committee tilts much more heavily toward the majority party, allowing it to control the flow of legislation on the floor of the House.

The rules under which the House considers legislation began to change in the 1970s. Previously, legislation often came to the House floor under open rules from the Rules Committee with no restrictions on germane amendments. But as the House became more partisan and divided after the 1980s, both parties when they enjoyed a majority on the Rules Committee began attaching increasingly restrictive rules to more and more legislation. Such rules have limited the time for debate and the amendments that can be offered on the floor of the House; approximately three in four bills now coming out of the Rules Committee prohibit amendments.

The Senate has no equivalent committee to schedule and set the terms of debate on the floor. Scheduling is largely the work of the Senate Majority Leader, but he or she requires **unanimous consent** to bring a bill up for Senate consideration. Individual senators who want to prevent passage of a bill can filibuster—that is, hold the Senate floor and not give it up until the offending bill is removed from consideration—unless 60 members vote to end debate. Usually, the threat of a filibuster, rather than an actual extended debate, is used to make it impossible to pass legislation unless a supermajority of sixty senators is prepared to vote for the bill. Such votes to end a filibuster most often take place on partisan lines, with neither party enjoying a 60-seat majority. Nor does the Senate limit and set the terms of debate on the Senate floor, as the Rules Committee does for legislation considered by the House. The rules of the Senate are much more freewheeling than those of the House.

Taken together, these various rhythms and traits produce different patterns of representation in each chamber. Members of the House are more likely than senators to work hard on behalf of local interests that reflect the makeup of their district, whether they be requests by farmers for better subsidies, by businesses who want less regulation or higher tariffs to restrict overseas competion, or by unions in their constituencies wishing to make it easier to organize workers. Senators, representing larger constituencies with all kinds of crosscutting pressures, tend to be more attuned to the demands of large groups that operate at the level of the states or the nation as a whole. In that way, they serve as more of a bridge between Congress and the president. Over time, however, the differences between the character of representation in the two chambers have been reduced because the size of House districts has grown. Since 1928, the size of the House of Representatives has been fixed at 435 members (plus five nonvoting representatives). In 1928, the average size of each House district was 275,000 persons; today, it is just over 700,000.

Even when the versions of a bill introduced in both the Senate and the House are the same, they may look very different after they come out of the committee process in both chambers. House and Senate committees mark up a bill without conferring with each other, and amendments to the draft that emerges from committee and is debated on the floors of the House and the Senate result in very different versions in the two chambers. As a result, the version of the bill passed by the House may differ considerably from the one passed by the Senate. The president can sign into law only bills that have been passed in identical form by both houses of Congress. Differences between the House and Senate versions of the bill are resolved in conference committees. **Conference committees**, composed of House and Senate members selected by the House Speaker and the Senate Majority Leader, respectively, meet to reconcile differences in the versions of a bill passed by the two chambers. If the conference committee can resolve the differences between the House and Senate versions of the bill, the new, reconciled version of the legislation is then sent back to the House and the Senate to be voted up or down, without amendment. If both houses vote to accept the conference report—that is, to accept identical versions of the bill—the final bill is then sent to the president. The bill becomes law if the president chooses to sign it; or it becomes law without the president's signature ten days after the president receives it, provided Congress is still in session. However, the president may choose to veto the bill. In that case, the veto can be overridden by two-thirds votes in both the House and the Senate, and the bill becomes law without the president's signature, a development that happens only rarely.

This legislative process is noteworthy for the number of choke points, or opportunities to block legislation, that it contains. "It is very easy to defeat a bill in Congress," President John F. Kennedy once observed. "It is much more difficult to pass one."[45] A bill may be waylaid at the subcommittee and committee levels; it may never be scheduled for consideration on the floor of the Senate or the House; it may fail to pass either the Senate or the House; a conference committee may not be able to reconcile differences between Senate and House versions of the bill; the Senate or House may find the conference bill objectionable; the president may veto the legislation; and the Senate and House may be unable to marshal the two-thirds majority necessary to overturn a presidential veto. And all of these potential choke points must be successfully negotiated within the two-year life span of a single Congress, or else the measure has to be reintroduced and the whole procedure repeated again when a new Congress is seated.

Following passage of a campaign-finance-reform bill in the Senate in 2001, Senator John McCain of Arizona, one of its principal sponsors, warned of the many dangers still ahead: "I think this is a victory, but I want to emphasize, I have no illusions about the House [of Representatives], about a conference, about the White House. We've just taken the first step, and as we enjoy this moment, tomorrow we'd better fully understand that we've got a long way to go."[46] His warning was prophetic, at least in the short term. That year, the campaign-finance-reform bill passed in the Senate but later died in the House. In 2002, the Bipartisan Campaign Reform Act, sponsored by senators McCain and Russell Feingold of Wisconsin, did successfully overcome procedural roadblocks and became federal law. But with the decision taken by the Supreme Court in 2010 in *Citizens United v. Federal Elections Commission*, which prohibited the government from limiting political spending by corporations and unions, spending on elections again skyrocketed.

A legislative process loaded with many points where new legislative proposals can be stopped is not politically neutral, but broadly serves to protect the status quo. The legislative process puts innumerable roadblocks in the way of those who seek to use the government to bring about change. Groups that are systematically disadvantaged and depend on political power and public policy to offset their lack of power in the marketplace often find themselves stymied by a legislative process that creates so many opportunities for blockage and defeat. They must build winning coalitions within both the House and the Senate at the committee level, on the floor of each chamber, at conference, and then within the executive branch. Opponents, on the other hand, need to win only once at any level to defeat the bill. A legislative process that creates so many opportunities for obstruction, that promotes failure rather than success, makes it difficult for the disadvantaged to enlist public power against corporate private power.

The procedures of Congress, its rules of the game, are constantly in flux as groups seek to adjust them and thus advance their interests. Political struggles about rules vitally affect prospects for legislative outcomes. Congress frequently reforms itself as legislators seek to change the process by which legislation is made in order to change the results. The most important of such recent rules changes concerns what is known as the **reconciliation** process, a procedure that was created mainly to deal with how the federal budget is approved.

The president submits a budget for the coming fiscal year. After amending it, Congress either passes a budget resolution or fails to, depending on whether majorities in the two houses can agree on the same resolution. If they do, the resolution is not signed by the president, because it is not a law; rather, it acts as an authorizing guideline for subsequent appropriations (which are signed into law by the president). Created by the Congressional Budget Act of 1974, reconciliation was first designed as a narrow procedure to bring revenue and spending under existing laws into conformity with the levels set in the annual budget resolution by directing various committees to develop legislation that is consistent with its priorities. A reconciliation bill follows these instructions. When it is reported out, the legislation is limited to 20 hours of debate in the Senate (ten hours on the conference bill) and thus cannot be blocked by a filibuster.

Over time, the use of this procedure has extended to major substantive law-making. During the Reagan presidency, reconciliation was employed to cut social-welfare spending. Later, in the Clinton years, reconciliation was deployed by Democrats to successfully reverse many of President Reagan's cuts to the welfare state, particularly Medicaid. President Clinton failed to overcome the objections of Senate stalwart Robert Byrd to using the reconciliation strategy for his comprehensive health-care reform in 1993. But in 1996, Clinton and a Republican Congress successfully used reconciliation to pass welfare reform; and in 1997, they amended Medicaid to create SCHIP, a health-care program for children. President George W. Bush and congressional Republicans later used reconciliation to pass nearly $1 trillion in tax cuts during his administration, and the Obama administration utilized the procedure to pass health-care reform.[47]

Overall, the legislative process is so daunting that Congress deviates from it quite often to avoid gridlock. According to the congressional scholar Barbara Sinclair, unorthodox lawmaking has become routine as Congress increasingly circumvents its own procedures. Committees are bypassed more frequently; bills are now more likely to be reworked after they emerge from committee; the content of legislation is more likely to be worked out in summits among executive and legislative leaders; and omnibus legislation, in which disparate bills are offered together in one legislative package, is now more common. Sinclair argues that it is no longer accurate to speak of one legislative process; rather, there are many.[48] The legislative process has become a maze in which bills may now take many different paths through Congress on the way to enactment.

Legislating, though, does not exhaust what Congress does. When we considered the presidency, we observed that the president manages the federal bureaucracy but that Congress creates it. Each new federal agency originates with an act of Congress, which describes what the agency is supposed to do and provides the funding to do it. Congress is usually quite vague in its legislative instructions for agencies because it cannot anticipate all the contingencies an agency might encounter, and because Congress hopes to avoid criticism and controversy by not being too specific. As a result of this delegation, agencies have a great deal of discretion in interpreting the mandate they receive from Congress. Thus, to help ensure that federal agencies interpret and implement the law as the legislature intended, Congress engages in **oversight** of the bureaucracy.

As government has grown, Congress has come to spend more time on oversight, especially during periods of divided government, when the party opposing the president is less sure that the executive branch will act in ways that reflect the legislature's preferences. Oversight is performed by congressional subcommittees and committees, which review the activities of agencies under their jurisdiction. They hold hearings at which members of Congress remind agency heads that Congress is the boss, that they get their appropriations from Congress, and that Congress expects deference from them.

SEEKING INFLUENCE

This maze and this pattern of oversight, combined with the reforms that made Congress more open to scrutiny and influence, have had the ironic effect of exposing the complicated legislative process to special interests that have the ability to fund **lobbying** efforts. The very openness of Congress to the social forces outside it means that the diversity and inequalities of the larger society are reflected within it. Those with the most political resources outside of Congress are in the best position to take advantage of Congress's accessibility, to cultivate relationships with its members, committee and subcommittee chairs, and party leaders. The legislative process is scrutinized carefully by a small army of lobbyists who seek to influence legislation. Spending on lobbying is immense, and it has been increasing by leaps and bounds. In 1998, total spending on lobbying reached $1.4 billion. In 2012, lobbying by companies, unions, and other interest groups cost $2.45 billion, as 12,016 registered lobbyists performed their work. Some special interests have their own in-house lobbyists, and the majority hire specialized lobbying firms located in Washington, D.C. (many of them on K Street).

Inasmuch as business has more political resources than other groups, it can best take advantage of Congress's openness to influence the legislative process. When the political scientists Kay Lehman Schlozman and John T. Tierney examined interest-group presence in Washington, they found that 70 percent of all the organizations represented in their sample were either businesses and trade associations or law and public-relations firms hired by corporations to represent them in Washington.[49] The largest Fortune 500 companies were the best represented. They maintained their own lobbying arms in Washington, were members of their industrial trade group, and participated in peak organizations like the Business Roundtable. Moreover, the Washington corporate office was no longer a dumping ground where corporate executives placed their incompetent relatives to keep them out of harm's way. To the contrary, managers of corporate public-affairs departments gained status within the corporate hierarchy. The *Wall Street Journal* found "the post of government-affairs executive has taken on added luster. A tour through the government-affairs department can be a quick route to the top."[50] Indeed, many corporate lobbyists are former government officials who can offer their new employers privileged access to former government colleagues and knowledge of agency or congressional procedures. Almost one-third of all retiring members who had served in the previous Congress and Cabinet-level officials from the departing Clinton administration signed with lobbying or government-relations firms during the Bush administration. A comparable process is at work today.

Compared to other interest groups, business is the most organized, hires the most lobbyists, has the most contact, and devotes the most money to influencing policy makers. Between 1998 and 2012, labor unions spent $528 million on lobbying. By contrast, the finance, insurance, and real-estate sectors of the economy spent over $5.2 billion, a sum nearly matched by health-insurance and pharmaceutical companies. In 2012, the biggest spender on lobbying, the U.S. Chamber of Commerce, spent $95.7 million. Single companies also spend princely sums to influence legislative outcomes. Notable examples include Blue Cross/Blue Shield, at $16.2 million; General Electric, at $15.6 million; and Google, at $14.4 million.[51]

Lobbying firms often employ or are headed by former influential governmental officials. Former Louisiana Senator John Breaux joined with former Senate Majority Leader Trent Lott to form a lobbying firm. Former aides to elected representatives also often go on to form lobbying firms. Chuck Brain, a former Clinton White House Director of Legislative Affairs and a longtime

WHAT DO YOU THINK?

Pressure-Group Lobbying

Lobbying, it is thought, provides legislators with information about the interests that care about bills, about the content of legislation, and about the intensity of preferences among members of the public. Yet lobbying, it also is thought, twists the democratic process out of shape by giving too much influence to those with the most vested interests. How can lobbying be made more fair and more effectively democratic? Would the legislative process be better if there were no lobbyists at all?

staffer at the House Ways and Means Committee, went on to serve as a lobbyist at Capitol Hill Strategies, Inc. Former New York Republican Senator Al D'Amato similarly went on to found his own lobbying firm. These firms emphasize the lobbyist's connections to insiders. For instance, the website of D'Amato's firm states the following: "Park Strategies cultivates influential and beneficial relationships through our years of experience and involvement with government and private sector industries. Our relationships, combined with our unprecedented resources, support and expertise, are the key factors to moving our clients successfully towards their business objectives."[52]

Lobbying is a sophisticated, multifaceted operation that requires an extraordinary amount of money to be effective. Following the lead of Microsoft, Google and Facebook are also active in hiring lobbyists.[53] In 2011, Google spent nearly $10 million in lobbying. Facebook too has rapidly accelerated its lobbying activities, especially with respect to privacy issues, online piracy, and restrictions on Internet access by foreign governments. In 2011, Facebook spent almost $1.4 million on lobbying—an 85-percent increase over the prior year. Facebook also expanded its Washington, D.C., presence by hiring former George W. Bush Deputy Chief of Staff Joel Kaplan as its Vice President of U.S. Public Policy. Such lobbying efforts cost companies tens of millions of dollars, much more than their opponents who lobby for public-interest groups can afford to match. But this expense pales in comparison to what industry trade groups spend to influence policy. The pharmaceutical industry has more registered lobbyists than there are members of Congress. When they go to work, they often find themselves lobbying former colleagues because more than one-half of all drug lobbyists are either former members of Congress or former staff members. Thomas A. Scully, who ran Medicare for President Bush, left government soon after Medicare reform passed to take a job with a law firm that represents companies in the health-care industry. Tom Daschle, the former Senate Majority Leader, a Democrat from South Dakota, lost his seat in 2004 and then went on to earn about $5 million over the course of the following four years, largely by consulting for health-care industries.[54]

There is no guarantee, of course, that efforts to secure influence will achieve the intended results; but frequently they do. Consider the passage in the House of Representatives of a comprehensive climate bill in late June 2009. The *New York Times* reported that the bill "grew fat with compromises, carve-outs, concessions, and out-and-out gifts intended to win the votes of wavering lawmakers and the support of powerful industries" that had lobbied hard to revise the legislation. The result "would funnel billions of dollars in payments to agriculture and forestry interests. Automakers, steel companies, natural gas drippers, refiners, universities, and real estate agents all got in on the fast-moving action."[55] The cumulative impact of these concessions—including the largest, which guaranteed that utilities could continue to build and operate coal-burning power plants without incurring new costs—sharply reduced the environmental impact of the legislation aimed at dealing with global warming.

CONCLUSION

In an ideal democracy, society is made up of equal interests, pursuing their own political goals, and government responds in an evenhanded way. The representative qualities of Congress—sharpened by regular elections, open hearings and procedures, and visible forms of debate—make the national legislature more responsive to public participation than do the bureaucracies of the executive branch or the Supreme Court. But political representation is contested on an uneven playing field. Few groups can match Microsoft or PRMA in the amount and variety of resources devoted to lobbying public officials. Few can donate substantially to political campaigns. Few can mobilize press attention. Even fewer can develop close ties with individual members of Congress.

Representation thus tends to be genuine and profound yet deeply uneven. The very structure and rules of Congress, and the multiplicity of pathways by which a bill becomes a law, can become sources of uneven advantage in gaining access and influence. Further, given the power of incumbency, the need to raise money to inhibit challengers, the polarization of the parties, and the fact that members of Congress are drawn largely from—and responsive to—the higher strata of society, it is no wonder that so many Americans judge Congress harshly. Many citizens are disaffected because they do not see their backgrounds, ideas, or their wish that a broad public interest be served reflected in congressional affairs. The local representation they get is often skewed to the most vocal, the best off, the leading interests. Yet these are not the only influences. Members of Congress and their constituents have preferences and goals that often are shared, and no member can afford to simply represent the powerful while needing the support of a majority. The politics of power in Congress thus are tense, charged, and contradictory. And the stakes are high.

CHAPTER SUMMARY

Introduction

Congress is both the most accessible branch of the federal government and the one that often scores highest in public distrust. This paradox is explained by how influence is wielded and why many Americans believe these patterns are not fair.

The Origin of Two Legislative Chambers

The Constitutional Convention, concerned that it was necessary to protect the country from excessive democracy, created a Senate that gives each state, large and small, two seats and that elects its members to serve for six-year terms. It also created a House of Representatives, whose members serve two-year terms and are intended to more directly reflect popular preferences.

Congress: Past and Present

The strength of Congress compared to the presidency, and the relative abilities of each house to legislate, has changed over the course of American history. Such changes are often a result of key procedural reforms; but they are also the product of the kinds of issues that come to the fore at any given moment, and of how much power Congress is willing to delegate to the executive branch.

Congressional Careers and the Electoral Connection

Members of Congress are almost constantly running for reelection or raising large sums of money to do so. Elections are designed to hold Congress accountable to voters. Election campaigns are expensive and thus tilt influence in the direction of those capable of funding them. In an age of polarization, most incumbents are reelected, therefore making the process less competitive than in the past.

Members of Congress

The social backgrounds of members of the House and Senate imperfectly reflect those of the population as a whole. They are unrepresentative with respect to gender, ethnicity, race, and class. Very few members come from working-class backgrounds.

Realignment and Polarization

Two closely related changes have altered the congressional landscape. The southern states, which persistently voted Democratic before the civil rights revolution, have increasingly supported conservative Republicans. In turn, each party has moved away from the political middle and from each other: Democrats, on average, have become more liberal; and Republicans, on average, are now more conservative.

The Legislative Process

The complex labyrinth any proposed legislation must navigate before becoming a law contains many choke points and opportunities to block legislation, thus favoring the status quo and providing many ways to influence the results.

Seeking Influence

The very openness and complexity of the congressional process make it possible for those interests with the most resources to sway how the legislature acts by organizing active and expensive lobbying campaigns. The number of lobbying firms has recently grown rapidly. They tend to specialize by party and by subject.

Critical Thinking Questions

1. What role has the South played in lawmaking at different moments in American history? How and why has this role been distinctive?

2. Why are American citizens so often skeptical about Congress and the work it performs?

3. How important are political parties in shaping the legislative process?

4. Does it matter when members of the House and Senate are different in class, race, and gender from the voters they represent?

Suggested Readings

E. Scott Adler and John Lapinski, eds., *The Macropolitics of Congress*. Princeton, NJ: Princeton University Press, 2006.

Robert A. Caro, *Master of the Senate: The Years of Lyndon Johnson*. New York: Random House, 2003.

Thomas G. Mann and Norman J. Ornstein, *It's Even Worse Than It Looks: How the American Constitutional System Collided With the New Politics of Extremism*. New York: Basic Books, 2012.

Keith T. Poole and Howard Rosenthal, *Congress: A Political-Economic History of Roll Call Voting*. New York: Oxford University Press, 2000.

Elizabeth Sanders, *Roots of Reform: Farmers, Workers, and the American State, 1877–1917*. Chicago: University of Chicago Press, 1984.

Eric Schickler, *Disjointed Pluralism: Institutional Innovation and the Development of the U.S. Congress*. Princeton, NJ: Princeton University Press, 2001.

Steven S. Smith, Jason M. Roberts, and Ryan J. Vander Wielen, *The American Congress*, 6th ed. New York: Cambridge University Press, 2009.

Charles Stewart III, *Analyzing Congress*. New York: W. W. Norton, 2001.

THE COURTS

INTRODUCTION

Everything about the case was unusual, and the stakes could not have been higher. Normally the Supreme Court gives lawyers for the plaintiff and defendant a half hour each to present their arguments and answer questions from the justices. But in this instance the Supreme Court scheduled six hours of oral argument, extended over three days. The Court typically hears oral arguments only in the morning. But on the last day of hearings it scheduled an unusual doubleheader, holding oral arguments in the morning and then reconvening for another round in the afternoon. The mood at Court is normally subdued, and exchanges between lawyers and justices tend to be dull. But in this case the atmosphere was electric, and exchanges between justices and attorneys were sharp and intense. On average, the Court receives about a dozen friend-of-the-court briefs, in which interested parties who are not directly involved in a case submit their legal opinions regarding it. But on this occasion, the Court received over a hundred such briefs—the most that a single case had generated in over 40 years—from sources as powerful as the AARP (formerly the American Association of Retired Persons) and as obscure as the Montana Shooting Sports Association. Normally the Court doesn't release transcripts of oral arguments until the end of the week. But in deference to the intense interest generated by the case, the Court changed its rules and released transcripts at the end of each day. The Court did, however, stick to its tradition of prohibiting the use of electronic devices in the courtroom, which meant no phones, no tablets, and no cameras. This led to the unusual scene of reporters dashing out of the chamber to describe what was happening inside, as if they were in some black-and-white movie from the 1950s or time travelers from the classic era of television.

The day on which the Supreme Court delivered its opinion—June 28, 2012—was just as extraordinary as the events leading up to it. People had been lined up outside the building since the night before—as if they were camped out for World Series or Beyoncé tickets—to be sure they would get a seat when the doors opened. One thousand opponents and supporters of the issue before the Court paraded outside with signs amid tourists, belly dancers, and people dressed like the Statue of Liberty, creating a raucous and festive atmosphere. Reporters from around the world jostled with one another as they awaited the Court's decision.

Nothing in the dull title of the case signaled its importance: *National Federation of Independent Business et al. v. Sebelius, Secretary of Health and Human Services, et al.* Yet nothing less than the constitutionality of the Patient Protection and Affordable Care Act—popularly known as Obamacare—was at stake. The case involved whether Congress and President Obama had exceeded their legal authority in enacting a law that required individuals to purchase health insurance. Obamacare was President Obama's most significant domestic achievement, and his legacy now depended on whether a majority of the Court found it constitutional.

Betting on how the Court would rule had shifted dramatically since the Court first heard oral arguments back in March. Three-quarters of the gamblers now predicted the Court would rule that the law was unconstitutional, whereas just two months before two-thirds of them bet that the Court would uphold the law.

The frenzy and confusion continued even after the Court issued its ruling. In an embarrassing moment reminiscent of the 1948 presidential election, when newspapers jumped the gun and incorrectly printed headlines announcing that Thomas E. Dewey had beaten Harry Truman, both Fox News and CNN initially issued inaccurate reports that the Court had overturned the law.

In fact, by a 5-4 decision the Court ruled that the Affordable Care Act, including its individual mandate that virtually all Americans buy health insurance, was constitutional. Five justices agreed that the penalty incurred if someone did not buy health insurance was the equivalent of a tax, something that Congress has the constitutional authority to impose. Moreover, a majority of justices held that the legislation did not actually require individuals to purchase health insurance, as people could always decide to pay the penalty instead.

The Supreme Court interprets the Constitution, the supreme law of the land, and its judgment is final. "We are under a Constitution," Chief Justice Charles Evans Hughes once remarked, "but the Constitution is what the judges say it is."[1] Those fortunate to be at Court when Chief Justice John G. Roberts, Jr., read the majority decision in the Affordable Care Act case were reminded of this as they entered the Supreme Court building. Above a bronze statue of

Chief Justice John Marshall (1801–35) in the building's Lower Great Hall, his remarks from the *Marbury v. Madison* (1803) decision are etched in marble: "It is emphatically the province and duty of the judicial department to say what the law is."[2] The principle of judicial review, that the courts are the law's final arbiter, was asserted as late as 2000 in *Dickerson v. United States*, when Chief Justice William Rehnquist wrote, "Congress may not legislatively supersede our decisions interpreting and applying the Constitution."[3]

The power of **judicial review** permits the courts to nullify or overturn any federal, state, or public law that conflicts with the Constitution—just as opponents were hoping the Court would do to Obamacare. By means of judicial review, the courts have invalidated state laws mandating segregation, presidential orders depriving alleged terrorists of their constitutional rights, and laws making it a federal crime to carry guns near schools.

The power of the courts is reflected not only in judicial review but also in the extraordinary independence granted federal judges. They are appointed to life terms, cannot have their salaries reduced, and cannot easily be removed from office. Consequently, they do not have to decide cases or tailor their decisions to suit donors, interest groups, voters, or even presidents. When Justice Antonin Scalia was asked whether he felt pressure from President Obama to uphold his health-care law he responded, "No. What can he do to me? Or to

Supporters of the Affordable Care Act demonstrate outside the Supreme Court during the hearings for the case in 2012.

any of us? We have life tenure. And we have it precisely so that we will not be influenced by politics, by threats from anyone."[4] Federal judges are protected from political retribution, so they are free to issue rulings without worrying about how their decisions might affect their careers.

Yet for all the judiciary's power and prestige, leading political observers have pointed to its limitations since the founding of the Republic. When John Jay resigned as the first Chief Justice to become Governor of New York, President George Washington offered the job first to Alexander Hamilton and then to Patrick Henry. Both dismissively turned it down. Hamilton stated his contemptuous view of the Court's powers bluntly: "Of the three powers . . . the judiciary is next to nothing."[5] He described the courts as the "least dangerous branch," having "no influence over either the sword or the purse; no direction either of the strength or of the wealth of the society." That is, the courts may rule on a case but must depend on other branches of government to implement their decision. For example, when President Andrew Jackson disagreed with a Supreme Court ruling, he reportedly snickered, "[Chief Justice] John Marshall has made his decision, now let him enforce it."[6] The Founders' lack of regard for the judiciary is also evident in where it appears in the Constitution. The judiciary is discussed in Article III after Congress and the presidency, and the Founders devoted half as many words to describing its powers as they did to the presidency in Article II, which itself is half as short as the description of Congress's powers in Article I.[7]

The courts are also hindered by a lack of democratic legitimacy. Unlike presidents or members of Congress, federal judges are appointed, not elected. Consequently, they cannot appeal to election results as the reason citizens should obey their decisions. Instead, Justice Tom C. Clark explained, "We have to convince the nation by the force of our opinions."[8] Finally, the courts are at the mercy of the other branches of government for their budget, staff, and jurisdiction. Their dependence on the other branches of government weakens the courts in relation to them.

The powers and limits of the courts place them in creative tension with the other branches of government. Nowhere was this more evident than in the conflict that pitted the courts against Congress and the president regarding the war on terror. The Supreme Court rejected President George W. Bush's claims that his power to detain terrorist suspects was not subject to judicial scrutiny, that military tribunals established to try suspects did not have to conform to domestic law, and that the president could detain American citizens without informing them of the charges against them. Legal pressure led to the release of over three-quarters of the suspects imprisoned at Guantanamo Bay, and to the recognition of the rights and improvement of the conditions of those who remained. The executive branch was forced "to clean up its act in order to appear more reasonable in court."[9]

Another source of tension for the courts is managing their role as both legal and political institutions. As legal institutions, the courts are supposed to be guided by precedent in neutrally and passively interpreting the law. Judges are supposed to be objective; they must not issue rulings designed to satisfy whoever is in power or to reflect their own personal beliefs. For example, Justice William J. Brennan privately opposed abortion, but he helped draft *Roe v. Wade,* the decision that decriminalized it. He was reluctant to hire women as law clerks but supported equal rights for women in his Supreme Court rulings, and although he was often enraged by the press's irresponsibility, he nevertheless defended freedom of the press in his decisions.[10] Chief Justice Roberts articulated the view of the courts as legal institutions at his confirmation hearings when he told the Senate Judiciary Committee, "Judges and justices are servants of the law, not the other way around. Judges are like umpires. Umpires don't make the rules; they apply them."[11]

But, in practice, judges are more than umpires. Through their decisions, they do make rules; and thus courts act as political as well as legal institutions. If the rules were always clear, there would be no need for judges to resolve differences over their meaning. And like other political actors, judges can't avoid bringing their own values to work or being influenced by the world outside their chambers when they issue rulings. The courts' legitimacy depends upon judges being courageous enough to resist the pull of public opinion and election results and yet wise enough to take them into account.

The courts' relationship to equality is similarly ambiguous and conflicted. On the one hand, the law is an arena of equality: the same rules apply to everyone, whether white, black, or brown; rich or poor; man or woman. No one is above the law. Justice is supposed to be blind. On the other hand, formal, legal equality is compromised when it operates in a society marked by racial, class, and gender inequalities. For example, individuals on death row are poor, almost to a person—not because rich or middle-class individuals never commit murder but because wealthy defendants can afford to hire high-priced lawyers to represent them, whereas poor suspects must depend on overworked and underpaid public defenders.

Finally, whether the law protects or threatens elites is also hard to pin down. On the one hand, the law may be dismissed as mere pretense, composed of false promises and pretty phrases behind which elites enforce their domination. But the formal framework of rights and procedures provided by the law creates tangible resources that ordinary people can draw upon to make claims on the rich and the powerful.[12] It is the law under the Constitution that grants people freedom of speech and assembly, that protects citizens from unreasonable search and seizure, and that requires the government to follow certain procedures when charging them with crimes. And ordinary citizens can appeal to the law in asserting these rights, as civil rights activists did in the 1960s, and as those imprisoned without due process did during the Bush administration's war on terror.

This chapter is organized differently from previous ones covering the presidency and Congress. Rather than beginning with a historical introduction, it starts by describing how the court system is organized. It then explores judicial power and weakness, and the tension between the courts as legal and political institutions. Finally, it clarifies how the law can both promote equality and offer an illusion of it, and be both a balm for the strong and a resource for the weak.

A DUAL COURT SYSTEM

If we are to understand the judiciary's many ambiguities, we need first to understand how the courts are organized.

The United States has a **dual court system**: state and federal systems of justice exist side by side. Each of the fifty states, as well as the federal government, maintains its own system of courts. The federal-court system has three tiers. At its base are 94 district courts, where full trials are conducted: witnesses are examined, testimony is taken, and exhibits are entered into the record. Most federal cases begin and end here. But litigants unhappy with a district-court decision can appeal to the next level, the court of appeals. There is one court of appeals for each of the United States' 12 judicial circuits, which have jurisdiction over several states. Most cases are heard on appeal from district courts by panels of three judges (rather than by a single judge, as at the district level). Only about one in ten cases makes it to this level. Finally, at the top of the federal-court system stands the Supreme Court. It is the court of last resort; there is none higher.

Federal courts hear about 400,000 cases each year. But this is less than 2 percent of the total U.S. caseload. State courts handle all the rest. "For most Americans," John Schwartz writes, "Lady Justice lives in the halls of state courts."[13] In 2010, about 100 million cases were filed in the nation's 15,500 state and local courts. They ranged from civil cases involving traffic infractions and custody disputes to criminal cases involving murder and rape. Given the amount of litigation at the state level, it is no surprise that about 90 percent of all people in prison, as well as 99 percent of those on death row, have been convicted in state court.

States are free to organize their courts as they please, name them as they wish, and establish their jurisdictions as they see fit.[14] Many states' court systems are modeled on the federal system, but others are not. Some states have only two levels of courts, with no intermediate or appeals court as in the federal-court system. Another important difference between federal- and state-court systems is the method of selecting judges. Federal judges are appointed by the president subject to confirmation by the Senate, whereas 87 percent of all state judges are elected. The appointment of judges is hard to reconcile with democratic theory, because judges selected in this manner are not accountable to voters.

But electing judges, as is the practice in 39 states, entails its own risks, which may compromise judicial legitimacy. Running for office is costly, and becoming a state-supreme-court judge has never been more expensive. Campaign contributions in state-supreme-court elections reached $38.4 million, an all-time high, in 2010. As the cost of campaigning increases, judges may be tempted to rule in favor of lawyers or litigants who contribute to their campaigns. John Grisham's recent novel *The Appeal* (2008), in which a chemical company receives a favorable ruling from a judge in return for campaign contributions, is (unfortunately) ripped straight from the headlines. In West Virginia, one member of the state's supreme court sat in judgment of a company after receiving $3 million in contributions from one of its executives.

Electing judges also tempts candidates to curry favor with the public. Two political scientists found that judges up for reelection tended to give harsher sentences in order to display their law-and-order credentials to the public.[15] In addition, judges running for office sometimes try to attract voters by pledging to rule in certain ways in future cases. Such pledges contradict the idea that judges are impartial: that they are guided by laws and not their own views, and that they will rule on the merits of the case and not to attract votes.

An incident that occurred in Iowa reveals the chilling effect elections can have on judicial decisions. In 2009, the Iowa state supreme court decided unanimously that same-sex marriage was legal. The American Family Association in Tupelo, Mississippi, which opposes same-sex marriage, provided almost all the funding for a local Iowa organization to campaign against the three judges running for reelection. The judges refused to campaign and defend themselves against the negative ads broadcast against them, arguing that to do so was

WHAT DO YOU THINK?

How Should Judges Be Selected?

What is the best process for selecting judges? Electing judges, as is done in many states, has the virtue of permitting citizens to hold judges accountable for their decisions. At the same time, however, the pressure to raise money for election campaigns or to issue popular decisions may taint judicial independence. Appointing judges to life terms, as is done at the federal level, may have the opposite effects. It promotes judicial independence at the expense of accountability. Which process do you prefer: the way many states elect judges, or the federal system of appointing them?

unseemly and would politicize the judiciary. All three lost. While removing the judges didn't change the law in Iowa, it intimidated other judges, who now have reason to fear that their decisions in controversial cases might attract outside money to prevent their reelection. This was evident in 2012, when state judges who had never campaigned before were out raising money to defend themselves from looming super-PACs that could write large checks with the intent of defeating them. One group tracking judicial elections at the state level described donating to judges' campaigns as "the single best investment in American politics" because "[a] few big spenders can really have an outsize effect."[16]

The United States has a federal system of government that reserves some powers to the states, which have their own laws, constitutions, and courts. But where does state law end and federal law begin? Take the case of marijuana use. According to the federal Comprehensive Drug Abuse Prevention and Control Act of 1970, it is a crime to manufacture, distribute, dispense, or possess substances such as marijuana. But in 1996, California approved by referendum the Compassionate Use Act, which permits the use of marijuana for medicinal purposes. After the law passed, Diane Monson, who suffered from severe chronic pain, was prescribed marijuana by her physician. Her condition improved dramatically, but in 2002 agents of the U.S. Drug Enforcement Administration (DEA) raided her home and confiscated her stash. Monson sued in state court for an injunction to prevent the federal government from enforcing drug laws that apply to the use of marijuana for medicinal purposes. California, not Congress, should rule in this area, she claimed. The case made it all the way to the Supreme Court (*Gonzalez v. Raich* [2005]), which ultimately upheld the federal government's authority to prohibit the local cultivation and use of marijuana under its power to regulate interstate commerce.

As a result of the Court's ruling, the federal government can still prosecute patients who consume marijuana for medicinal purposes, but the California law did not completely go up in smoke. It still offered marijuana users protection from prosecution by state authorities. Because 99 percent of all marijuana arrests are by local police officers and not by DEA agents, California has a thriving business of marijuana production and distribution for medicinal use, offering the drug by prescription.[17] In 2012, Colorado and Washington went one step further than California and legalized marijuana for recreational use. But citizens in those states, like those in California, would still be subject to arrest by federal agents for using or selling marijuana, even though it is legal under state law.

THE FEDERAL COURT SYSTEM

Each tier of the federal-court system—district, appellate, and Supreme—plays an important policy making role. District courts, readers may recall, are trial courts, where the record and facts of a case are established. Following the trial, judges apply the law to the case at hand. Because the Supreme Court typically restricts itself to articulating general principles, district-court judges enjoy broad discretion in applying Supreme Court rulings and deciding which rulings apply to which cases. For example, in *Brown v. Board of Education of Topeka, Kansas*, which outlawed state-sanctioned racial segregation in public schools, the Supreme Court did not fix a date for ending segregation but instead instructed the district courts to "act with all deliberate speed." But many district courts in the South reflected the region's opposition to *Brown* and used their discretion to forestall desegregation. Consequently, ten years after *Brown* only 1 percent of all southern black children were in nonsegregated schools. The district courts acted with "entirely too much deliberation and not enough speed," according to Justice Hugo Black, in requiring southern school districts to comply with the Court's ruling.[18]

Courts of appeals (see Figure 8.1 for the jurisdiction of different courts of appeal) also are important policy makers. Most of their decisions are final, because the Supreme Court denies 98 percent of the petitions it receives to review appeals-court decisions. Where appellate courts hear more than 28,000 cases a year, the Supreme Court normally hears fewer than 100. Consequently,

FIGURE 8.1

COURTS OF APPEALS CIRCUIT BOUNDARIES

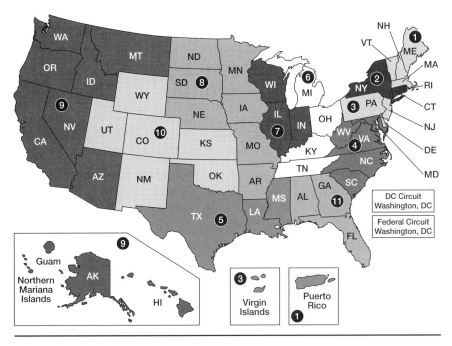

SOURCE: Robert A. Carp and Ronald Stidham, *The Federal Courts*, 2nd ed. (Washington, DC: CQ Press, 1991), 18.

federal appeals courts usually have the final say in most matters of law. One important difference, however, between the Supreme Court and courts of appeals is that decisions by appellate courts apply only to the specific states covered by the deciding court, whereas Supreme Court decisions apply to the entire country. For example, in 2009 the Ninth Circuit Court of Appeals in San Francisco ruled that the Constitution's Second Amendment protecting the citizens' right to bear arms applied to the states, while the Seventh Circuit Court of Appeals in Chicago found that it did not. This left citizens in Alaska, Arizona, California, and other western states covered by the Ninth Circuit Court with the right to bear arms despite state laws outlawing them, whereas citizens in Illinois, Indiana, and Wisconsin, who were under the jurisdiction of the Seventh Circuit, had to respect local laws limiting guns. The issue was finally settled in 2010 when the Supreme Court ruled that local laws limiting guns are in fact trumped by Second Amendment guarantees on the right to bear arms.

More recently, appellate courts issued contradictory rulings with regards to the constitutionality of the Obama administration's signature piece of legislation, the Patient Protection and Affordable Care Act of 2010. The Eleventh Circuit Court of Appeals in Atlanta ruled that the law's mandate requiring people to buy health insurance was unconstitutional. The Sixth Circuit Court in Cincinnati and the D.C. Circuit Court both disagreed, ruling that the law was constitutional because Congress did not exceed its power to regulate commerce by requiring people to buy insurance.

When federal appeals courts disagree, the Supreme Court often takes the issue up and renders a decision that applies nationally to all federal courts. As described in the beginning of this chapter, the Supreme Court in 2012 ultimately upheld the law (although on grounds different from those the Appeals Courts had used to sustain it).

Article II of the Constitution empowers the president to nominate federal judges, subject to the "advice and consent" of the Senate, meaning that the Senate must vote to approve judicial appointments. Appointments to the federal bench are especially consequential because federal judges have lifetime tenure. Unlike an administration's legislative successes, which can be undone in the next Congress, a president's judicial appointments have a long-term and enduring effect. Lifetime tenure of federal judges permits presidents to leave a legacy regarding how laws are interpreted. As Table 8.1 reveals, President Ronald Reagan was very successful at leaving his stamp on federal courts, appointing

TABLE 8.1

PRESIDENTIAL LEGACIES ON FEDERAL COURTS

President	Appointed to Supreme Court	Appointed to Courts of Appeals*	Appointed to District Courts†
Johnson (1963–69)	2	40	122
Nixon (1969–74)	4	45	179
Ford (1974–77)	1	12	52
Carter (1977–81)	0	56	202
Reagan (1981–89)	3	78	290
Bush (1989–93)	2	37	148
Clinton (1993–2001)	2	66	305
G.W. Bush (2001–09)	2	62	261
Obama (2009–June, 2012)	2	30	121

*Does not include the U.S. Court of Appeals for the Federal Circuit.
†Includes district courts in the territories.

half of all federal judges by the time he left office. Because federal judges enjoy lifetime tenure, the courts tend to lag behind other political institutions and act as a drag on political change. Judges appointed by long-departed presidents may continue to issue decisions for decades based on values that have long since been repudiated by voters at the polls.

As the courts have become more active in recent years, setting policy in areas such as abortion, guns, and religious practice, the selection process of federal judges has become more public, divisive, and intense. Under President Ronald Reagan, for the first time in American history White House aides were involved in screening the credentials of potential judges.[19] Under President Clinton, the White House staff did not participate in the selection of judges as actively as its predecessors had, nor were his appointees as liberal as his predecessors' were conservative.[20] Yet despite selecting a politically moderate group of judges, the Clinton presidency was marked by a dramatic increase in Senate scrutiny of judicial nominations. When Republicans gained control of the Senate in 1994, the average time to confirmation for a nominee to federal district and appellate courts more than doubled.

When George W. Bush became president, he moved quickly and aggressively to follow the same strategy that Reagan had adopted. Bush announced that he would no longer consult with the American Bar Association (an impartial organization of distinguished lawyers) on judicial appointments, as past presidents had done. Rather, judicial appointments would be reviewed by a White House team that would seek advice from the Federalist Society, a group of conservative legal jurists, lawyers, and academics. This resulted in Bush's submitting a list of extraordinarily conservative and highly controversial nominees for Senate confirmation. Democrats proceeded to filibuster and prevent consideration of some of Bush's nominees in the same manner that Republicans had obstructed Clinton's appointments. But the Bush administration's efforts to remake the judiciary in its own conservative image proceeded apace. By the time Bush left office in 2009, he had appointed 40 percent of all sitting federal judges. Bush's judicial appointees were regarded as "the most conservative on record," especially in the area of civil liberties and rights.[21]

The Obama administration has been assertive in diversifying who sits on the bench. President Obama nominated a higher percentage of ethnic minorities and women than any other president. Forty-four percent of Obama's appointments were women, almost a quarter were black, and his nominees included a higher percentage of Asians and Hispanics, as well. "The President wants the federal courts to look like America," explained White House Counsel Kathryn Ruemmier.[22]

But a recurring problem for Obama's administration has been the number of vacancies on the courts. The Constitutional Accountability Center complained in 2011, "Never before has the number of vacancies risen so sharply and remained so high for so long." Obama left 82 vacancies unfilled at the end of his first term, almost three times more than the 29 openings Bush left after his first term. At first, the Obama administration was slow to nominate judges. Later, Congress was slow to confirm them.[23] In Obama's first term, it took, on average, seven months for judicial candidates to go from nomination to confirmation—much longer than an average of just one month under President Reagan. Senate Republicans placed "holds"—threats to filibuster—on many of Obama's nominees, thus preventing the Senate from ever voting on them. Even judges who were not particularly liberal were blocked by Republicans.

THE SUPREME COURT

At the top of the judicial system is the Supreme Court. The late Justice Robert H. Jackson said that judgments by members of the Supreme Court are "not final because we are infallible; we know that we are infallible only because we are final."[24] The Court receives the vast majority of its cases from the federal district and appellate courts. As Table 8.2 reveals, many more cases are filed with the Court each year than it has the time or inclination to hear. The number of petitions the Court receives has increased while the number of cases the Court

TABLE 8.2

U.S. SUPREME COURT CASES FILED AND DISPOSED: 1980–2011

Action	1980	1990	2000	2005	2007	2008	2009	2010	2011
Total cases on docket	5,144	6,316	8,965	9,608	9,602	8,966	9,302	9,066	8,952
Cases argued	154	125	86	88	75	87	82	86	75
Number of signed opinions	123	112	77	69	67	83	77	83	65

SOURCE: U.S. Census Bureau, "The 2010 Statistical Abstract," at www.census.gov/compendia/statab/2010/tables/lOs0322.pdf (accessed March 17, 2010). For 2007–2010 statistics see www.uscourts.gov/uscourts/statistics/judicial.business/2011/appendices/aoisept11.pdf. For 2011 statistics see scotusblog.com (accessed July 1, 2012).

actually decides has declined. In 2011, the Court received 8,952 petitions but agreed to fully review only 75 of them, and it issued only 65 signed opinions, the fewest in recent memory. The Court carefully chooses its cases, applying what is called the **rule of four**. That is, the Court will consider only those cases that at least four justices consent to hear.[25] The Supreme Court does not consider cases involving trivial issues, regardless of how consequential they may be for the parties involved. Nor is the Court concerned with correcting errors made by lower courts. In choosing which cases to decide, Chief Justice William Howard Taft (1921–30) explained, the Court should devote its resources to cases "that involve principles, the application of which are of wide public importance or governmental interest, and which should be authoritatively declared by the Court."[26] In 1949, Justice Fred Vinson provided a fuller statement of the guidelines the Court has followed in selecting which cases to review:

> The function of the Supreme Court is . . . to resolve conflicts of opinion on federal questions that have arisen among lower courts, to pass upon questions of wide import under the Constitution, laws and treaties of the United States, and to exercise supervisory power over lower courts. If we took every case in which an interesting legal question is raised, or our prima facie impression is that the decision below is erroneous, we could not fill the Constitutional and statutory responsibilities placed upon the Court. To remain effective, the Supreme Court must continue to decide only those cases which present questions whose resolution will have immediate importance far beyond the particular facts and parties involved.[27]

The Supreme Court has had as few as five justices, when it was first organized in 1789, and as many as ten. Its membership, set by Congress, has been fixed at nine since 1869. The Court is presided over by the chief justice of the United States, who is appointed by the president—subject to confirmation by the Senate. Although chief justices are the official leaders of the Court, they are only first among equals in their relationship to the other eight justices. In a 2006 interview, Chief Justice Roberts, who had been on the job just one year, acknowledged, "There is this convention of referring to the Taney Court, the Marshall Court, the Fuller Court, but a chief justice has the same vote that everyone else has. . . . The chief's ability to get the Court to do something is really quite restrained."[28]

The chief justice is in effect the conductor of the orchestra, but he cannot tell the other justices what music to play. Some chief justices, however, are better than others at getting their colleagues to play the same tune. For example, Chief

Justice Earl Warren used every personal and political argument he could muster to convince two reluctant members of the Court to sign what then became a unanimous opinion in the *Brown v. Board of Education* decision. Other chief justices have not been so successful. The Court sometimes leads, more than it is led by, the chief justice.

Decision making on the Court begins after lawyers on each side plead their case in oral argument. Like students having to suffer through a bad presentation in class, the justices may find their attention flagging while listening to the lawyers. To divert themselves, the justices sometimes pass notes to one another commenting on the courtroom proceedings or news from the world outside. On October 10, 1973, in the midst of the baseball playoffs and an investigation of Vice President Spiro Agnew, Justice Potter Stewart passed this note to his colleague Harry Blackmun during oral argument: "V.P. Agnew just resigned! Mets 2, Reds 0."[29]

Following oral argument, the justices discuss the case in private. No law clerks or secretaries attend this confidential conference. Privacy is designed to promote a frank and full exchange of views. The chief justice leads the discussion, during which justices offer reasons for their respective conclusions. According to Justice Antonin Scalia, "[N]ot much conferencing goes on" at conference anymore.[30] Views are stated rather than argued. There is less collective deliberation and more expounding of individual convictions. After the conference reveals each justice's tentative vote on a case, the chief justice, if in the majority, assigns the writing of the Court's opinion to a justice in the majority. Chief Justice Roberts referred to his ability to assign opinions when in the majority as "not my greatest power, it's my only power."[31] (If the chief justice is not in the majority, the senior member of the majority assigns the opinion.)

Chief justices value the power to assign cases. It allows them to select the justice most likely to make an argument that can sustain the tentative majority established during conference. Former Justice John Paul Stevens recalls that when the chief justice was in the minority and Stevens was the senior member of the majority he would frequently ask Justice Anthony Kennedy to write the opinion because "I thought that if he wrote it out himself he was more sure to stick to his first vote."[32] Chief Justice Warren Burger was suspected by the other justices of voting frequently with a majority he actually disagreed with just so that he could select who would write the majority opinion.

Justices assigned to write the majority opinion circulate a draft to their colleagues, who review and respond to it. As a result of written exchanges among the justices, the rationale for the decision may be modified and votes may be switched, so that a completely different decision emerges from the process. For example, the 1989 *Webster v. Reproductive Health Services* case threatened to overturn the 1973 *Roe v. Wade* decision establishing a woman's constitutional right to an abortion. A majority of five justices at conference voted to uphold a Missouri law that would have placed restrictive conditions on abortions. Chief Justice William H. Rehnquist assigned himself the task of writing the majority opinion. But as memos circulated among the justices in response to Rehnquist's draft, Justice Sandra Day O'Connor switched her vote. What was once a 5–4 majority to effectively overturn *Roe* became, after an exchange of views among the justices, a 5–4 majority to reaffirm *Roe* (while still upholding some of the restrictions in the Missouri law). A similar shift occurred in an otherwise inconsequential case called *Huddleston v. United States* (1974), in which a 5–4 majority for Huddleston at conference turned into an 8–1 majority against him after briefs circulated among the justices. Justice Lewis F. Powell, Jr., who had voted to acquit Huddleston at conference, sent a note to Justice Blackmun (who wrote the dissenting opinion): "Although I voted the other way at Conference, upon a mature consideration and in light of your excellent opinion, I am persuaded to join you."[33]

The process in the *Webster* and *Huddleston* decisions reveals that conference votes are not carved in stone. Indeed, the Supreme Court scholars Lee Epstein and Jack Knight contend that justices change their minds frequently as a case proceeds from conference to final decision.[34] Allegedly, Chief Justice Roberts voted to overturn Obamacare at conference and changed his mind to affirm it as opinions circulated among justices.

In the early days of the Republic, presidents would select justices who shared their views; but they also nominated them with an eye to regional balance on the Court. An informal tradition developed in which certain seats were reserved for people from New England, New York, and the South. As regional conflicts dissipated and immigration increased, diversity on the Court came to be defined in religious, not regional, terms. A new informal tradition emerged in which there was a Catholic and a Jewish seat on the Court to reflect the emergence of these groups. Today, presidents are much less concerned with regional and religious balance than they are about gender and race. For example, no Protestant currently sits on the Court even though Protestants are the largest religious group in the United States, and four of the current justices come from New York City. The notion of diversity on the Court continues to be modernized and redefined to reflect a changing society. Today, the Court has more women than it has ever had and far more racial and ethnic diversity. Thurgood Marshall was the first black to join the Court, in 1967, Sandra Day O'Connor was the first woman appointed to the Court, in 1981, and, in 2009, Sonia Sotomayor was the first Hispanic to be confirmed.[35]

Although the notion of diversity on the Court is constantly being updated, ideology continues to drive the selection process. Presidents select justices who share their values and policy preferences. And far from being friendly or familiar with presidents prior to their nomination, many justices have not even met them before interviewing for the job.

Although presidents try to appoint justices whom they believe will reflect their views, sometimes they are spectacularly wrong in their predictions. President Harry Truman, for example, did not mince words over his disappointment with Justice Tom Clark: "Tom Clark was my biggest mistake. No question about it. . . . I don't know what got into me. He was no damn good as Attorney General, and on the Supreme Court . . . it doesn't seem possible, but he's even worse. He hasn't made one right decision that I can think of. . . ."[36] When asked what his biggest mistake was while in office, President Dwight Eisenhower replied, "The appointment of . . . Earl Warren."[37] Sometimes presidents guess right, only to have appointees change their views over time. Justice Harry Blackmun voted with his friend Chief Justice Warren Burger, another conservative Nixon appointee, 90 percent of the time when he first came on the Court in 1970. But his views changed, and by the time he retired, in 1994, he had become its most liberal member.[38] Judicial scholars have noted that Supreme Court justices deviate over time from the values of the president who appointed them, but the differences are not great.[39] Most justices reflect pretty well the politics of the president who appoints them.

Presidential appointments to the Supreme Court are more contentious today than they were in the past. Before the Senate's rejection of two of President Richard Nixon's Supreme Court nominees, in 1969 and 1970, one has to go back to 1930 and the Hoover administration to find the last time the Senate rejected a presidential nominee. Most Senate confirmation hearings resembled that for Justice "Whizzer" White in 1962: the Senate Judiciary Committee hearing lasted a total of 90 minutes, the committee then met in executive session for another 5 minutes, and White's nomination was confirmed by the Senate that same afternoon. In contrast, Senate confirmation hearings today are long, contentious affairs that are more like fierce rugby scrums than polite cricket matches. Pitched battles were fought in 1987 over President Reagan's nomination of Robert Bork, and in 1991 over President George H. W. Bush's nomination of Clarence Thomas. The former was rejected as too conservative by a Democratic Senate, and the latter was confirmed by the Senate despite charges of sexual harassment against him. Supreme Court appointments have drawn increasing scrutiny in part because more political issues are being placed at the Court's door. Groups are litigating what they cannot legislate. More and more, the Court is being called on to choose between competing policies in areas of profound disagreement. This, in turn, calls attention to the people appointed to the Court, who are increasingly perceived as making public policy when they decide cases. The frequency of divided government, when one party controls one or both branches of Congress and another controls the presidency, as well as the partisan and ideological polarization within Congress, have also made battles over judicial appointments more contentious.

JUDICIAL ACTIVISM AND RESTRAINT

We have seen how the Constitution established the Supreme Court and left it to Congress to create lower federal courts as needed. But the Constitution did not stipulate the number of members of the Supreme Court or what its specific powers would be. For example, the power of judicial review, in which the courts can nullify any federal, state, or public law that they believe conflicts with the Constitution, is not explicitly granted by the Constitution. This key power was first asserted by the Supreme Court in the landmark case of *Marbury v. Madison* (1803), in which the Court ruled that Thomas Jefferson's secretary of state, James Madison, had failed to convey the commission appointing William Marbury to a government post as a last-minute act of President John Adams. In his *Marbury* decision, Chief Justice John Marshall wrote, "It is emphatically the province and duty of the judicial department to say what the law is. . . . A law repugnant to the Constitution is void; . . . courts as well as other departments are bound by that instrument."[40] Even after *Marbury*, however, judicial review was slow to institutionalize. The Court waited 54 years before attempting to invalidate another act of Congress, in its infamous *Scott v. Sanford*, or Dred Scott, decision (1857) confirming slavery, and it was not until the late-nineteenth century that the principle was fully established.

The principle of judicial review is in tension with democratic theory inasmuch as it gives unelected judges the power to overrule laws made by elected officials. Courts are criticized for nullifying the will of the people, and of practicing unwarranted **judicial activism**, when they overturn laws passed by elected officials. But while opponents of judicial review claim that it is irreconcilable with democracy, supporters contend that it actually enhances democracy by protecting fundamental rights. Judicial review permits courts to nullify laws that conflict with the Bill of Rights or that subject minorities to the tyranny of the majority, as was the case in *Brown v. Board of Education*.[41]

The opposite of judicial activism is **judicial restraint**, which occurs when courts defer to the will of the people as expressed through legislative majorities.

Justice Oliver Wendell Holmes, Jr., for example, believed that democratic politics produced many bad laws that judges had no business changing. If his fellow citizens wanted to go to hell, Holmes once remarked, it was his job to help them on their way.

Most expressions of judicial activism have been conservative, preserving and protecting property rights. The Supreme Court's 1905 *Lochner v. New York* decision, which vacated a state law that restricted working hours, and its rulings that initially struck down New Deal legislation are examples. But there is no automatic identification of judicial activism with conservative results or, correspondingly, of judicial restraint with liberal outcomes. The law professor Philip B. Kurland has suggested that "[a]n 'activist' court is essentially one that is out of step with legislative or executive branches of the government," and whether it is liberal or conservative depends on "which role its prime antagonist has adopted."[42] The political complexity of the issue was apparent when President George W. Bush celebrated the fiftieth anniversary of the *Brown* decision—in which activist judges nullified state segregation laws. That same day, his office issued a press release criticizing the Massachusetts Supreme Court's ruling in favor of gay marriage on the grounds that "[t]he sacred institution of marriage should not be redefined by a few activist judges."[43] Like President Bush, most people do not consistently support judicial activism or restraint in principle; rather, the approach they favor depends on whether they agree or disagree with the Court's ruling in a particular case.

THE SUPREME COURT IN HISTORY

Marbury v. Madison settled a question that had divided the country along clear partisan lines. Judicial review was supported by the Federalist Party, which was dominated by northern manufacturing, finance, and mercantile interests. Southern and western farmers, planters, and small landowners in the Republican Party favored the principle of legislative supremacy and opposed judicial review. But Federalists and Republicans were also divided over the scope of national and state power. This question came before the court in *McCulloch v. Maryland* (1819). In *McCulloch*, the Court ruled that federal law was supreme. State law would have to give way when federal and state laws were in conflict. Thus, just as *Marbury* confirmed the power of the Supreme Court, *McCulloch* confirmed the power of the national government. Both marked a triumph of the Federalist Party's national industrial interests over the Democratic Party's local agrarian interests.

After Chief Justice John Marshall's death in 1835, President Andrew Jackson appointed Roger Taney to lead the Court. The Court over which Taney presided, in contrast to the Marshall Court, tilted toward states' rights and southern interests. This was particularly evident in its notorious Dred Scott decision (1857), when the Court voted 7–2 that no black could be an American citizen, that a black was "a person of an inferior order," and that blacks were slaves and possessions of their owners, whether they were in a state that outlawed or permitted slavery. The Dred Scott decision provoked an outcry in the North and hastened the onset of the Civil War.

Following the Civil War, the Court was in the hands of northern Republicans, who were chiefly concerned with safeguarding property and providing a legal environment for the development of capitalism. For example, the Fourteenth Amendment, adopted in 1868, was intended to protect black's civil rights from hostile state actions. But its famous "due process" clause—no state shall "deprive any person of life, liberty, or property, without due process of law"— served corporate interests more than it did blacks following Reconstruction. The clause precipitated a wave of judicial activism by courts that relied on it to hold that laws regulating business or protecting workers were unconstitutional because they deprived business of due process.[44] The courts not only nullified efforts to regulate the private marketplace but limited the reach of antitrust laws and restricted the ability of unions to organize and to strike. In recognition of the Supreme Court's service to business, a New York bank president told an audience of capitalists in 1895, "I give you, gentlemen, the Supreme Court of the United States—guardian of the dollar, defender of private property, enemy of spoliation, sheet anchor of the Republic!"[45]

But the Court's defense of property rights and freedom of contract could not withstand the popular momentum of Franklin Roosevelt's New Deal. Initially, the Court repeatedly struck down New Deal legislation. It outlawed the Agricultural Adjustment Act, a New York State minimum-wage law, and the National Industrial Recovery Act, which were enacted to relieve the Depression. The outlook was grim for other New Deal legislation whose constitutionality was also being challenged, such as the Social Security Act and the National Labor Relations Act. The more the Court stood in the way of the New Deal, the more popular frustration with the Court's undemocratic character grew. Senator George Norris of Nebraska expressed this common complaint when he denounced the Court on the Senate floor, saying, "The members of the Supreme Court are not elected by anybody. They are responsible to nobody. Yet they hold dominion over everybody."[46]

Never before had a president been so stymied by the Court in implementing his agenda. Yet Roosevelt was unable to alter the Court's decisions, because there were no vacancies and he could not change its composition. In desperation, Roosevelt proposed what came to be known as "court packing" legislation. His plan would have permitted the president to appoint a new justice, up to a total of 15 for each justice who reached age 70 and did not retire. Since six of the nine justices were over 70 at the time, this would have enabled Roosevelt to add six new like-minded justices to the Court. Roosevelt lost the battle to reform the Court but he won the war. Justice Owen Roberts, who had voted against New Deal legislation and written key opinions striking them down, now voted to uphold such laws as constitutional. Justice Roberts's about-face is often referred to as the "switch in time that saved nine." One member of Congress noted that Justice Roberts had effectively amended the Constitution and changed the lives of millions simply "by nodding his head instead of shaking it."[47] This reversal gave Roosevelt a majority on the Court, upon which he later expanded. By the end of his presidency in 1945, thanks to vacancies on the Court created by death and retirement, he had appointed more Supreme Court justices than any president since George Washington.

The contest between the Court and the president reveals much about the power and limits of the judiciary. The Court can nullify the will of the people, as it initially did regarding New Deal legislation. But if the Court stands too hard and too long against public opinion, it risks losing legitimacy and its prestige and stature suffer.

After 1936, the Supreme Court upheld every New Deal statute whose constitutionality was challenged. Judicial activism was replaced with judicial restraint. In the course of confirming the New Deal, the Court initiated a constitutional revolution that greatly expanded the power of the federal government over business and the states.

THE MODERN COURT: FROM WARREN TO ROBERTS

The Warren Court

On March 16, 1948, 20 black citizens assisted by the National Association for the Advancement of Colored People (NAACP) filed suit in U.S. district court in Florence County, South Carolina. They claimed that racial segregation practiced by the Clarendon County Board of Education violated the equal-protection clause of the Constitution's Fourteenth Amendment. Simple justice, they claimed, required the government to give black children the same educational opportunities it provided to whites. In Clarendon County, in 1949–50, the local board of education spent less than one-third of its budget to maintain

61 schools for blacks; the remaining revenue was allocated to support just 12 schools for whites. While white schoolchildren rode to school in buses, black schoolchildren had to walk because the school board failed to provide them with transportation.

The suit was filed under the name of Henry Briggs, the first plaintiff in alphabetical order, who worked as a gas-station attendant. Before the litigation was over, he would be fired from his job. Maisie Solomon, another plaintiff, also lost her job. Other plaintiffs faced retribution too: John McDonald could not get a loan for his tractor, Lee Richardson could not secure credit for his farm, and no one would rent land to William Ragin for growing cotton. The doors of justice may be open to everyone, but sometimes it requires uncommon courage to walk through them.

After two years of delay and defeat in the lower courts, the school-segregation case reached the Supreme Court of the United States. There, the suit joined similar cases, from Delaware and Virginia, which the Court was also hearing on appeal. These cases were consolidated with a fourth school-segregation case from Kansas: *Brown v. Board of Education of Topeka*. This case was listed first because the justices did not want the issue of segregation to appear as a purely southern matter.

On May 17, 1954, Chief Justice Earl Warren read the Supreme Court's unanimous opinion in the group of school-segregation cases known collectively as *Brown*. He told the assembled spectators and reporters that the Court had asked itself if racial segregation in public schools deprived black children of equal opportunity. "We believe that it does," he declared. His closing remarks left no doubt where the Court stood: "We conclude

The three attorneys (from left to right, George E.C. Hayes, Thurgood Marshall, and James Nabrit Jr.) who argued the case against school segregation, standing and smiling in front of the U.S. Supreme Court building after the Court issued its *Brown* decision.

that in the field of public education, the doctrine of 'separate but equal' has no place. Separate educational facilities are inherently unequal. Therefore the plaintiffs . . . have been . . . deprived of the equal protection of the laws guaranteed by the Fourteenth Amendment."[48]

The *Brown* decision was only one of many by the Warren Court that resonated across the country and whose principles still stand today. The issues the Warren Court wrestled with no longer involved government regulation of business, as had been the case for the New Deal era that preceded it, when the Court had decisively settled the matter of regulation in the government's favor. Now the Court concerned itself with issues of civil liberties and extending the principle of political equality to new areas. From just 9 percent of the Court's agenda in 1933, cases involving civil rights and civil liberties accounted for 65 percent of the Court's docket in 1971. The "rights revolution" had begun.[49]

The Warren Court's effort to realize the promise of legal equality for all Americans was evident in a number of landmark decisions. *Brown*, of course, led the way in civil rights. The Warren Court also acted to expand the notion of legal equality and ensure the effectiveness of each citizen's vote by requiring equally apportioned legislative districts. Some legislative districts included many more voters than others. In *Baker v. Carr* (1962), the Court ruled that it was appropriate for federal courts to hear cases challenging malapportioned state election districts. Two years later, in *Reynolds v. Sims*, the Court took the next logical step, declaring that the "one person, one vote" principle, which governed congressional districting, should also apply to state legislatures.

The Warren Court was also responsible for extending the boundaries of democracy by requiring states to abide by virtually every provision of the Bill of Rights. State law-enforcement and criminal procedures would also now have to meet federal due-process requirements, giving defendants charged with crimes certain procedural rights and protections. In *Mapp v. Ohio* (1961), the Court ruled that the police could not conduct searches for evidence without a court order. Two years later, in *Gideon v. Wainwright* (1963), the Court declared that states must provide legal counsel to all defendants charged with serious crimes. Finally, in *Miranda v. Arizona* (1966) the court decided that a confession obtained from a criminal suspect during interrogation is not admissible as evidence in court unless the accused person has been informed of his or her rights to remain silent and to be represented by a lawyer. But the rights revolution extended beyond banning states from trying defendants without lawyers and preventing police from conducting searches without court authorization or from eliciting confessions without informing defendants of their rights. It also meant states could no longer outlaw the sale of contraceptives, or segregate schools by race. State laws that did so were now regarded as violations of fundamental constitutional rights.[50]

Some of the Warren Court's decisions have become national standards. It is hard to imagine the law today tolerating government-sanctioned racial segregation or deviating from the principle of one person, one vote. Even Chief Justice William Rehnquist, who was opposed to much of the Warren Court's jurisprudence, acknowledged in 2000 that some of its rulings were now so embedded in American political culture that respect for precedent weighed heavily against overruling them. Although many Warren Court decisions provoked tremendous controversy, they prevailed because they were in tune with the activist, liberal wing of the Democratic Party, which was the governing coalition at the time.[51] And while subsequent Supreme Court decisions have chipped away at the Warren Court's jurisprudence in recent years, its legacy lives on.

The Burger Court

Conservatives attacked the Warren Court for coddling criminals, tying the hands of police and prosecutors, being irreligious, violating states' rights, and promoting civil unrest. Richard Nixon pledged to remold the Court in his 1968 presidential campaign, and within a year of his election he had a chance to deliver on that promise. In 1969 Earl Warren retired, and President Nixon appointed Warren E. Burger, a critic of many Warren Court decisions, to replace him as chief justice. By the end of Burger's service as chief justice in 1986, Republican presidents had appointed six members to the Supreme Court. Only two members of the liberal bloc from the Warren Court, justices William Brennan and Thurgood Marshall, remained on the bench, along with the moderate Byron White.

Circumstances were ripe for conservatives to undo the work of the Warren Court. But the anticipated counterrevolution never happened. The power of judicial precedent, the lack of leadership by Burger, and the skill of the liberal justice William Brennan in coaxing a majority of his colleagues to follow the Warren Court's rulings were enough to hold the line. In a review of the Burger Court, the political scientists Mark Silverstein and Benjamin Ginsberg concluded that "[t]he most controversial decisions of the Warren era involving school prayer, reapportionment, desegregation, and criminal procedure remain the law of the land. The Burger Court nibbled at the edges of several Warren Court precedents, often seeking to confine their application, but overt attempts at overruling were either avoided or defeated."[52]

Nowhere was the Burger Court more faithful to its predecessor than in the area of civil rights. In *Swann v. Charlotte-Mecklenburg County Board of*

Education (1970), the Court made clear there would be no retreat from *Brown*, unanimously upholding the use of busing to achieve racially balanced schools. The Court also gave constitutional approval to affirmative-action plans as a way to remedy past and ongoing discrimination against minorities and other protected groups. But the Burger Court's most famous decision, *Roe v. Wade* (1973), most clearly expresses the degree to which it followed the legal reasoning of its predecessor. The Warren Court first recognized a constitutional right to privacy in *Griswold v. Connecticut* (1965), when it struck down a state law barring the use of contraceptives. In *Roe v. Wade*, the Burger Court applied the same logic to strike down state laws denying a woman's right to an abortion.[53]

The Rehnquist Court

In 1986, Republicans pulled the equivalent of a double steal in baseball. Justice Burger retired and was replaced as chief justice by William Rehnquist, the most conservative member of the Court. Controversy over Rehnquist's nomination to chief justice erupted at his Senate confirmation hearings. Questions regarding his integrity, honesty, and respect for minority rights distracted attention from the appointment of Antonin Scalia, who was even more conservative, to fill the seat Rehnquist had occupied.[54]

William Brennan, the most liberal member of the Court, stepped down in 1990. President George H. W. Bush replaced him with David H. Souter. When Thurgood Marshall, the last liberal holdover from the Warren Court, resigned a year later, he was replaced with another African American, Clarence Thomas. Skin color may have been the only thing that Marshall and Thomas had in common. Marshall opposed the death penalty and supported affirmative action and reproductive rights. Thomas, on the other hand, favored the death penalty and opposed abortion and government programs to remedy the effects of discrimination. Marshall was esteemed within his profession, but the American Bar Association's judiciary committee gave Thomas the lowest rating ever given a confirmed justice; none of its members rated him well-qualified.

Justices Scalia and Thomas perceive their role as undoing what they regard as the perfidious work of the Warren and Burger Courts. Both justices regard the law as moving dangerously away from what the Founders intended, and they hope to restore its original meaning. Other Supreme Court justices appointed by Republican presidents to the Rehnquist Court—Sandra Day O'Connor, David Souter, John Paul Stevens, and Anthony Kennedy—were conservative but not counterrevolutionary like Scalia and Thomas, and they resisted too great a turn away from precedents. To simply discard the legal legacy of the

Warren and Burger courts, this group believed, would damage the Supreme Court as an institution, exposing it to the charge that its decisions reflected election results rather than Constitutional principles. Thus, in 1991 justices O'Connor, Souter, and Kennedy wrote an unusual joint opinion upholding *Roe* in the abortion case *Planned Parenthood of Southeastern Pennsylvania v. Casey*. They argued that since *Roe* had been decided people "had ordered their thinking and living around that case" and that no legal principle weakening *Roe*'s constitutional basis had emerged in the intervening years. "A decision to overrule *Roe*'s essential holding under the existing circumstances," their opinion continued, would be "at the cost of both profound and unnecessary damage to the Court's legitimacy and to the rule of law."[55]

President Bill Clinton was the first Democrat to appoint a justice to the Supreme Court in 26 years. When Byron White retired, in 1993, President Clinton replaced him with Ruth Bader Ginsburg, the second woman appointed to the Court. A year later, when Harry Blackmun retired, Clinton appointed Stephen Breyer to replace him.

The Rehnquist Court reflected a shift in public opinion to the right and the Republican Party's resurgence, just as the Warren Court epitomized the liberalism of its day and the Democratic Party's dominance. It revived states' rights, looked with suspicion on affirmative action, approved the death penalty and certain restrictions on abortions, treated the rights of criminal defendants with indifference, and relaxed the constitutional separation of church and state. It did not overturn Warren and Burger Court precedents but instead hollowed them out and limited their application.

Although the Rehnquist Court's record was conservative, it was not overly so. The Court struck a blow for long-established legal rights when it rejected President George W. Bush's arguments that he had the power as commander-in-chief to detain suspected terrorists indefinitely without their knowledge of the charges against them or even access to a lawyer. The Court, in effect, ruled that the president was not above the law. The Rehnquist Court also compiled a strong record on First Amendment cases. According to the legal scholar Burt Neuborne, the Rehnquist Court "echoed and deepened the powerful First Amendment doctrine [it] inherited . . . and has been among the strongest free speech courts in the nation's history."[56] Its most famous ruling in this arena was *Texas v. Johnson* (1989), which held that burning the American flag is protected by the First Amendment. And in *Lawrence v. Texas* (2003), the Court strongly reaffirmed the Warren Court's right-to-privacy doctrine to strike down a Texas anti-sodomy law. This ruling was a constitutional watershed that made gay sex legal and overruled the Court's *Bowers v. Hardwick* decision (1986).

The Rehnquist Court drew the ire of liberals for undermining, in practice if not in principle, the Warren Court legacy. It also attracted their fury because of its 5–4 decision in *Bush v. Gore* (2000), which suspended a recount in Florida of disputed presidential-election returns, effectively making George W. Bush the 43rd president of the United States. The Court overruled state courts, state laws, and local canvassing boards to reach a decision. The bare majority in favor of stopping the recount lacked such confidence in the principles they used to justify their decision that the Court said they should not apply in future cases. Justice Stevens, writing for the minority, wrote a scathing rebuttal to the Court's decision, warning that it "can only lend credence to the most cynical appraisal of the work of judges throughout the land. . . . Time will one day heal the wound to that confidence that will be inflicted by today's decision. One thing, however, is certain. Although we may never know with complete certainty the identity of the winner of this year's Presidential election, the identity of the loser is perfectly clear. It is the Nation's confidence in the judge as an impartial guardian of the rule of law."[57] Summarizing the extraordinary role that the one-vote majority on the Court played in elevating George W. Bush to the presidency, the comedian Mark Russell mused, "We have a new president. In this democracy of 200 million citizens, the people have spoken. All five of them."[58]

The Roberts Court

Upon Chief Justice Rehnquist's death in 2005, President Bush nominated John G. Roberts, Jr., to fill his post. Roberts had impeccable legal and political credentials. He graduated from Harvard Law School, served as a Supreme Court clerk for Rehnquist, and worked in the Reagan Justice Department before becoming a successful corporate lawyer. In 2000, he advised the Bush team on its legal challenges in the contested presidential election; three years later, he was appointed by President Bush to the United States Court of Appeals for the District of Columbia.

The Court experienced further turnover following Rehnquist's departure when Sandra Day O'Connor retired. She was replaced in 2006 by Samuel Alito, who had served on the U.S. Third Circuit Court of Appeals. The irony of Alito's appointment as a replacement for O'Connor did not escape veteran court watchers. In Alito's first major opinion on the appeals court, he was the only one of the three judges hearing the case to uphold all the abortion restrictions of a new Pennsylvania law, including spousal-notification requirements. When the state law eventually came to the Supreme Court in *Planned Parenthood v. Casey*, this was the only restriction that the Court struck down, and O'Connor wrote a blistering critique of the law's requirement that husbands be notified. Now she was being replaced by a judge whose views on abortion she had ridiculed earlier.[59]

In 2009, David Souter announced his retirement, permitting President Obama to make his first Supreme Court appointment. He chose U.S. Court of Appeals Judge Sonya Sotomayor, a Latina of Puerto Rican descent, as Souter's replacement. A year later, in 2010, Justice John Paul Stevens announced his retirement. Elena Kagan, the former dean of Harvard Law School and the solicitor general of the United States, was confirmed to replace him.

The Roberts Court has rewarded the faith of conservatives with sympathetic rulings. It has provided corporations more protection against lawsuits, defended states' rights from federal encroachment, lowered the wall of separation between church and state, interpreted campaign contributions as free speech, reduced protections for criminal defendants, established a personal right to possess guns, and been hostile to efforts to remedy the effects of discrimination. The rightward drift of the Roberts Court is also evident in the methodology it uses to reach its decisions. Justices are more apt to issue opinions that reflect the conservative approach of originalism, in which Justices try to take the founders' words from 240 years ago and apply them to contemporary issues, such as internet privacy.[60]

But the Roberts Court has also disappointed conservatives at times. This is particularly true in regard to the restrictions it has placed on presidential powers. It has repeatedly ruled that "no prisoner is beneath the law, and no president above its limits."[61] In four separate decisions, the Roberts Court has ruled that detainees—alleged enemy combatants whom the Bush administration imprisoned in its war on terror—are entitled to due process of law, and when Congress tried to narrow the Court's jurisdiction by suspending rights for detainees, it struck down that provision, too. The Court also upset conservatives when it voted to uphold the Obama administration's Affordable Care Act as constitutional. But the Roberts Court is still considered the most conservative in modern times. A ratings system found that the Roberts Court issued conservative decisions 60 percent of the time, compared to 55 percent for both the Burger and Rehnquist courts and just 35 percent for the Warren Court.[62]

The Roberts Court is also an outlier compared to previous courts when it comes to life experience. All of its members had already been judges before joining the Supreme Court, with the exception of Elena Kagan. Their resumes shine with degrees from and teaching positions at the best Ivy League law schools, but no members ever served in a legislature, ran for public office, or spent much time in private practice. According to one analyst, their "cloistered and

The current Justices of the Supreme Court.

neutral experiences offer limited opportunities for the development of the most critical judicial virtue: practical wisdom."[63] The lack of practical wisdom that experience in politics would have provided was evident in Justice Kennedy's opinion for the Court in the 2010 *Citizens United* decision, previously discussed in Chapter 4. Kennedy proclaimed confidently that "independent expenditures [in federal elections], including those made by corporations, do not give rise to corruption or the appearance of corruption."[64] The effect of *Citizens United* was the very opposite of what Kennedy's naive statement predicted—which anyone familiar with how politics works in the real world would have anticipated. *Citizens United* opened the floodgates for the wealthy and corporations to spend unlimited money in federal elections, which increased people's fears that candidates were for sale and elections could be bought.

Although their backgrounds as brilliant legal technicians are supposed to reassure the public that the Court is nonideological and will be modest in its rulings, the Roberts Court has been as polarized as any other Court and not at all shy about overturning precedents and public laws.[65] In 2010, for example (as discussed above and in earlier chapters), the Court ignored legal precedents and by a 5–4 vote in *Citizens United* overturned federal laws limiting corporate campaign activity on behalf of candidates, claiming such laws limited corporations' free-speech rights under the First Amendment. Nor has the Roberts Court been reluctant to enter political thickets. In 2011, it chose to hear cases challenging redistricting maps that would influence which party has an advantage in the House of Representatives, cases challenging President Obama's health-care bill, and cases pertaining to the controversial issue of immigration. This is not a bashful Court willing to leave politics to elected officials.

The Roberts Court is exquisitely balanced between its right wing (Alito, Roberts, Scalia, and Thomas) and left wing (Breyer, Ginsburg, Kagan, and Sotomayor), with Justice Kennedy often serving as the swing vote between them. In 2010, the Court decided 14 cases, about 20 percent of its load, by a 5–4 vote. In 12 of those cases, the four liberals lined up against the four conservatives, with Kennedy casting the deciding vote. In 2011, the Court again decided about 20 percent of its cases by 5–4 votes, with the liberals and conservatives often lining up in blocs and Kennedy providing the deciding vote in two-thirds of them. Given the frequency with which Kennedy's vote makes the majority in 5–4 decisions, it is his views that define the court more than any other justice, including Chief Justice Roberts.

But this familiar description of the Court as evenly balanced ideologically, with Kennedy in the center, does not capture how far the Court's center of gravity has moved to the right. Compared to the Warren Court, the left on today's Court would be considered moderates, the center would be on the right, and those now on the right would be off the scale entirely.[66] When Justice Stevens retired in 2010, he noted that every justice appointed since he joined the Court in 1975 was more conservative than the person he or she replaced. A 2009 study confirmed that hunch, finding that in the last quarter century Republican presidents have chosen justices who are more conservative than the justices that Democrats have appointed are liberal. Four of the five most conservative justices on the bench since 1937 are currently on the Court. By contrast, none of the current liberal members of the Court made the list of top five liberals since 1937, and only Justice Ginsburg was included in the top ten.[67]

Each term adds a new wrinkle to our picture of the Roberts Court, which evolves as new members join it and new issues come before it. But as much as the Court is independent, it also reflects its political environment. As parties polarized and became more ideological, partisan affiliation increasingly came to define the Roberts Court. Whether Democratic or Republican presidents nominated them became an accurate predictor of how Justices on the Court would vote. Not only did the Roberts Court reflect hardening partisan divisions in the country at-large, but fewer unanimous decisions and more dissenting and concurring opinions reflected a more contentious and belligerent political culture.[68] As Linda Greenhouse, a former judicial-affairs reporter for the *New York Times*, wrote in her farewell column covering the Court: "The court is in America's collective hands. We shape it; it reflects us. At any given time, we may not have the Supreme Court we want. We may not have the court we need. But we have, most likely, the Supreme Court we deserve."[69] This applies to the Roberts Court as much as to its predecessors.

POLITICS BY LAWSUIT

Americans are known to be litigious, settling their disputes in court. The degree to which Americans engage in lawsuits is not a cultural trait but a reflection of the many rights they enjoy and the openness of the judicial system to their complaints. Recently, corporate America has tried to reduce the prevalence of lawsuits, claiming they are often frivolous and expensive. Lobbyists for business have encouraged members of Congress to pass bills that would cap punitive-damages awards by juries and discourage lawsuits by making plaintiffs pay if they lose. The most famous example of a justice system that is ostensibly out of control is the 1994 case of a woman who won a multimillion-dollar award from McDonald's after she spilled a cup of their hot coffee on herself. But the general perception that her claim was trivial is a myth. In fact, McDonald's had received over 700 complaints about burns from their coffee, which was 20 degrees hotter than in most other restaurants; and the woman required skin grafts for third-degree burns that took more than a year to heal. Moreover, she had offered to settle before the trial, but despite encouragement from the judge McDonald's refused to do so. Only after it lost did McDonald's claim to be the victim of a process that it chose to pursue. While the $2.9 million jury award received extensive coverage in the media, not many newspapers reported that the woman actually received only $600,000 after the judge reduced the jury's punitive-damages award. Although the law may serve the interests of corporations, it can also be used to hold them accountable for coffee that burns badly enough to require hospitalization, as well as for unsafe cars, cancerous cigarettes, and dangerous drugs.

Victims of corporate wrongdoing are not the only ones turning to the courts for restitution. More and more groups are looking to the courts to resolve political issues. This is particularly so during extended periods of divided government, when Congress and the executive branch are deadlocked. Political activists then look to the courts to settle issues that politicians can't. But activists also go to court when they believe they will get a more favorable decision there than from the other branches of government. For example, when George W. Bush became president, environmentalists began filing expensive lawsuits against polluters because they had little faith that the Bush administration would enforce environmental regulations designed to police them.[70] The court-room has become another field for political battle once it spreads past the electoral, legislative, and administrative arenas. More than 150 years ago, Alexis de Tocqueville noted this peculiar trait when he observed, "There is hardly a political question in the United States that does not sooner or later turn into a judicial one."[71]

The federal courts have encouraged political activists to litigate their disagreements by relaxing previous restrictions about what kind of cases could be brought to court and who could bring them. This change, according to the political scientists Benjamin Ginsberg and Martin Shefter, has "given a wider range of litigants access to the courts, has rendered a broader range of issues subject to judicial settlement, and so has greatly increased the reach of the courts in American life."[72] The new openness of the courts has contributed to a broader involvement of the courts in policy and politics. The political scientist and legal analyst Paul Frymer writes, "Judges are now used to resolve conflicts as various as international terrorism, war crimes, presidential elections, and congressional redistricting, all of which were routinely handled by politicians only fifty years ago."[73] For example, federal district courts have gone so far as to take over local school systems, constructing elaborate plans for their desegregation when local school boards have dragged their feet. Courts have become involved in deciding what schools would close, where new ones would be constructed, and which schools students would attend.

Finally, the courts' growing involvement in policy and politics is evident in the lack of deference courts now show to federal administrative agencies. Courts today are less willing to accept the expertise of administrative agencies in how legislation is interpreted and implemented. Of course, the more courts substitute their judgment for that of administrative agencies, the more they invite litigation. Groups seeking vigorous enforcement of the law and those resisting regulation now engage in politics by lawsuit, appealing to the courts to overturn administrative decisions they oppose.[74]

Although groups have had some success in pursuing reform through the courts, those who attempt to do so should come with lots of patience and low expectations. Fifteen years after the *Brown* decision, which began with a suit in Clarendon County, South Carolina, that county's public school system enrolled 3,000 black children and just a single white child. White students in the county had deserted the public schools and attended private segregated academies. In 1979, 25 years after the *Brown* decision, a new school-desegregation suit was filed in Topeka, Kansas, by Linda Brown—the school girl and original plaintiff in the school-desegregation case that bears her name—on behalf of her children!

WHAT DO YOU THINK?

Are the Courts an Appropriate Site to Settle Political Issues?

More and more political questions that divide society are being resolved by the courts, from abortion and gun control to immigration and campaign finance. The two most vivid examples of this tendency are the Supreme Court's decisions to halt the 2000 election recount and to uphold President Obama's health-care law. Do you think putting the courts into the mix and adding another check to existing checks and balances makes policy better? Or is it inappropriate for courts to settle political issues because federal judges are not elected and are not accountable? Does political engagement of the courts come at the expense of democracy?

The same story is true with regard to abortion. Despite the pro-choice victory in *Roe*, the number of abortions actually grew faster in the years preceding that landmark decision than they did afterward. The political scientist Garrett Epps argues, "In the great sweep of American history, obstructing social change has been, more often than not, the high court's chosen task."[75] The courts don't create reforms, but they can remove obstacles to them. Legal victories can confirm changes that have occurred in the halls of Congress, at elections, and in the minds of citizens, but they are no substitute for them.

THE COURTS IN COMPARATIVE PERSPECTIVE: INCARCERATION NATION

The American justice system is distinctive in many ways. Other countries grant their courts the power of judicial review, but few do so through the regular court system, as occurs in the U.S. In Germany and France, constitutional questions are handled by special courts created for that purpose. By contrast, in the United States the question of whether a law is constitutional or not is heard in the same federal court where all other types of cases are tried. Another unusual quality of American courts is the way that judges are chosen. Few other countries select judges through elections, as is typically done at the state and local (but not federal) levels in the United States. Instead, other countries try to insulate judges from political influences by having their peers select them on the basis of professional criteria. In still other systems, when politicians do appoint judges, political influences are mitigated by making their term of appointment nonrenewable. When judges know they are appointed for only one term, they do not have to look over their shoulders and worry about how particular rulings will affect their judicial careers.

But in no respect is the United States more unique than in its criminal-justice system. No other developed country has such a vast prison complex to warehouse such a large number of prisoners; and no other country inflicts such harsh and punitive sanctions on offenders. Even as the state was being rolled back in other arenas beginning in the 1970s, it was expanding dramatically in terms of incarceration and severity of punishment. The number of prisoners has increased fivefold since 1973, and sentences meted out by judges have become longer. With more than 2 million adults in jail, the United States has a larger proportion of adults in prison than any country in the world. In 1980 there were about 228 people in jail per 100,000 Americans; by 2010 that number had more than tripled, to 731. More than half of those in prison are black, and more black men are behind bars than are enrolled in college. And the cost of maintaining this vast penal colony has not been cheap. Over the past two decades the rate of spending on prisons has risen six times faster than on higher education.[76]

The American criminal-justice system is not simply on a different scale from that found elsewhere. It is also more punitive. Nonviolent offenders in Europe comprise a smaller proportion of the prison population than they do in the United States. Offenders in the United States receive longer sentences than they would receive elsewhere for the same crime. Moreover, many people in the United States temporarily or permanently lose their rights as well as their freedom when they enter prison. For example, in some states a citizen with a prison record cannot vote and is ineligible for social services, such as student loans.

Finally, the United States is unique among developed countries in its use of capital punishment. Europe had its last execution in 1977. In contrast, about 3,000 people currently sit on death row in American prisons, awaiting execution. The appetite for the death penalty has declined worldwide, and more countries are abolishing capital punishment; but the United States remains a leader, in such dubious company as Iran and China, in executing its own citizens.

The preference of the American criminal-justice system for retribution over rehabilitation can be traced to a variety of factors. First, law-and-order politicians have stoked the public's taste for vengeance. Politicians trolling for votes promise to get tough on crime. Second, the prison-industrial complex—comprised of private corporations that supply and run prisons, prison guards and staff, and local communities that depend on prisons for jobs and income—is a powerful interest group that promotes and profits from prison expansion. Third, the prison boom arose as a means of crime prevention, of removing offenders from the street and thereby making society more secure. Finally, the victims'-rights movement also contributed to the race to incarcerate by pitting the rights of victims against the rights of offenders. Victims'-rights proponents have framed the issue as a zero-sum game in which punishing offenders is designed to compensate victims for their losses.[77]

CONCLUSION

The courts are mostly conservative institutions that support the status quo. Their decisions usually consolidate reforms rather than initiate them. Based on a study of civil rights, women's rights, and reapportionment, the political scientist Gerald Rosenberg concluded that in the United States "courts can almost never be effective producers of significant social reform. At best, they can second the social reform acts of other branches of government."[78] The law, in other words, usually follows politics, not the other way around. In addition, the social-reform potential of the courts is diminished because they need to respect precedent, fit their rulings to the specific contours of a case, wait for cases to be brought to them, and obtain the cooperation and support of other political actors to implement their decisions. They cannot go much farther than the institutions they depend on are willing to go.

Yet, as we argued in the introduction to this chapter, it would be a mistake to dismiss the significance of the courts or the degree to which the law can be a tool of social change. The *Brown* decision, for example, gave impetus and legitimacy to black demands for political equality. Blacks were more willing to challenge segregation when they had the law behind them. In addition, new legal principles expounded in one circumstance can be applied in different contexts to win new rights. For example, the right to privacy that was first developed in a case permitting the use of contraceptives became the constitutional basis for a later case that made abortions legal. Constitutional principles can take on a life of their own, applying to issues beyond the circumstances in which they were first articulated. Finally, courts are an important check that the weak can appeal to in challenging those who have power. After all, even the powerful cannot do as they please but must submit to the rule of law. Presidents cannot simply ignore citizens' rights when ordering them to be detained; companies cannot simply pollute in violation of environmental laws; and employers cannot simply indulge their prejudices and discriminate when hiring and firing workers. Citizens can appeal to the courts to assert their rights of due process, the public can sue companies that violate environmental laws, and workers who are the victims of discrimination can turn to courts for restitution. Of course, successfully asserting these rights inside courts depends on the resources people have outside of them. Still, as much as the law may reflect and confirm the powers that be, it can also be a tool to hold them accountable.

CHAPTER SUMMARY

Introduction

The courts are riddled with ambiguity. First, they are both powerful and weak in relation to the other branches of government. Courts have the power of judicial review, and federal judges enjoy lifetime tenures ensuring their independence. But the courts depend on other branches of government to implement their decisions, and the decisions of courts whose judges are not elected lack democratic legitimacy. Second, the courts are both legal and political institutions. They are supposed to follow the letter of the law but must also be mindful of the political context in which they decide cases. Third, the courts reflect both equality and inequality. Citizens have equal rights, but they also have unequal resources to take advantage of those rights. Finally, the courts can act as both a conservative and a progressive force. The law often reflects the interests of the powerful, but it is also a resource people can use to make legal claims against them.

A Dual Court System

Each of the 50 states has its own judicial system—with its own laws, courts, and constitution—alongside that of the federal government. State courts are the real workhorses of the judiciary because most cases are decided here rather than in federal courts. One important difference between state and federal courts is the way judges are selected. Most states elect judges, whereas federal judges are appointed.

The Federal-Court System

The federal-court system is divided into three tiers. District courts are the lowest level, where trials are held, followed by courts of appeals, which hear cases on appeal from district courts. At the apex is the Supreme Court, the court of last resort. Federal judges are appointed by the president but must be confirmed by the Senate. Today, more judicial appointments to federal courts are challenged and delayed by the Senate than in the past, and the process of appointing judges to federal courts has become increasingly partisan and contentious.

The Supreme Court

The Supreme Court hears cases that are approved by four justices and that often involve important constitutional issues. The Court has nine members and is led by the chief justice, who is only first among equals. Presidents appoint justices who share their values, but sometimes justices issue decisions that unpleasantly surprise those who appointed them. Even so, the process of judicial appointments is highly ideological and has become more contentious than in the past.

Judicial Activism and Restraint

The Supreme Court's power of judicial review is not explicitly granted in the Constitution; rather, it was first asserted in the landmark case *Marbury v. Madison* (1803). The principle of judicial review is sometimes argued to be in tension with democratic theory, inasmuch as it gives unelected judges the power to overrule laws made by elected officials. When courts do overturn such laws, they are said to practice judicial activism. When courts defer to legislative majorities and let laws stand, they are said to practice judicial restraint.

The Supreme Court in History

McCulloch v. Maryland (1819) established that federal law was the supreme law of the land, superseding state laws where the two conflicted. However, in the mid nineteenth century, the Court tilted toward states' rights and southern interests, and then later toward northern business interests. Even initially during the New Deal, the conservative Court struck down legislation passed by a liberal Congress and administration. But the Court, pressured by FDR, eventually reversed itself to fend off critics and upheld New Deal legislation that greatly expanded the power of the federal government over business and the states.

The Modern Court: From Warren to Roberts

The Warren Court greatly expanded citizen rights and conceptions of political equality during the 1950s and 1960s. The Burger Court that followed disappointed conservatives because it affirmed many Warren Court rulings. But as the country shifted from liberal to conservative, so did the Court. The Rehnquist Court began to hollow out many Warren Court precedents by limiting them in practice. The current Court, led by Chief Justice Roberts, has been even more conservative, in both its approach to the law and its rulings.

Politics by Lawsuit

More U.S. citizens bring suit in court than people in other countries because American courts have relaxed restrictions on the kinds of cases they will accept and who can bring them. Consequently, the court's openness has encouraged groups to achieve through lawsuit what they could not achieve through legislation.

The Courts in Comparative Perspective: Incarceration Nation

Unlike the United States, most countries do not have judicial review or elect judges. But the United States legal system differs the most from other developed countries' when it comes to its criminal-justice system, which is more punitive, puts more people in prison, and still has the death penalty.

Critical Thinking Questions

1. Should the Senate interpret its "advice and consent" role in judicial appointments as one that gives it a veto over nominess, or should it defer to the president except in extraordinary circumstances?

2. Is judicial review compatible with democracy or antithetical to it? Supporters argue that it is necessary to prevent majorities from depriving minorities of their rights. Opponents argue that it thwarts democracy by permitting judges to overrule the people's representatives.

3. Was Franklin Roosevelt correct in trying to pack the court? Some argue that Roosevelt threatened the constitutional system of checks and balances when he did so. Others believe it was necessary because the Court thwarted popular legislation that was designed to address the problems posed by the Great Depression.

4. Should we be concerned about how representative the Supreme Court is of the American public? Should its membership reflect the full diversity of American society?

5. Are prisons an effective deterrent to crime? Is punishment an appropriate form of justice for victims of crime? Under what circumstances, if any, should the death penalty be invoked?

Suggested Readings

Charles Epp, *The Rights Revolution: Lawyers, Activists and Supreme Court Cases in Comparative Perspective.* Chicago: University of Chicago Press, 1998.

Lee Epstein and Jack Knight, *The Choices Justices Make.* Washington, DC: Congressional Quarterly Press, 1998.

Linda Greenhouse, *Becoming Justice Blackmun: Harry Blackmun's Supreme Court Journey.* New York: Times Books, 2007.

Kermit L. Hall and Kevin T. McGuire, eds. *The Judicial Branch.* New York: Oxford University Press, 2005.

Gerald N. Rosenberg, *The Hollow Hope: Can Courts Bring About Social Change?* Chicago: University of Chicago Press, 1991.

Jeffrey Toobin, *The Oath: The Obama White House and the Supreme Court.* New York: Doubleday, 2012.

PART IV

PUBLIC POLICY

I f political participation is the motor that drives the machine of political institutions, public policy charts the direction the machine takes. Some policies reduce inequality, while others generate new and deeper inequities. Some extend the scope of public responsibility, while others contract it. Some project American power abroad while others reduce it. Part IV analyzes three of the most important policy arenas: Economic policy creates the framework within which capitalism operates and allocates resources; social policy and the welfare state determine how patterns of risk and the distribution of income and wealth are modified by politics; and foreign policy describes how the United States manages its relations with other countries. Because these policy domains are so important, they are among the most contested sites of a politics of power.

Public policies are the outcomes of political struggles among citizens, groups, and public officials. They help determine who gets what, where, and how. Policies also matter because they help shape future outcomes. They create arrangements that are advantageous to some political actors and harmful to others. Contenders struggle over policy armed with the weapons that previous policies have given them.

Public policy is not made in a vacuum. In the United States, it occurs in a context of tensions between capitalism and democracy, which are analyzed in Chapters 2 and 3, and within the settings of political participation and institutions that are analyzed in Chapters 4 through 8. Because policies are debated openly and determined within democratic institutions, outcomes are sometimes responsive to public opinion and group demands. But the democratic features of American government are often constrained and distorted by the advantages capitalism confers, by patterns of inequality, and by uneven access to political institutions. At such moments, policies diverge from the preferences of the public and reflect those of people who hold economic power.

ECONOMIC POLICY

INTRODUCTION

The recent recession, whose effects continue to linger, was the worst economic disaster to strike the U.S. since the Great Depression of the 1930s. Real-estate prices collapsed, foreclosures rose, unemployment increased, major financial institutions filed for bankruptcy, and stocks plummeted. Few Americans escaped its distress. Citizens who were fortunate enough to retain their jobs and homes had to tighten their budgets and delay plans that involved major expenses, such as sending children to college or scheduling major surgery. For less fortunate Americans, the recession was a catastrophe. Desperation replaced mere uncertainty. People were left with no job, no home, and no income. Thus, one group emerged from the recession poorer than before, but feeling lucky they were still working and in their homes; the other group absorbed the recession's full fury.

The onset of recessions and the extent of their pain are influenced by economic policies. Indeed, no actions by government—except, perhaps, mobilizing for war—touch the lives of more Americans more profoundly than economic policy. Jobs, incomes, and standards of living depend on government performance in this area. Americans prosper when the government's economic policies succeed. They seek refuge from the storm when these programs fail.

This chapter reviews economic policy through which government sets the rules and influences private production. It concentrates on three ways that government tries to shape economic performance: fiscal policy, which entails taxes and spending by the government; monetary policy, which involves setting interest rates; and regulation, which mandates or prohibits certain activities.

THE GOVERNMENT AND THE ECONOMY

In 2010, governments at all levels—federal, state, and local—collected $3.6 trillion in revenues and spent $5.1 trillion in outlays. With the government collecting and spending so much money, many believe it is too big, confiscating too much money in taxes and spending too much on wasteful programs. Indeed, government has grown dramatically since 1950, as Table 9.1 indicates. Total government outlays, which were just 22.7 percent of **gross domestic product (GDP)** in 1950, were 29.2 percent of GDP 50 years later, in 2000, and grew to 35 percent by 2010. As the activities of government have increased, especially in the realms of social welfare and defense, so have the expenses required to pay for them.[1]

The magnitude of spending and its growth over time have given rise to frequent complaints about "big government." Yet the size of the public sector in the United States is comparatively quite small. For example, the tax burden on American citizens is light compared to that in other advanced industrial countries. The United States collects a lower proportion of its GDP in the

TABLE 9.1

GOVERNMENT SPENDING AS A PERCENTAGE OF GDP

Year	Total Government Receipts	Government Receipts % of GDP	Total Government Expenditures	Government Expenditures % of GDP
1950	56.4	20.7	62.0	22.7
1955	90.8	22.9	97.6	24.7
1960	130.7	25.2	135.8	26.2
1965	172.6	25.1	181.9	26.5
1970	286.5	28.3	298.3	29.5
1975	428.9	27.5	499.8	32.0
1980	756.7	27.8	853.5	31.3
1985	1,117.9	26.9	1,347.4	32.5
1990	1,585.7	27.6	1,862.1	32.5
1995	2,092.7	28.6	2,318.3	31.6
2000	3,006.2	31.0	2,834.0	29.2
2002	2,887.1	27.8	3,209.9	30.9
2004	3,040.0	26.4	3.594.8	31.2
2006	3,758.3	28.9	4,115.0	31.6
2008	3,995.2	28.1	4,669.9	33.0
2010	3,558.1	24.7	5,078.4	35.0

NOTE: Numbers are in billions of dollars.

SOURCE: *Historical Tables: Budget of the U.S. Government, Fiscal Year 2012* (Washington, DC: Office of Management and Budget, 2012), 340–345, tables 15.1, 15.2, and 15.3.

form of taxes than any other affluent country, and it spends less as a percent of GDP than any other except for Australia, Ireland, Japan, and Switzerland (see Figure 9.1).

The smaller public sector in the United States, in terms of revenue collected and money spent, is reflected in lower benefit levels, tighter eligibility requirements, and fewer public services. For example, in many other rich democracies, the government either provides child-care services directly or provides more generous subsidies for it.

The comparatively small size of the government in relation to the economy is also apparent when one measures it by the number of government jobs. Public-sector employees at federal, state, and local levels combined comprised only 15 percent of total employment, which placed the U.S. in the bottom third of 18 Western democracies.[2]

Not only is the government comparatively small, but it also has less leverage to influence the economy. Compared to their counterparts in other advanced economies, U.S. firms are subject to fewer and less invasive government regulations. A standard measure used to compare the regulatory burden from one country to another is the number of procedures and days it takes to start a new business. The U.S. ranks among the easiest countries in the world to open a new business, requiring only an average of five steps lasting five days.[3] Another standard measure of the thickness of the regulatory environment compares laws governing job termination. Nowhere else does the absence of government regulations give employers so much power to fire or lay off workers and leave them unprotected from summary job loss.

Alongside regulatory controls, the government also relies on indirect mechanisms, notably fiscal and monetary policy, to intervene in the economy. The government uses **fiscal policy** to manage the economy by adjusting the government's budget, and it uses **monetary policy** to influence the economy by adjusting interest rates. But the ability of policy makers to utilize these tools effectively is undermined by their institutional design. Control over fiscal policy is divided between Congress and the president, while control over monetary policy is vested in the Federal Reserve Board (popularly known as the Fed). Because fiscal and monetary policies are assigned to independent institutions, there is no assurance that these policies will be coordinated—that is, that they will push in the same direction at the same time.[4]

Economic policy is subject to a politics of power, a shifting balance of forces that can retard or promote change. For example, the sharp recession beginning in the last quarter of 2007 triggered pain and cries for help throughout the country, as people lost their jobs and their homes. The government's normal restraint was replaced by a new aggressiveness. It flexed its economic muscles and even

FIGURE 9.1

TOTAL TAX REVENUE AS A PERCENTAGE OF GDP, 2010

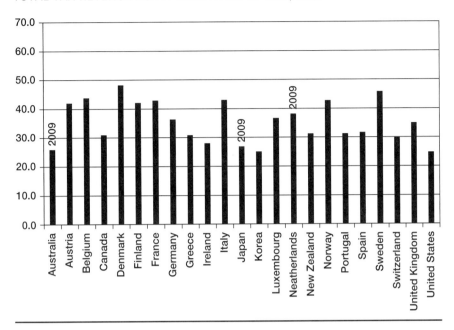

SOURCE: OECD (2011), Revenue Statistics: Comparative Tables, OECD Tax Statistics.

GENERAL GOVERNMENT TOTAL OUTLAYS AS PERCENTAGE OF GDP, 2010

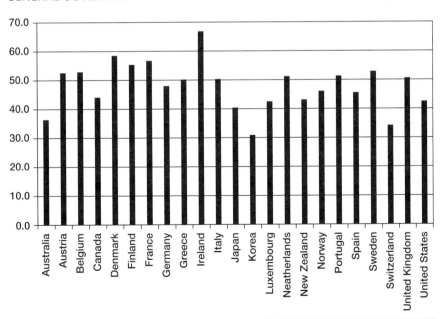

SOURCE: OECD (2011), Economic Outlook, Volume 2011, Issue 2, no. 90, Statistical/ Annex Table 25, December 7, 2011.

developed new ones. The government brokered marriages between failing and healthy banks, supervised the reorganization of the automobile industry, became the majority owner of mortgage companies, pumped money into the economy with new spending and tax breaks, and guaranteed corporate loans. Policies of minimal intervention based on the premise that government was the problem were replaced by a new activism that regarded government as the solution.

FISCAL POLICY

Fiscal policy manipulates the total amount of government revenue and spending to manage overall demand in the economy. Government can either stimulate the economy by running a **budget deficit** or restrain it by running a **budget surplus**. Budget deficits pump money into the economy, encouraging more spending, while surpluses take money out, discouraging investment and consumption. Fiscal policy is a kind of thermostat that policy makers adjust to counteract the economy's market swings. But the federal budget is more than a fiscal tool to bring the economy into balance, cooling it down when **inflation** gets too high and revving it up when employment gets too low. It also establishes the priorities and values of decision makers, depicting in black and white who the winners and losers in society will be. Some groups will shoulder a larger share of the tax burden while others will receive more in benefits. The budget reveals who has power in the way it distributes costs and benefits among different groups. For example, the budgets submitted by President George W. Bush gave the wealthiest Americans the largest tax cuts, while President Obama's budgets imposed the largest tax increases on them. Spending priorities also shifted: Bush's budgets devoted proportionally more money to defense while Obama's called for a higher proportion of spending for health care and education.

The budget process is a long, difficult, and intensely political affair that involves partisan conflict between Democrats and Republicans, institutional conflict between the legislative and executive branches, jurisdictional conflict within each of these branches, and interest-group conflict among an immense array of pressure groups. The process begins in the Executive Office of the President (described in Chapter 6), where the Office of Management and Budget (OMB) formulates the president's budget. The OMB negotiates with federal agencies to reconcile differences between their requests and the president's projections. It then submits a draft budget to the president for review and approval. The president then makes whatever changes are deemed necessary before presenting a budget proposal to Congress. The budget that President Obama submitted to Congress in 2012 consisted of five volumes and weighed in at over 11 pounds.

The president's budget, reflecting the administration's priorities, becomes the point of departure for consideration by Congress, which is free to reject or amend it. Conflict between Congress and the administration over the budget is inevitable as each tries to impose its own priorities. But it is especially intense when the presidency and one or both houses of Congress are controlled by different parties. In 1995, when Bill Clinton, a Democrat, occupied the White House and Congress was controlled by the Republicans, disagreement over the budget led to a temporary shutdown of the federal government. Federal offices and national parks were closed for 26 days because without a budget agreement between Congress and the president there was no authority to pay workers to keep them open.[5] More recently, since 2011, divided government has prevented passage of a budget on which President Obama and the Republican majority in the House of Representatives could agree on. Consequently, the government has depended on continuing resolutions approved by Congress and the president to provide funding to federal agencies at current levels.

Relations between Congress and the president do not often deteriorate to the point of shutting down the federal government for lack of funds. More typically, after the president's budget is presented to Congress, the budget committees in the House and the Senate adopt a joint budget resolution that specifies the total amount of money the government intends to raise and spend. Expenditures are distributed across 20 broad categories of government activity, such as defense, energy, and agriculture. In essence, the budget resolution is a general plan of spending and revenue targets. Committees within Congress are then charged with amending existing law to reflect tax and spending changes consistent with the totals called for in the joint resolution. "For example," Daniel J. Palazzolo writes, "it is one thing to agree that $35 billion in tax breaks will go towards tuition assistance for higher education; it is another thing to determine who is eligible, how much each person will be eligible for, how the tax credits will be structured and the like."[6] The appropriations committees in the House and Senate review these changes and stipulate the actual funding levels for particular programs, with an eye to keeping total spending within the guidelines set by the joint budget resolution. An appropriations bill is then submitted to the president, who signs or vetoes it.

The final budget agreed to by the president and Congress is simply an estimate of what the government will spend and how much revenue it will collect. No one really knows, for example, what the final cost of disaster relief will be in any given year, whether the United States will enter a war that it did not anticipate fighting when the budget was passed, or exactly how much revenue certain taxes will raise. Budgets are intentions that the future sometimes respects and at other times mocks.[7]

TAXES

Nobody likes taxes. Americans, like citizens in other countries, complain that they pay too much, that the tax system is unfair and too complicated.[8] Yet taxes are necessary to pay for government: both for the services we receive from it, such as police protection, and for the benefits we collect from it, such as Social Security. Taxes are the fuel that keeps the machinery of government running. Just as no one likes paying money to fill up their car with gas, no one likes paying taxes. But cars cannot run without gas and government cannot function without taxes. "Taxes," Chief Justice Oliver Wendell Holmes once wrote, are "the price we pay for civilized society."[9]

Tax policy is highly contentious, as groups seek to influence what the overall level of taxation should be, what types of taxes should be imposed, and who should pay them. As we saw in Figure 9.1 and Table 9.1, American citizens are lightly taxed compared to citizens in other Western democracies and to past generations. Tax receipts at all levels of government amounted to 20.7 percent of GDP in 1950. They rose fairly steadily for the next 50 years to 31.0 percent of GDP by 2000, with federal taxes accounting for two-thirds of government receipts and state and local governments the remaining third. But tax revenues fell to just a little more than a quarter of GDP by 2004. The Bush administration's tax cuts reduced federal revenue as a percent of GDP to its lowest level since 1951 (16.1%) and accounted for the entire decline in tax receipts. Total tax revenue proceeded to recover somewhat, but it nose-dived again when the recent recession reduced economic activity, lowering tax receipts to 24.7 percent of GDP in 2010, their lowest level since 1959. The federal portion of tax revenue fell even faster, dropping to just 14.9 percent of GDP.[10] Not only are federal taxes a much smaller percentage of the economy (GDP) now than in the past, but they are a smaller proportion of people's income. In 2009, the average rate people paid in federal taxes on their income was just 17.4 percent, the lowest average tax rate in more than 30 years. It is ironic that the Tea Party–fueled antitax sentiment, which played such a large role in propelling Republicans to victory in the 2010 congressional elections, should coincide with years in which people were actually paying *less* in federal taxes as a proportion of their income than they had in more than a generation.[11]

With expenditures as a proportion of GDP growing and tax revenue as a percentage of economic activity declining, deficits ensued, especially at the federal level. Tax cuts, the wars in Iran and Afghanistan, and a new prescription-drug benefit that was not paid for with new taxes contributed to rising federal deficits under President Bush. The deficit rose even faster under President Obama due to lower tax receipts as a result of the recession and increased spending to help revive the economy. Deficits require the government to borrow money to pay its bills, and creditors naturally charge interest for the money they lend it. The government then must dip into current revenues to pay off interest charges on the debt it owes, leaving less money in the budget to support vital services such as health care, environmental protection, and homeland security. In 2010, the federal government paid $196 billion in interest to holders of the national debt. This was 5.7 percent of all federal outlays, more than the federal government spent on any agency or department except for Defense and Health and Human Services.

Deficits are not necessarily bad; at times, they are even appropriate. Everything depends on how well the economy is doing and what the government spends the money on. When the economy is in recession, deficits stimulate commerce that puts people back to work. People have more money to spend, consumer demand increases, employers hire workers to fill increased orders, and tax receipts recover as employment, spending, and incomes all rise. Deficits are also appropriate when they allow the government to invest in the future. Some government spending yields a high social and economic return that makes borrowing money worthwhile. It can contribute to future economic growth. In short, whether deficits are good or bad depends on the state of the economy as well as on how wisely the money is invested.

Not only has the amount of taxes the government collects as a proportion of GDP changed, but so has the composition of taxes. There are different streams of tax revenue. State and local governments, for example, rely primarily upon sales and property taxes to raise revenue. By contrast, the federal government raises most of its money from individual income taxes (see Table 9.2). From 1945 to the present, it has collected between 40 and 50 percent of all its money from this one source. But in 2010, the personal income tax accounted for only 41.5 percent of all federal revenue, the lowest it had been since 1946. Lower tax rates, more exemptions, and stagnant incomes have reduced the amount income taxes contribute to the government's revenue stream.

TABLE 9.2

PERCENTAGE COMPOSITION OF TAX RECEIPTS BY SOURCE

Year	Individual Income Tax	Corporate Income Tax	Social Insurance and Retirement Receipts	Excise Tax	Other
1950	39.9	26.5	11.0	19.1	3.4
1960	44.0	23.2	15.9	12.6	4.2
1970	46.9	17.0	23.0	8.1	4.9
1980	47.2	12.5	30.5	4.7	5.1
1990	45.2	9.1	36.8	3.4	5.5
2000	49.6	10.2	32.2	3.4	4.5
2002	46.3	8.0	37.8	3.6	4.3
2004	43.0	10.1	39.0	3.7	4.2
2006	43.4	14.7	34.8	3.1	4.1
2008	45.4	12.1	35.7	2.7	4.2
2010	41.5	8.9	40.0	3.1	6.5

SOURCE: *Historical Tables: Budget of the U.S. Government, Fiscal year 2012* (Washington, DC: Office of Management and Budget, 2012), table 2.2, pp. 30–33.

The contribution that corporate income taxes make to total federal revenues has declined even more precipitously. Corporate income taxes accounted for one-quarter of all federal tax receipts in 1950. By 2010, they accounted for less than half that amount: only 8.9 percent of federal revenue. The federal tax rate for big corporations is officially 35 percent on profits, one of the highest corporate tax rates in the West, but loopholes, credits, and accounting gimmickry have cut the effective corporate tax rate to about 25 percent, one of the lowest rates among Western democracies.[12] Sometimes tax shelters permit corporations to avoid taxes altogether. One study found that only a quarter of the largest 280 American corporations paid the 35-percent corporate tax rate; another quarter paid less than 10 percent; and over a tenth paid no taxes at all, making American companies world leaders in tax avoidance. For example, the General Electric Corporation, which made $14.2 billion worldwide and $5.1 billion in the U.S. in 2010, paid nothing that year in corporate taxes.[13]

Along with corporate taxes, the proportion of taxes the federal government raises through excise taxes (federal sales taxes on such items as alcohol, cigarettes, and gasoline) has fallen. The federal government collected about one-fifth of its money through these kinds of consumption taxes in 1950. By 2010, they amounted to a negligible 3.1 percent of total federal revenue.

The decline in the proportion of federal revenue raised through income, corporate, and excise taxes has been compensated for by a rise in payroll taxes. The Social Security payroll tax, which finances retirement and health benefits for the elderly and disabled, accounts for the largest portion of these contributions. It is the second largest federal revenue stream and now makes almost the same contribution to federal coffers as the individual income tax. Whereas social-insurance contributions amounted to about 10 percent of all federal taxes in 1950, in 2010 they amounted to 40 percent of all federal revenue.[14]

Any form of taxation will place a greater burden on some groups than others. Some people argue that the tax system should be **progressive**, requiring the rich to pay a larger proportion of their income in taxes. Others believe the tax system should be **regressive**, meaning that tax rates should not increase as personal income rises. As Table 9.3 reveals, when all types of taxes are considered together—federal and state income taxes, Social Security contributions, sales taxes, property taxes, and others—the distribution of the tax burden among the rich, poor, and middle class in 2011 was mildly progressive. The bottom 20 percent of income earners, with an average income of $13,000, had an effective tax rate of 17.4 percent; the middle quintile, whose average income was $42,000, paid about 25 percent of their income in taxes; while the top 1 percent,

TABLE 9.3

INCOMES AND FEDERAL, STATE, AND LOCAL TAXES IN 2011

| | Average Cash Income | TAXES AS A PERCENTAGE OF INCOME | | |
		Federal Taxes	State & Local Taxes	Total Taxes
Lowest 20%	$13,000	5.0%	12.3%	17.4%
Second 20%	26,000	9.5%	11.7%	21.2%
Middle 20%	42,000	13.9%	11.3%	25.2%
Fourth 20%	68,700	17.1%	11.2%	28.3%
Next 10%	105,000	18.5%	11.0%	29.5%
Next 5%	147,000	19.7%	10.7%	30.3%
Next 4%	254,000	20.6%	9.9%	30.4%
Top 1%	1,371,000	21.1%	7.9%	29.0%

NOTE: Taxes include all federal, state, and local (personal and corporate income, payroll, property, sales, excise, estate, etc.).

SOURCE: Institute on Taxation & Economic Policy Tax Model, April 2012, by Citizens for Tax Justice.

averaging $1,371,000 in income, was taxed at an effective rate of 29 percent. While the poor pay a smaller percentage of their income in taxes than everyone else, the middle class are taxed at a rate close to what those who are much richer pay. The mild progressivity of the tax burden—which becomes less progressive as income increases—is due entirely to federal taxes. The tax burden that state and local taxes impose across income groups is virtually flat. That is, the wealthy pay almost the same proportion of their income in state and local taxes as the middle and lower classes. Federal taxes have more progressive effects than state and local taxes because they rely on different taxes to raise revenues. The federal government depends more on income taxes, which are progressive, while state and local governments rely more on regressive taxes, such as the sales tax, to raise revenues.

Tax fairness, an issue that figured prominently in the Occupy Wall Street movement, entered the mainstream when Democrats and President Obama took it up. The issue also arose in debates about the so-called Buffett Rule, which was supported by President Obama. Obama agreed with Warren Buffett, one of the richest men in the world, who complained that it wasn't right that he should be taxed at a lower rate than his secretary. The Buffett Rule would require those in the highest tax bracket to pay a higher minimum tax rate to insure that they pay a greater share of their income in taxes than less affluent Americans.

While the federal income-tax code is somewhat progressive, supposedly assessing the incomes of those in the highest bracket at 39.6 percent, very few rich people actually pay that much. Most of their income takes the form of capital gains (profits from investments), which are taxed at a lower rate— 15 percent—than the rich pay on ordinary income. For example, according to Mitt Romney's 2010 tax return, he earned $21 million, placing him in the highest tax bracket. But his actual tax rate was only about 14 percent—what an American earning $80,000 would pay—because almost all of his income took the form of capital gains.

Not only does tax policy permit a rich family like the Romneys to pay lower taxes than Americans who earn much less, but recent changes to tax policy have also permitted rich families to pay a lower tax rate than their predecessors. For example, Mitt Romney pays a much lower tax rate than did his father, George Romney, a wealthy automobile executive and governor of Michigan. George Romney, who died in 1995, paid an average federal tax rate of 37 percent, according to tax forms that he released when he was alive. His son's rate is far lower because of changes to the tax code in the intervening years that have benefited the rich: the rate for taxpayers in the highest bracket was 50 percent for George Romney, compared to 35 percent for his son, and profits on investments were taxed as ordinary income and not at lower rates, as they are today.[15]

Finally, tax policy is not simply about how much money to collect, how to raise it, and how the burden should be distributed. It is also about creating incentives for certain types of behavior by offering tax exemptions, rebates, and deductions. For example, the government encourages home ownership by permitting homeowners to deduct the interest they pay on their mortgages from their tax bill. It encourages saving for retirement by permitting citizens to shield from taxes income that they contribute to a retirement account, and it encourages donations to charity by permitting people to deduct charitable contributions from their income. In sum, government often makes policy through the tax code by subsidizing activities it wants to encourage. Policy makers often prefer to offer what are called **tax expenditures**—public subsidies through favored tax treatment—rather than authorize normal expenditures for the same purpose because tax breaks are less likely to arouse conflict.[16] New tax breaks can be hidden in larger revenue bills, whereas new spending faces greater procedural hurdles, requiring approval in multiple congressional committees as part of the budget process. The cost to taxpayers is the same in either case, whether it takes the form of direct spending or decreased tax revenue. But the political consequences are very different.

According to Suzanne Mettler, the use of tax expenditures, or what she calls "the submerged state," has pernicious effects. Making policy through the tax code by giving favored tax treatment to certain activities is not as visible as new spending for programs. The costs of tax expenditures are diffuse and their effects not easily traceable. Consequently, citizens don't give government the credit it deserves for solving problems, such as making saving for retirement easier or making home owning more affordable. At the same time that the submerged state fosters passivity among the public, it energizes well-organized groups to obtain hidden subsidies through the tax code. The result, Mettler argues, is that the submerged state "exacerbates inequality, intensifies interest group activity, and undermines informed and engaged citizenry."[17]

The increased use of tax expenditures as a way to make policy has complicated the tax code and filled it with an array of exemptions, deductions, and rebates. Once perceived simply as a way to raise revenue, the tax code has become a more concealed and more frequent means by which government makes policy. Moreover, tax expenditures are very expensive. The federal government gave up about $1 trillion in revenue in 2011 through tax expenditures. This is just a bit less than the total deficit it ran in 2011.

EXPENDITURES

Taxes are one side of the government budget. The other side is spending. Political conflict over spending is as pervasive and bitter as it is over taxes. Groups struggle over how much money the government should collect and what it should spend it on. These conflicts are evident in how government expenditures have changed over time. Federal expenditures, which were just $42 billion (15.6 percent of GDP) in 1950, increased to $3.5 trillion (23.8 percent of GDP) by 2010. The federal government spends more today because it does more. Sixty years ago, Social Security coverage was not as broad, Medicare for seniors and Medicaid for the poor did not exist, and offices like the Environmental Protection Agency had not yet been created.

The federal government accounts for about two-thirds of all government expenditures, with state and local governments together responsible for the remaining third. Just as the revenue sources from which the federal government raises money have changed, so have the categories in which the national government spends it. Some federal activities that once captured a large share of the federal budget now get less, while other activities receive more. Consider, for instance, how spending for national defense and the welfare state—the two largest charges on the federal budget—have changed through the years (Table 9.4). In 1954, in the midst of the Cold War, 69.5 percent of all federal

TABLE 9.4

FEDERAL OUTLAYS FOR DEFENSE AND THE WELFARE STATE (IN MILLIONS OF DOLLARS)

Year	Defense	% of Federal Expenditures	Welfare State	% of Federal Expenditures
1954	49,266	69.5	13,076	18.5
1960	48,130	52.2	26,184	28.4
1970	81,692	41.8	75,349	38.5
1980	133,995	22.7	313,374	53.0
1990	299,331	23.9	619,329	49.4
2000	294,495	16.5	1,115,481	62.4
2002	348,555	17.3	1,317,437	65.5
2004	455,847	19.9	1,485,870	64.8
2006	521,840	19.7	1,672,076	63.0
2008	616,097	20.7	1,895,740	63.6
2010	693,586	20.1	2,385,731	69.0

SOURCE: *Historical Tables: Budget of the U.S. Government, Fiscal Year 2012* (Washington, DC: U.S. Government Printing Office, 2012), 48–55.

outlays were devoted to defense spending. From that peak, the share of federal spending committed to the military declined steadily to 16.1 percent in 1999, climbing back to 20.1 percent of federal spending in 2010 to finance the wars in Afghanistan and Iraq.

In the interim, the percentage of the federal budget dedicated to welfare-state spending, which includes federal expenses for health care, education, income support, Social Security, and veterans' benefits, increased considerably. Welfare-state expenses comprised only 15.6 percent of the federal budget in 1954 but accounted for more than two-thirds (69 percent) of all federal spending by 2010.

Although the balance between welfare and warfare has shifted over time, spending in these two areas, along with interest on the debt, totaled about 87 percent of all federal outlays in 2010. All the other tasks the federal government performs, from maintaining the national parks to paying the salaries of federal judges, are responsible for the remaining 13 percent of federal spending.

Another way of looking at how federal money is distributed is to divide it between mandatory and discretionary accounts. Two-thirds of all federal spending is mandatory. Spending for these programs, Daniel J. Palazzolo writes, is "governed by formulas or criteria set forth in authorizing legislation" passed by Congress "rather than by appropriations."[18] In other words, these programs are the result of previous commitments that Congress is obligated to meet. For example, **mandatory spending** includes payments on the national debt. To retain its access to credit, the government must pay off its debt when it comes due. But the most expensive form of mandatory spending takes the form of **entitlement programs**. Entitlement programs provide benefits to citizens as long as they meet certain eligibility requirements. Their cost is open-ended. The government will provide benefits to all those who qualify, regardless of how many there are or what the final cost may be. Social Security, for example, is an entitlement program. Citizens who have contributed to the Social Security program receive checks from the government when they apply and become eligible. SNAP (formerly food stamps) and Medicare are other examples of entitlement programs.

Mandatory spending consumes so much money that not much is left over for discretionary spending. Unlike entitlement programs, discretionary spending is under the jurisdiction of the House and Senate Appropriations committees, which provide authority for "federal agencies to incur obligations and make payments out of the treasury for specified purposes."[19] The largest portion of the federal government's discretionary spending (60 percent) is allocated to defense. The other 40 percent includes everything from the national park service to environmental protection, the federal courts to foreign aid, and

WHAT DO YOU THINK?

What Is the Right Size for Government?

Are Americans better or worse off because government spending and revenues account for such a small percentage of GDP compared to other affluent democracies? Some argue that when government directs so much money it chokes off innovation, promotes inefficiency, and leads to decision making based on what yields the biggest dividends for politicians, not for society. Others believe that the market is too unstable and leads to outcomes that are too unequal without the moderating and guiding hand of government. Are Americans better off with less or more government?

homeland security to college loans. The small share of federal outlays devoted to discretionary programs makes it very hard for Congress to direct expenditures through its annual appropriations process. It also makes it difficult for Congress to control spending without reducing the cost of entitlement programs. Government outlays increase each year because the cost of entitlement programs grows each year. And that growth is automatic as more people qualify for Social Security and Medicare, the two largest and most expensive entitlement programs.

MONETARY POLICY

Along with fiscal policy, the government tries to manage the economy through monetary policy. Monetary policy attempts to fine-tune the economy by manipulating interest rates, the cost of borrowing money. High interest rates tend to slow down the economy by discouraging spending. Low interest rates, on the other hand, encourage borrowing and spending by making credit cheap and easy to obtain. Like fiscal policy, monetary policy is used to counteract tendencies toward economic instability. If the economy is tending toward inflation or excessive demand, raising interest rates will cool it down. Conversely, if demand is slack and a recession appears imminent, reducing interest rates will help revive the economy by making loans more attractive for consumers wanting to purchase new goods and for businesses wanting to make new investments.

But manipulating interest rates is not simply about trying to counteract tendencies toward inflation and recession. Like fiscal policy, monetary policy affects different groups in different ways. For example, affluent people with savings in the bank generally benefit from high interest rates—so-called "tight money"—because it increases the value of their investments. The opposite is often true for working-class people, who are more likely to go into debt than to have savings: lower interest rates on loans reduce the interest charges they have to pay on their debt. Similarly, entrepreneurs who need credit to start or expand a business do better when interest rates are low, whereas banks profit more when interest rates are high. Thus, whether to err on the side of setting interest rates high or low is not simply a technical matter of managing the economy but a political one of rewarding some groups at the expense of others. For example, with interest rates currently low, retirees with savings accounts complain that their investments are yielding meager rates of return that jeopardize their retirement, while consumers trying to secure mortgages for new homes and firms seeking loans to expand their businesses appreciate low interest rates because they reduce their borrowing costs. A key question, then, is who decides, and on what basis, if the economy needs higher or lower interest rates?

Monetary policy is in the hands of the Federal Reserve Board (or Fed), whose mandate is to maximize employment, stabilize prices, and moderate long-term interest rates. The Fed determines the rate of interest that the Federal Reserve Bank charges other banks to borrow money. When the Federal Reserve Bank raises the rate it charges banks for loans, the banks correspondingly increase the rate they charge borrowers. The result is that fewer loans are made, and economic growth slows. Similarly, when the Fed lowers the interest rate for banks, banks can give customers easier credit terms, increasing the flow of money in the economy. For example, in 2008, as unemployment rose and stock prices dropped sharply, the Fed reduced interest rates as fast as it could—at one point even hurriedly arranging an unscheduled meeting to cut rates. The interest rate it charged banks dropped from 5.75 percent in August 2007 to an unprecedented 0.50 percent by December 2008—and the Fed has subsequently announced that it will hold interest rates near zero until it sees marked improvement in unemployment. In essence, the Fed was trying to revive the economy by virtually loaning money free to banks in hopes of easing the lending terms they charge their customers.

Aside from lending money to banks, the Fed affects the money supply through open-market operations, which involve buying and selling government bonds. Bonds are loans that the government promises to repay with interest when the debt is due. Buying government bonds puts more money into circulation, while selling bonds withdraws money from the economy. Finally, the Fed influences the money supply by setting the reserve rate that banks must hold on deposits. The reserve rate is the proportion of money that banks must keep on hand in the event that depositors withdraw funds from their accounts. An increase in the reserve rate means that banks have to hold more of their funds in reserve and therefore have less money to lend out, decreasing the money supply. Lowering the reserve rate has the opposite effect: it permits banks to lend out a higher proportion of their deposits as loans to creditors, thereby increasing the money supply.

But the Fed expanded its playbook dramatically in response to the recent recession. The Fed rescued the insurance giant AIG when it could not pay its debt to large banks, which themselves could have gone under if AIG had defaulted. The Fed loaned AIG $85 billion so it could meet its commitments in exchange for an 80 percent share of the firm. The Fed also engaged in quantitative easing, which entails buying government and private-sector assets. In 2008, the Fed bought hundreds of billions of dollars of mortgage-backed securities and government bonds in order to drive down interest rates and ease credit conditions. Since then the Fed has announced two additional rounds of quantitative easing to lower long-term interest rates and encourage lending.

The different methods the Fed uses to manipulate the money supply send ripples through the economy, affecting the direction of the stock and bond markets, the rate of interest that banks charge on mortgages and that credit-card companies charge on unpaid balances. But the ripples continue far beyond this, affecting whether companies hire more employees or prune their payrolls, whether wages and salaries go up or down, and whether the economy expands or contracts. The fact that so little is known about the operation of the Fed is an extraordinary feature of American politics. Henry Ford, Sr., once observed, "It is well enough that the people of the nation do not understand our banking and monetary system for, if they did, I believe there would be a revolution before tomorrow morning."[20]

According to the journalist William Greider, the Fed is "the crucial anomaly at the very core of representative government, an uncomfortable contradiction with the civic mythology of self-government."[21] When the Fed was created in 1913, it was deliberately insulated from democratic pressures and the influence of elected officials. To this day, the Fed enjoys more political independence from both Congress and the president than any other government agency. It does not have to depend on Congress for money, because it is self-financing through the interest it collects on the government bonds it holds; and members of its board of governors are appointed for lengthy, 14-year terms. It owes this enviable position to the idea that monetary policy—adjusting interest rates—is a technical matter beyond politics, and to the fear that elected representatives would simply print money to please constituents regardless of whether the economy required it. But exempting monetary policy from democratic accountability does not mean that politics has disappeared. In the absence of democratic control, monetary policy tends to be captured by banks.

The Fed often adopts the perspective of banks because they are its primary constituency: over 2,000 banks belong to the Federal Reserve System, and most Federal Reserve Board members either worked for banks or are economists trained in finance. The Fed, after all, is a bank itself, the central bank of the United States. Moreover, representatives from the banking community participate and vote when the Fed deliberates over monetary policy. Commercial banks select members of the Federal Open Market Committee (FOMC), which sets interest-rate targets. In 1993, Representative Henry B. Gonzalez, chair of the House Committee on Banking, wrote an open letter to President Clinton deploring the presence of bankers on the FOMC and the lack of influence the public has over its composition. Gonzalez wrote:

> In general, the Federal Reserve decision makers are bankers or friends of bankers. Decision makers representing the concerns of agriculture, small business, labor, and community groups are almost unheard of. . . . Last week, the Fed selected one of their [sic] own, William J. McDonough, as president of the New York Federal Reserve Bank. Mr. McDonough's qualifications and his views on monetary policy . . . will not be debated in public. His expertise in central bank monetary policy will not be questioned in Senate confirmation hearings. However, because he has been selected through the Fed's internal private mechanisms, he will manage our nation's money supply without ever going before the American people or their representatives.[22]

But the direct influence of representatives from the banking community participating in policymaking discussions of the FOMC is only insurance that the Fed reflects the views of bankers. The Fed tends to promote the interests of banks because it believes that what is good for banks is good for the economy. After all, banks supply money to the industrial muscles of the economy, just as the heart pumps blood to the physical muscles of the body. In each case, the muscles cannot function unless they receive the sustenance they require. Thus, there is a structural basis for the Fed's support of banks. The health of the economy, the Fed believes, depends on the health of the banks that circulate money through it.

Nowhere was this structural dependence on banks more apparent than in the way the Fed responded when major Wall Street investment firms seemed poised to fail during the 2008 financial crisis. Willem H. Buiter, a professor of finance at the London School of Economics, argues that the Fed was so accommodating to Wall Street's distress—offering to come to its rescue in exchange for very little—because it had "internalized the objectives, concerns, world views and fears of the financial community."[23] The Fed wasn't bought, blackmailed, or bribed when it offered to save AIG, Citigroup, Bear Stearns, Bank of America, and other financial institutions that were about to collapse due to bad loans they had made. Rather, the Fed provided a lifeline because it had adopted the "objectives, interests, and perceptions" of the financial community as its own. It viewed the needs of the broader economy through the needs of the banking community it was supposed to regulate.

The independence and authority of the Fed has elevated its chair to what some regard as the second most powerful position in the government. No one earned that reputation more than Alan Greenspan, who chaired the Fed from 1987 to 2006. He was called "the Maestro" and received rock-star adulation for the way he guided the economy through recessions and financial crises. At Greenspan's final meeting as Chair in 2006, just before the economy collapsed, the other members of the Fed Board gushed in tribute to his alleged brilliance. In words that are embarrassing to repeat today, Fed Board member Janet Yellin said the situation Greenspan was handing off to his "successor is a lot like a tennis racquet with a gigantic sweet spot."[24] But the holes in the racquet were bigger than Yellin ever imagined, and Greenspan's tenure as chair swiftly came under attack once the housing market collapsed. It was as if the curtain had been pulled back, revealing the wizard to be a fraud. Greenspan endorsed Bush's tax cuts, which contributed to the deficit; kept interest rates low, which contributed to the bubbles in the housing and credit markets; and opposed regulations that would have prevented banks from taking on too much risk, which contributed to their bad debts and need for a bailout. As the recession deepened, even Greenspan recognized "a flaw in [his] model of how . . . the world works" when he admitted to the House Committee on Oversight and Government Reform that "[t]hose of us who looked to the self-interest of lending institutions to protect shareholders' equity—myself included—are in a state of shocked disbelief."[25] In other words, Greenspan acknowledged that government regulation was necessary and that banks could not be trusted to regulate themselves, because the self-interest of banks is insufficient to ensure safe, prudent lending practices.

In 2006, President Bush appointed Ben Bernanke, chair of the President's Council of Economic Advisors, to succeed Greenspan as the new chair of the Fed. Although Bernanke was a protégé of Greenspan's, he has diverged from many of Greenspan's policies. First, Bernanke reversed course and now supports increased regulation of the financial sector. Second, he has tried to make the Fed more transparent so that investors can take Fed policy into account when they make their plans. Third, he made clear that the Fed would take reducing unemployment as seriously as it did preventing inflation. In 2012, Bernanke announced that the Fed would keep interest rates low until the recovery took hold. Finally, he transformed the Fed into the lender of last resort. To avert financial panic, the Fed extended loans to banks and insurance companies that were about to collapse but were deemed too big and too interconnected to fail. But then the Fed went further and proceeded to extend credit to a wider variety of ailing firms that remained sick because the normal medicine the Fed prescribed was no longer working. As described earlier, the Fed cut interest rates to almost zero. When this was not enough to get credit flowing so that business could meet payrolls, make purchases, and roll over debt, the Fed proceeded to purchase assets in order to pump money into the economy. It offered loans to companies in exchange for stock; bought securities containing home mortgages and auto, credit-card, student, and small-business loans; lent money to banks; and guaranteed money-market funds that underwrite short-term loans to businesses. The Fed amassed nearly $3 trillion in assets—far outstripping any bailout money approved by Congress—and another $2 trillion in loan guarantees. The Fed's activism revealed how powerful the chair is in "making any loan he wants under any terms to any entity or individual in America that he thinks is economically justified."[26] The *New Yorker* described Bernanke's efforts to stem the financial crisis as "the boldest use of the Fed's authority since its inception, in 1913."[27] After learning that the Fed had committed the U.S. government to investments in the real estate, insurance, banking, automobile, and other industries, one Republican, Senator Jim Bunning of Kentucky, was so appalled that he complained, "I thought I woke up in France. But, no, it turned out it was socialism here in the United States of America."[28]

This is not your father's Fed anymore. The Fed has become more active, stretching its authority into new realms. It has gone beyond its traditional tools of influencing the money supply to engage in more regulatory oversight of the financial sector, such as engineering mergers of failing banks with healthy ones. It has improvised and aggressively pumped money into the economy by purchasing stock in companies, issuing short-term loans to businesses, and making investment guarantees. It has made a much stronger commitment to reducing unemployment, and it has become more transparent.

But this new assertiveness is not without risk to the Fed. As the Fed becomes more involved in the process of picking winners by deciding which industries

WHAT DO YOU THINK?

Should the Fed Be More Democratically Accountable?

Critics of the Fed's independence believe that it is too important not to be accountable to the public. Moreover, in the absence of accountability to Congress and the president, the Fed is responsive to the interests of banks by default. Defenders of the Fed believe that greater accountability to Congress and the president would lead to bad policy, that the Fed would not act prudently if it had to answer to public officials, who would always keep the money flowing for political reasons, leading to inflation. Should the Fed's independence be protected or should it be more democratically accountable?

to support, it becomes more of a target for lobbying and congressional scrutiny. It loses its mystique and jeopardizes its independence. The politicization of the Fed was evident in 2010 when President Obama's nominee to the Fed Board of Governors, the M.I.T. economics professor and 2010 Nobel Laureate Peter Diamond, was blocked by Senate Republicans.

REGULATION

Fiscal and monetary policies affect economic actors only indirectly, by influencing the conditions in which they operate. Policy makers use these tools to create an environment of stable prices and high employment levels that people can count on. But government can also use more direct means to influence what economic actors do. When authorized by Congress to do so, federal agencies engage in regulation, setting explicit rules of conduct that firms and workers must follow. Regulations dictate what economic actors can and cannot do. For example, regulations stipulate that firms cannot sell unsafe products, issue misleading financial statements, or engage in deceptive advertising. Other regulations require firms to accurately label foods and drugs, post safety notices, and pay a minimum wage to their workers.

Complaints about "big government" often refer to regulation. Conservatives and businesses grumble that the American economy is overregulated. They suggest that rules governing firms are proliferating, imposing unnecessary costs in terms of compliance, discouraging innovation with a maze of bureaucratic requirements, and promoting inefficiency by distorting the normal operation of the market. Yet in truth the United States is one of the least regulated markets in the world. According to the Fraser Institute, a conservative Canadian think tank, the hand of regulation in the United States is not heavy at all, but exceedingly light. The United States ranked twentieth out of 141 countries surveyed in terms of having the least regulated credit, labor, and product markets.[29]

The federal government's authority to issue regulations stems from the power the Constitution gave Congress to regulate commerce among the states and with foreign nations. But this power was largely dormant until 1887, when, under popular pressure, Congress created the Interstate Commerce Commission (ICC) to regulate railroad rates and routes. This agency was followed by a host of others created by Congress in response to outcries about the abuse of corporate power. In 1914, Congress established the Federal Trade Commission (FTC) to protect consumers from deceptive business practices. The Food and Drug Administration (FDA) was created in 1931 to prevent firms from selling tainted food and harmful drugs, and the Securities and Exchange Commission (SEC) was created in 1934 to prevent investors from being defrauded by stock-market manipulation. But these efforts often led to the opposite of what reformers intended. Officials in government agencies developed close ties with the very industries they were supposed to regulate.[30] The FDA became responsive to the pharmaceutical industry and the SEC to Wall Street brokerage houses. Watchdogs for the public became guard dogs for industry. Nor has much changed since the first regulatory agencies were created. Recently, Neil Barofsky, head of the Troubled Assets Relief Program, left his position in frustration, complaining that "regulatory capture exists, dominates our system and needs to be eradicated."[31]

Regulatory failure can have catastrophic consequences. In 2009, BP's Deepwater Horizon oil rig blew up in the Gulf of Mexico, killing 11 people and releasing 5 million barrels of oil into the water. It was the worst oil spill in American history. Investigators found that the Minerals Management Service (MMS), which was created to manage and oversee offshore drilling, ignored studies that questioned the reliability of blowout preventers— the fail-safe equipment that failed on the Deepwater Horizon rig.[32] They also found that agency inspectors routinely accepted gifts and trips from oil representatives, sidelined proposals that might have increased costs but improved safety, and adopted language provided by the industry trade group, the American Petroleum Institute, for rules to govern offshore drilling and safety. Worse, there was a fear that MMS officials were pulling their punches in regulating the oil industry because so many of them went on to take more lucrative jobs in it.

The first wave of regulatory agencies created during the Progressive and New Deal eras—such as the FDA and SEC—were engaged in **economic regulation**. Congress created these agencies to regulate specific industries, a process that often involved managing competition and setting standards, such as fuel efficiency standards for cars. In the 1960s, however, a new surge of popular protest emerged, demanding **social regulation** by the government. The civil rights movement pressed Congress to create agencies that would enforce new laws preventing discrimination. In 1970, the environmental movement prevailed upon Congress to establish the Environmental Protection Agency (EPA), which would develop and enforce environmental-quality standards. That same year, the labor movement convinced Congress to create the Occupational Safety and Health Administration (OSHA) to monitor workplace safety and health standards. And two years later, in 1972, the consumer movement used its growing influence in Congress to create the Consumer Products Safety Commission.

While the earlier and later waves of regulation both stemmed from popular dissatisfaction with free markets, economic and social regulation have very different logics and impacts. Economic regulations fixed prices, managed competition, set standards, and issued licenses for specific industries. The FDA regulated the pharmaceutical industry and the SEC regulated stock-market brokerage firms. But the social regulation of the 1960s and 1970s cut across industries to affect all businesses. All firms, regardless of the industry to which they belonged, now had to abide by antidiscrimination laws, environmental regulations, and workplace-safety rules. "The result," the political scientist David Vogel writes, "was a fundamental restructuring of both the politics and the administration of government regulation of corporate social conduct."[33]

But the reach of agencies like the EPA and OSHA across industrial lines also helped forge a united front against them by business interests. The second wave of regulation soon awakened a sleeping giant. Business mobilized in the 1970s to roll back what it perceived as intrusive and costly new social regulations. Campaign contributions from business soared, corporate lobbying increased, and efforts to sway public opinion against social regulations were launched. A counteroffensive by a mobilized and cohesive business community in favor of regulatory reform was moving across all fronts.

The politics of regulation are evident not only in the presence or absence of rules but also in how vigorously rules are enforced. In the same way that fiscal and monetary policies can be adjusted in response to economic circumstances, the zealousness with which the government pursues regulation depends on political circumstances. There is regulatory slack in the system that can expand or contract depending on the political pressures brought to bear on it.

The government can aggressively look for environmental violations or passively wait for citizens to file complaints; it can issue large fines to those who violate labor laws or merely slap them on the wrist; and it can send out enough inspectors to ensure that food meets safety standards or employ too few. Whether regulations are enforced rigorously or administered indifferently is as much a source of political conflict among advocates and opponents as the regulations themselves. Standard setting and enforcement by regulatory agencies stretch and bend in response to the political pressures applied to them.

Take the case of the SEC, which was created in 1934 to protect investors in the stock market against fraud. In the 1987 movie "Wall Street," the SEC brings the unscrupulous corporate raider Gordon Gecko to justice for insider trading on the stock market. That's Hollywood. In the real world, the SEC is not so vigilant. Most recently, the SEC failed to bring to light Bernie Madoff's Ponzi scheme, in which investors were paid not with actual earnings on their investments but with money coming in from new investors. Madoff's trickery fleeced investors of over $65 billion. The SEC had been tipped off about Madoff's scam as early as 1999, and had even investigated his firm three times, but the commission gave it a clean bill of health after each examination. Indeed, one of the SEC lawyers who investigated Madoff and found no wrongdoing received the SEC's highest performance rating, in part for her ability "to understand and analyze the complex issues of the Madoff investigation."[34] As if that were not embarrassing enough, Madoff then used SEC clearances as a selling point to assure investors that his investment practices were legitimate.

Nor did the SEC carefully scrutinize the finances of failing investment banks like Lehman Brothers or Bear Sterns, or the credit-rating agencies that gave deceptive AAA ratings to debt-ridden companies and risky assets. When the SEC finally did take action against banks who engaged in deceitful and fraudulent transactions during the recent financial crisis, the courts were stunned by its timidity. In one famous case, Citicorp bet against $1 billion in mortgage securities that it promoted and sold to investors. When the value of those securities collapsed, clients lost $700 million while Citi made $160 million in profit. The SEC obtained a settlement with Citi in which the bank did not admit to doing anything wrong but agreed to pay a fine and to never do it again. But Citi was already a repeat offender, having promised never to defraud customers again in 2005, 2006, and 2010, in similar settlements. Yet the SEC never brought contempt-of-court charges against Citi for chronic violations. Nor has the SEC succeeded in bringing criminal charges against anyone involved in the mortgage fraud that the banks engaged in. As one critic remarked incredulously, "The institutions can't be culpable without someone making a culpable decision, but

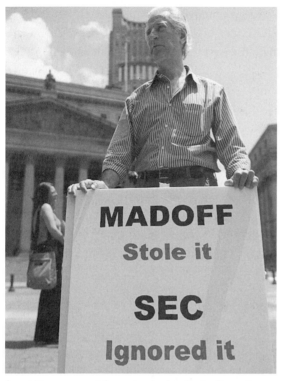

A protestor appears at the sentencing hearing for Bernard Madoff, who was convicted of eleven felonies that defrauded thousands of investors of billions of dollars.

the SEC seems to be emulating Inspector Clouseau and is constantly losing the trail."[35]

The problem stems partly from the close ties binding the SEC to the industry it is supposed to regulate. One study found that former SEC employees routinely took jobs with corporations and then helped their new employer "try to influence SEC rulemaking, counter the agency's investigations of suspected wrongdoing, soften the blow of SEC enforcement actions, block shareholder proposals, and win exemptions from federal law."[36]

Perhaps the best justification for hiring industry insiders is the one President Franklin Delano Roosevelt reportedly offered when he appointed the financier Joseph Kennedy chair of the newly created SEC in 1934: "It takes a thief to catch a thief." The revolving door between the SEC and finance is so busy that 219 former SEC staffers filed 789 "post-employment statements indicating their intent to represent outside clients before the commission" from 2006 to 2010.[37] It is not difficult to imagine that enforcement officers might be lax in going after investment banks that they recently worked for or hope will be their next employer.

CONCLUSION

In the United States, the production and allocation of goods and services is largely determined by the market. Yet no economy, not even a capitalist one that operates according to the laws of supply and demand, can exist without government. Government is needed to create a common currency that facilitates trade and exchange, to enforce contracts that promote security and predictability, and to supply public goods that society needs but the market will not provide because it is unprofitable to do so. As a congressman from Mississippi once acknowledged without a hint of irony, "The free enterprise system is too important to be left in the hands of private individuals."[38]

Economic policy sets the balance between markets and government. What is so remarkable about U.S. economic policy is the degree to which markets are empowered to determine who gets what and how much. Despite all the complaints about "big government," the size of the government in relation to the economy is comparatively quite small. Government spending as a proportion of GDP is relatively small and Americans pay less in taxes than citizens do in most advanced Western democracies. Not only does the government direct less of the flow of money through the economy in the U.S. than elsewhere, but it has weaker levers with which to direct. The value of fiscal and monetary policies for managing the economy is undermined by their institutional design. Fiscal and monetary policies are assigned to different institutions, with Congress and the president in charge of the former and the Federal Reserve Board in charge of the latter. There is no assurance that these institutions will work in conjunction with one another. Regulations are a more direct means of influencing what business does than fiscal and monetary policy. But regulation in the United States is not pursued with the vigor found in other countries. Firms must comply with fewer regulations, and the regulations that do exist are often not aggressively enforced.

The predominance of markets in America's political economy is due to the political power of business. But business interests must constantly defend the latitude granted markets. Social regulations of the 1960s and 1970s, which left a legacy of environmental, workplace, consumer, and civil rights protections, rolled back the private power of business. Although business regained enormous freedom beginning in the 1980s, the recent financial crisis contributed to demands for more regulation. It revealed how lax regulation of the financial sector had become, letting banks take on too much bad debt and permitting scam artists to fleece investors.

The 2008 recession had a similar effect on fiscal and monetary policy. The government became much more aggressive and interventionist. Government, which was previously regarded as the problem, was now expected to provide the solution. The Fed bought stock in companies that buy and sell mortgages, engineered mergers between failing and healthy banks, guaranteed loans, and bought bad debts that banks carried on their books. The Obama administration became the de facto overseer of the auto industry as it supervised the bankruptcy and reorganization of General Motors and Chrysler. And Congress became more assertive by extending unemployment insurance and reducing payroll taxes to stimulate spending. The trench warfare of economic policy between those who advocate reliance on markets and those who want to give more power to government never abates.

CHAPTER SUMMARY

Introduction

The recession that began in 2008 demonstrates the significance of economic policy. When policies that influence the production and allocation of goods and services work well, families have income to pay for food, housing, health care, and some amenities. When they do not work well, unemployment rises, foreclosures increase, and the demand for government and charitable assistance grows.

The Government and the Economy

The U.S. government's role in the economy is quite small compared to that of governments in other affluent democracies. Government revenues and expenditures are a smaller percentage of GDP, public-sector employment is a smaller proportion of total employment, and businesses have to comply with fewer regulations. But in response to the 2008 recession, government has become more active and interventionist, involving itself more directly in the management of firms and their strategies.

Fiscal Policy

Fiscal policy is the government's use of the budget to fine-tune the economy—to run deficits to stimulate it and promote employment and to run surpluses to slow it down and ward off inflation. The budget is negotiated between the president and Congress. The budget is significant because it reveals relations of power in society by depicting which groups must pay a higher share in taxes and which groups receive a larger share of benefits.

Taxes

As the responsibilities of government have grown, so have revenues as a percentage of GDP to pay for them. In addition, sources of revenue have shifted from excise and corporate income taxes to payroll taxes on workers. Finally, tax policy is used not only to raise revenue but also, increasingly, to make policy. The government favors certain activities and discourages others by treating them differently through the tax code.

Expenditures

The government spends more money today as a proportion of GDP because it does more than it did in the past. Almost 90 percent of all federal outlays are spent on just three items: welfare expenditures, defense spending, and payments on the national debt to creditors. The little that remains is devoted to all other federal programs.

Monetary Policy

The Federal Reserve Board is responsible for monetary policy, which influences interest rates and is supposed to regulate the banking industry. The Fed is politically independent of Congress and the president, which means it is subject to very little democratic oversight. The Fed tends to identify the welfare of the economy with the welfare of banks, which leads to monetary policies that are pleasing to them.

Regulation

Regulations that require or prohibit certain activities are weak in the United States, and their enforcement is often quite lax. Regulations take the form of economic regulations, which apply to certain industries, or social regulations, which apply to all firms in all industries. Regulators are often captured by the businesses they are supposed to regulate.

Critical Thinking Questions

1. Why are Americans so concerned about big government when the actual size of the government is smaller than in almost any other developed country?

2. To what degree do the size and intrusiveness of the state affect economic performance? Other developed countries, such as Sweden and Germany, have more regulations, higher taxes, and more government spending, yet they are no less economically efficient or competitive than we are. If the size and intrusiveness of the state mattered so much why aren't we performing better than they are?

3. The United States spends far more on defense and much less on welfare than other developed countries. Do you think the way we allocate our budget among these different functions is appropriate?

4. Control over economic policy is shared by the executive and legislative branches, as well as the Federal Reserve Board. Are we better off with policy fragmented among independent institutions, or should it be consolidated in one?

Suggested Readings

Dean Baker, *Plunder and Blunder: The Rise and Fall of the Bubble Economy.* Sausalito, CA: PoliPointPress, 2009.

William Greider, *Come Home America: The Rise and Fall (and Redeeming Promise) of Our Country.* New York: Macmillan, 2009.

Suzanne Mettler, *The Submerged State: How Invisible Government Policies Undermine American Democracy.* Chicago: University of Chicago Press, 2011.

John Howell Harris, *Right to Manage: Industrial Relations Policies of American Business in the 1940s.* Madison: University of Wisconsin Press, 1982.

Jonas Pontusson, *Inequality and Prosperity: Social Europe vs. Liberal America.* Ithaca, NY: Cornell University Press, 2005.

10

SOCIAL POLICY

INTRODUCTION

People hope to grow old. When they do, their quality of life depends in part on diet and exercise, but also on uncertain circumstances affecting their health and finances. Some risks of aging are inevitable. Some are less certain. Accidents can happen at work. Firms disappear, and with them go many jobs. Spouses die prematurely, leaving financial problems for their families. Other risks, like the chance of being poor, are strongly shaped by family history, racial background, neighborhood location, education, and access to work. Much of the time, people deal with these perils by private action. Those who can afford it often invest for their old age and take out private health, life, and disability insurance policies. Some adults pay for schooling to retrain and gain new skills. Private charities, both secular and religious, direct assistance to the homeless and the destitute.

For all but the wealthiest, however, private solutions are either insufficient or inaccessible. For this reason, all the democracies in countries wealthy enough to afford such policies sponsor programs to minimize risk and provide citizens with security. Across the political spectrum, almost all Americans support national policies—and much spending—that cushion citizens against the dangers that come with age, ill health, unemployment, or the death of a spouse. The federal government offers Social Security to the elderly and to surviving spouses in the form of a monthly pension. Medicare provides payments to doctors and hospitals, and prescription drugs, for people over 65. When workers lose their jobs, unemployment insurance softens the blow, helping tide them over until they land a new one. On a state-by-state basis, workers' compensation provides medical care for persons injured at work.

These programs of **social insurance** are the largest part of the **welfare state**. They step in when markets are unable to offer material security in the face of life's hazards. Most welfare-state spending of this type benefits the working class and middle class. Social-insurance programs are based on contributions workers make in the form of payroll taxes, which the government holds in trust in the event of a worker's death, injury, unemployment, or retirement. These programs cover almost all those in the labor force and their families. Their benefit levels tend to keep up with the cost of living. Although the level of support varies in some social-insurance programs, including unemployment insurance and workers' compensation, the largest programs tend to have uniform benefit levels. Since the early 1970s, **Social Security** payments, which are set nationally, have been indexed; that is, they increase in step with the previous year's rate of inflation. Social-insurance programs enjoy broad levels of support, both because large groups of Americans are beneficiaries and because beneficiaries are regarded as "deserving," having worked and contributed toward their benefits through the payroll taxes they paid.

Other social policies compensate for the limits and failures of the marketplace in more targeted ways. As we have discussed, the United States is characterized by an unusual degree of inequality as well as by significant **poverty**. To counteract and offset hardship, a cluster of programs that transfer funds to the poor offers a safety net to especially disadvantaged citizens. These programs include the Supplemental Nutrition Assistance Program (SNAP)—formerly known as food stamps—which provides debit cards that the poor can redeem for food; housing assistance; child-welfare payments; and **Medicaid**, which offers health insurance to the needy. These **public-assistance programs**, which help citizens not covered by social insurance, are available only to Americans whose income or wealth is below a particular level set by law. Unlike Social Security, public-assistance-program benefits are not indexed, nor is there a national standard of support. That is, benefit levels in public-assistance programs often are eroded by inflation and are unequal across the states. Under **Temporary Assistance to Needy Families (TANF)**, a federal program administered by each of the fifty states, the maximum monthly benefit for a family of three ranges from a high of nearly $1,000 in Alaska to a low of just under $300 in Georgia.[1] Such programs, which lessen the burdens of poverty and deprivation, are controversial. Many Americans believe that government's efforts to alleviate poverty relieve the poor of responsibility for their own situations; this belief is so strong that the very word *welfare*, despite its positive dictionary meaning as something that promotes well-being, often is used as a negative term.

Passed in March 2010, the **Patient Protection and Affordable Care Act**, known as "Obamacare," does not fit neatly into these distinctions between public and private provisions for social welfare, and between the social-insurance and transfer policies of the welfare state. This significant legislation, discussed later in this

WHAT DO YOU THINK?

What Is the Proper Role of Government?

Many Americans believe that economic and social well-being is not the concern of government. How Americans deal with deficiencies in income, security, health, and education should largely be the responsibility of families, churches, and organized charities. Many others, by contrast, believe that a critical role must be played by governmental policies because only the government has the resources to effectively compensate for deep inequalities or minimize a wide range of risks, including those associated with unemployment, aging, education, and housing. Where do you stand on this question?

chapter, keeps the provision of health care largely in the hands of private insurance, while also expanding eligibility for Medicaid. Moreover, it uses public funds to subsidize the purchase of private insurance, and it increases the federal government's ability to regulate the type and quality of insurance private companies provide.

Government also provides for schooling. Long thought a basic feature of citizenship, education prepares children to enter the worlds of work, community, and politics by conferring knowledge and skills that are indispensable for an effective adulthood. Public school systems are primarily a state-and local-government responsibility, but the federal government has been playing an increasingly significant role in this area of social policy as Washington has come to provide funds, encourage reforms, and set standards.

There is also what might be called a hidden or private welfare state. Although private arrangements to deal with risks are inadequate, most Americans continue to depend on welfare benefits that flow through the private sector. Some, for example, receive health insurance and a pension from their employer as part of the compensation package attached to their job. More money is distributed to pensioners from private retirement plans than from Social Security. The political scientist Jacob Hacker writes, "In no other nation do citizens rely so heavily on private benefits for protection against the fundamental risks of modern life."[2] But the private welfare state is not really so private. The government subsidizes the private welfare state through the tax code. Employer-sponsored health care and pension contributions are not taxed as income. Exempting income from taxation to support the private welfare state costs the federal government over $400 billion in revenue each year. The tax system also subsidizes mortgages, allowing homeowners to deduct mortgage-interest payments from their federal income tax.

The relatively large scale of the private welfare state is a hallmark of American social policy. Many benefits that citizens in other rich democracies receive from their government are provided to Americans either through their job or through personal savings and investments. The difference between these two approaches is substantial. When governments provide benefits, everyone who qualifies is eligible. But when private firms and persons are the source of benefits, only those workers who have the market power to make employers provide health insurance and private pensions receive them from their companies. Most of the health-care and pension benefits provided by employers go to those who are better off, while lower-paid employees receive less generous fringe-benefit packages. In other words, the private welfare state is more inequitable than government programs in terms of who benefits and how much they benefit.

Spending on social-insurance and public-assistance programs, as well as on state-subsidized private welfare programs, has expanded dramatically. By 2020, the country plans to spend an additional 940 billion federal dollars on health care than it did in 2012. Yet the United States spends and will continue to spend much less on public welfare than most European countries. Comparatively, the U.S. welfare state is small; it captures a more limited share of tax revenues and national wealth than does welfare spending in other advanced capitalist countries (Figure 10.1). In 2012, the United States devoted an estimated 19.5 percent of its gross domestic product (GDP) to public social expenditures. Most other rich democracies spend considerably more: some, including Italy, Finland, Belgium, Germany, France, Sweden, Austria, and Denmark, devote 25 to 30 percent of their GDP to such programs. American spending is just above the level of South Korea, Mexico, and Turkey.

The American welfare state is distinctive in other ways as well, such as the degree to which a person's well-being depends on the labor market. Some societies provide social rights, such as a right to health care, to all their citizens regardless of their position in the labor market. In other societies, including the United States, the amount and kind of benefits depend more heavily on one's job. Overall, Americans enjoy fewer and less generous social rights than citizens in many other industrial societies. Although some benefits (like Social Security pensions) are quite generous, many other benefits tend to be low, stigmatizing, and of short duration. They hardly provide a reprieve from the market. An example is the long-standing system of employer-based health insurance. Those with good jobs usually have enjoyed employer-based health insurance, but an increasing number of jobs, especially those that are poorly paid and nonunion, lack such insurance. This situation, which closely ties health insurance to employment, contributed to the result that nearly 50 million Americans—16.3 percent

FIGURE 10.1

PUBLIC SOCIAL EXPENDITURE AS A PERCENTAGE OF GDP

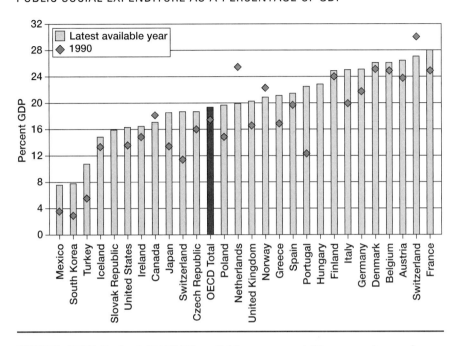

SOURCE: OECD Factbook 2011/2012, available at www.oecd-ilibrary.com (accessed October 8, 2012). The figures for latest available year are based on public social expenditures as a percentage of 2007 GDP.

of the population—had no health insurance in 2010. (The new health-care law is aimed at changing this.) Thus, the interaction of the public and private welfare states often reinforces the way the marketplace distributes income and wealth, instead of offering an alternative to it.[3]

THE HISTORICAL WELFARE STATE

The perception that the American welfare state is a laggard, a late addition to the family of welfare states, is based on when key social policies—workers' compensation, **unemployment insurance**, disability insurance, and old-age pensions—first were enacted. These welfare-state programs were created at the federal level in the United States with the passage of the Social Security Act in 1935, well after they were established in many European countries.

But this comparison gives a false impression that the federal government was not involved in social assistance before the enactment of Social Security.

In fact, an unusual sort of welfare state, one that diverged from Europe's, existed before 1935. West European welfare states were aimed at workers and provided everything from unemployment insurance in the event of layoffs to workers' compensation in case of an industrial accident. A consequence of targeting workers was that these welfare programs predominantly covered men, who were far more likely to participate in the labor force than women. In the United States, on the other hand, the early American welfare state did not target working men but rather extended social protection to veteran soldiers and mothers.

Between 1880 and 1910, the federal government spent more than a quarter of its entire budget on pensions for Union Civil War veterans and their dependents. In fact, the federal government spent more money on pensions for former Union Army soldiers and their dependents than on any other category except for interest payments on the national debt. By 1910, more than 500,000 Americans—28 percent of all men over age 65—received federal benefits averaging $189 per year, which was a tidy sum at the time. An additional 30,000 orphans, widows, and dependents of Civil War soldiers also received payments from the federal government.[4] These coverage rates were as high as those in comparable European old-age programs, and the benefits Americans received were more generous than those some pensioners received in Europe.

This unusual social-assistance program, in the form of veterans' pensions, expired when the generation of Civil War veterans passed away. As these payments were ending, a "maternalist" welfare state developed that promoted motherhood. During the Progressive Era, the first two decades of the twentieth century, a program of mothers' pensions provided income assistance to poor single mothers so they could stay home and raise their children. Providing income support to single mothers was perceived as preferable to having

WHAT DO YOU THINK?

Markets and Morals

Supporters of extensive welfare states offer three kinds of arguments. Some are based on making markets, especially the labor market, work more efficiently. Others center on the rights that come with citizenship, making the case that people suffering insecurity and deprivation cannot be active participants in public life. Still others have a moral basis, claiming that social policy has an ethical component of responsibility for other human beings. How would you assess such arguments and choose among them?

a woman work outside the home or give up her children to an orphanage or foster home. Each of these options would have undermined the mother's role, which advocates of mother's pensions sought to preserve.

But not all mothers were treated alike. To qualify for assistance, they had to prove themselves worthy. Widows could easily do this, because they were not perceived as responsible for their plight; but unwed mothers were often excluded. Benefits, moreover, were made contingent on the behavior of mothers. They had to display moral character by showing "intelligence, willingness to learn English, piety, celibacy," compliance with directions from social workers, and dedication to "full-time child-centered domesticity."[5] The price mothers paid for pensions was state regulation of their lives to ensure they conformed to traditional gender roles. Further, the maternalist welfare state was marked by deep racial discrimination. As the political scientist Deborah Ward has demonstrated, many states and localities, especially in the South, where most African Americans still lived, excluded black mothers from the rolls of recipients.[6] Mothers' pensions thus are an example of how certain roles—in this case, roles based on gender and race—can be inscribed by social policy.

THE NEW DEAL AND BEYOND

The shock of the Great Depression provided the impetus for the most dramatic expansion of the U.S. welfare state to date. When President Franklin D. Roosevelt declared in 1937 that "one-third of [the] nation" was "ill-housed, ill-clad, ill nourished," his estimate understated the problem. The proportion of the population that fit this description in the midst of the Depression, contemporaries agreed, was actually closer to one-half.[7] The main source of this distress was the staggering unemployment that afflicted the nation. In 1933, almost 13 million workers—a quarter of the workforce—were jobless, looking for work. Unemployment bred poverty and poverty bred despair. One man wrote to relief officials in Washington and inquired, "Can you advise me as to which would be the most humane way to dispose of myself and family, as this is about the only thing that I can see left to do."[8]

Poverty, low wages, and unemployment led some to abstain from politics. But it led others to take political action. Thousands of workers occupied factories to demand union recognition, the unemployed marched to demand food and shelter, and farmers dumped their produce to demand higher prices. The Roosevelt administration responded to these challenges by offering federally funded jobs and social-welfare programs to help the needy. The corporate community balked at these reforms, claiming they were a threat to private enterprise. But with the prospect of mass unrest growing, Roosevelt ignored their misgivings. The president recognized that a safety net providing citizens with a modicum of economic security was necessary both to alleviate suffering and to save capitalism, even if promoting such programs meant opposing conservatives who urged thrift and passivity in the face of distress.

There was an ironic quality to this hostility to the New Deal. As the business magazine *Fortune* observed in 1935, "it was fairly evident to most disinterested critics" that the New Deal "had the preservation of capitalism at all times in view."[9] Social reform was part of the administration's strategy to keep the market economy functioning. When the threat of civil disorder arose, the federal government expanded work-relief programs. When the threat of disorder waned, federally funded jobs diminished. Some social-welfare concessions were extended when the poor disrupted the status quo and were then retracted once the threat passed.[10]

But enduring legacies, especially the Social Security Act, have continued to shape American life. Passed in 1935, this law offered pensions and unemployment compensation to qualified workers, provided public assistance to the elderly and the blind, and created a new national program for poor single mothers, called Aid to Dependent Children (ADC; later called **Aid to Families with Dependent Children**, or **AFDC**). The protection and support the government provided through the Social Security program made it possible for the blind, the unemployed, the elderly, and poor single mothers to live with a modicum of security and dignity.

Yet even as the Social Security Act blazed new paths, it reinforced many conservative ideas about poverty from the previous period. First, it continued the American tradition of localism. States were given the authority to set benefit levels and eligibility requirements for ADC and unemployment insurance. This discretion led to wide variations in benefits between states. Citizens in identical circumstances were treated differently, depending solely on which state they lived in.

Second, benefits were set quite low. Benefit levels continued to follow the "least eligibility" principle, which held that no one should be better off on welfare than at work. Benefits should be set below the wage of the lowest-paid worker, so that the poor would rather offer themselves to any employer on any terms than accept relief.[11] Welfare should be made as undesirable as possible to reinforce the work ethic and ensure an abundant supply of cheap labor.

Third, the Social Security Act institutionalized the invidious distinction between deserving and undeserving welfare recipients. Programs organized on the principle of

A U.S. government poster displayed in post offices and other public buildings instructing citizens on how to apply for the old-age benefits of the Social Security Act.

social insurance, like Social Security, were for workers who deserved them. These programs were financed through payroll taxes on employers and employees. Recipients "earned" their benefits through their contributions while they worked. Public-assistance programs, on the other hand, were financed out of general tax revenues. These programs were means-tested and stigmatized the poor. While social-insurance programs for workers enjoyed political support, public-assistance programs for the poor were deplored as government handouts for the unworthy.

The Social Security Act reinforced gender inequalities. The separation of the poor into public-assistance programs and workers into social-insurance programs distinguished how most men fared from how most women accessed the welfare state. With relatively few women in the wage-labor force, men were more likely to qualify for social-insurance programs like Social Security and unemployment compensation, which depended on contributions from earnings and paid benefits only to individuals who had to leave the labor force because they were laid off or retired. Women, by contrast, were more likely to receive their benefits from public-assistance programs that were neither well–funded nor well–regarded.

Finally, Social Security, in tandem with other key policies of the 1930s and 1940s, also had a profound racial content. Inflected by the preferences of the southern wing of the Democratic Party, these policies massively advantaged American whites while often excluding African Americans, especially the majority who still lived in the 17 states that mandated racial segregation. During Jim Crow's last hurrah in the 1930s and 1940s, when members of Congress from these 17 southern states controlled the gateways to legislation, policy decisions dealing with welfare, work, and war excluded or differentially treated the vast majority of African Americans. Farmworkers and maids, who made up most of the southern black workforce, were denied Social Security pensions and access to labor unions. Benefits for veterans were administered locally. For example, the famous GI Bill of 1944 provided a substantial array of educational and financial benefits to returning GIs. It adapted to "the southern way of life" by accommodating to segregation in higher education, to the job ceilings local officials imposed on returning black soldiers who came home from a segregated army, and to an unwillingness to offer loans to blacks even when they were insured by the federal government. Of the 3,229 GI Bill–guaranteed home, business, and farm loans made in 1947 in Mississippi, for example, only two were offered to black veterans.[12]

With most blacks left out of social-welfare programs, the damage to racial equity was immense. Social Security, which excluded the majority of blacks until well into the 1950s, quickly became the country's most important social legislation. Perhaps most surprising and most important, the treatment of veterans after the war, despite the universal eligibility for the benefits apparently offered by the GI Bill, perpetuated the blatant racism that had marked the still segregated military during the war. At no other time in American history have so much money and so many resources been put at the service of the generation completing education, entering the workforce, and forming families. At the very moment a wide array of public policies were providing most white Americans with valuable tools to insure their old age, get good jobs, acquire economic security, build assets, and gain middle-class status, black Americans were mainly left to fend for themselves, with the exception of their growing participation in public-assistance programs aimed directly at the poor.

The last major New Deal social-policy initiative was the Fair Labor Standards Act of 1938, a law that established the first national minimum wage (25 cents per hour) and a 40-hour work week. Soon, World War II brought a halt to social reform as the country fixed its attention on defeating Germany, Italy, and Japan. When the war ended, liberals hoped to restore the momentum of the New Deal. But a politically resurgent business community, in tandem with an increasingly conservative Congress, resisted new social initiatives. Supporters of federal welfare programs were thrown on the defensive and effectively denounced in the early years of the Cold War as being the opening wedge of communism and a threat to freedom. In 1946, conservatives in Congress weakened a bill that would have committed the government to a full-employment policy. In 1949, a national health-insurance bill proposed by the Truman administration was defeated in Congress.[13] No comparably broad program of national health insurance would be enacted for another 60 years. Other parts of President Truman's Fair Deal—his program to extend the New Deal welfare state—met a similar fate.

Upon being defeated politically, unions and other liberals who supported national health insurance tried to obtain from employers what they could not secure from Congress. Unions in large corporations began to negotiate fringe-benefits packages in collective bargaining with employers; the benefits included health insurance, employer-funded pensions, and supplementary unemployment for their members. Between 1948 and 1959, the number of workers who received health insurance and private pensions as part of their employment contracts tripled. A private welfare system, in which social protections such as health insurance and pensions were tied to jobs through labor contracts between employers and employees, began to develop. As we noted earlier, the United States is distinctive in its mix of public- and private-sector welfare spending, which is weighted heavily toward the private sector. Approximately 25 percent of all welfare spending in this country comes from the private sector, compared to just 5 percent in France and Sweden.

The private welfare system of employer-based benefits made workers dependent for their social protection—health insurance and pensions—on the firms that employed them. This pattern of social provision not only tied workers to their employers but also divided workers from each other. Only workers employed in the corporate sector of the economy received extensive social protections from their employers. Workers who toiled for firms in the competitive sector of the economy often did not receive such fringe benefits, because small firms could not afford to pay health-insurance costs or contribute to private pensions for their workers. Consequently, workers in the corporate sector of the economy, who were receiving social protection from their employers, had less of a stake in improving, expanding, and adding new government programs that workers in the competitive sector and the poor depended on. The private welfare system of employer-based benefits siphoned off political pressure from corporate-sector workers—the most organized and politically powerful section of the American working class—to increase the level of protection the American welfare state provided beyond the minimum necessary for social peace.

Although the New Deal may not have advanced under President Truman, a Democrat, neither did it go backward under his successor, President Dwight Eisenhower, a Republican. Under Eisenhower, conservatives did not try to revoke the Social Security Act or return to the pre-Depression style of minimal government.[14] Corporations that had adamantly opposed Social Security in the 1930s now acknowledged that it could help stabilize the economy and was preferable to more radical, or conservative, alternatives. Moreover, attempts to roll back Social Security would have been futile, given its broad popular support. The issue for Republicans was striking the proper balance between private welfare plans run by employers and public welfare programs run by the government. Republicans were determined that the welfare state should not displace welfare capitalism in the form of private, employer-based welfare plans. According to Marion B. Folsom, an Eastman Kodak executive who became Eisenhower's secretary of health, education, and welfare, government should provide only "basic minimum protection and it should not be intended to cover all the needs of everyone." He argued that benefits in government programs should be low and that businesses should be offered tax incentives to subsidize their own employer-based welfare plans. Limited public benefits would encourage the need for and reliance on private, corporate welfare plans. These plans, in turn, would act as a brake on the further extension of governmental public welfare programs.[15]

THE NEW POVERTY

The publication in 1962 of Michael Harrington's *The Other America: Poverty in the United States* roused the nation's conscience. Using statistics that were widely available but had drawn little attention, Harrington exposed a disturbing truth: despite unprecedented prosperity, 40 to 50 million people—one-quarter of all Americans—remained mired in poverty. In previous decades, full employment had reduced poverty. But by the mid-1960s, the traditional correlation between low unemployment and low AFDC welfare rates no longer applied. Throughout the 1960s, in the midst of one of the most prosperous decades in the nation's history, the number of families needing income assistance grew by almost 10 percent per year.[16]

One reason that welfare caseloads grew even as the economy boomed was the changing color of poverty. A disproportionate and increasing number of the poor now were African Americans who lived in urban ghettos. Once blacks migrated from the South to join the modern industrial economy in northern cities like Cleveland, New York, and Chicago, they faced greater discrimination and larger obstacles to social mobility than the immigrant groups, such as Italians, Poles, and Jews, who preceded them. Race proved a more visible and powerful marker of difference than ethnicity and nationality.[17]

Blacks, moreover, entered the modern industrial economy at the very moment it was passing from the scene. When previous immigrant groups had arrived with little education, the economy needed their unskilled labor to dig canals, lay railroad tracks, and work in the industrial plants of Detroit, Philadelphia, and Chicago. That was no longer true by the time blacks migrated north. Technology had reduced the need for labor in manufacturing. Capital had replaced labor in production. Economic restructuring now put a premium on education that many urban blacks lacked. In addition, factories no longer were located in cities accessible to blacks. Manufacturing plants were now located in the suburbs, where taxes and land were cheaper. This put many blue-collar manufacturing jobs beyond the reach of poor black residents located in inner cities.[18] At the same time that postindustrial capitalism was producing well-compensated white-collar jobs requiring education, it was also creating service-sector jobs that failed to pay a living wage. Many of those who worked hard and played by the rules were consigned to poverty by a lack of skills, a lack of unions that could bargain for higher wages on their behalf, and a lack of government regulations that could assure them an adequate income.[19]

The color of welfare was changing, becoming darker as job discrimination and economic changes conspired to restrain black mobility, and so was its gender. Women now increasingly filled the ranks of the poor. This development, dating back a half-century, has continued to shape the contours of poverty today. Almost one-third of all female-headed households are poor. These families comprise more than one-half of all families in poverty.[20] Single mothers are likely to be poor either because women earn lower wages when they work or because they need to stay home to care for their children and are unable to work.

The poor also became younger—much younger than they once were. The great success of the American welfare state in reducing the poverty rate among

WHAT DO YOU THINK?

Responsibility for Poverty

Some argue that poverty is largely caused by structural factors over which individuals have little or no control. These factors include family background, educational opportunities, the state of the job market, and differences in economic life chances in different cities and states. Others argue that poverty is mostly caused by bad choices individuals make about schooling, job training, and family formation. How would you judge these differences in emphasis?

the elderly has only underlined its greatest failure: the high and persistent poverty rate that remains among children. The poverty rate among those who are 65 and older has declined by almost two-thirds in just four-and-a-half decades, from 29.5 percent in 1967 to 9 percent in 2012.[21] In the same period, the poverty rate among children has hovered stubbornly around 20 percent—more than twice the current poverty rate for the elderly.[22] The American poverty rate among children is three times the rate in Western Europe. Poverty among children in Europe is so much lower than in the United States because European countries spend more money on more programs for families with children, thus raising above the poverty line children who otherwise would be below it. No other developed welfare state is as generationally skewed as that of the United States, where benefits flow to the elderly through such relatively expensive programs as **Medicare** and Social Security while fewer and less expensive efforts are made to insulate children from deprivation and its corrosive effects.[23]

Poverty has remained persistent. As we saw in Chapter 2, both good and bad jobs in postindustrial capitalism have been growing at the expense of blue-collar jobs in the middle. The service-sector jobs available to unskilled workers (e.g., fast-food worker, maid, and security guard) are characterized by low wages, low or no fringe benefits, and irregular and temporary employment. A single parent with two children who worked steadily for 40 hours a week, 52 weeks a year at a minimum-wage job in 2012 would have earned only $15,080 before taxes, which is 86 percent of what the government defined as the poverty line for such a family ($17,568). Indeed, over time, the value of the federal minimum wage has declined, as indicated in Table 10.1.

THE GREAT SOCIETY PROGRAM

The last concerted effort to grapple with poverty as a national priority, the Great Society program initiated by President Lyndon Johnson in 1964, happened a half-century ago. Like the first great wave of social reform, the New Deal, which was made possible by the sweeping Democratic electoral realignment spearheaded by President Roosevelt in the 1930s, this wave of reform also was the result of a thorough Democratic electoral victory. Another key factor was the pressure exerted in each era by mobilized protests, led especially by labor during the New Deal and the civil rights movement during the Great Society.

In 1964, 51 freshmen Democrats were elected to Congress on President Johnson's coattails. Liberals now had enough votes to overcome the veto that

TABLE 10.1

FEDERAL MINIMUM WAGE RATES, 1959–2012

Year	Value of the Minimum Wage		Year	Value of the Minimum Wage	
	Current Dollars	Constant (1996) Dollars		Current Dollars	Constant (1996) Dollars
1959	1.00	5.39	1986	3.35	4.80
1960	1.00	5.30	1987	3.35	4.63
1961	1.15	6.03	1988	3.35	4.44
1962	1.15	5.97	1989	3.35	4.24
1963	1.25	6.41	1990	3.80	4.56
1964	1.25	6.33	1991	4.25	4.90
1965	1.25	6.23	1992	4.25	4.75
1966	1.25	6.05	1993	4.25	4.61
1967	1.40	6.58	1994	4.25	4.50
1968	1.60	7.21	1995	4.25	4.38
1969	1.60	6.84	1996	4.75	4.75
1970	1.60	6.47	1997	5.15	5.03
1971	1.60	6.20	1998	5.15	4.96
1972	1.60	6.01	1999	5.15	4.85
1973	1.60	5.65	2000	5.15	4.69
1974	2.00	6.37	2001	5.15	4.56
1975	2.10	6.12	2002	5.15	4.49
1976	2.30	6.34	2003	5.15	4.39
1977	2.30	5.95	2004	5.15	4.28
1978	2.65	6.38	2005	5.15	4.14
1979	2.90	6.27	2006	5.15	4.04
1980	3.10	5.90	2007	5.85	4.41
1981	3.35	5.78	2008	6.55	4.94
1982	3.35	5.78	2009	7.25	5.47
1983	3.35	5.28	2010	7.25	5.22
1984	3.35	5.06	2011	7.25	5.06
1985	3.35	4.88	2012	7.25	4.97

NOTE: Adjusted for inflation using the CPI-U (Consumer Price Index for All Urban Consumers).
SOURCE: Infoplease, at www.infoplease.com/ipa/A0774473.html (accessed October 8, 2012).

the conservative coalition of Republicans and southern Democrats in Congress had exercised over social-welfare legislation in the 1950s. A liberal Democratic president with concurring large majorities in the Senate and the House could now overcome the obstacles that opponents had used to stymie welfare-state initiatives in the past.[24]

In his 1964 State of the Union address, President Johnson declared a **War on Poverty** that would result in a Great Society, free of hunger and privation. The AFL-CIO reflected the sentiment of other liberals when it crowed, "The New Deal proclaimed in 1933 has come to a belated maturity now under LBJ in 1965."[25] After a 30-year hiatus, the federal government was building on the legacy of the New Deal and assuming new responsibilities in almost every area of social welfare. Federally funded health insurance, in the form of Medicare and Medicaid, was established for the aged and the poor. New educational opportunities for the disadvantaged, such as Head Start and Upward Bound, were enacted. Job-training programs, such as the Job Corps, were legislated. New initiatives in housing and urban development, such as the Model Cities program, followed suit. The aim of these initiatives was to enhance opportunities for the poor, "to open up doors, not set down floors; to offer a hand up, not a handout," according to the historian James T. Patterson.[26] Federal social-welfare expenditures almost doubled from 1965 to 1975 in support of these efforts. Social-welfare costs, which amounted to one-third of the entire federal budget in 1965, accounted for more than one-half ten years later.[27]

But like the social-reform period of the New Deal, the War on Poverty was short-lived. Initially, the War on Poverty drew its moral and political energy from the civil rights movement. But as the moral power of the civil rights movement declined amid violence and internal strife, so did the impetus behind the Great Society. Equally important, the Johnson administration became distracted by the war in Vietnam. The more the war against communism in Asia escalated, the more the war against poverty at home lost momentum. A conservative backlash against the Great Society first appeared in the 1966 congressional election, which restored the blocking power of the conservative coalition of Republicans and southern Democrats in Congress.[28] Two years later, in 1968, Richard Nixon (a Republican) was elected president on a platform skeptical about the Great Society and the moment of social reform effectively came to an end.

According to many conservatives, the War on Poverty failed; worse, its antipoverty programs were harmful. Welfare rolls, they noted, continued to increase, not decrease; crime became worse, not better; more single mothers appeared, not fewer; and illegitimacy rates continued to rise, not decline. The country's cities burned as violent urban protests rocked the nation in the late 1960s. During his 1968 campaign, Nixon captured this sense of disappointment when he charged, "For the past five years we have been deluged by government programs for the unemployed, programs for cities, programs for the poor, and we have reaped from these programs an ugly harvest of frustration, violence and failure across the land."[29]

Backlash against the Great Society also developed because the War on Poverty had polarized the electorate along the fault lines of the division between social-insurance and public-assistance programs. Workers covered by social insurance had little stake in the Great Society programs that aided the poor. As the prosperity of the 1960s turned into the stagflation of the 1970s, resentment over these expenditures and their tax burden grew. Race compounded this resentment. Many New Deal programs excluded blacks, but the War on Poverty targeted them for inclusion.[30] The political consequences of the Great Society program pitted taxpayers, who were part of the social-insurance system, against tax recipients, who received public assistance; the private sector was set against the public sector, workers against the jobless, and whites against blacks.[31] Politicians in both parties exploited and exacerbated these tensions, using *welfare* as a code word to appeal to some voters' fears concerning crime, taxes, morality, and race.

The recoil against the Great Society reached its peak during the Reagan administration (1981–89). President Ronald Reagan came to office pledging to shrink the federal government. His administration quickly aimed its fire at the poor and the Great Society programs they depended on. Some federal programs, such as funding for public-service jobs and revenue sharing for the states, were eliminated completely; other poverty programs were cut back drastically.[32]

Reagan's attack on the welfare state overreached, however. Tax cuts for the rich and spending cuts for the poor exposed his administration to charges of unfairness, even meanness. As poverty became more visible due to government cutbacks and rising unemployment, the public became more upset with the results. As David Stockman, Reagan's budget director, observed, "The abortive Reagan revolution proved that the American electorate wants a moderate social democracy to shield it from capitalism's rough edges."[33]

In fact, far from failing, the War on Poverty had succeeded in reducing the number of people living in poverty. The poverty rate dropped from 19 percent in 1964 to less than 12 percent in 1979. The number of people living below the poverty line declined until President Reagan signaled retreat in a war the country was winning. Government income-support programs, not economic growth, accounted for the largest part of this decline. Before taking such income supports into account, the number of households in poverty fell by 900,000 between 1965 and 1971. But with these programs, the number of poor families declined by 2.6 million.[34] The federal government's antipoverty programs not only lifted families out of poverty but also raised the quality of their lives by reducing malnutrition, increasing access to medical care, improving housing, and opening up educational opportunities that previously had not been available.[35]

Despite these dramatic changes, critics of the War on Poverty were suspicious of the type of difference such programs made in poor people's lives and were opposed to government "handouts" that were not earned by contributing to social-insurance programs. Poverty programs, they argued, may have improved poor people's lives materially, but they did not change their behavior, which led to welfare dependency, illegitimate babies, and broken families. Even granting that more of the poor's basic needs may have been met as a result of Great Society initiatives, the critics insisted this success came at the cost of the recipients' character. This line of argument, however, does not hold up to close scrutiny. Larger cultural forces regarding sexuality and parenthood, not welfare policy, drove the trend toward more female-headed households. Moreover, poverty, low wages, and the growing insecurity of the market weakened the ties that bound families together. As the noted economist Lester Thurow put it, "The traditional family is being destroyed not by misguided social welfare programs coming from Washington . . . but by a modern economic system that is not congruent with 'family values.'"[36]

Inaccurate impressions of welfare dependency also abounded. In fact, of the people on welfare, most received benefits for short periods rather than over the long term.[37] People moved in and out of the welfare rolls not because they wanted to be there but because personal and economic setbacks including divorce, abandonment, unemployment, lack of child care, or sickness placed them there. And all the disadvantages of being poor that afflict one generation affect the next. What was passed from one generation to the next among the poor was their poverty, not welfare dependency.[38] This was evident in the classic study of poor urban black men by the anthropologist Eliot Liebow, who found that they had followed in the failed footsteps of their fathers not because a *culture* of poverty had been handed down, but because the same social and educational *deficits* of poverty that had prevented their fathers from succeeding were visited on them.[39]

FROM REAGAN TO CLINTON

During the Reagan administration, a concerted effort to reduce the size and scope of the welfare state proved only a partial success. Welfare-state spending was slowed but not reversed. Great Society poverty programs took heavy cuts, mostly surviving in truncated form, while New Deal social-insurance programs emerged relatively unscathed.[40] But the Reagan administration's impact on the welfare state was more profound than can be gleaned from looking at welfare-state spending alone.

Republicans succeeded in placing the welfare state on the defensive as conservatives now set the terms of debate over social policy. The solution to poverty was redefined from increasing the poor's resources to changing their behavior, from blaming their circumstances on the inadequacies of the economy to blaming it on the perverse incentives of the welfare state.

The public mood changed so much that even Democrats were prepared to renounce their own New Deal and Great Society legacies. In March 1990, members of the Democratic Leadership Council (DLC), a group of moderate and conservative Democrats, announced they were ready to bury their party's past. Meeting in New Orleans, they dismissed the relevance of New Deal and Great Society programs, claiming that "the political ideas and passions of the 1930s and 1960s cannot guide us in the 1990s." At that meeting, the DLC selected a new council president to present this view, putting a little-known governor from a small southern state on the national stage for the first time. His name was William Jefferson Clinton.[41]

President Clinton's social policy was shaped decisively by these two inheritances from Republican administrations: a large federal deficit and a conservative definition of the welfare problem. To reassure financial markets that he was serious about cutting the federal deficit, Clinton sacrificed his 1992 campaign promise to invest in domestic programs. Even as the budget began to run surpluses toward the end of the 1990s, the Clinton administration continued to give priority to fiscal responsibility over restoring cuts to welfare-state programs.

The welfare state during the Clinton presidency was not simply mortgaged to deficit reduction but also conducted within a conservative definition of the welfare problem that the president adopted as his own—the view that public-assistance programs undermined the character of the poor. From this perspective, the best way to build their character was to remove the welfare crutch they depended upon. This view was embodied in a major reform of the welfare system, the Personal Responsibility and Work Opportunity Reconciliation Act (PRWORA), which President Clinton signed in 1996.

When the old welfare program, Aid to Families with Dependent Children (AFDC), was replaced by a radically different welfare policy, the debate in Congress was charged. "This isn't welfare reform," Senator Daniel Patrick Moynihan of New York thundered in dismay as the overhaul of the existing welfare system wound its way through Congress. "This is welfare repeal."[42] Conflict on the House Ways and Means Committee over eliminating the guarantee of welfare benefits to every eligible poor American was so furious that the sergeant at arms had to be called to restore order. When the bill reached the floor of the House, the debate reached uncommon levels of acrimony. Some Democrats compared Republican welfare proposals to Nazism, and some Republicans likened welfare recipients to wild animals. This debate was overwrought because it was freighted with many meanings, from relationships between the sexes to relationships between races to relationships between the states. Eventually, the Republican Congress—seizing the initiative from President Clinton "to end welfare as we know it," which Clinton had promised to do during the 1992 presidential campaign—sent the president a welfare bill that did what he pledged, but in ways he never intended. Forced to choose between breaking his campaign promise to reform welfare and repudiating his own more generous welfare proposals, President Clinton chose the latter and signed the PRWORA. This legislation created a new welfare program, Temporary Assistance to Needy Families (TANF), to help impoverished children and their families.

AFDC had been an entitlement program that required the federal government to provide income assistance to poor families for as long as they were eligible. The amount of federal money for welfare would adjust automatically to cover some of the money that states gave to poor families, regardless of the number of families on the rolls and regardless of how long they had been there.[43] Under TANF, states now receive fixed sums of money from the federal government in the form of block grants to help pay for welfare. These sums do not increase automatically with the welfare rolls. When more people qualify, raising the number of clients, and when states spend all of their federal money but choose not to supplement it, poor families who are eligible for income support may not receive any. TANF has given states more discretion on how to spend federal welfare money and devise their own welfare policies, but with one important condition required by Congress. The law sets a limit of two years on welfare, after which recipients must work, and it establishes a lifetime limit of five years during which people may receive welfare.

The promise of a Democratic president and a Republican Congress to "end welfare as we know it" thus was redeemed. Welfare as an entitlement was eliminated by setting time limits on benefits and by removing the guarantee that the federal government would reimburse the states for each eligible recipient, regardless of how many there were.

Proponents of this law have pointed to declining welfare rolls—they were cut in half during the program's first decade—as a sign that its work promotion has been effective.[44] But the welfare rolls had begun to decrease in 1993, well before the new welfare bill was signed. Moreover,

WHAT DO YOU THINK?

Consensus and Controversy

Some vital public policies, including Social Security and Medicare, once were keenly opposed as inappropriate intrusions by government into private markets. Today, they have become a part of the social contract that almost no citizen or political leader is against. What happened? How did this shift from contestation to agreement occur? And why did it not happen with regard to AFDC?

most of the credit for lower welfare rolls belongs to the period's surging economy, which pulled the most able people off the welfare rolls and into work. Tellingly, when the deep recession of 2008 hit, welfare rolls jumped upward. Caseloads rose in 23 of the 30 largest states. Oregon's total jumped 27 percent from the prior year, South Carolina's 23 percent, and California's 10 percent.[45] Given these circumstances, President Obama's stimulus package provided funding for states whose caseloads were growing beyond budgetary expectations.

FROM BUSH TO OBAMA

During the past decade, the shape of the welfare state has changed substantially. The federal role in public education has expanded. Most notably, a series of important changes, culminating in the landmark Patient Protection and Affordable Care Act in 2010, has dramatically transformed the role of the federal government with respect to medical-insurance issues for all Americans.

Elementary and high school education in the United States is mostly financed by localities, especially by property taxes. This pattern of support results in enormous disparities in the amounts spent by different school districts. In part to help rectify these inequalities, Congress passed the Elementary and Secondary Education Act (ESEA) in 1965 to provide, for the first time, significant federal funding for K–12 education. This law was renewed seven times before a substantial revision, called No Child Left Behind (NCLB), was proposed by President George W. Bush. NCLB was passed with bipartisan support by Congress in January 2002 with the stated purpose of "[c]losing the achievement gap" between economically advantaged and disadvantaged schoolchildren. The law requires states to administer annual math and reading tests beginning in the third grade and to move toward a 100-percent passage rate within 12 years.

The law further imposes severe consequences for schools that do not achieve adequate yearly progress, including providing parents with alternatives to failing schools. During the first term of the Bush administration, the Department of Education's budget grew dramatically, increasing spending by the Department of Education on K–12 education from $27.3 billion in 2001 to $44 billion in 2009.[46] Yet states still charged that NCLB's onerous testing imposed an "unfunded mandate" on their budgets, particularly at a time of fiscal crisis. By one estimate, offered by the American Federation of Teachers, the federal government had shortchanged NCLB by more than $70.9 billion in its first decade. Even though federal spending had increased, the fiscal demands placed on the states by the new law had grown even faster. A disillusioned Senator Ted Kennedy, a Massachusetts Democrat and one of the original cosponsors of the bipartisan bill, observed that "we called the law the No Child Left Behind Act because we meant just what it said—no child means no child. The tragedy is that these long overdue reforms are finally in place, but the funds are not."[47]

Despite its strong history of cross-party support, NCLB has become more contentious. As he was launching his presidential campaign in 2007, Barack Obama called "no child left behind" "one of the emptiest slogans in the history of politics" due to its insufficient funding.[48] Efforts to increase spending on education that year by the White House and sympathetic members of Congress, including Senator Kennedy, failed to renew the act because reauthorization was delayed until a new administration would take office.

During President Obama's first term, a new initiative called Race to the Top was added to the federal government's portfolio of education programs. Announced by Secretary of Education Arne Duncan in July 2009, it created a competition for funds among the 50 states, rewarding those that created innovations in kindergarten through high school education. Since its inception, applicant states have been awarded points for developing high standards and effective curricula, identifying and rewarding top teachers and school principals, turning around low-achieving schools, and demonstrating gains in student achievement. As a result, many states have made it easier to open charter schools, adopt common standards, and introduce merit-pay systems for teachers.

The second, and most dramatic, extension of the welfare state during the Bush and Obama presidencies has been in the area of health care. In January 2004, the Medicare Prescription Drug, Improvement, and Modernization Act was passed into law. In creating a new "Part D," the statute offered the largest and most expensive overhaul of Medicare since its inception in 1965 and provided prescription-drug coverage to all Medicare recipients. Strongly supported by pharmaceutical manufacturers who stood to gain many new customers, and funded by a combination of government funding, increased premiums assessed monthly on Medicare beneficiaries, and higher deductibles, the law reduced the proportion of elderly without drug coverage from 24 percent in 2004 to 7 percent in 2006, and offered subsidies to those with low incomes.[49] The law's content was shaped strongly by the pharmaceutical industry, which lobbied strenuously and successfully to avoid price controls and price regulation and to forbid the federal government from negotiating with drug manufacturers to secure lower prices for Medicare beneficiaries. To be sure, recent studies have found that Medicare Part D has reduced out-of-pocket costs for seniors and has led them to be more likely to actually get their prescriptions. Yet without the provisions supported by the pharmaceutical industry, Jacob Hacker and Theodore Marmor of Yale University estimated that the bill could have delivered twice as much coverage for the same price.[50]

This period also witnessed a significant increase in spending on children's health. Pioneered during the Clinton presidency, this focus significantly expanded at the start of Barack Obama's first term. President Clinton proposed and Congress passed the State Children's Health Insurance Plan (SCHIP) in 1997. This program enlarged Medicaid through increased financial support from the federal government, so that the states could provide health insurance to an additional 5 million children under the age of 18 whose families met its income requirements. Though the plan originally passed with strong bipartisan support, efforts by Democrats to expand SCHIP were thwarted by President Bush in 2007. Only after two vetoes to prevent what the president saw as an "irresponsible plan that would dramatically expand this program beyond its original intent" did he sign into law a temporary extension of the program through March 2009.[51] President Obama made SCHIP a top priority immediately after taking the oath of office on January 20, 2009. By February 4, Congress had passed and he had signed the Children's Health Insurance Program Reauthorization Act of 2009. Paid for by substantial increases in tobacco-related taxes and a reduction in payments to doctor-owned hospitals, the statute extended the program through 2013 and brought the total of covered children to 10 million.

With Medicare Part D and SCHIP, as well as significant increases in Medicare and Medicaid spending, health care became the area of fastest welfare-state growth—so much so that this part of the federal budget has been increasing far faster than any other. This escalation of costs (Figure 10.2) in the public sector, combined with dramatically escalating private health-care costs, places the United States at the top of the league table of expenditures in this area—quite a contrast to its relatively meager welfare state as seen in comparative perspective (Figure 10.3). The high and escalating cost of health care was one of the main

FIGURE 10.2

GOVERNMENT SPENDING ON HEALTH CARE IN THE UNITED STATES, 1960–2012, IN BILLIONS

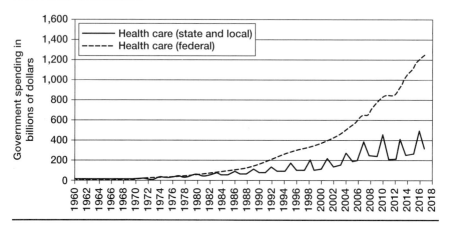

NOTE: Intergovernmental transfers from the federal government to the state or local government are counted as part of federal spending for purposes of this graph.

SOURCE: Christopher Chantrill, "Government Spending in the United States of America," at www.usgovernmentspending.com (accessed October 7, 2012).

reasons offered by President Obama in support of his plan to create universal access to health insurance, which, he claimed, would be a key means to contain costs and distribute them across the age spectrum.

But the primary reason for health-care reform—the most significant extension of the American welfare state since the creation of Medicare and Medicaid in 1965—was to reduce the number of Americans who stood outside the system of health insurance. Culminating an effort that had begun with President Theodore Roosevelt at the beginning of the twentieth century, the transformation of the health-care system that was passed in March 2010 by the House and Senate, at the behest of President Obama, fundamentally reshaped the rules for this aspect of American life.

Starting in 2014, employers with more than 50 workers must provide affordable insurance or pay a penalty of up to $3,000 per employee. The smallest firms will receive subsidies to make it easier for them to provide health insurance for their workers, especially those who earn low wages. Americans will be required to carry health insurance or pay a fee of 2.5 percent of their income, topping out at $695 for individuals and $2,085 for families. To make sure that insurance is affordable, low-income persons whose income does not exceed

FIGURE 10.3

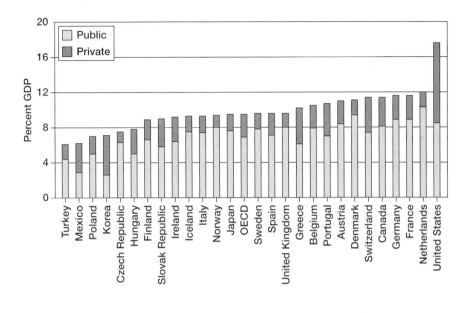

SOURCE: OECD Factbook 2011/2012, at www.oecd-library.org/sites/factbook-
2010-en/10/02/02/index.html?contentType=&itemId=/content/chapter/factbook-2010-
76-en&containerItemId=/content/serial/18147364&accessItemIds=&mimeType=text/html
(accessed March 5, 2012).

133 percent of the federal poverty level ($14,404 for individuals and $29,326
for a family of four when the bill was passed) will be eligible for Medicaid.
For individuals and families with incomes between 133 and 400 percent of the
poverty levels, the federal government will provide subsidies on a sliding scale
to help cover the cost of buying health insurance, which will be sold in new
state-based insurance marketplaces called exchanges (states that choose not to
create such exchanges will have federally run exchanges instead). Insurers will
not be allowed to reject applicants based on their health status, nor will they
be able to place lifetime limits on coverage. The Medicare prescription-drug
benefit also has been improved, and all Medicare preventive services, such as
screening for breast, prostate, and colon cancer, will be free to beneficiaries.
Some provisions have already taken effect. For instance, children can stay on
the policies of their parents until they reach the age of 26.

This dramatic expansion of health-care coverage is expensive—some
$940 billion over the first ten years. But because of new fees, taxes on

high-income earners, and reductions to Medicare spending (by phasing out the private-plan part of Medicare and reducing the rate of increase in payments to hospitals and doctors), the Congressional Budget Office estimated that the legislation actually will narrow the federal budget deficit in this period by $138 billion.

This sweeping social legislation was immensely controversial, exposing sharp partisan divisions. The House moved first, passing a health-care overhaul by a 220–215 vote on November 7, 2009, without any Republican votes. The Senate passed its version of health-care reform on December 24, 2009, on a strict 60–39 party-line vote. Three months later, on March 21, 2010, with demonstrations for and against the bill unfolding on Capitol Hill, the House passed the Senate version on a close 219–212 vote. Again, no Republican voted yes, and 34 Democrats joined them to also vote no. The opponents argued that the proposed law was too expensive, too complex, and broadened the powers of government too much. Some also worried that it would expand access to abortion. To secure sufficient votes, the president issued an executive order affirming that no federal funds would be used for this purpose. Following passage, the House and Senate passed modifying language through the reconciliation process that brought the content of the new act closer to the House bill than the version the Senate originally had passed.

Given the scope and significance of this legislation, an immense lobbying effort was mounted, primarily by opponents, to either stop or reshape the bill to make sure it would not contain a public-insurance option that would

Protesters, for and against, gathered outside the U.S. Capitol in Washington, D.C., on March 21, 2010 as the House of Representatives was about to vote on healthcare reform.

compete with private providers. In the fourth quarter of 2009, the Chamber of Commerce spent some $70 million to fight health-care reform, the Pharmaceutical Research and Manufacturers of America (PhRMA) spent $26 million, and the leading health-insurance lobby, America's Health Insurance Plans (AHIP), spent nearly $9 million. For every member of Congress, there were six health-care lobbyists trying to influence the course of the legislation.[52]

This massive lobbying effort had some success. It helped prevent the inclusion of a public-insurance option. But it did not defeat such provisions as those for a federal rate-review board to check steep increases in premiums. Nor, of course, did it ultimately succeed in derailing the bill.

The result, the *New York Times* reported, was "the federal government's biggest attack on economic inequality since inequality began rising more than three decades ago." In those years, this evaluation observed, "government policy and market forces have been moving in the same direction, both increasing inequality." By contrast, "nearly every major aspect of the health bill pushes in the other direction."[53] This legislation thus stands out for the way it raises questions central to any analysis of the politics of power, including, most notably, what the role of government should be in seeking to reduce income and wealth gaps among Americans through the instruments of social policy.

CONCLUSION

The welfare state has a conservative and a liberal side. The welfare state is conservative in that it stabilizes the corporate capitalist system. Welfare, the British politician Joseph Chamberlain once said, is the ransom the rich must pay in order to sleep peacefully in their beds at night. The welfare state alleviates but does not correct the basic structural inequalities that are part and parcel of American capitalism. It reinforces the market by making the inequalities and insecurities of a capitalist economy tolerable. Yet the welfare state also offers a more egalitarian alternative to the marketplace. The welfare state can make workers' standards of living less dependent on the wages they receive, thus reducing the power that employers exercise over their employees. For this reason, business generally has opposed extensions of the welfare state while working-class and poor-people's movements have supported it. In addition, where welfare states are extensive—as they are in Scandinavian countries, which provide such benefits as a modest income to all citizens—workers are less tolerant of inequality.[54] The egalitarian logic of the welfare state can spread to other activities, progressively infringing on areas that once operated according to market principles based on the ability to pay.[55] In the United States, meanwhile, the welfare state has exhibited both liberal and conservative aspects. It has extended new social protections to vulnerable groups, but often in a way that has reinforced divisions between workers and the poor, whites and blacks, men and women.

The future of the country's welfare state is uncertain. Each of its parts is under strain. During the first decade of this century, budget surpluses turned into massive budget deficits, and inequality continued to grow. With the economic collapse that began in 2008, demand for governmental assistance grew significantly, from unemployment insurance to SNAP food assistance to TANF grants to poor families. Concurrently, the employer-centered private welfare state has come under great pressure as more and more companies find themselves hard-pressed to sustain rapidly growing health and pension costs. Further, one of the best-supported parts of the welfare state, Medicare, has experienced dramatic fiscal strain as medical costs for an aging population rise much more swiftly than the rate of inflation. By 2020, the cost of Medicare benefits will outrun the program's accumulated pool of money paid for by payroll taxes, especially if health-care costs continue to increase at a rate far higher than inflation. Based on the current law, Medicare will be unable to pay the benefits it now promises by 2024.

Some also question the long-term viability of Social Security, but it does not face a fiscal crisis until much further into the future. Still, there is reason for concern. With the baby boom generation reaching retirement age, and with their numbers over age 65 growing faster than the number of workers who pay for benefits, the program's commitments are mounting more rapidly than the economy is growing and revenues are being generated. By 2030, Social Security will have grown as a fraction of GDP from today's 4 percent to 6 percent, and projected spending will exceed the monies in the Social Security Trust Fund. Without changes to the scale and eligibility for benefits, some scholars estimate that the fund will run out by 2040. It is estimated that by 2080, Medicare and Social Security will have grown to fully 20 percent of GDP, which is a number hard to sustain.

This unprecedented shortfall in the near and longer term makes it harder to find monies to tackle the persistence of poverty. Such initiatives have been made even more difficult as a result of the tax cuts advocated by the Bush administration at the start of the twenty-first century and weighted toward the highest earners. Even when the stock market was soaring to new highs in the late 1990s and early 2000s—when the American economy's growth far outpaced that of any rival, when unemployment and inflation were low and the economy was creating millions of jobs per year—more children grew up in poor families in the U.S. than in any other Western industrialized nation, and the country's overall poverty rate remained in the mid-teens. Moreover, during the first ten years of the twenty-first century fully four in ten Americans found themselves living in poverty at some point, and to date a remarkable six in ten find themselves in such circumstances at least once during their adult lives.[56]

Economic growth alone cannot reduce poverty. Only government programs in tandem with a successful economy can do that. Poverty rates are sensitive to political choices governments make about the welfare state. The welfare state is here to stay. Perhaps one should say multiple welfare states are here to stay, including social insurance and public assistance, government spending and private provisions linked to employment, and national programs and spending at the state and local level. Together, these welfare states have an important impact on class, regional, generational, and racial inequalities, sometimes easing them and sometimes exacerbating them.

Health-care reform has transformed a key part of the welfare state. Yet the sharp partisan polarization that shaped its passage, the public's uncertainty about its merits, and the long period of implementation have created a situation in which the future of the welfare state remains unclear, including the balance of ways to manage risk. Also not conclusively settled is the set of goals the welfare state should try to accomplish—should it support the private economy to increase economic growth, compensate for inequalities generated by the political economy, provide security against inevitable and probable hazards, enhance and equalize opportunities, or ensure that the income and wealth gaps that separate Americans get sharply reduced? Some of these decisions are practical, but others are concerned with fundamental values and choices about privileges and power.

CHAPTER SUMMARY

Introduction

The United States possesses four types of programs that are geared to increase material security—social insurance against risks of age, illness, disability, and unemployment; targeted transfers to alleviate hardship; schooling to provide citizens with skills to earn a living; and private-sector benefits tied to work. Compared to that in other countries, the scale of spending in the U.S. is modest and the mix of elements unusual.

The Historical Welfare State

Before the New Deal of the 1930s, most social-welfare spending was directed either to military pensions or programs to support mothers and children. With the Social Security Act of 1935, which provided old-age and unemployment insurance and welfare payments to needy families, a modern American welfare state was created. These policies, which secured most Americans against deprivation, lacked universal health insurance and discriminated against racial minorities and women.

The New Deal and Beyond

Faced with economic emergency and motivated by an ambition to bring more security to the lives of ordinary Americans, Franklin Roosevelt's New Deal utilized welfare-state programs not only to stimulate the economy and put people to work but also to build a framework that could protect individuals who faced unemployment and poverty as well as persons who had reached retirement age.

The New Poverty

Despite prosperity after World War II, tens of millions of Americans were living in poverty a quarter-century later, and welfare caseloads had begun to grow. In this period, the poor became younger, more black, and more female.

The Great Society Program

With nearly one in five Americans poor at the start of the 1960s, President Lyndon Johnson led a legislative effort to fight a "War on Poverty" and make it a national priority to improve the circumstances of those at the bottom. Federal spending on social welfare increased dramatically, and a dent was made in the poverty rate. The War on Poverty became a political target when conservatives claimed that it had both overreached and created incentives for poor people not to help themselves.

From Reagan to Clinton

In response to a backlash against federal efforts to strengthen the welfare state, the Reagan administration made an active effort to reduce the size and scope of national social-policy programs. The Clinton administration successfully sponsored "welfare reform" that made it more difficult for the poor to receive assistance.

From Bush to Obama

In the new century, the welfare state has continued to develop. During the presidency of George W. Bush, new programs were initiated that increased the federal role and the level of funding for education, and a prescription-drug benefit was added to Medicare. Early in his presidency, Barack Obama succeeded in passing health-care reform that would extend insurance to virtually all Americans.

Critical Thinking Questions

1. How important is it to secure the long-term fiscal future of Social Security and Medicare?

2. How broad should the federal role be in setting standards for primary schooling and for high school education?

3. How has the welfare state affected gender relationships, and how have such changes affected the further development of the welfare state?

4. What are the best ways to pay for social programs?

Suggested Readings

Jacob S. Hacker, *The Divided Welfare State.* New York: Cambridge University Press, 2002.

Gwendolyn Mink, *Wages of Motherhood: Inequality in the Welfare State, 1917–1942.* Ithaca, NY: Cornell University Press, 1995.

James O'Connor, *The Fiscal Crisis of the State.* New York: St. Martin's Press, 1973.

James T. Patterson, *America's Struggle against Poverty in the Twentieth Century.* Cambridge, MA: Harvard University Press, 2000.

Paul Pierson, *Dismantling the Welfare State? Reagan, Thatcher, and the Politics of Retrenchment.* New York: Cambridge University Press, 1994.

Frances Fox Piven and Richard Cloward, *Regulating the Poor: Functions of Social Welfare.* New York: Pantheon Books, 1971.

Theda Skocpol, *Protecting Soldiers and Mothers: The Political Origins of Social Policy in the United States.* Cambridge, MA: Harvard University Press, 1992.

William Julius Wilson, *More than Just Race: Being Black and Poor in the Inner City.* New York: W. W. Norton, 2009.

FOREIGN POLICY

INTRODUCTION

Two sets of statistics—military and economic—provide the context for understanding American foreign policy. The United States has by far the most powerful military force in the world, and, with about 1.4 million men and women in uniform, it has the world's second-largest number of military personnel after China, a country with over four times the population of the U.S. The U.S. maintains 20 large military bases overseas and 642 smaller ones.[1] Nearly 200,000 American military personnel, the world's best trained and equipped, are stationed in 148 countries around the world. U.S. naval ships and submarines patrol every ocean, reconnaissance satellites circle the globe, thousands of missiles equipped with nuclear weapons can be launched in minutes, and American warplanes enjoy uncontested supremacy in the skies. Military treaties link the U.S. to over 40 countries. The 2012 U.S. military budget of over $700 billion exceeded military spending by the next 15 nations combined and constituted 41 percent of the entire world's military expenditures.[2] (This figure does not include the $4 trillion spent for fighting wars in Afghanistan, Pakistan, and Iraq since September 11, 2001.)[3] Military spending accounts for about half of all U.S. federal-government spending.

These immense resources are devoted to maintaining American global preeminence. Just how preeminent the U.S. is can be gleaned from statistics charting its economic position. With 5 percent of the world's population, the United States accounts for one-third of the world's wealth. The richest 1 percent of the world's population owns 40 percent of global assets. Over one-third of this group is American.[4] The average American is wealthier (as can be seen in Table 11.1), enjoys better housing, is less apt to be hungry, and receives more education than most other people in the world. Note that this description does not take account of economic inequality *within* the U.S., the focus of other chapters.

TABLE 11.1

PER CAPITA INCOME, SELECTED COUNTRIES, 2012 (ESTIMATED)

Country	Per Capita Income (in dollars at PPP: Purchasing Power Parity)
Brazil	12,000
Canada	41,500
China	9,100
Dominican Republic	9,600
Ghana	3,300
India	3,900
Italy	30,100
Mexico	15,300
Russia	17,700
Senegal	1,900
Sweden	41,900
United States	49,800

SOURCE: CIA, *The World Factbook*, 2013.

When American political leaders proclaim the need to maintain world order and stability, they are referring to the order and stability of a world in which the U.S. enjoys a highly privileged position. A principal goal of American foreign policy, and the primary mission of the military establishment, is to maintain that position. The U.S. government spends relatively little for nonmilitary foreign-policy purposes. For example, U.S. government expenditures in 2010 to assist economic and social development in poor regions of the world were under 4 percent of the military budget. The U.S. ranked fourth from the bottom that year among member countries of the Organisation for Economic Co-operation and Development (OECD), an organization of 23 rich, democratic countries, in the proportion of the gross domestic product (GDP) spent on development aid. The U.S. contribution of .21 percent of its GDP was proportionately less than that contributed by Portugal and Spain, under half of that contributed by France and Germany, and under one-third of that spent by Britain, Denmark, Norway, and Sweden.[5]

There have been conflicts about the appropriate ends of American foreign policy.[6] Yet since the establishment of the U.S. in the eighteenth century, virtually all of its political leaders have placed the highest priority on enabling the U.S. to achieve and maintain a favored position in the global political economy. When the U.S. became the dominant world power in the twentieth century, it did not just happen; it was *made* to happen.

The first decade of the twenty-first century marked a turning point in the international position of the U.S. Americans had long been accustomed to thinking of the country as invulnerable. That comforting belief was shattered on September 11, 2001, when suicide bombers belonging to the Islamic fundamentalist movement al Qaeda hijacked four U.S. airliners and used them as missiles. Two were flown into the twin towers of the World Trade Center in New York City, setting the massive buildings on fire and causing them to crumble. The attack claimed nearly 3,000 lives. The third plane crashed into the Pentagon, killing 184 people and producing extensive damage. The fourth plane never reached the hijackers' intended destination of the nation's capital. Passengers and crew overpowered the hijackers, and the plane crashed in a field in Pennsylvania, killing everyone aboard.

For more than half a century after World War II, the U.S. ranked first in virtually every significant dimension of power: military, political, and economic. This was often described as U.S. hegemony—that is, a situation in which U.S. domination rested not only on "hard power" (primarily, coercion or military force) but also on "soft power," involving the use of nonmilitary resources, such as economic pressure, to sustain America's leadership.[7] Some analysts suggest that U.S. hegemony is giving way to a "post-American world," in which the U.S. is forced to share power with other power centers, such as the European Union (EU—a political and economic alliance of European countries) and rising powers like China and India.[8] This chapter surveys the changing international position of the U.S., as well as how American foreign policy has affected that position. We begin by describing the process of making foreign policy.

MAKING FOREIGN POLICY

The process of developing foreign policy has elements in common with the domestic-policy process. However, foreign policy is usually made with much less public debate. The number of public and private actors involved is far smaller and the process is far more centralized within the executive branch. Previous chapters have described the extensive limits on democratic decision making regarding domestic policy. The process by which policy is formulated and implemented in the sphere of foreign policy is much less subject to open debate and democratic decision making.

The president is at the center of the foreign-policy process, assisted nowadays by agencies and advisors within the Executive Office of the President—notably, the National Security Council, National Intelligence Council, and national security advisor. Other key executive officials include the secretaries of Defense, State, and Homeland Security, as well as the director of the Central Intelligence Agency and the U.S. ambassador to the United Nations. In developing foreign policy, presidents must balance conflicting demands involving domestic partisan and political issues, ideological preferences, financial constraints, and the preferences and pressures of allied and other foreign governments.

Although the executive usually has the upper hand in the realm of foreign policy, Congress plays an influential role because of its authority to appropriate funds, pass legislation, and summon military and civilian leaders to testify before congressional committees. Important congressional figures include the two chambers' leaders, especially those belonging to the majority party, and the chairs and minority leaders of the armed services, intelligence, and foreign-affairs committees in both houses. These officials generally have extensive foreign-policy expertise. However, compared to the substantial influence that Congress exercises in the sphere of domestic policy, its role in relation to foreign policy is quite limited.

Finally, private interests seek to shape foreign policy. As in domestic policy, there is a strong contrast between rank-and-file citizens and more organized, affluent, and powerful interests. The most influential participants are large defense contractors, whose interests are vitally affected by foreign and defense policy, and **transnational corporations (TNCs)**, that is, U.S.-based firms with worldwide operations. In addition, international-relations scholars, think tanks like the Council of Foreign Relations, and nongovernmental organizations (NGOs) like Human Rights Watch provide analyses and policy recommendations. As in the domestic-policy process, the constellation of groups involved is issue specific. For example, defense contractors focus on maintaining high levels of military spending; the American Israel Public Affairs Committee (AIPAC) seeks to ensure American support for policies that it claims will enhance Israel's security.

AMERICAN FOREIGN POLICY BEFORE WORLD WAR II

What explains the U.S. rise to power? The development is especially puzzling because throughout the eighteenth and nineteenth centuries, the U.S. generally did not join European countries in engaging in foreign conquest and the search for colonies. American foreign-policy makers faithfully followed the advice that George Washington offered in his farewell presidential address, when he urged Americans to profit from the good fortune that geography provided, in the form of an ocean separating the U.S. from Europe, to avoid "entangling alliances" with other countries. However, the U.S. was never a passive bystander in world politics. According to the historian Andrew Bacevich, American expansionism goes back to the beginning: "If the young United States had a mission, it was not to liberate [despite frequent proclamations that this was its goal] but to expand."[9]

What obscured this situation is that, unlike European powers, the U.S. did not acquire a colonial empire. First, the U.S. expanded by staking out an informal sphere of influence. The initial target was the Western Hemisphere. In 1823, President James Monroe issued a statement that came to be known as the **Monroe Doctrine**, in which he warned European powers not to intervene in Latin America. According to the historian Richard Van Alstyne, "[I]t is not the negatives [in the Monroe Doctrine] that really count. It is the hidden positive to the effect that the United States shall be the only colonizing power and the sole directing power in both North and South America."[10]

Second, in the early years of the republic, the U.S. exercised power directly by integrating within its boundaries Native American territory that had been forcibly conquered by the military and settled by U.S. citizens. According to Bacevich, "Depending on the circumstances, the United States relied on diplomacy, hard bargaining, bluster, chicanery, intimidation, or naked coercion. We infiltrated land belonging to our neighbors and then brazenly proclaimed it our own. We harassed, filibustered, and, when the situation called for it, launched full-scale invasions."[11] As a result of westward expansion, the U.S. quadrupled in size during its first half century.

The violent conquest and forced resettlement of Native Americans deserves special mention. In the fifteenth century, Christopher Columbus sought to repay the Spanish Crown for financing his expeditions by capturing, enslaving, and bringing to Spain over 1,000 Native Americans.[12] During the settlement of North America in the following centuries, Europeans slaughtered 3 million Native Americans, nearly the entire indigenous population of North America. Many revered early heroes, including George Washington, John Quincy Adams, and Andrew Jackson, directed this brutal campaign. Along with the centuries-old institution of slavery—embraced by most Northern and Southern whites from the first days of European migration to North America—the genocidal violence directed against Native Americans ranks among the most shameful aspects of the formation of the U.S.

During the nineteenth and the early twentieth centuries, preoccupied with consolidating control in its own backyard, the U.S. mostly confined foreign intervention to the Western Hemisphere, and it exercised relative restraint in its dealings with European powers. This policy was commonly described as

isolationism. However, an important threshold was crossed in 1898, when the U.S. initiated war with Spain. The historian Michael Hunt observes that "in the span of two decades [the U.S.] made a colony of Puerto Rico, imposed protectorates on Cuba and Panama, and converted into fiscal dependencies Haiti, Nicaragua, and the Dominican Republic."[13]

Gunboat diplomacy, as it became known, consisted of dispatching the U.S. Navy to foreign ports to install and protect client regimes favorable to American business interests. Between 1801 and 1904, the U.S. engaged in 101 military actions in Latin America. The journalist Stephen Kinzer observes that "[n]o nation in modern history has [overthrown foreign regimes] so often, in so many places so far from its own shores."[14]

Toward the end of the nineteenth century, the U.S. further extended its international influence as the power of Britain—the world's dominant country at the time—began to wane. After the two world wars of the twentieth century ravaged the leading European nations, the U.S. achieved global dominance. The only industrial power whose territory escaped destruction during World War II, the U.S. achieved a position of virtually unchallenged preeminence after the war. It possessed the world's most powerful armed forces, assisted by advanced weaponry, including a monopoly of nuclear weapons. After the war, the U.S. quickly replaced Britain as the dominant capitalist power and the hub of world manufacturing, commerce, and banking.

AMERICAN FOREIGN POLICY AFTER WORLD WAR II

World War II was a watershed in American foreign policy because of two fundamental changes: the assertion of global political leadership and the expansion of American economic influence abroad. The wartime presidents Roosevelt and Truman, influential public and private officials, and most foreign-policy analysts agreed that the U.S. needed to abandon the relatively passive stance it had occupied until then in the global arena. Instead, they recommended that it assume a more activist role in response to the decline of the major European capitalist powers, the challenge posed by the Soviet Union, the growth of nationalism in newly independent countries in Asia and Africa, and the risk of a resumption of prewar economic depression. Chapters 3, 9, and 10 have described how policies were devised during the New Deal and after World War II to promote economic and social stability at home. In addition, U.S. policy makers crafted foreign policies to deal with a rapidly changing global situation that included anticolonial movements in the areas in Asia and Africa formerly controlled by Western European countries, as well as demands for economic development and social justice throughout the world. The new U.S. foreign-policy orientation included three elements: opposing communism, integrating the non-communist world under U.S. leadership, and creating international regulatory institutions.

Opposing Communism: The Cold War

The most apparent feature of world politics in the period following World War II was the bitter rivalry between the U.S. and the Soviet Union (USSR), which became known as the **Cold War**. Each country had an extensive sphere of influence: the U.S. in Western Europe, North America, and Latin America; the USSR in Eastern and Central Europe, Cuba (following the Cuban Revolution in 1959), and the People's Republic of China (following the Communist Revolution in 1949, although the USSR and China split in the 1960s). The U.S. and USSR also had client states in the third world.

Ideological rivalry pitted the liberal-democratic, capitalist U.S. against the USSR, which had a command economy and an authoritarian Communist Party. The two blocs faced off across an iron curtain (so named by the British prime minister Winston Churchill) that ran through the heart of Europe. The U.S. sponsored the **North Atlantic Treaty Organization (NATO)** to coordinate military planning by Western European and North American countries; the USSR organized the Warsaw Pact, a parallel organization of its allies in Central and Eastern Europe.

Beginning in the Cold War, the world has faced the awful possibility of nuclear devastation. Ever since the U.S. developed atomic weapons and unleashed two of them against Japan in the closing months of World War II, and the USSR deployed nuclear weapons in the 1950s, the future of the world has hung by a thread. During the half century of the Cold War, the U.S. and USSR possessed tens of thousands of nuclear-equipped intercontinental ballistic missiles targeting each other's armed forces and civilian populations. This created the constant possibility of nuclear catastrophe by accident or irresponsible design. Indeed, the two superpowers approached the brink of nuclear war during the Cuban Missile Crisis of 1962, when leaders of both countries came perilously close to unleashing a nuclear attack.

The Cold War had an important impact on the economy, politics, and culture of the U.S. In the past, when wars ended, military mobilization was quickly followed by a return to a civilian economy. However, the Cold War ushered in a situation that persists to this day of permanent mobilization for war, what the economist Seymour Melman described as "the permanent war economy."[15] This pattern was identified, named—and lamented—by none other than the two-term president Dwight D. Eisenhower, the five-star general whom Franklin Roosevelt named Supreme Commander of allied forces in Europe and who directed the invasion of Normandy in 1944, which was a turning point in World War II. In his farewell address in 1961, after serving as president for eight years, Eisenhower warned Americans, "We must guard against the acquisition of unwarranted influence, whether sought or unsought, by the military-industrial complex." The phrase "military-industrial complex" referred to the close alliance of the Pentagon and corporate weapons producers, who shared a common interest in boosting military spending.

More than half a century later, Eisenhower's warning remains relevant. The government lavishes an enormous amount on the military and defense contractors. Further, military and martial values pervade American cultural life: witness the popularity of war-themed video games like "Medal of Honor" and "Call of Duty."[16]

The term "Cold War" is somewhat misleading in that, during the heyday of the Cold War, U.S.-Soviet conflict was often white hot. The two countries fought numerous "proxy wars" in the third world—including in Africa (Angola, Mozambique, and Ethiopia) and in Central America (Nicaragua, El Salvador, and Guatemala). These conflicts often pitted authoritarian client governments supported by the U.S. against insurgent movements backed by the USSR. The U.S. provided friendly regimes with financial assistance and trained their military, intelligence, and police officials. In addition, the U.S. engaged in two large-scale conventional wars with Soviet allies after World War II: the Korean War (1950–53) and the Vietnam War (mid-1960s–1973).

Vietnam proved to be a nightmare. The U.S. massively intervened to prevent the communist regime in the North from unifying the partitioned country. The war claimed several million Vietnamese casualties and the lives of over 50,000 American troops. It divided the U.S. more intensely than any previous war since the Civil War.

Since World War II, the United States has also engaged in military intervention, not all linked to the Cold War, in Laos and Cambodia (connected to the Vietnam War), the Dominican Republic, Lebanon, Grenada, Panama, Libya, Somalia, Yugoslavia, Iraq, and Afghanistan.[17]

Although the dominant feature of the half century after World War II was Cold War rivalry between the U.S. and the Soviet Union, a related development was a more global assertion of American power. The historian David Callahan suggests that

> [w]hether the Cold War had occurred or not, it is clear that the United
> States would still have played a much greater global leadership role

after World War II than it did after World War I. . . . For quite apart from the problem of security, postwar U.S. economic growth was seen as requiring international economic order that could only be guaranteed if the United States took over the position of a declining Britain.[18]

Writing in 1970, the foreign-policy analyst Graham Allison observed, "Historians in the year 2000, looking back with detachment on the Cold War, are apt to conclude that the main feature of international life in the period 1945–1970 was . . . the global expansion of American influence: military, economic, political and cultural.[19]

Beginning in the late 1980s, momentous changes occurred in the Soviet Union and its allies when economic stagnation provoked popular opposition to economic austerity and authoritarian rule. By 1991, widespread protest had culminated in the dissolution of the USSR and its replacement by the much smaller non-communist Russian Federation. Regions in East-Central Europe and Central Asia formerly incorporated within the USSR or in its sphere of influence became independent states, and former Soviet client states in East-Central Europe, such as Poland and Hungary, broke free of Soviet control. The implosion of the USSR and defeat of communism left the U.S. as the world's sole superpower—a "hyperpower," in the words of a French foreign minister. The strategic analyst Richard Betts observes, "Only the collapse of the Soviet pole [in the 1990s] . . . marked the real arrival of U.S. global dominance."[20]

Integrating the Non-Communist World

After World War II, the U.S. informally achieved a commanding position in non-communist regions of the world, a result of the American government's activist political and military posture as well as economic penetration by U.S.-based transnational corporations operating in Western Europe and the developing world. The two forms of influence were often complementary. According to the political economist Robert Gilpin, the income generated by American investments abroad in the postwar period was used "to finance America's global political and military position. The income from foreign investments, in other words, had become an important factor in American global hegemony."[21]

Following the war, the U.S. helped rebuild the war-damaged economies of the industrialized capitalist countries of Western Europe and forged an alliance with their governments under U.S. leadership. The policy proved a brilliant success. One element involved a generous aid package known as the **Marshall Plan**, which enabled Western European countries to finance reconstruction of their economies. The Marshall Plan also encouraged countries that had formerly clashed, especially France and Germany, to engage in economic and political cooperation. Its success laid the groundwork for the European Union (EU), an organization that integrates the economies of most European countries and promotes political coordination. Following World War II, Western Europe became a haven of peace, prosperity, and stability after centuries of intense internal strife.

After World War II, the U.S. government informally extended the scope of the Monroe Doctrine from South America to what was described at the time as the third world—the less developed regions in Asia, Africa, and Latin America. (A common classification at the time consisted of the industrialized capitalist world [the first world], the Soviet bloc [the second world], and the less developed regions [the third world]). The U.S. pursued the ambitious goal during this period of reshaping the entire world in a manner that both conformed to American ideals of self-determination and maximized U.S. influence. It pressured Britain, France, Belgium, and the Netherlands to dismantle their colonial empires in the name of national self-determination and democracy. Dozens of colonies in Africa and Asia became independent countries in the decade after World War II. Once the former colonies became independent states, the U.S. frequently intervened to ensure that they were led by pro-U.S. regimes, the way it had in Latin America. (One study tabulates 70 cases of U.S. intervention in third-world countries since World War II.)[22]

The goal of U.S. intervention was to install and shield friendly regimes in developing countries, oppose Soviet influence, promote democracy, and bolster capitalism. The U.S. was not always successful. In 1949, a communist movement overthrew an American-backed regime in China. In the 1950s, U.S. forces were stalemated in Korea. The most dramatic instance was the costly and agonizing U.S. defeat in the Vietnam War of the 1960s and 1970s. After nearly two decades of military intervention—at its peak, 500,000 U.S. troops served in Vietnam—immense destruction, and the loss of enormous numbers of lives, the U.S. withdrew from Vietnam in 1973, only to see the regime in the North quickly reunify Vietnam under communist control.

An important goal of postwar foreign policy was to help U.S. oil companies gain control of the Middle East petroleum reserves, the largest in the world. In 1940, Great Britain controlled 72 percent of Middle East oil, the United States 10 percent, and other countries the remainder. Thanks to alliances that the U.S. government formed with oil-rich states in the Middle East who depended on the U.S. for political and military support, U.S. companies wrested control from British companies. By 1967, U.S. companies controlled 59 percent of Middle

East oil deposits while Britain's share had tumbled to 29 percent.[23] The U.S. attacked Iraq in 1991 after Iraq invaded Kuwait, an American ally. Following a swift U.S. victory, the American government created military bases in Kuwait, Saudi Arabia, and Bahrain. After the September 11 attacks, the U.S. established military bases in the oil-rich "Stans" of Central Asia: Uzbekistan, Tajikistan, and Kyrgyzstan. One reason the U.S. toppled Saddam Hussein's regime in Iraq in 2003, after 9/11, is that Iraq has the second-largest petroleum reserves in the world.[24]

The U.S. continues to give high priority to protecting access to overseas supplies of petroleum for itself and its allies. As the strategic analyst Michael Klare points out, "Oil makes this country [the U.S.] strong; dependency [on oil] makes us weak."[25] Although the International Energy Agency has recently reported that the U.S. will overtake Saudi Arabia as the world's largest producer of oil by 2025, other countries—especially newly developing ones like China and India—are desperately seeking new energy sources.[26] Protecting the free flow of oil worldwide remains an important U.S. goal for domestic reasons—the price of oil is set within global markets, and if Middle East oil could not reach markets in Europe and Asia, the price of oil would rise for all consumers, including Americans. Moreover, if the U.S. is to remain a superpower, it must safeguard oil supplies for its allies in Europe and Asia.

An oil refinery in Basra, Iraq.

Creating International Regulatory Institutions

After World War II, the U.S. took the lead in creating international organizations designed to regulate the world's political and economic order. Among the most important were the United Nations (UN), an umbrella organization comprising the General Assembly, Security Council, and other agencies; the International Monetary Fund (IMF), whose mission is to provide financial assistance to member states experiencing financial crises; the International Bank for Reconstruction and Development (known as the World Bank), created to reduce poverty and promote economic development of poor countries and regions; the Organisation for Economic Co-operation and Development (OECD), which includes the major capitalist countries; and the organization that later became the World Trade Organization (WTO). The WTO's mission is to eliminate barriers to global trade and commerce. The U.S. government has used its influence in these institutions to promote stability and market-friendly policies throughout member states.

The sharp increase in the American government's global power after World War II initially outstripped the expansion of foreign operations by most American-based corporations. Although many U.S. corporations did a brisk export trade, in part because World War II had decimated industrial capacity abroad, the bulk of American productive capacity remained located within American borders and most corporations produced for domestic American markets. This situation changed in the 1980s, when American-based corporations substantially increased foreign trade, investment, and finance; Americans began buying more imported goods and services; and foreign companies stepped up investments in the U.S. These developments are often regarded as constituting a new era, commonly described as globalization.

A NEW ERA OF GLOBALIZATION?

Did the world enter a new (globalized) era beginning in the 1980s? One can identify two groups, which we label globalists and skeptics, who defend opposite sides of this issue. Globalists claim, in the title of one feisty account, that we are now "one world, ready or not."[27] Advances in transportation (such as containerized shipping) and communication (above all, the Internet) enable people, commodities, capital, and information to circle the globe at great speed and relatively low cost. Globalization also has a powerful political impact. States are less able to control their borders in an electronically interconnected world. Globally integrated markets make it difficult for states to pursue autonomous economic policies. At best, they can seek to position their economies at the cutting edge internationally and help their citizens adjust to globalization. At worst, if states ignore the importance of global economic competition and slip behind the global leaders, their citizens pay the price in lower living standards.

Although skeptics question some of the globalists' claims, they agree that there has been a sharp increase in key global economic flows. Exports of OECD countries have tripled since 1960. Foreign direct investment in OECD countries has grown even faster—at triple the rate of increase of international trade.[28] Large as they are, these changes are dwarfed by increases in transnational financial flows, including loans to foreign governments and firms, purchases of foreign government bonds, and currency exchange. The magnitude of these transactions has increased from several billion dollars daily in the 1970s to nearly $2 trillion today!

However, skeptics disagree with globalists about the causes and significance of these changes. For globalists, globalization follows developments in technology and transportation the way night follows day. For skeptics, on the other hand, economic and policy changes have depended on politics, that is, proglobalization decisions, institutions, and policies.[29] Skeptics also emphasize that most production in the world remains geared to domestic consumption. Guess what proportion of U.S. GDP is exported these days—less than one-fifth, about half, over half? The first answer is correct, and then some: only about 10 percent of U.S. GDP is exported.

With that said, there is no denying the substantial increase in international economic interdependence in recent decades that has deeply affected all nations and people. In the U.S., globalization has fractured established interest alignments, such as when the traditional cleavage between business and labor unions is replaced by industry- or firm-specific coalitions of business and labor. For example, when the Air Force decided to replace its aging fleet of refueling aircraft, a fierce competition to land the $35 billion contract pitted the management and unions at Boeing against the management and unions at Northrop Grumman, a U.S.-based subcontractor for the European aerospace company Airbus.

In conclusion, the political economists Leo Panitch and Sam Gindin provide a fine overview of what caused and maintains globalization:

> The American state has played an exceptional role in the creation of a fully global capitalism and in coordinating its management, as well as restructuring other states to these ends. . . . It was the immense strength of U.S. capitalism which made globalization possible, and what continued to make the American state distinctive was its vital role in managing and superintending capitalism on a worldwide plane.[30]

Transnational Corporations

Transnational corporations (TNCs) are the Goliaths of globalization. The 500 largest TNCs control over one-third of the world's global assets. Most are head-quartered in the U.S. [31] Although American corporations began creating foreign subsidiaries after World War II, the largest growth has occurred since the 1980s. By 2000, TNCs outnumbered countries on the list of the world's 100 largest entities, as measured by countries' GDP's and TNCs' sales revenues.

Most large American-based corporations are TNCs. For example, General Electric, one of the world's largest companies, operates in over 100 countries and derives over half its revenue from its foreign operations.

To gain access to skilled labor and infrastructure, and to locate themselves close to consumers who purchase their commodities, TNCs direct most invest-ment to affluent countries north of the equator (the region often described as the global north). However, to obtain access to raw materials and cheap labor, TNCs also make substantial investments in poor countries.

TNCs have enabled South Korea, Taiwan, India, and China to achieve enor-mous economic expansion and significant poverty reduction. China deserves special mention because of its enormous population and astonishingly rapid economic growth. A backwater until the 1980s, China leapfrogged to a position as one of the world's leading economic, political, and military powerhouses.

Much of the economic growth of China and other newly industrializing countries is facilitated by investments and outsourcing arrangements by TNCs. Although TNC operations in many poor countries provide welcome infusions of capital and technology, TNCs locate in these areas to take advantage of low wages, lax labor laws, and poor enforcement of environmental regulations.

The other side of the coin of American-based TNC investments abroad is for-eign-based TNC investments in the U.S. TNCs employ over 5 million American workers. In the auto industry, for example, they employ over one-quarter of all workers.[32] The U.S. depends on foreign investment to maintain job levels and financial stability. In recent years, American companies and consumers have purchased $600 billion more imported goods and services annually than U.S. firms have exported to other countries. (This pattern is called the trade deficit.) To balance the books, the U.S. depends on new foreign investment in the U.S. and purchases of U.S. treasury bills by foreign governments and investors.

A Post–Cold War Clash of Civilizations?

The concept of globalization helps make sense of the contemporary world. Another perspective proposed to explain contemporary global tensions is the concept of the "clash of civilizations." The political scientist Samuel Hunting-ton popularized this view in what the international-relations expert Peter Kat-zenstein has described as "arguably the most influential book published in international relations since the end of the Cold War." Huntington asserted that the world's major cultures or civilizations embrace divergent political and cultural values. In particular, he claimed that a fundamental conflict existed between the Judeo-Christian West, which has championed the importance of individualism and freedom, and Islamic culture, which Huntington character-ized as displaying intolerant and authoritarian values.[33]

We question this claim. For one thing, cultural values are not static. Although freedom, individualism, and secularism may now be dominant values in the West, they became widespread quite recently in most Western countries. For centuries, the West was the site of violent religious clashes, at a time when the Muslim rulers of the vast Ottoman Empire granted non-Muslim communities extensive autonomy and religious freedom.

For another thing, cultures are not monolithic. The economist and philoso-pher Amartya Sen points out that "[d]iversity is a feature of most cultures in the world. . . . Islam is often portrayed as fundamentally intolerant and hostile to individual freedom. But the presence of diversity and variety within a tradi-tion applies very much to Islam as well."[34]

Conflicts nowadays frequently occur *within* rather than *between* civilizations. These disputes pit moderate, liberal elements in a religious community against groups championing what members claim is traditional, orthodox religious practice.

If the clash of civilizations is a misleading template for understanding con-temporary global conflicts, is there a preferable alternative? Although contem-porary conflicts do not neatly align along a single divide, one major source of conflict pits the U.S. and its allies, who seek to preserve the status quo, against states and nonstate networks that challenge the U.S. government. A key instru-ment that underpins American hegemony in this regard is the military.

THE MILITARY ESTABLISHMENT

During the Cold War, the U.S. military establishment's major goal was to check the USSR (through a policy of **containment**). Both the United States and the USSR possessed thousands of strategic nuclear warheads and several times that number of tactical nuclear weapons. After the Cold War, the two sides con-cluded the START treaty, which substantially reduced their nuclear stockpiles, although enormous quantities of nuclear weapons and delivery systems remained, including intercontinental missiles, nuclear-armed submarines, and long-range bombers. In 2010, President Obama concluded another agreement with Russia, called "New START," that involved modest additional reductions in long-range nuclear weapons. President Obama also proposed that Russia and the United States cooperate to achieve the distant goal of worldwide nuclear disarmament.

The danger of nuclear war has been reduced by nuclear-weapons agreements between Russia and the U.S. to limit their nuclear weaponry, as well as a nuclear nonproliferation treaty (NPT) ratified by 190 nations that commits signatories not to develop nuclear weapons or assist other nations to develop them. However, the risk of nuclear catastrophe has increased because of nuclear proliferation. In addition to the five members of the nuclear-power club that have signed the NPT—the U.S., Russia, Britain, France, and China—four nations who are not signatories of the NPT have developed nuclear weapons: India, Pakistan, North Korea, and Israel. Other countries, notably Iran, probably aspire to do so. An even more ominous risk is that nonstatist groups like al Qaeda might hijack a nuclear-power facility or obtain radioactive material in order to unleash a "dirty bomb."

What has been the U.S. military's mission in the post–Cold War period? An authoritative indication was provided by the Department of Defense 2000 report "Joint Vision 2020." The report identified the goal of the U.S. military as "full spectrum dominance," meaning global superiority in every militarily strategic sphere: land, sea (both surface and underwater), air, space, and electromagnetic spectrums. Paul Rogers, a strategic analyst, describes the aim as "'global reach'—the ability to project power around the world."[35] The journalist George Easterbrook claims that the American military establishment is distinctive among those of other major countries in that its "primary military mission is not defense. Practically the entire military is an expeditionary force, designed not to guard borders—a duty that ties down most units of other militaries, including China's—but to 'project power' elsewhere in the world."[36] However, the distinction between defense and offense, as well as between offensive and defensive weapons, has become blurred in the post-9/11-era war on terrorism.

The military specialist Mary Kaldor has described how the military retooled to confront current challenges: "the end of the Cold War led to a feverish technological effort to apply information technology to military purposes, known as the Revolution in Military Affairs (RMA)."[37] RMA involves "the interaction between various systems for information collection, analysis, and transmission and weapons systems—the so-called 'system of systems.'"[38] Key interrelated elements include unmanned precision-guided weapons, like those unleashed by unmanned aerial vehicles (UAVs)—that is, drones—and sophisticated surveillance systems.

According to the *Washington Post* reporter Greg Miller, since 2010 "the Obama administration has institutionalized the highly classified practice of targeted killing, transforming ad-hoc elements into a counterterrorism infrastructure capable of sustaining a seemingly permanent war." The intelligence agencies directing the counterterrorism campaign have developed a "disposition matrix," a highly classified list of militants around the world targeted for killing by U.S. special-operations forces. Miller notes that the Obama administration "is the first [administration] to embrace targeted killing on a wide scale. . . ."[39]

To implement the disposition matrix, the Central Intelligence Agency (CIA) has dispatched drones to Pakistan, Afghanistan, Yemen, Somalia, and the Philippines to kill alleged militants of the Taliban, al Qaeda, and associated networks. For example, 320 drone strikes in Pakistan between 2004 and 2012 killed over 2,500 people, including numerous civilians.[40] The administration has claimed that the attacks have been highly effective; critics charge that they violate international law by invading other countries' airspace, targeting those whose responsibility for military operations or terror has not been determined by judicial procedures, and producing civilian casualties.

The use of high-tech weapons raises especially important questions when they violate other nations' boundaries and target militants who are not clearly combatants: who is legally authorized to deploy these weapons, what is their status under international law, and do the benefits of using them outweigh the risks and costs of doing so? These questions are rarely raised and are even less often subject to public debate. While it is not self-evident how open discussion and determination of classified matters should be, vast and vital areas of government policy and activity are presently off-limits to democratic discussion and decision making.

Most U.S. military forces, other than those stationed in Afghanistan and Iraq, now consist of mobile, rapid-intervention units transported by aircraft based in the U.S. and capable of flying long-range missions thanks to aerial refueling. For example, the U.S. Central Command, which directs the wars in Afghanistan and Iraq, is based in Tampa, Florida, thousands of miles from the theaters of operations. Another vital component of the globally mobile military force is the U.S. Navy, whose tonnage and firepower exceed those of all other major naval powers combined. Finally, as noted earlier, the United States maintains hundreds of military bases abroad.

The military's mission now includes involvement in unconventional conflicts, such as counterinsurgency, and in ethnically and religiously based violence. The military has also been delegated responsibilities for state and **nation building**, tasks even further removed from traditional combat. In Iraq and

Afghanistan, military personnel train police and teachers, build schools and roads, and provide economic-development aid.

The military's broadened mission has contributed to the Pentagon's swollen budget. The funds going to the military dwarf the budgets of civilian agencies concerned with foreign policy. For example, there are more members of marching bands in the U.S. military than U.S. Foreign Service diplomatic officers! The title of a news report describes the result: "The Pentagon has all but eclipsed the State Department in setting U.S. foreign policy."[41]

One aspect of foreign policy unrelated to maintaining military superiority is strengthening human rights and democracy around the world. Liberal presidents like John F. Kennedy and Jimmy Carter calculated that democratic regimes would be more inclined to support U.S. political and economic policies. On the other hand, when democratic governments have opposed U.S. leadership and market-friendly policies, the American government has at times orchestrated regime change. The U.S. government has also ignored human rights abuses and undemocratic practices by U.S. allies, such as Bahrain and Saudi Arabia.

What other goals might U.S. foreign policy pursue? Clearly, a priority must be to keep Americans safe. Indeed, before 9/11 the government ignored repeated warnings by its own experts regarding likely attacks of the kind that occurred. Another goal that has received little attention is the attempt to reduce nuclear stockpiles. While President Obama convened a conference on the issue in his first term and negotiated a nuclear-arms-reduction agreement with Russia, the danger of nuclear conflagration persists. In addition, the issue of climate change—which threatens the well-being of the entire planet—has received relatively little attention.

WHAT DO YOU THINK?

Promoting Global Well-Being versus Exercising Self-Restraint

How many resources (financial and political) should the American government devote to seeking to eliminate nuclear weapons; taking the lead in promoting alternative-energy sources and other steps to deal with global warming; protecting the world's battered ecosystem; reducing poverty, hunger, disease, and economic inequalities; and/or strengthening democracy and human rights? Can the U.S. exert leadership without dictating to others? If so, how? Alternatively, should the U.S. adopt a more modest profile, consistent with what physicians are taught in medical school: "First, do no harm"?

CLIMATE CHANGE, GLOBAL WARMING, AND ECOLOGICAL CRISIS

There is ample evidence that the volume of greenhouse gases released into the atmosphere from burning fossil fuels and other human activities is causing temperatures to increase, the polar ice caps and glaciers around the world to melt, sea levels to rise, and violent storms to become increasingly frequent.[42] The environmental expert Lester Brown asserts that we must "redefine security in twenty-first century terms. The time when military forces were the prime threat to security has faded into the past. The threats are now climate volatility, spreading water shortages, continuing population growth, spreading hunger, and failing states."[43]

U.S. domestic and foreign policies have utterly failed to confront these urgent challenges. There are many measures that the U.S. might take to preserve the world's battered ecosystem, including developing alternative energy sources, reducing carbon emissions, and assisting other countries to reduce deforestation. Brown estimates that the U.S. could resolve most major environmental problems at a cost of about 20 percent of the U.S. military budget. However, successive presidents of both parties have failed to give climate change and the accelerating environmental crisis the priority they deserve.

One major initiative in addressing climate concerns has been the mandating of higher fuel-economy standards in cars. The Honda Fit EV, an electric vehicle, is charged via solar power.

In his first term, President Obama did little to promote green policies, partly because there was little chance that Congress would support the necessary legislative and fiscal reforms. One change that he sponsored—which did not require congressional approval—was to mandate a substantial increase in fuel-economy standards for automobiles. In his first post-reelection speech in 2012, and second Inaugural Address in 2013, Obama announced that he planned to deal more forcefully with climate change in his second term.

THE SHIFT TO UNILATERALISM

Every president since World War II has sought to maintain U.S. global superiority, but successive presidents have interpreted and pursued this goal in quite different ways. For example, Jimmy Carter emphasized the importance of promoting human rights throughout the world. Ronald Reagan at first adopted a bellicose policy and then sought greater accommodation with the USSR toward the end of his presidency. George W. Bush's attempt to expand American power, however, was far more aggressive than any other postwar president's.

All presidents since Harry Truman proclaimed the value of participating in **multilateral** institutions—that is, intergovernmental organizations to develop and implement common economic, political, and military policies. George W. Bush broke with this tradition by championing a **unilateral** approach by which the U.S. acted alone rather than in concert with its allies. The new orientation was evident from the first days of Bush's presidency, well before 9/11, when he announced that the U.S. would not ratify the Kyoto Protocol, an agreement designed to slow global warming that most nations had ratified. The president further isolated the U.S. by refusing to recognize the jurisdiction of the International Criminal Court (ICC). The ICC was created to try cases of genocide, war crimes, and crimes against humanity.

The Bush administration sought to profit from Russia's weakened position following the Cold War—and thereby laid the groundwork for future conflict with a revitalized Russia. Bush provoked Russia by proposing to admit its neighbors Georgia and Ukraine into the NATO military alliance. He rejected previously negotiated limits on antiballistic-missile development and announced plans to build a nuclear antimissile shield in Poland and the Czech Republic, two more of Russia's neighbors. The president shelved a comprehensive nuclear-test-ban treaty signed by President Clinton. These measures increased tension between Russia and the U.S. so sharply that some analysts spoke of a new Cold War.

The turn to unilateralism isolated the U.S. and produced a steep drop in U.S. standing around the world, especially when the U.S. attacked Iraq in 2003 despite strong opposition from Russia and many other countries. In 2004, the former national security adviser Zbigniew Brzezinski observed, "We're more unpopular in the world today than at any time in our history, and our policies are more unpopular than those of any country in the world."[44]

In the United States, initial support for the Iraq War soon turned into opposition. Antiwar sentiment contributed to the Democrats' takeover of Congress in the 2006 midterm elections. Early opposition to the war by a little-known state senator from Illinois named Barack Obama was a principal reason why Obama gained the Democratic presidential nomination and was elected president.

Beyond the question of the Iraq War, one can identify two important changes in American foreign and security policy sponsored by the Bush administration: an aggressive assertion of U.S. power to preserve its global dominance and expansion of the government's internal security and coercive apparatus. These policy changes were a powerful legacy confronting President Obama when he took office in 2009.

Aggressive Assertion of U.S. Power

There has often been a tension within U.S. foreign policy between the government's claim to provide a global framework of freedom that enables other governments to develop as they wish and its attempt to shape other countries' regimes and policies in ways that advance American interests. The Bush administration shifted the balance toward a more aggressive posture.

In 2002, the government issued the "National Security Strategy of the United States," a policy statement designed to guide U.S. policy makers.[45] The document claimed that "[to] forestall or prevent hostile acts by our adversaries, the United States will, if necessary, act preemptively." This meant that, for the first time in American history, the government proclaimed the right to launch preventive war—that is, to initiate hostilities despite the absence of an imminent attack. The new posture became known as the **Bush Doctrine**.

The new doctrine was not idle words. Richard Clarke, U.S. counterterrorism chief during the Bush administration, describes his astonishment when he participated in discussions at the White House the day after 9/11. Instead of focusing on a response to al Qaeda and the Taliban regime that supported al Qaeda in Afghanistan, where al Qaeda was based, much of the conversation involved Iraq. President Bush urged Clarke to uncover any evidence of Iraq's involvement in the attack even though Clarke insisted that there was no link between Saddam Hussein and al Qaeda.[46] Over a year later, despite the continued absence of evidence that Iraq was involved in 9/11 or attempting to develop weapons of mass destruction (WMDs), Secretary of State Colin Powell delivered a speech at the UN urging support for an attack on Iraq. Powell cited what he described as "incontrovertible proof" that Iraq possessed WMDs. However, after the United States toppled Saddam Hussein's regime, a massive search failed to produce evidence of WMDs in Iraq or an active program to produce them. Years later, Powell ruefully confessed that the UN speech was the biggest mistake of his career.

Given the failure to find WMDs, the president offered a new defense for launching the war: to increase American security. He claimed that fighting terrorists abroad spared the United States from having to fight them within its borders. To this, Clarke replied, "Nothing America could have done would have provided al Qaeda and its new generation of cloned groups a better recruitment device than our unprovoked invasion of an oil-rich Arab country [Iraq]."[47]

Expansion of the Government's Internal Security Apparatus

Immediately after 9/11, the Bush administration asserted that the government needed additional powers to deal with the unprecedented threat represented by international terrorism. David Cole, a professor of constitutional law, described the administration's response as involving "a full-scale assault on the courts, on international law, and on the rule of law."[48] The constitutional scholar Ronald Dworkin agreed. In his words, "Since September 11, the government has enacted legislation, adopted policies, and threatened procedures that are not consistent with our established laws and values and would have been unthinkable before."[49]

One important example was the Patriot Act, sponsored by the Bush administration and passed by an overwhelming vote of Congress. According to Dworkin, the law created "a new, breathtakingly vague and broad definition of terrorism and of aiding terrorists."[50] A *New York Times* commentator suggested that if the law "sounds as if it's directed more toward effigy-burning, or Greenpeace activity, than international terror, it's because it is. International terror was already illegal."[51] The Patriot Act freed the Bush administration from judicial and congressional constraints. For example, the law authorized the government to conduct surveillance of American citizens without obtaining judicial authorization. President Bush devised a new category, "unlawful combatants," that most legal scholars believe violates international law. Despite objections from lawyers in the Pentagon, President Bush issued an order authorizing the government to hold unlawful combatants indefinitely and to deprive them of rights and protections guaranteed to prisoners of war by the Geneva Convention, a solemn international agreement to which the U.S. is a party. Hundreds of U.S. aliens and several American citizens were imprisoned under these procedures and subjected to harsh interrogation techniques that amount to torture.

In 2004, an especially ugly illustration of how the new policies might encourage lawless behavior came to light, when photographs were made public depicting prisoners in sexually humiliating poses at the Abu Ghraib U.S. military prison in Iraq. Official investigations reported that prisoners were routinely stripped naked, hooded, held in stressful positions, submerged in water, attacked by guard dogs, and placed in solitary confinement in dark, extremely hot or cold rooms.

Government officials declared that these abuses were the regrettable excesses of rogue prison guards. However, official investigations and reports by independent journalists documented that many were common practices at U.S. military prisons in Afghanistan and Iraq. For example, an FBI memorandum described "abuse of prisoners by military personnel in Iraq that included detainees being beaten and choked, and having lit cigarettes placed in their ears."[52] Methods of interrogation included slamming prisoners against a wall, conducting mock executions, threatening to abuse prisoners' families, and subjecting them to waterboarding, a technique that induces near drowning. Other tactics included **extraordinary rendition**—sending prisoners to countries with authoritarian regimes where they were subjected to torture—and sending suspects for interrogation to secret detention centers run by the CIA. These practices are prohibited by the Geneva Convention, the Universal Declaration of Human Rights, and the UN Convention against Torture—agreements ratified by the United States. However, Bush's attorney general, Alberto Gonzales, declared, "[A] new paradigm renders obsolete [the Geneva Convention's] strict limitations on questioning of enemy prisoners and renders quaint some of its provisions."[53] The *New York Times* legal commentator Anthony Lewis observed, "Instead of a country committed to law, the United States is now seen as a country that proclaims high legal ideals and then says that they should apply to all others but not to itself."[54]

Pushback began to occur in 2004 following revelations of prisoner abuse. The Supreme Court reversed some initial decisions and restored some detainee rights stripped away by the Bush administration. Pressure increased to trim executive power after the Democrats gained control of Congress in 2006 and Obama was elected in 2008.

OBAMA'S FOREIGN POLICY: CONTINUITY OR CHANGE?

Barack Obama was elected president in part because he promised to reverse the aggressive foreign policy of the Bush administration and to restore America's tarnished standing abroad. The change was symbolized on Obama's first day in office, when he announced his intention to close the Guantánamo Bay military prison in Cuba by year's end. (Congress blocked the administration's attempt to do so, in part because the government could not arrange for prisoners to be transferred elsewhere.) Obama ordered coercive interrogation techniques to end and closed CIA-run secret prisons. He announced a deadline for withdrawing combat troops from Iraq.

Obama sponsored other initiatives to restore traditional restraints on legal abuses as well as to regain the respect of the international community. The Obama administration rejected the legal opinions issued by the Bush administration authorizing interrogation techniques amounting to torture. The president abandoned the Bush administration's plan to build a missile-defense system in Poland and the Czech Republic. More broadly, he rejected the Bush administration's unilateralism in favor of multilateral cooperation. For example, he negotiated a second Strategic Arms Reduction Treaty (New START) with Russia that mandated a steep reduction in the two countries' nuclear weapons. Bush had suspended talks with Russia aiming to conclude such an agreement. Obama convened a conference of world leaders aimed at combating nuclear terrorism and seeking nuclear disarmament. He directed administration officials to participate in international conferences seeking reductions in greenhouse gases. These policies constituted an about-face from the Bush administration's approach to foreign affairs.

Obama was highly popular abroad. When he and Michelle Obama visited Europe in 2009, large crowds turned out to give them an enthusiastic welcome. The president delivered a speech in Cairo, Egypt, in 2009, in which he called for mutual understanding between Muslims and members of other faiths. Judging by public opinion polls and declarations by world leaders, Obama helped the U.S. to regain ground lost during the Bush presidency. These factors help explain why President Obama was awarded the Nobel Peace Prize in 2009.

Yet the Obama administration also continued to practice many of the Bush administration's sweeping and unregulated executive powers. Like the Bush Justice Department, the Obama Justice Department invoked the doctrine of state secrets to oppose lawsuits challenging the government's alleged torture and warrantless wiretapping. Like its predecessor, the Obama administration practiced **preventive detention**, which involves imprisoning detainees without

Detainees at Camp X-Ray, Guantánamo Bay Naval Base, Cuba, 2002.

access to lawyers, judicial review, or trial. It also defended the practice of extraordinary rendition. Contrary to President Obama's campaign pledge, the government announced that it would try foreign prisoners held at Guantánamo in military tribunals, where defendants possess significantly fewer rights than they do in civilian courts. The government continued to engage in warrantless surveillance of U.S. citizens suspected of having links to terrorism. In an editorial noting the continuity between the two administrations, the *New York Times* warned, "The Obama administration has clung for so long to the Bush administration's expansive claims of national security and executive power that it is in danger of turning President George W. Bush's cover-up of abuses committed in the name of fighting terrorism into President Barack Obama's cover-up."[55]

In 2011, Congress passed the National Defense Authorization Act (NDAA). It replaced a vote by Congress after 9/11 that authorized the government to use military force against perpetrators of the 9/11 attacks. The NDAA codified the conditions of detention of suspected terrorists and authorized the government to imprison indefinitely those whom the executive suspects might have "substantially supported" al Qaeda and its allies. The statute provided the government with even greater power than did the earlier Congressional vote.

WHAT DO YOU THINK?

What Drives American Foreign Policy?

Ever since the first years of the Republic, there has been tension involving U.S. foreign policy. On the one hand, political leaders have often proclaimed that the U.S. is distinctive—"a city upon a hill"— with a unique mission to promote freedom at home and abroad. On the other hand, U.S. foreign policy and behavior often appear to be motivated not by noble principles but by the attempt to maximize U.S. power and promote conditions in the world that will enable the U.S. to prosper. What do you think motivates U.S. foreign policy and behavior?

Critics claim that the NDAA does not define what constitutes "substantial support" and deprives suspects of a right to trial. They also charge that it chills free speech, since it imposes severe penalties for expressing opinions that might be construed as supporting terrorism. A federal judge issued a permanent injunction in 2012 barring the government from invoking this provision of the law for those with no connection to the 9/11 attack.

By doubling the number of U.S. troops in Afghanistan, President Obama went beyond President Bush. The aim of the surge was to eradicate al Qaeda and prevent the Taliban from toppling a U.S.-backed government and regaining control of Afghanistan.

Obama did emphasize limits to waging war in Afghanistan by setting a deadline of 2014 for withdrawing all combat troops from the country. The debate continues whether the great material and human costs of the decade-long war have increased U.S. security; promoted the establishment of a stable, democratic, and effective regime in Afghanistan; and prevented Afghanistan from serving as a base for terrorist training and operations.

The Obama administration also vigorously waged a quasi-war against al Qaeda and the Taliban in Pakistan, a nuclear-armed country ruled by a fragile and corrupt state. Although Pakistan was officially an ally of the U.S. and the recipient of considerable U.S. military and economic assistance, key elements of its infamous government intelligence agency, Inter-Services Intelligence (ISI), were known to work hand-in-glove with members of the Taliban and al Qaeda. In light of this situation, the U.S. did not inform Pakistani officials when in 2011 U.S. intelligence services pinpointed the location in Pakistan of the compound of Osama bin Laden, the head of al Qaeda and mastermind of 9/11.

Obama ordered a team of elite Navy Seals to raid the compound where bin Laden was hiding. During the raid, bin Laden was killed. The U.S. did not seek authorization from Pakistani officials or inform them of the raid in advance for fear that bin Laden would be warned and enabled to flee.

The Obama administration further angered Pakistani authorities and citizens, as described earlier, by directing drone strikes to kill suspected militants of al Qaeda and the Taliban inside Pakistan. The definition of "militant" is imprecise: one administration official stated that the government assumed that all men of fighting age in Pakistan's tribal areas qualified as militants and could be targeted. Although U.S. officials claimed that the drone campaign was highly effective, it violated Pakistani sovereignty and international law, produced numerous civilian casualties, and provoked a strong anti-American backlash in Pakistan and elsewhere.

Obama's greatest foreign-policy challenge in his first term was how to deal with the wave of uprisings in the Arab world that began in Tunisia in 2011 and quickly spread throughout North Africa and the Middle East. The tidal shift collectively became known as the Arab Spring.

Obama publicly supported the protests against authoritarian regimes in the region. For example, when Hosni Mubarak, long-time dictator in Egypt—and an ally that U.S. governments had supported for decades—refused to comply with Obama's demand that he adopt reforms to deal with huge demonstrations protesting his rule, Obama bluntly declared on television that Mubarak's 30-year reign should "end now."

Obama carefully limited support for the Arab Spring mainly to verbal pronouncements. Above all, he refused to dispatch U.S. troops to support the uprisings. The most active U.S. intervention occurred in the campaign to oust Libyan dictator Muammar Gaddafi. Although opposition forces were fighting a losing battle to oust Gaddafi, Obama did not provide the rebels with assistance until he received a mandate from the Arab League (an alliance of Arab countries) and the UN Security Council. The U.S. and several European allies then enforced a no-fly zone to prevent Gaddafi's regime from bombing rebel strongholds, and Obama authorized the launch of 112 Tomahawk cruise-missile strikes against military targets. Soon, Obama encouraged NATO to direct opposition to Gaddafi. At the same time, a coalition of 17 countries, including the U.S., managed ground-unit attacks.[56] A member of the administration described the U.S. policy as "leading from behind," a phrase that conservatives quickly seized upon to criticize the lack of a more aggressive U.S. posture. The opposition toppled the Gaddafi regime in 2011, and the Obama administration was praised for its skillful and measured actions during the civil war.

However, Libya was the scene of a tragic and humiliating incident involving the U.S. in 2012. On the anniversary of 9/11, J. Christopher Stevens, U.S. ambassador to Libya, and three other U.S. diplomatic officials who were visiting the U.S. consulate in Benghazi, were killed when the consulate was overrun and set on fire. The State Department first announced that the deaths were linked to a popular demonstration at the consulate that evening that was protesting the online posting of a video made in the U.S. ridiculing the Prophet Mohammed and the Muslim religion. However, the administration changed the official version within a week. It now described the attack on the consulate as a well-planned offensive by pro–al Qaeda militants. The incident figured in the 2012 presidential campaign when Mitt Romney charged that the administration had failed to provide adequate security for the ambassador and had fabricated an explanation of how it occurred to cover up its negligence.

In 2012, Syria became another Arab country with an authoritarian regime that provoked widespread opposition. The regime responded by unleashing brutal repression against opposition forces and the civilian population. Here again the U.S. helped organize sanctions and diplomatic isolation of the regime, but it refrained from military intervention.

While President Obama's approach to foreign policy was low-key, moderate, and pragmatic, he did launch some important foreign-policy initiatives. For example, while on a trip to Asia in November 2011, he announced a "pivot" in the U.S. foreign-policy focus from Europe to Asia. After his reelection, Obama's first trip abroad was to Asia.

WHAT DO YOU THINK?

Should the U.S. Provide Assistance to Regimes Emerging from the Arab Spring?

A *New York Times* editorial has advocated that the U.S. should provide more economic assistance to the regimes that replaced dictatorships in the Arab Spring. However, the editorial cautioned that "American support should be calibrated based on their [the rulers of these countries'] commitment to human rights and the rule of law" [*New York Times*, editorial, 12 November 2012]. Do you agree that more assistance should be given? Why or why not? If you support providing aid, should it be conditioned on these countries complying with human rights and the rule of law? Provide one or two reasons that support each of the opposing positions in this debate.

The Two Facets of the Obama Doctrine

Does the Obama administration have an overall vision of America's place in the world, and of when, how, and what U.S. government resources should be deployed abroad? Put otherwise, can one identify an Obama Doctrine in the sphere of foreign policy? According to the *New York Times* foreign-policy analyst David Sanger, there is an Obama Doctrine. It involves "a redefinition of the circumstances under which the United States will use diplomacy, coercion, and force to shape the world around it."[57] Sanger believes that this approach comprises "a lighter footprint around the world [compared to that sought by George W. Bush], and a reliance on coalitions to deal with global problems that do not directly threaten American security. . . ."[58]

The Obama Doctrine has two distinct facets, according to Sanger: "When confronted with a direct threat to American security, Obama has shown he is willing to act unilaterally—in a targeted, get-in-and-get-out fashion that avoids, at all costs, the kind of messy ground wars and lengthy occupations that have drained America's treasury and spirit for the past decade."[59] Examples include the bin Laden raid, drone strikes, and the Stuxnet worm (computer virus) that the U.S. is reported to have unleashed against Iran in 2010 to cripple its nuclear-weapons development. The second facet of the doctrine is a more cautious stance: "If a threat does not go to the heart of America's own security—if it is a threat to the global order but not to the country—Obama has been far more hesitant."[60] The two elements are opposite: the first involves a "willingness to strike unilaterally, and often in secret;" the second involves an "embrace of working in coalitions to support shared goals. . . ."[61]

Another two opposing facets of Obama's approach are a lofty, inspiring vision, and a hardheaded pragmatism. On the one hand is the Obama who was awarded the Nobel Peace Prize, who promotes peace, prosperity, mutual respect among nations, and a greener planet. On the other is the Obama who calculates the costs and benefits of any action for the U.S. and for his own political standing. This duality was echoed by scholars who described Obama's approach to the Middle East in terms that could be used to describe his overall approach to foreign policy (and possibly also to domestic politics): "When it comes to speaking, his rhetoric is visionary; but when it comes to delivering, his approach is pragmatic."[62]

DECLINING HEGEMONY?

Empire is the term usually used to describe one country's control over other countries and regions. To suggest that the U.S. exercises imperial power borders on the unpatriotic. Political leaders typically proclaim that, unlike powerful countries like France and Britain in past centuries, the U.S. does not possess foreign colonies. This claim is not accurate. Although the U.S. never acquired colonies on a grand scale, its colonial possessions include Puerto Rico, Guam, the Marshall Islands, American Samoa, and the Virgin Islands. More important, the fact that the U.S. is an imperial power is still not generally recognized. The historian and sociologist Thomas J. Sugrue summarizes the widely held myth: "The United States is a nation builder, not an empire builder; a world power that benignly brought democracy to the world by sowing the seeds of capitalism; a beacon of persuasion rather than coercion."[63] Whatever term is used, the U.S. has been the most powerful nation in the world for a century and exercises vast influence throughout the world.[64]

Many international-relations specialists claim that the position of the U.S. is as secure as ever, thanks to its great productive capacity, enormous resources, and technological edge in military and civilian sectors. This chapter has provided the evidence that is used to defend this claim. However, other international-relations specialists question whether the U.S. remains preeminent today and assert that the era of American dominance is coming to an end. They have defended the claim in publications with titles like *The Limits of Power*, "Waving Goodbye to Hegemony," and *The Post-American World*.[65]

An authoritative assessment reflecting this position was provided in a 2008 CIA report predicting that "[a]lthough the United States is likely to remain the [world's] single most powerful actor [in 2025], the United States' relative strength—even in the military realm—will decline and U.S. leverage will become more constrained."[66] Two trends suggest that the U.S. is losing global dominance. First, consider the changed nature of security threats. If firepower alone was the measure of dominance, the debate about U.S. preeminence would be over. However, since 9/11 Americans do not need reminding that small, nonstatist networks can pose a deadly threat. One possibility is cyberattacks directed against the Pentagon's computers, as well as U.S. electricity grids, financial systems, and complex communications networks. Another is sabotage of the U.S. transportation system and water supply. There is also an ever-present possibility of unconventional attacks like detonating a dirty bomb.

Climate change also involves a host of new security threats. According to one report, "Climate-induced crises could topple governments, feed terrorist movements or destabilize entire regions. . . . [E]xperts at the Pentagon and intelligence agencies for the first time are taking a serious look at the national security implications of climate change."[67]

Dealing with the new threats militarily may be not only ineffective but also counterproductive. The international-relations analyst Parag Khanna suggests:

> Many saw the invasions of Afghanistan and Iraq as the symbols of a global American imperialism; in fact, they were signs of imperial overstretch. Each expenditure has weakened America's armed forces, and each assertion of power has awakened resistance in the form of terrorist networks, insurgent groups and "asymmetric" weapons like suicide bombers. America's unipolar moment has inspired diplomatic and financial countermovements to block American bullying and construct an alternate world order. That new global order has arrived. . . .[68]

The foreign-policy analyst Joseph Nye, Jr., who coined the term *soft power*, has suggested why security nowadays cannot be obtained merely by superior weaponry:

> Not all the important types of power come out of the barrel of a gun. . . . [M]any of the transnational issues, such as climate change, the spread of infectious diseases, international crime, and terrorism, cannot be resolved by military force alone. Representing the dark side of globalization, these issues are inherently multilateral and require cooperation for their solution.[69]

A second challenge to U.S. dominance involves economics. The EU's combined GDP now exceeds that of the U.S. Likewise, China's and India's growth rates are several times higher than that of the U.S. (although, because their economies are much smaller, the absolute increase in the U.S. GDP exceeds theirs). Moreover, because of anemic U.S. savings and growth rates, coupled with massive purchases of imports, the U.S. has become a debtor nation. Large annual government deficits have produced a huge U.S. debt, which further weakens the international economic position of the U.S. No less an authority than the Chairman of the U.S. Joint Chiefs of Staff, Michael Mullen, identified the "burgeoning national debt as the single largest threat to the U.S. national security."[70]

U.S. economic stability has come to hinge on the willingness of other countries to provide the resources to balance its international economic ledger. Such dependence is hardly the posture that one expects of a hyperpower.

The savior is China, whose trade surplus with the U.S. exceeds $200 billion annually. What keeps the U.S. economy afloat—and prevents the government from falling into bankruptcy—is the willingness of the Chinese government to recycle its trade surplus by purchasing U.S. treasury bills. If China were to reduce its purchases of U.S. debt, the results might be catastrophic. One of Obama's foreign-policy goals has been to assure China's continued cooperation and to persuade its leaders to assume greater responsibility for promoting international peace and stability.

While China is the most successful new player in the global economy, India, Brazil, Turkey, Venezuela, and other countries have also become more economically developed and willing to challenge U.S. economic leadership. In recent years, the so-called BRICS countries—Brazil, Russia, India, China, and South Africa, the five largest developing economies—have begun to coordinate opposition to some U.S. policies.

Given that the U.S. no longer has the resources to compel the compliance of other countries, a prudent strategy might be to devise a transition to a world in which other countries share responsibility with the U.S. for promoting peace and prosperity. Barack Obama probably accepted the wisdom of this path, and even took modest steps toward facilitating such a global shift. However, the steps were halting and offset by other actions that reflected the more traditional goal of trying to maintain American dominance. And, of course, any U.S. president who explicitly spoke of seeking to guide the U.S. toward becoming a nation among equals rather than the sole hyperpower would provoke a firestorm of domestic opposition.

WHAT DO YOU THINK?

Is American International Power Singular or Plural?

Is the U.S. less powerful in the twenty-first century than it was in the late twentieth century? How and why? In answering this question, it might be useful to discuss how you think power should be measured. For example, should power be thought about in the singular or plural? That is, are various dimensions of power, such as economic, military, political, and cultural, different facets of a single whole? Or are they sufficiently distinct that American power cannot be thought of as a single entity because, for example, its military position might be preeminent but its economic standing might have declined? What difference does it make to regard American international power as singular or plural?

CONCLUSION

In 1630, the Puritan minister John Winthrop preached a sermon to the founders of the Massachusetts Bay Colony in which he declared that "we shall be as a city upon a hill." Worshippers knew that Winthrop was alluding to the Sermon on the Mount, in the Book of Matthew (5:14), where Jesus told his followers, "You are the light of the world. A city on a hill cannot be hidden." Ever since Winthrop, American political leaders have loudly praised the United States as unique, endowed with a divine mission, a city upon a hill. These stirring words, however, should not obscure a more complex reality: although many imperial powers have been more brutal than the U.S., and have provided fewer benefits to those whom they dominated, the U.S. is far from exempt from criticism. It assumed its present boundaries by exercising violence on a grand scale, and it achieved and maintained its preeminent position in the world not by chance, providence, or moral superiority but by the relentless use of power.

There have been some important continuities in foreign policy from one president to the next. First and foremost has been the goal of expanding the political and economic influence of the U.S. During the nineteenth century, the U.S. sought to make Latin America its personal preserve. Following World War II, the U.S. extended its sphere of influence to Western Europe and the third world. U.S. political leaders attempted to promote an international economy favorable to U.S. capitalism by persuading foreign governments and international organizations to promote market-friendly policies. The government also gave a helping hand to U.S.-based transnational corporations (TNCs), especially in the era of globalization beginning in the 1980s. For a decade after the end of the Cold War, some analysts thought that U.S. hegemony and liberal democracy would extend throughout the world forever. The claim was famously developed in an essay by the international-relations analyst Francis Fukuyama, "The End of History?" (The question mark was dropped when Fukuyama expanded the article to a book.)[71]

However, 9/11 was a cruel reminder that, like nature, history cannot be fully controlled. President George W. Bush's aggressive military action was designed to buttress U.S. dominance, but it probably left the U.S. in a weaker position. Although President Obama partially reversed President Bush's unilateral and aggressive assertion of U.S. power, some of his administration's policies and actions have provoked an international backlash. It remains an open question whether the Obama administration will rise to the challenge of fashioning a multilateral approach to dealing with immense global challenges, including a fast-growing crisis of the global ecosystem and a world in turmoil.

CHAPTER SUMMARY

Introduction
Despite many changes in American foreign policy since the founding of the republic, a constant goal has been to achieve and maintain a preeminent position for the U.S. in the world.

Making Foreign Policy
The process of making foreign policy is highly concentrated within the executive branch, especially in the Executive Office of the President, the National Security Council, intelligence agencies, and the departments of Defense, State, and Homeland Security. Given the large imbalance in resources between military and civilian agencies, there is a tendency for foreign policy to give priority to military solutions to international problems. Outside the Executive Branch, other influential participants in shaping foreign policy include congressional leaders of the defense and foreign-affairs committees, large defense contractors, and, to a lesser extent, policy intellectuals in universities and foreign policy–oriented think tanks.

American Foreign Policy before World War II
From the founding of the U.S. through the nineteenth century, American political leaders proclaimed that the U.S. should remain isolated from Europe's intrigues and conquests. At the same time, the U.S. assumed its present boundaries by annexing adjacent land through westward expansion, defeating and displacing Native Americans, and waging war against Mexico. The Monroe Doctrine created an informal sphere of U.S. influence in South America that excluded European countries. To achieve its commanding position, the U.S. frequently resorted to military force.

American Foreign Policy after World War II
Following World War II, the U.S. was the world's most powerful country. It pursued three major goals: checking the USSR during the Cold War; integrating the non-communist world, including the industrialized countries of Western Europe and the newly independent countries in the developing world; and creating international regulatory institutions to maintain worldwide peace and stability. These diverse goals aimed to maintain American international dominance.

A New Era of Globalization?

After the Soviet Union crumbled in the late 1980s, the U.S. was so dominant that it was commonly described as the world's only hyperpower. The U.S. used its commanding position to promote closer integration of global markets, which produced a vast increase in international trade, investment, and finance. The new era was fueled by advances in technology, including rapid communication and information processing, and an increase in the number and international penetration of transnational corporations (TNCs) based in the United States and other industrialized countries. It also involved economic development by newly developing countries like China and India. The changes during this period are commonly described as globalization. Along with enormous economic changes, globalization has generated intense international conflict, epitomized by the destruction of the World Trade Center in New York on September 11, 2001, followed by the U.S. invasions of Afghanistan and Iraq.

The Military Establishment

A core element of American international dominance is the military establishment. As noted above, the U.S. military budget of $700 billion nearly equals the combined military expenditures of all other countries in the world. The U.S. has an immense arsenal of nuclear-equipped intercontinental missiles, an unrivaled navy, rapid-interventionist forces, and cutting-edge high-tech or "smart" weapons. The major missions of the military are to protect the U.S. from attack, to deter and subdue challenges to U.S. dominance, and to maintain global stability.

Climate Change, Global Warming, and Ecological Crisis

One might not think that the issue of climate change belongs in a chapter on foreign policy. Yet, in addition to the social and human costs of climate change, the rise in global temperatures and related climate changes threaten U.S. security by increasing global competition for scarce resources like water, causing increased hunger and migration, and thereby weakening the capacity of states around the world. The Obama administration proposed some policy reforms in response but the issue of climate change will doubtless require more forceful measures in the future.

The Shift to Unilateralism

In the period after World War II, the U.S. sought to develop common positions with allies and gain the support of international organizations. In part because of 9/11, President George W. Bush sponsored a sharp turn toward unilateralism. The new policy involved an aggressive assertion of American power, an expansion of the domestic-security apparatus, and interrogation techniques used on detainees that are generally regarded as torture and as violations of international laws and treaties. Congress, the Supreme Court, and popular pressure forced the Bush administration to partially curtail some of these measures.

The Obama Presidency: Continuity or Change?

Barack Obama partially reversed the Bush administration's unilateral and aggressive foreign-policy stance. He negotiated an agreement with Russia to reduce nuclear weapons, and gave higher priority to international agencies like the UN. When confronted with challenges like the Arab Spring, he sought to develop multilateral alliances rather than act unilaterally. However, there were also important elements of continuity in American foreign policy, such as maintaining many of the questionable powers developed by the Bush administration, and seeking to shield the executive from scrutiny and accountability.

Declining Hegemony?

The U.S. remains the world's greatest military power. But judged by some other important standards—for example, comparative economic performance—the U.S. no longer occupies the position of global preeminence that it held for decades following World War II. The critical question is whether the U.S. will use its immense resources to deal with global challenges such as an accelerating crisis of the global ecosystem.

Critical Thinking Questions

1. When you survey the history of American foreign policy, what features have changed and what elements remain the same? Which tendency has predominated—continuity or change?

2. To what extent and how has globalization affected U.S. domestic politics and foreign policy? A suggestion: instead of trying to generalize, choose a specific issue to analyze.

3. President George W. Bush's policies in response to 9/11—for example, domestic surveillance, the treatment and interrogation of detainees, and military action in Afghanistan and Iraq—were highly controversial. Were they justified? Why or why not?

Suggested Readings

Andrew J. Bacevich, *The Limits of Power: The End of American Exceptionalism.* New York: Metropolitan Books; Henry Holt, 2008.

Jagdish Bhagwati, *In Defense of Globalization.* New York: Oxford University Press, 2004.

Lester R. Brown, *World on the Edge: How to Prevent Environmental and Economic Collapse.* New York: W. W. Norton, 2011.

Mark Danner, *Stripping Bare the Body: Politics, Violence, War.* New York: Nation Books; Perseus, 2009.

Joshua B. Freeman, *American Empire: The Rise of a Global Power, the Democratic Revolution at Home, 1945–2000.* New York: Viking, 2012.

Thomas L. Friedman, *The World Is Flat.* New York: Farrar, Straus and Giroux, 2005.

George C. Herring, *From Colony to Superpower: U.S. Foreign Relations since 1776.* New York: Oxford University Press, 2008.

G. John Ikenberry, *Liberal Leviathan: The Origins, Crisis, and Transformation of the American World Order.* Princeton, NJ: Princeton University Press, 2011.

Martin S. Indyk, Kenneth G. Lieberthal, and Michael E. O'Hanlon, *Bending History: Barack Obama's Foreign Policy.* Washington, D.C.: Brookings Institution Press, 2012.

Robert Kagan, *The World America Made.* New York: Knopf, 2012.

Leo Panitch and Sam Gindin, *The Making of Global Capitalism: The Political Economy of American Empire.* London: Verso, 2012.

David Rothkopf, *Superclass: The Global Power Elite and the World They Are Making.* New York: Farrar, Straus and Giroux, 2008.

David E. Sanger, *Confront and Conceal: Obama's Secret Wars and Surprising Use of American Power.* New York: Crown Publishers, 2012.

Robert Singh, *Barack Obama's Post-American Foreign Policy: The Limits of Engagement.* New York: Bloomsbury Academic, 2012.

Joseph E. Stiglitz, *Globalization and Its Discontents.* New York: W. W. Norton, 2003.

David C. Unger, *The Emergency State: America's Pursuit of Absolute Security at All Costs.* New York: Penguin Press, 2012.

Fareed Zakaria, *The Post-American World.* New York: W. W. Norton, 2008.

12

DEMOCRACY'S CHARACTER AND FUTURE

INTRODUCTION

The rules are the same for every baseball team: three strikes and you're out; three outs to a side; whoever scores the most runs wins. The pitcher's mound is the same 60 feet 6 inches from home plate in Yankee Stadium as it is in Wrigley Field, where the Chicago Cubs play. The distance between the bases is the same 90 feet for the home team as it is for the visitors. All teams must abide by the same rules, which apply uniformly to all of them. No team is permitted four outs to an inning, a smaller strike zone for their batters, or ten players on the field.

And yet the same teams continue to win. Some teams, like the Chicago Cubs, have not been in a World Series since 1945—and the last time the Cubs *won* a World Series was 1908. The New York Yankees, on the other hand, have been in 40 World Series—and have won 27 times. Indeed, the lack of competitive balance was regarded as such a problem that Baseball Commissioner Bud Selig appointed a blue-ribbon panel to investigate. The panel reported in 2000 that inequality threatened the integrity of the nation's pastime. From 1995 to 1999, no team in the bottom half of payrolls ever won a divisional series or league championship game, and only teams in the top quartile of payrolls ever won a World Series game. Even worse, the gap between wealthy and low-budget teams was growing. Whereas the average payroll of clubs in the richest quartile grew by $28 million between 1995 and 1999, the average payroll of clubs in the lowest quintile increased by only $4 million. By 1999, the richest team had a payroll equal to the payroll of the five lowest teams *combined*.[1] This situation continues to hold true today. The rules were fair; the game was not.

When baseball owners got hit where it hurt, in their pocketbooks—because the obviously unfair system resulted in falling attendance, and therefore declining revenue—they took action. In 2002, they initiated a revenue-sharing plan that redistributed income from the wealthiest teams—those in large television markets with lucrative TV contracts—to the poorest teams. In 2010, the New York Yankees, baseball's wealthiest team, paid about $110 million to Major League Baseball in the form of revenue-sharing and luxury-tax payments; under the new collective-bargaining agreement that came into effect in 2012, this single team is expected to pay over 27 percent of such future payments. Overall, revenue sharing has gone some distance toward leveling the steeply sloped playing field. The ratio of the highest to the lowest team revenue has decreased, and there has been a small increase in the overall performance of poorer teams. But the plan went only some distance. The Yankees' $196 million payroll in 2012 (the highest in Major League Baseball) was nearly six times larger than the payroll of the Kansas City Royals, the team with the lowest payroll (also in 2009, the Yankees managed to win yet another World Series). Compared to the situation ten years earlier, this represents progress; but the new system hardly can be said to have resulted in circumstances that give all teams an equal chance to compete for the best players.

And yet no matter how great the economic inequalities among teams, the game is not decided by whoever has the largest payroll or highest revenue. It still has to be played on the field, where players must hit, run, pitch, and catch. In the end, high-spending teams are challenged to translate their higher payrolls into more runs. In 2011, none of the nine highest-spending teams made it to the World Series. The team that ranked tenth out of 30 in payroll, the St. Louis Cardinals, won their division and went on to play in the World Series, in which they beat the Texas Rangers (ranked thirteenth). But in 2012, the more familiar pattern returned. The team with the seventh-highest payroll, the San Francisco Giants, defeated the team with the sixth, the Detroit Tigers. Even though money is not the only factor in determining outcomes, its influence cannot be ignored. Low-payroll baseball teams sometimes win—but only occasionally. High-payroll teams may not win all the time, but the odds continue to be in their favor. They still win most of the time.

Like baseball, the politics of power offers structural advantages to players and teams with more assets. Large companies and banks have an advantage over smaller political interests, just as baseball teams in large markets do over teams in small markets. Teams that enjoy a structural advantage are able to accumulate higher revenues from television and other sources and use the money to hire better players. So, too, corporations that enjoy a structural advantage can utilize it to shape public opinion, lobby policy makers, contribute to candidates, and create supportive interest groups. The political conflict that ensues is unfair, just as the contest on the baseball diamond is unfair because of economic inequality, even though the rules are the same for everybody.

But higher payrolls do not guarantee sports victories, and political advantages do not translate automatically into political success. Outcomes are not predetermined. Politics still matters. Change is possible. The political game plays on, with important consequences for the lives, and life chances, of more than 300 million people in the United States—and, given America's global role, for billions more around the globe.

CAPITALISM, AND DEMOCRACY REVISITED

Like the situation in organized baseball, American political institutions and processes are partially open and fair. Yet because of disproportionate resources, they are also partially closed and unfair. Though the law and politics ostensibly treat all citizens as equals, they often interact to produce deep, and widening, patterns of economic inequality. The character and quality of American democracy thus depend on how various dimensions of inequality affect the opportunities citizens have to participate effectively in making political decisions, in having their interests adequately represented, and in grappling with the advantages of class, race, and gender by promoting a more level playing field in the political, economic, and social spheres.

Our treatment of these concerns has highlighted what we identify as a tension at the very core of American politics: between capitalism, which tends to generate systemic inequalities, and democracy, which tends to promote equality. We also have stressed the ways in which the relationship between capitalism and democracy has varied quite a lot. American politics is not fixed or static.

With its limited regulation of business, declining unions, comparatively low taxes, and small safety net, the United States tilts more toward market capitalism than other Western countries. That tendency gives private markets, rather than the public sphere, an uncommon degree of organizing power. Because the relationship of capitalism and democracy is dynamic, a central political question concerns why and how changes in their relationship have occurred, and might further occur.

One can distinguish between structural change and conscious, voluntary political activity. Structural changes that result from political conflicts and decisions alter the basic framework within which politics is conducted, including the shape of political institutions; the broad distribution of economic, political, and social resources; and the composition and social identities of the citizenry. When the Department of Homeland Security was created in 2003 by the Bush administration and Congress, a structural change resulted. The size and power of executive agencies concerned with safeguarding the country from the threat of terrorism were expanded and transformed. When Chrysler and General Motors passed through bankruptcy with federal assistance between 2009 and 2012 to become much-changed car companies, the distribution of economic resources, including jobs and their benefits, changed substantially. When the population grows older on average, new challenges to health care and the welfare state emerge.

Such structural alterations can be distinguished from intentional political activity aimed at protecting or changing the status quo. During most of his first year as president, Barack Obama sought to convince the American public and Congress to transform the country's health-care system. This mobilization of attention produced large-scale change. In the American political system, elections stand out as an important means for candidates and parties to stand for, and promote, different policies. Other means involve campaign contributions, efforts to influence public opinion, lobbying by interest groups, and participation by citizens in change-oriented organizations and social movements including those directed at affecting civil rights, the environment, women's rights, matters of public morality such as abortion, and issues of war and peace.

Structural features and political activity are not independent of each other. When political activity is sufficiently powerful, it can alter structural features. Since the 1970s, the environmental movement has succeeded in introducing a host of public regulations to safeguard water and the air we breathe, protect consumer safety, increase occupational health and safety, and begin to address the great challenge of global warming. Changes the movement advocated have affected the structure of the political and economic system. These range from heightened fuel efficiency and safety standards in automobiles to the requirement that industries install technology to minimize pollution. But given the deeply rooted structural features in American political institutions that tilt the field on which political struggles are waged, attempts at reform frequently face steep uphill battles, especially when they involve challenges to concentrations of wealth and power.

Most Americans subscribe to both democracy and capitalism. They overwhelmingly support a political system based on consent, elections, free speech, the rule of law, fair procedures, protection against arbitrary action by government, and moral and religious freedom. Despite many disagreements about particular issues, the status of liberal democracy as the way Americans wish to govern themselves is strong and secure. So, too, is the powerful emphasis on freedom in the country's political culture. Furthermore, the great majority of Americans have a high degree of tolerance for the expression of minority opinions and unconventional ideas.[2] Indeed, over the course of American history, the scope of liberty in religion, in the press, and in matters that concern morals and sexuality has grown as public tolerance has increased.[3]

Further, set against the country's history of slavery and segregation, and long-standing patterns of discrimination against women, ethnic minorities, and homosexuals, the country today seems deeply committed to political equality and to the dignity and human worth of each person. The great majority think it goes against the American idea of equality to teach that some kinds of people are better than others or that some people are undeserving of equal treatment. Some 95 percent subscribe to the view that "every citizen should have an equal chance to influence government policy." More than 90 percent think that "everyone should have a right to hold public office."[4]

Americans also tend to strongly support the existence of a capitalist economic system. Survey after survey has shown strong backing for the view that people should be free to earn as much as they can and for the view that values achievement, ambition, and a strong work ethic. When asked to respond to such statements as "there is nothing wrong with a [person] trying to make as much money as he honestly can" and "the profits a company or a business can earn should be as large as they can fairly earn," huge majorities of Americans—of all political persuasions—say yes. To the proposition that "government should limit the amount of money any individual is allowed to earn in a year," nine out of ten say no. Furthermore, well over 80 percent believe that the "private ownership of property is necessary for economic progress" and that a system of free enterprise is "necessary for free government to survive."[5]

As a result of these strong commitments to both democracy and capitalism, the country's political culture experiences deep frictions between its various priorities and values. When two leading students of public opinion, Herbert McCloskey and John Zaller, introduced their powerful study of these two traditions of belief, they observed that they are not mutually consistent or harmonious. Rather, democracy and capitalism represent two traditions—one maximizing freedom and participation, the other maximizing earnings and profit—that offer discordant, often clashing priorities. "Capitalism tends to value each individual according to the scarcity of his talents and his contributions to production," they write, whereas "democracy attributes unique but roughly equivalent value to *all* people." Further, these authors state that "capitalism stresses the need for a reward system that encourages the most talented and industrious individuals to earn and amass as much wealth as possible; democracy tries to ensure that all people, even those who lack outstanding talents and initiative, can at least gain a decent livelihood." Finally, they observe, "capitalism holds that the free market is not only the most efficient but also the fairest mechanism for distributing goods and services." By contrast, "democracy upholds the rights of popular majorities to override market mechanisms when necessary to alleviate social and economic distress."[6]

Often, Americans hold fast to both sets of commitments without directly confronting how they might be incompatible. Sometimes they debate the relative priority that democratic and capitalist values should have. How free should the market be? When should government act to ensure that political equality is backed by a sufficient degree of economic equality to make it meaningful? Such questions define the choices our politics offer.

The dominant way most Americans manage these tensions is by subscribing to a cluster of values often gathered under the heading of "the American dream." These values stress the importance of equality of opportunity, the chance for all Americans to freely and actively pursue their ambitions in the public and private realms. Of course, there are mythical qualities to this dream. Not everyone can participate equally in the quest for success. People tend to blame themselves, rather than more impersonal and distant forces, for their shortcomings. But given the depth of commitment Americans have to both democracy and capitalism, no other ideological position successfully competes with this vision of equal opportunity.[7]

This broad perspective permits more than one kind of public policy. At times, as in the New Deal of the 1930s, the quest for equal opportunity strongly supported the push for a more effective government that could limit and tame the inequalities generated by the economic system. During, and for two decades after, the presidency of Ronald Reagan in the 1980s, equal opportunity underpinned an assault on big government. It was coupled with the argument that the people, not the national state, should keep as much of the money they earn as possible and that this orientation will best help expand the economy and spread opportunity. Since the deep economic crisis that began in 2008, matters concerning inequality—including outrage over the compensation of bankers and CEOs of failing companies—have again come to the fore, triggering much greater willingness by political leaders and the public alike to grapple with disparities in income and wealth through policy changes and action by the federal government.

Over time, the way that Americans' belief in equal opportunity informs their views about the role of the federal government has changed quite a lot. In the early years of the Republic, most Americans thought that a strong central state would become the tool of the privileged. Equal opportunity thus required a small national state that would undertake only basic responsibilities for defense, trade, and internal communications. But with industrial development in the late nineteenth and twentieth centuries, combined with the growth of new patterns of inequality as capitalism expanded, more and more Americans looked to the federal government to pass laws and institute regulations to level the playing field and create conditions that allowed the notion of equal opportunity to be realized. Today, large majorities of Americans—more than two out of three—support increased spending for education and child care as well as programs to assist the elderly, improve health care, and fight poverty.[8] Although opinions often differ about how this should be done, government has achieved a durable role in promoting the norm of equal opportunity. Government thus can reduce tension between democracy and capitalism; but this friction has not disappeared, nor can it ever be entirely eliminated.

Much of the time, the relationship between capitalism and democracy is managed by distinguishing between issues thought to be political, and thus subject to democratic life and popular control, and those considered to be economic, and thus largely placed in private hands. But more and more, that distinction is difficult to sustain. Government policy plays a huge role in economic life. In turn, the largest enterprises that dominate the country's economy possess enormous political clout; and as the rescue of GM and Chrysler recently showed, these firms are not permitted to collapse even after they fail. As the political scientist Robert Dahl observes, "A large firm is . . . inherently a *political* system because the government of the firm exercises great power, including coercive power. The government of a firm can have more impact on the lives of more people than the government of many a town, city, province, state."[9]

So the tension remains. The politics of power proceeds in the crucible of tough-to-resolve differences between capitalism and democracy. Whereas both sets of institutions command high regard by the public, Americans are often divided—frequently against others, sometimes against themselves—about how to find the proper balance between the two. Although significant majorities (about two-thirds) believe that the private-enterprise system is "generally fair and efficient" and that "workers and management share the same interests in the long run," a slightly larger majority thinks both that corporations and the wealthy don't pay their fair share of taxes and that "corporations and people with money really run the country."[10]

AMERICAN DEMOCRACY IN THEORY AND PRACTICE

This book has identified three elements that comprise a fuller approach to democracy than the usual standard requiring that all citizens have the right to participate in electing key political representatives. Our more expansive approach considers the impediments citizens face when they wish to help make decisions, participate in deliberations, shape political life, and affect public policy. Judging the politics of power and assessing whether citizens' interests are adequately represented requires taking stock of these three elements.

The first element concerns the need for procedures to ensure the full and fair expression of political views (especially unpopular ones) and strict adherence to rules for electing representatives. The record is uneven. During the past generation, there has been a prevailing trend toward the enormous concentration of media control in a few giant corporations, making it increasingly difficult for viewpoints outside the mainstream to be heard on network television or radio. Yet the centralization of the mainstream media has been offset, if only partially, by more decentralized means of electronic communication, including cable television, Internet news sources, and bloggers. Most of the time, elections are open and fair; but there also have been shocking violations of fair and honest electoral procedures. When dirty tricks are used to prevent citizens from registering to vote or from casting their ballot, and when votes are not counted—abuses practiced in recent presidential elections—the United States fails an elementary test of democracy. Other practices also underrepresent substantial groups of citizens. We have seen how the Constitution specifies that every state elect two senators, a rule that makes the votes in sparsely populated states worth several times as much as votes in large states like California, New York, Texas, and Florida. Further, many states deprive convicted felons, even after their release from prison, of the right to vote; thus, those states are collectively disenfranchising millions of citizens.

The second element assesses whether political leaders broadly reflect major social identities based on class, race, ethnicity, religion, gender, and region. Clearly change was afoot in the 2008 presidential campaign when a woman, Hillary Clinton, and an African American, Barack Obama, vied for the Democratic Party nomination for president—and when Obama ultimately won the presidency, then was reelected in 2012. Congress, though—despite minority gains—largely remains a club for affluent white men. The mismatch between its demography and that of the country at large means that the national legislature inadequately reflects the concerns of a diverse American electorate, especially the interests of African Americans, Hispanics, and women.

The third element focuses on effective political responsiveness, the requirement that representatives promote the interests of their constituents. In several chapters, we have seen how economic inequalities and political contributions by affluent citizens and organized interests powerfully influence the political agenda, thus making the representation of interests skewed and less efficient for those who lack money, power, and influence. The unevenness of representation is compounded by how the political system, with its multiple points of access and multiple opportunities for blocking reform, can fail to meet widespread demands for change.

Overall, it is precisely because the country's political system offers the most vibrant potential to check deep inequality that shortcomings of democratic representation are disquieting. All too often, the politics of power reflects and even contributes to inequalities instead of narrowing them. Unless the democratic side of the equation is strengthened, reversing the trend toward growing inequality will be difficult.

As the twenty-first century continues to unfold, the dynamics of political life are being vitally affected by the large-scale patterns of change we identified in the introduction to this chapter. These patterns have reshaped the agenda of American politics; moreover, they have opened new dimensions for political deliberation, conflict, and possibilities for change. As the lone superpower (albeit one whose relative power may be declining) confronting a more interconnected and more unpredictable world, the United States faces difficult decisions: which weapons to build, where to deploy its armed might, how to raise funds to pay for its overseas ventures, which means are best to project American power as well as secure the nation against attack by armed groups, how to organize global trade, whether to make the environment a worldwide priority, and whether to promote more equal distribution of wealth and resources across the globe. The choices range from ever assertive foreign and military policies aimed at securing the country's global reach to much more modest aims based on a reduction of overseas ambitions.

As politics has become more polarized, and as a realignment has occurred across regional lines, making decisions about such issues has become more difficult and more charged by deep ideological differences and diverse policy preferences. What is less clear is whether these splits that have become characteristic of debates among political leaders and in the media, especially cable news, reflect or are much sharper than divisions in the population as a whole. Either way, it has become harder to reach agreement across party lines about how to manage the economy, shape the welfare state, deliver health care, deal with immigration, consider controversial social issues like abortion and stem-cell research, and grapple with the country's great diversity of people.

As economic crisis has returned, calling into question both the virtues of markets and the promise of government, questions about the future of the country and its politics of power also have deepened. At stake is the degree of structural change, the ways capitalism will be regulated and risk managed, the character of social policies to cushion economic change, and, most fundamentally, how democracy and capitalism will engage with each other within the ambit of public policy. Economic troubles have widened the scope of possible answers, but the degree of involvement by the government in shaping the future of capitalism has yet to be determined.

CONCLUSION

Outcomes are uncertain. Answers to these challenges will be produced by political action within the framework of American politics—that is, by the politics of power. Such challenges will require knowledge, judgments, and decisions—hopefully informed judgments and decisions—about how American politics works; about what constraints and pressures affect its institutions, processes, and policies; and about which policies might be selected at home and abroad.

There are reasons for hope, but no grounds for complacency, especially because public knowledge is uneven and the information citizens have is not always accurately presented. Much of the time, the clash of opinion, the range of information, and the thoughtfulness of debate about public policy help produce an informed public; but the country's history over the past half-century has been punctuated by efforts that do not meet a standard of truthfulness. As a presidential candidate in 1960, John F. Kennedy erroneously declared a missile gap with the Soviet Union; even after his administration knew that this scenario was false, it repressed the information to justify a rapid buildup in weapons. In 1964, President Lyndon Johnson misleadingly claimed that North Vietnam had attacked two U.S. destroyers in the Gulf of Tonkin in order to persuade Congress to authorize war in Vietnam. In 1985 and 1986, President Ronald Reagan disguised covert efforts to trade arms and hostages with Iran in a complicated and illegal scheme to help arm rebels in Nicaragua fighting a guerrilla war against the elected leftist government. Before the United States went to war against Iraq in 2003, President George W. Bush exaggerated the military threat from that country in his State of the Union address, even to the point of citing forged documents about an Iraqi attempt to obtain nuclear fuel in the African country of Niger.[11]

The judgment announced in the classic work on public opinion by the political scientist V. O. Key, Jr., still holds. "Politicians," he wrote, "often make of the public a scapegoat for their own shortcomings; their actions, they say, are a necessity for survival given the state of public opinion. Yet that opinion itself results from the preachings of the influentials, of this generation and of several past generations." He further noted that political "leaders who act as if they thought the people to be fools responsive only to the meanest appeals deserve only scorn."[12] Critical responsibility for the depth and quality of political life lies with the character of education provided by our schools, the range and rigor of reporting by the mass media, the standards used by experts who care about public policy, and the thoughtfulness and responsibility exhibited by political leaders.

Understanding how the country's democracy currently falls short need not produce a cynical or resigned view that little can be done to challenge the uneven distribution of wealth and power. Just as there have been moments of great change in the past, we can be confident that the future will be very different from the present. How such changes will unfold depends in large part on political participation—or nonparticipation. We thus urge students of American politics to be both critical and engaged: critical because the promise of American democracy remains to be fulfilled; engaged because inequalities will intensify without robust critical engagement.

Informed and active political participation can be both politically effective and politically infectious. Ample opportunity exists to extend and deepen democratic possibilities. When we apply an understanding of the politics of power, Americans can work to realize the rousing promise of American democracy.

ENDNOTES

Chapter 1

1. These figures are reported by the September 2011 U.S. Census report, "Income, Poverty and Health Insurance in the United States, 2010," issued September 2011, Table A-3; data from the 2011 "Current Population Survey Annual Social and Economic Supplement." www.census.gov/prod/2011pubs/p60-239.pdf. Also see the 2011 Congressional Budget Office Report, http://money.cnn.com/2011/10/26/news/economy/cbo_income/index.htm; http://economix.blogs.nytimes.com/2012/01/17/measuring-the-top-1-by-wealth-not-income/; www.federalreserve.gov/pubs/feds/2011/201117/201117pap.pdf; www.forbes.com/sites/christopherhelman/2011/10/12/americas-25-highest-paid-ceos/; www.vanityfair.com/society/features/2011/05/top-one-percent-201105; http://money.cnn.com/2012/03/30/markets/top-earning-hedge-fund-managers/index.htm (accessed March 7, 2012).

2. www.statcan.gc.ca/pub/13f0026m/13f0026m2006001-eng.pdf; http://blogs.reuters.com/felix-salmon/2011/03/25/swedish-inequality-datapoint-of-the-day/; www.census.gov/prod/2011pubs/p60-239.pdf; "Searing Poverty Casts Spotlight on 'Lost Decade,'" *New York Times*, 13 September 2011 (accessed March 7, 2012).

3. *New York Times*, 1 June 1999; Angus Deaton, "Health, Income, and Inequality," National Bureau of Economic Research, "Health, Income, and Inequality," Spring 2003 at www.nber.org/reporter/spring03/health.html (accessed March 7, 2012).

4. www.census.gov/prod/2011pubs/p60-239.pdf. The best data broken down by race comes from the Pew Research Center, which mounted a survey that compared 2005 and 2009 circumstances. The report was released on July 26, 2011; http://pewresearch.org/pubs/2069/housing-bubble-subprime-mortgages-hispanics-blacks-household-wealth-disparity (accessed March 7, 2012).

5. http://money.cnn.com/2011/09/14/news/economy/poverty_government_assistance/index.htm; http://money.cnn.com/2011/09/13/news/economy/poverty_rate_income/index.htm?iid=HP_LN; http://stats.oecd.org/Index.aspx?DataSetCode=POVERTY (accessed March 7, 2012).

6. John Paul Stevens, "Should We Have a New Constitutional Convention?," *The New York Review of Books*, 11 October 2012. The best recent discussion of the debates and compromises at the Constitutional Convention is David Brian Robertson, *The Original Compromise: What the Constitution's Framers Were Really Thinking* (New York: Oxford University Press, 2013).

7. Charles E. Lindblom, *Politics and Markets: The World's Political-Economic Systems* (New York: Basic Books, 1977), 171, 172.

8. Ibid., 175.

9. www.nytimes.com/2012/02/17/business/gm-reports-its-largest-annual-profit.html (accessed March 7, 2012).

10. Robert Dahl, *Who Governs? Democracy and Power in an American City* (New Haven, CT: Yale University Press, 1961), 3–4.

11. Ibid., 1, 3.

12. Ibid., 86, 311.

13. Carole Pateman, *Participation and Democratic Theory* (New York: Cambridge University Press, 1970), 25.

14. Hanna Fenichel Pitkin, *The Concept of Representation* (Berkeley: University of California Press, 1967).

15. www.acq.osd.mil/ie/download/bsr/bsr2010baseline.pdf (2010 Base Inventory; (accessed March 7, 2012).

16. www.ncpa.org/sub/dpd/?Article_ID=18745 (accessed March 7, 2012).

17. Nolan McCarty, Keith Poole, and Howard Rosenthal, *Polarized America: The Dance of Ideology and Unequal Riches* (Cambridge, MA: MIT Press, 2008); Larry M. Bartels, *Unequal Democracy: The Political Economy of the New Gilded Age* (Princeton, NJ: Princeton University Press, 2008).

18. In all, Republicans have tended to be more consistently ideologically conservative, and Democrats have been consistently liberal. For discussions, see Jacob S. Hacker and Paul Pierson, *Off Center: The Republican Revolution and the Erosion of American Democracy* (New Haven, CT: Yale University Press, 2005), and Thomas A. Mann and Norman J. Ornstein, *It's Even Worse Than It Looks: How the American Constitutional System Collided with the New Politics of Extremism* (New York: Basic Books, 2012).

19. Robert L. Bartley, "Liberalism 1976: A Conservative Critique" (paper prepared for the Conference on the Relevance of Liberalism, Columbia University Research Institute on International Change, New York, January 1976).

20. David Leonhardt, "Greenspan's Mea Culpa," *New York Times*, 23 October 2008; www.npr.org/blogs/itsallpolitics/2012/09/27/161818462/2012-gender-gap-could-be-historic-but-not-necessarily-why-you-think (accessed March 7, 2012).

Part I

1. Good accounts of Flint can be gleaned from Ronald Edsforth, *Class Conflict and Cultural Consensus: The Making of a Consumer Society in Flint, Michigan* (New Brunswick, NJ: Rutgers University Press, 1987); Ben Hamper, *Rivethead: Tales From the Assembly Line* (New York: Warner Books, 1991); and Steven P. Dandaneau, *A Town Abandoned: Flint Michigan Confronts Deindustrialization* (New York: State University of New York Press, 1996).

2. Don Pemberton and Robert Schnorbus, *Genesee County and the Transformation of the Auto Industry* (Chicago: Federal Reserve Bank of Chicago, 1996).

3. George E. Lord and Albert C. Price, "Growth Ideology in a Period of Decline: Deindustrialization and Restructuring Flint Style," *Social Problems* 39, no. 2 (May 1992): 155–69.

4. Ronald Edsforth, "Review of Roger & Me," *American Historical Review* 96 (October 1991): 1145–47.

5. David Streifeld, "As One City Accelerates Its Loss, Another Relishes Its Rare Boom," *New York Times,* 22 April 2009.

6. Bill Vlasic and Nick Buntley, "The Last Holdouts Cast Their Lot with GM," *New York Times,* 23 May 2008.

Chapter 2

1. Smith is quoted in Robert L. Heilbroner, *The Nature and Logic of Capitalism* (New York: W. W. Norton, 1985).

2. Thomas L. Friedman, *Hot, Flat and Crowded: Why We Need a Green Revolution and How It Can Renew America* (New York: Farrar, Strauss and Giroux, 2008), 53.

3. Diamond is quoted in Friedman, *Hot, Flat and Crowded*, 67.

4. See *Stern Review Executive Summary* at www.hm-treasury.gov.UK /Sternreview_summary .htm (accessed November 20, 2012).

5. Jacob S. Hacker and Paul Pierson, "What Krugman and Stiglitz Can Tell Us," *New York Review of Books,* 27 September 2012, 55.

6. Peter S. Goodman, "Late Fee Profits May Trump Plan to Modify Loans," *New York Times,* 30 July 2009.

7. Marc Linder and Ingrid Nygard, *Void Where Prohibited: Rest Breaks and the Right to Urinate on Company Time* (Ithaca: Cornell University Press, 1998).

8. Joshua Altman, "Obama: A Plan for Those Passionate about 'Job Creators,'" *The Hill* 8 September 2011.

9. Elizabeth Sanders, *Roots of Reform: Farmers, Workers and the American State, 1877–1917* (Chicago: University of Chicago Press, 1999), 387.

10. James C. Cobb, *The Selling of the South: The Southern Crusade for Industrial Development, 1936–1980* (Baton Rouge: Louisiana State University Press, 1982).

11. Louise Story, "Empty Words, Empty Workplaces," *New York Times,* 2 December 2012.

12. James Surowiecki, "Corporate Welfare Queens," *New Yorker* 8 October 2012, 42.

13. Ethan Epstein, "A Schilling Pitch That Went Awry," *Weekly Standard* 17 September 2012, vol. 18, no. 1.

14. Peter Eisenger, *The Rise of the Entrepreneurial State: State and Local Economic Development Policy in the United States* (Madison: University of Wisconsin Press, 1988), 128–73.

15. M. D. Platzer and G. J. Harrison, *The U.S. Automotive Industry: National and State Trends in Manufacturing Employment* (Washington, DC: Congressional Research Service, 2009), 28.

16. John McMillen, *Reinventing the Bazaar: A Natural History of Markets* (New York: W. W. Norton, 2002), 28.

17. Melody Peterson, "New Medicines Seldom Contain Anything New, Study Finds," *New York Times,* 29 May 2002.

18. Steve Striffler, "Inside a Poultry Processing Plant: An Ethnographic Portrait," *Labor History*, vol. 43, no. 3 (August 2002), 306.

19. Tawney is quoted in Heilbroner, *The Nature and Logic of Capitalism*, 100.

20. Richard B. Freeman and Joel Rogers, *What Workers Want* (Ithaca: Cornell University Press, 1999), 1.

21. Charles Lindblom, *Politics and Markets: The World's Political-Economic Systems* (New York: Basic Books, 1977), 172.

22. Richard W. Stevenson and David Leonhardt, "Biggest Hurdle: Uncertainty," *New York Times*, 22 September 2002.

23. Louis Uchitelle, "Uncle Sam Wants You . . . to Have a Job," *New York Times*, 31 January 2010.

24. Neil J. Mitchell, *The Conspicuous Corporation: Business, Public Policy and Representative Democracy* (Ann Arbor: University of Michigan Press, 1997), 167.

25. Ibid., 167–89.

26. John Bellamy Foster, Robert W. McChesney, and R. Jamil Jonna, "Monopoly and Competition in Twenty-First Century Capitalism," *Monthly Review*, vol. 62, no. 11 (April 2011), 1–39.

27. www.census.gov/econ/smallbus.html. Table 2b (accessed September 20, 2012).

28. Eric Schultz, *Markets and Power: The 21st Century Command Economy* (Armonk: Sharpe, 2001).

29. Foster, McChesney, and Jonna, "Monopoly and Competition in Twenty-First Century Capitalism."

30. Jeffrey E. Garton, "Megamergers Are a Clear and Present Danger," *Business Week* 25 January 1999, 28.

31. William Lynch, an executive at the stockbrokerage house Dean Witter Reynolds, interviewed by the *Voice of America*, 3 February 1985.

32. 2010 Alliance for Board Diversity Census, *Missing Pieces: Women and Minorities on Fortune 500 Boards* at: http://theabd.org/Missing_Pieces_Women_and_Minorities_on_Fortune_500_Boards.pdf (accessed September 23, 2012).

33. E. E. Schattschneider, *Politics, Pressure and the Tariff* (New York: Prentice Hall, 1935), 287.

34. G. William Domhoff, *The Higher Circles: The Governing Class in America* (New York: Random House, 1970).

35. Michael Useem, *The Inner Circle: Large Corporations and the Rise of Business Political Activity in the U.S. and the U.K.* (New York: Oxford University Press, 1984), 56.

36. Kay Lehman Schlozman and John T. Tierney, *Organized Interests and American Democracy* (New York: Harper & Row, 1986), 401.

37. Ronald Edsforth, *Class Conflict and Cultural Consensus: The Making of a Mass Consumer Society in Flint, Michigan* (New Brunswick: Rutgers University Press, 1987), 39–71.

38. Daron Acegmolu and David Auter, "Skills, Tasks and Technologies: Implications for Earnings and Employment," NBER Working Paper 16082 (June 2010).

39. Kay Lehman Schlozman, Sidney Verba, and Henry E. Brady, *The Unheavenly Chorus: Unequal Political Voice and the Broken Promise of American Democracy* (Princeton: Princeton University Press, 2012), 82.

40. See www.doingbusiness.org/custom-query#hReprtpreview (accessed September 23, 2012).

41. Peter Osterman, Thomas A. Kochan, Richard Locke, and Michael J. Piore, *Working in America: A Blueprint for a New Labor Market* (Cambridge: MIT Press, 2001), 55.

42. Seymour Martin Lipset and Gary Marks, *It Didn't Happen Here: Why Socialism Failed in the United States* (New York: W. W. Norton, 2000), 279.

43. OECD, "Growing Income Inequality in OECD Countries: What Drives It and How Can Policy Tackle It?" (Paris: OECD, 2011).

44. Jacob S. Hacker and Paul Pierson, *Winner Take All Politics: How Washington Made the Rich Richer and Turned Its Back on the Middle Class* (New York: Simon & Schuster, 2010), 38–40.

Chapter 3

1. Bruce Laurie, *Artisans into Workers: Labor in Nineteenth Century America* (New York: Noonday Press, 1989), 15–47.

2. Guy S. Callender, "The Early Transportation and Banking Enterprises of the States in Relation to the Growth of Corporation," *Quarterly Journal of Economics* 77 (November 1902), 111–62. Quoted in Colleen A. Dunlavy, *Politics and Industrialization: Early Railroads in the United States and Prussia* (Princeton: Princeton University Press, 1994), 97.

3. See the important article by Harry N. Scheiber "Federalism and the American Economic Order, 1789–1910," *Law & Society Review* (Fall 1975), 57–119.

4. Stephen Skowroneck, *Building a New American State: The Expansion of National Administrative Capacities, 1977–1920* (Cambridge: Cambridge University Press, 1982), 23.

5. Quoted in Melvyn Dubofsky, *Industrialization and the American Worker, 1865–1920* (Arlington Heights, IL: Harlan Davidson, 1985), 53.

6. James R. Green, *Grass Roots Socialism: Radical Movements in the Southwest, 1895–1943* (Baton Rouge: Louisiana State University Press, 1978), 228–70.

7. Elizabeth Sanders, *Roots of Reform: Farmers, Workers and the American State, 1896–1917* (Chicago: University of Chicago Press, 1999).

8. Lawrence Goodwyn, *The Populist Moment* (New York: Oxford University Press, 1979).

9. Woodrow Wilson, *The New Freedom: A Call for the Emancipation of the Generous Energies of a People* (New York: Doubleday, 1918, Page & Co), 15.

10. Roosevelt is quoted in Arthur Schlesinger, Jr., "A Question of Power," *American Prospect,* 23 April 2001, 27.

11. Frank Drobbin, *Forging Industrial Policy: The United States, Britain and France in the Railway Age* (Cambridge: Cambridge University Press, 1994), 28–91.

12. Ibid., 324–33.

13. Irving Bernstein, *A History of the American Worker, 1920–1933: The Lean Years* (Boston: Houghton Mifflin, 1960), 47–83.

14. Alan Brinkley, *The End of Reform: New Deal Liberalism in Recession and War* (New York: Knopf, 1995), 230–31. See also John W. Jeffries, "The 'New' New Deal: FDR and American Liberalism, 1937–1945," *Political Science Quarterly*, vol. 105, no. 3 (1990): 397–418.

15. Andrew Shonfeld writes, "The New Dealers . . . perceived the future as a new mixture of public and private initiatives, with the public side very much reinforced but still operating in the framework of a predominantly capitalist system. Considering the opportunities for radical experiment offered by twenty years of uninterrupted Democratic administration from 1933 to 1952, it is surprising how little follow-through there was from this original impulse into the postwar world." See Andrew Shonfeld, *Modern Capitalism* (London: Oxford University Press, 1970), 308.

16. Alan Wolfe, *America's Impasse: The Rise and Fall of the Politics of Growth* (Boston: South End Press, 1981), 52–53.

17. Quoted in ibid., 51.

18. Judith Stein quotes President Lyndon Johnson telling a group of business people, "We put some of the money back for people to spend instead of letting the government spend it for them. We put some of the money back for business to invest in new enterprise instead of the government investing it for them." See Judith Stein, *Running Steel, Running America: Race, Economic Policy and the Decline of Liberalism* (Chapel Hill: University of North Carolina Press, 1998), 75.

19. Herbert Stein, *Presidential Economies: The Making of Economic Policy from Roosevelt to Clinton* (Washington, DC: American Enterprise Institute, 1994), 135.

20. Jack Metzger, *Striking Steel: Solidarity Remembered* (Philadelphia: Temple University Press, 2000), 210.

21. Robert B. Reich, *The Wealth of Nations: Preparing Ourselves for 21st Century Capitalism* (New York: Knopf, 1991), 67.

22. Taylor Dark, *The Unions and the Democrats: An Enduring Alliance* (Ithaca: Cornell University Press, 1999), 113.

23. Jacob S. Hacker and Paul Pierson, "Tax Politics and the Struggle over Activist Government," in Paul Pierson and Theda Skocpol, eds., *The Transformation of American Politics: Activist Government and the Rise of Conservatism* (Princeton: Princeton University Press, 2007), 156.

24. See the interview of supply-sider Grover Norquist by Jodie T. Allen, "Found Treasure," *U.S. News & World Report* 14 July 2003, 113.

25. For data on the financialization of the American economy, see Benjamin M. Friedman, "The Failure of the Economy and the Economists," *New York Review of Books,* 28 May 2009, 42–45; Simon Johnson, "The Quiet Coup," *Atlantic* May 2009, 46–56; and Jacob S. Hacker and Paul Pierson, *Winner-Take-All Politics* (New York: Simon & Schuster, 2010).

26. Figures on the debt ratio and savings rate are from the Federal Reserve Bank of San Francisco Economic Letter, "U.S. Household Deleveraging and Future Consumption Growth," No. 2009–16, May 15, 2009.

27. Charles R. Morris, *The Trillion Dollar Meltdown: Easy Money, High Rollers and the Great Credit Crunch* (New York: Public Affairs, 2009).

28. Greenspan is quoted in Morris, *The Trillion Dollar Meltdown,* 54.

29. David Leonhardt, "Economic Health: It's Relative," *New York Times,* 17 October 2012.

30. Robert Draper, *Do Not Ask What Good We Do* (New York: Free Press, 2012).

Part II

1. Joseph Schumpeter, *Capitalism, Socialism and Democracy* (New York: Harper & Row, 1942).

Chapter 4

1. In order to achieve their goal, the founders relied not only on representative procedures but also on the configuration of core political institutions that comprise the American political system—notably federalism, the division of powers, an indirectly elected president, and checks and balances among the three branches of the national government. We focus here on political parties and participation, and analyze political institutions in other chapters.

2. The founders looked for inspiration to some historical cases of indirect election—that is, representative institutions—and, for theoretical inspiration, to the writings of the English philosopher John Locke and the French philosopher Baron de Montesquieu.

3. Kay Lehman Schlozman, Sidney Verba, and Henry E. Brady, *The Unheavenly Chorus: Unequal Political Voice and the Broken Promise of American Democracy* (Princeton, NJ: Princeton University Press, 2012), 8.

4. E. E. Schattschneider, *Party Government* (New York: Holt, Rinehart and Winston, 1942), 1.

5. Richard Hofstadter, *The Idea of a Party System: The Rise of Legitimate Opposition in the United States, 1780–1840* (Berkeley: University of California Press, 1969), 53.

6. Ibid., 2.

7. John H. Aldrich, *Why Parties? The Origin and Transformation of Political Parties in America* (Chicago: University of Chicago Press, 1995).

8. Richard P. McCormick, "Political Development and the Second Party System," in *The American Party Systems: Stages of Political Development,* eds. William Nesbitt Chambers and Walter Dean Burnham (New York: Oxford University Press, 1977), 102.

9. Michael Schudson, *The Good Citizen* (Cambridge, MA: Harvard University Press, 1998), 112.

10. Walter Dean Burnham, *Critical Elections and the Mainsprings of American Politics* (New York: W. W. Norton, 1970), 21.

11. The classic account of the theory of critical elections is Walter Dean Burnham, *Critical Elections.*

12. Stephen Skowronek, *Building a New American State: The Expansion of National Administrative Capacities, 1877–1920* (New York: Cambridge University Press, 1982), 24, 25.

13. Burnham, *Critical Elections,* 71–73.

14. Ira Katznelson, "The Crisis of the Capitalist City: Urban Politics and Social Control," in *Theoretical Perspectives on Urban Politics,* eds. Willis D. Hawley and Michael Lipsky (Englewood Cliffs, NJ: Prentice-Hall, 1976), 224–25; Ira Katznelson, *City Trenches: Urban Politics and the Patterning of Class in the United States* (New York: Pantheon, 1981).

15. Frances Fox Piven and Richard Cloward, *Why Americans Don't Vote* (New York: Pantheon, 1988), 28–41.

16. J. Morgan Kousser, *The Shaping of Southern Politics: Suffrage Restrictions and the Establishment of the One-Party South* (New Haven, CT: Yale University Press, 1974).

17. Piven and Cloward, *Why Americans Don't Vote.*

18. Andrea Louise Campbell, "Parties, Electoral Participation, and Shifting Voting Blocs," in *The Transformation of American Politics: Activist Government and the Rise of Conservatism*, eds. Paul Pierson and Theda Skocpol (Princeton, NJ: Princeton University Press, 2007), 68.

19. Ira Katznelson, *When Affirmative Action Was White* (New York: W. W. Norton, 2005).

20. Earl Black and Merle Black, *Politics and Society in the South* (Cambridge, MA: Harvard University Press, 1987), 241.

21. Ibid.

22. John Petrocik, "Realignment: New Party Coalitions and the Nationalization of the South," *Journal of Politics* 49 (May 1987): 347–75.

23. Lisa McGirr, *Suburban Warriors: The Origins of the New Right* (Princeton, NJ: Princeton University Press, 2001), 157.

24. Mary C. Brennan, *Turning Right in the Sixties: The Conservative Capture of the GOP* (Chapel Hill: University of North Carolina Press, 1995), 141.

25. Jeffrey M. Stonecash, *Class and Party in American Politics* (Boulder, CO: Westview Press, 2000), 26.

26. Jacob S. Hacker and Paul L. Pierson, "Tax Politics and the Struggle over Activist Government," in Pierson and Skocpol, eds., *The Transformation of American Politics,* 263.

27. Christine Todd Whitman, *It's My Party, Too: The Battle for the Heart of the GOP and the Future of America* (New York: Penguin, 2005), quoted in Jacob S. Hacker and Paul Pierson, *Off Center: The Republican Revolution and the Erosion of American Democracy* (New Haven, CT: Yale University Press, 2006), 4.

28. Both speeches were quoted in the *New York Times,* 6 November 2008.

29. Charles Blow, "G.O.P. Nightmare Charts," *New York Times,* 23 May 2012.

30. Nicholas D. Kristof, "Can Republicans Adapt?," *New York Times,* 8 November 2012.

31. *New York Times,* 15 September 2012.

32. Andrew Gelman and Avi Feller, "Red Versus Blue in a New Light," Campaign Stops, *New York Times,* 13 November 2012.

33. The analysis that follows draws on 2012 exit polls sponsored by the *New York Times,* available at http://elections.nytimes.com/2012/results/president/exit-polls, as well as a series of exit polls published in the *New York Times* on 11 November 2012. The CBS exit poll referred to in the text is available at www.cbsnews.com/election-results-2012/exit.shtml?tag=context Main;contentBody (accessed December 28, 2012).

34. John Harwood, "Political Memo: Demographics in Key States Could Aid Obama in Fall," *New York Times,* 8 August 2012 (online edition accessed August 8, 2012).

35. Michael D. Shear, "As Electorate Changes, Fresh Worry for G.O.P.," *New York Times,* 8 November 2012.

36. James Poniewozik, "Lights, Camera, Traction: A Few Pivotal Moments Proved That Live TV Still Matters," *Time*, 19 November 2012.

37. Editorial, *New York Times*, "Mitt Romney, Class Warrior," 19 September 2012.

38. Editorial, *New York Times*, 8 November 2012.

39. Romney adviser Eric Fehrnstrom, in a CNN interview, 21 March 2012.

40. Steven Rosenfeld, "Advertising on Television Rockets, as Super PACs Pour in the Dough," at www.alternet.org/election-2012/advertising-television-rockets-super-pacs-pour-dough-total-total-spending-5-billion?akid=9501.237106.Yvk1hl&tf=18src+newsletter; 722971&t=3 (accessed December 28, 2012).

41. Richard Parker, "Social and Anti-social Media," Campaign Stops, *New York Times*, 15 November 2012.

42. Trip Gabriel, "Campaign Boils Down to Door-to-Door Voter Drives in Battleground States," *New York Times*, 22 October 2012.

43. Jim Rutenberg, "To Obama Workers, Winning Takes 'Grunt and Math,'" *New York Times*, 26 October 2012.

44. Russell J. Dalton, *Citizen Politics: Public Opinion and Political Parties in Advanced Industrial Democracies,* 3rd ed. (New York: Chatham House, 2002), 36. For comparative turnout levels, see "International Voter Turnout, 1991–2000," at http://archive.fairvote.org/turnout/intturnout.htm (accessed March 11, 2010).

45. Michael S. Lewis-Beck, William G. Jacoby, Helmut Norpoth, and Herbert F. Weisberg, *The American Voter Revisited* (Ann Arbor: University of Michigan Press, 2008), 104.

46. Ian Urbina, "Hurdles to Voting Persisted in 2008," *New York Times*, 1 March 2009, A14.

47. Michael D. Martinez, "Why Is American Turnout So Low, and Why Should We Care?," in Jan E. Leighley, ed., *The Oxford Handbook of American Elections and Political Behavior* (New York: Oxford University Press, 2010), Ch. 7.

48. Adam Liptak, "The Vanishing Battleground," *New York Times*, Sunday Review, 4 September 2012.

49. For a popular account of this trend, see Sasha Issenberg, *The Victory Lab: The Secret Science of Winning Campaigns* (New York: Crown Publishing, 2012). For a scholarly analysis of the impact of campaigns, see Robert S. Erikson and Christopher Wlezien, *The Timeline of Presidential Elections: How Campaigns Do (and Do Not) Matter* (Chicago: University of Chicago Press, 2012).

50. Rutenberg, "To Obama Workers, Winning Takes 'Grunt and Math.'"

51. Walter Dean Burnham, "The 1980 Earthquake: Realignment, Reaction or What?," in *The Hidden Election: Politics and Economics in the 1980 Presidential Campaign*, eds. Thomas Ferguson and Joel Rogers (New York: Pantheon, 1981), 126–27.

52. Jan E. Leighley and Jonathan Nagler, "Socioeconomic Class Bias in Turnout, 1964–1988," *American Political Science Review* 86 (1992): 725–36.

53. Stephen Wayne, *Is This Any Way to Run a Democratic Election?* (Washington, DC: CQ Press, 2007), 36.

54. Lee Drutman, "The Political One Percent of the One Percent," http://sunlightfoundation.com/blog/2011/12/13/the-political-one-percent-of-the-one-percent/. Cited in Schlozman et al., *The Unheavenly Chorus*, 591, fn 4.

55. David Corn, "The Fight Goes On," *The Nation*, 6 December 2004. For scholarly analyses, see Joel Bleifuss and Steven F. Freeman, *Was the 2004 Presidential Election Stolen? Exit Polls, Election Fraud, and the Official Count* (New York: Seven Stories Press, 2006); Mark Crispin Miller, ed., *Loser Take All: Election Fraud and the Subversion of Democracy, 2000–2008* (Brooklyn, NY: Ig Publishing, 2008).

56. For an excellent review of historical and current practices, see Tova Andrea Wang, *The Politics of Voter Suppression: Defending and Expanding Americans' Right to Vote* (Ithaca: Cornell University Press, 2012).

57. The newspaper was the *Palm Beach Post*; reported in an editorial in the *New York Times*, 4 November 2012.

58. Bill Marsh, "Data Points," *New York Times*, 21 October 2012. The figure was provided by an official from New York University's Brennan Center for Justice, the most authoritative source of information on voter suppression.

59. *New York Times*, 22 September 2012.

60. Charles Blow, "Election Data Dive," *New York Times*, 10 November 2012.

61.Quoted in Frank J. Sorauf and Paul Allen Beck, *Party Politics in America* (Glenview, IL: Scott Foresman, 1988), 101.

62. Lyle Denniston, quoted in James Hyatt, "Citizens United and Political Contributions: The Story So Far," *Business Ethics*, business-ethics.com/2010/04/15/1523-citizens-united-and-political-contributions-the-story-so-far (accessed January 9, 2013).

63. This statistic was provided by the public-interest research group Public Citizen in an e-mail sent 3 November 2012 to Mark Kesselman.

64. *New York Times*, 8 July 1998.

65. Quoted in Elizabeth Drew, *Politics and Money: The New Road to Corruption* (New York: Macmillan, 1983), 78.

66. Joe Nocera, "Buying the Election?" *New York Times*, 9 October 2012.

67. Reported on the National Public Radio news broadcast Morning Edition, 12 November 2012.

68. Nicholas Confessore and Jess Bidgood, "Little to Show for Cash Flood by Big Donors," *New York Times*, 8 November 2012.

69. These figures are from www.opensecrets.org/pressreleases/04results.asp (no longer available in the Open Secrets archives).

70. Jonathan Weisman and Derek Willis, "With Control of Senate at Stake, Last-Minute Money Pours into Races," *New York Times*, 5 November 2012.

71. Mark Bittman, "The Food Movement Takes a Beating," *New York Times*, Sunday Review, 11 November 2012.

72. Jacobs and Skocpol, eds., *American Democracy*, 9.

73. Charles Blow, "Bullies on the Bus," *New York Times*, 23 June 2012.

74. Earl Black and Merle Black, *Divided America: The Ferocious Power Struggle in American Politics* (New York: Simon & Schuster, 2007), 258.

75. Quoted in Edward M. Kennedy, *True Compass: A Memoir* (New York: Twelve, 2009), 217.

76. Morris Fiorina, with Samuel J. Abrams and Jeremy C. Pope, *Culture War? The Myth of Polarized America* (New York: Pearson Longman, 2006).

77. David Leonhardt, "The Caucus: Party Affiliation Is the Big Polarizer," *New York Times*, 5 June 2012. Leonhardt draws on the Pew Research Center for the People & the Press, *Trends in American Values: 1987–2012: Partisan Polarization Surges in Bush, Obama Years*, available at www.people-press.org/files/legacy-pdf/06/04-12$20values%20Release.pdf.

78. Jacob S. Hacker and Paul Pierson, *Winner-Take-All Politics: How Washington Made the Rich Richer—and Turned Its Back on the Middle Class* (New York: Simon & Schuster, 2010); Geoffrey Kabaservice, *Rule and Ruin: The Downfall of Moderation and the Destruction of the Republican Party, from Eisenhower to the Tea Party* (New York: Oxford University Press, 2012); and Thomas E. Mann and Norman J. Ornstein, *It's Even Worse Than You Think: How the American Constitutional System Collided with the New Politics of Extremism* (New York: Basic Books, 2012).

79. Jacobs and Skocpol, "American Democracy in an Era of Rising Inequality," 1, 9.

80. Mann and Ornstein, *It's Even Worse Than You Think*.

81. Verba, Schlozman, and Brady, *Voice and Equality*, 189.

82. www.Bartleby.com/73/1593.html/ (accessed December 28, 2012).

Chapter 5

1. Bill McKibben, "The Reckoning: Global Warming's Terrifying New Math," *Rolling Stone* 2 August 2012, 52.

2. Quoted in Aaron M. McCright and Riley E. Dunlap, "Challenging Global Warming as a Social Problem: An Analysis of the Conservative Movement's Counter Claims," *Social Problems* 47, no. 2 (November 2000), 505.

3. Riley E. Dunlap and Aaron M. McCright, "Organized Climate Change Denial," in *Oxford Handbook of Climate Change and Society*, eds. John S. Dryzek, Richard B. Norgaard, and David Schlosberg (New York: Oxford University Press, 2011), 145.

4. Jane Meyer, "Covert Operations: The Billionaire Brothers Who Are Waging a War against Obama," *New Yorker*, 30 August 2010, 45–56.

5. www.sourcewatch.org/index.php?title=Heartland_Institute (accessed May 13, 2012).

6. www.csmonitor.com/Science/2012/0507/Heartland-Institute-s-digital-billboards-make-bombastic-comparisons-video (accessed May 13, 2012).

7. Inhofe is quoted in Dunlap and McCright, "Organized Climate Change Denial," 153.

8. John C. Berg, "Waiting for Lefty: The State of the Peace Movement in the United States," paper presented to the annual conference of the New England Political Science Association, Portland, Maine, 8–9 May 2009.

9. Kay Schlozman, "Interest Groups," in *The Oxford Companion to Political Science*, 2nd ed. (New York: Oxford University Press, 2001), 400–01.

10. Kay Lehman Schlozman, Sidney Verba, and Henry E. Brady, *The Unheavenly Chorus: Unequal Political Voice and the Broken Promise of American Democracy* (Princeton: Princeton University Press, 2012), 349.

11. Gordon Adams, *The Iron Triangle: The Politics of Defense Contracting* (New York: Council on Economic Priorities, 1991).

12. Joseph A. Pika, "Interest Groups and the Executive: Presidential Intervention," in *Interest Group Politics*, eds. Allan C. Cigler and Burdett A. Loomis (Washington, DC: Congressional Quarterly Press, 1983), 303.

13. Bayard Rustin, "From Protest to Politics: The Future of the Civil Rights Movement," *Commentary* (February 1965), 25–31.

14. Benjamin N. Freidman, "The Oligarchy in America Today," *New York Review of Books* 11 October 2012, 36–39.

15. David Vogel, *Fluctuating Fortunes: The Political Power of Business in America* (New York: Basic Books, 1989).

16. Schlozman, Verba, and Brady, *The Unheavenly Chorus*, 328.

17. Ibid., 438.

18. Jacob S. Hacker and Paul Pierson, *Winner Take All Politics* (New York: Simon and Schuster, 2010), 66.

19. Adam Davidson, "It's Not Technically an Oligopoly," *New York Times Magazine*, 22 December 2011, 16–18.

20. Kate Phillips, "Google Joins the Lobbying Herd," *New York Times*, 28 March 2006.

21. Nicholas Perltoth, "Google Spends $5.03 Million on Lobbying," *New York Times*, 24 April 2012.

22. Michael Tomasky, "The Money Fighting Health Care," *The New York Review of Books*, 8 April 2010, 10–14.

23. Quoted in Thomas E. Mann and Norman J. Ornstein, *It's Even Worse than It Looks: How the American Constitutional System Collided with the New Politics of Extremism* (New York: Basic Books, 2012), 69.

24. Eric Lichtblau, "Lawmakers Regulate Banks, Then Flock to Them," *New York Times*, 14 April 2010.

25. Jeffrey H. Birnbaum, "Oil Lobby Reaches Out to Citizens Peeved at the Pump," *New York Times*, 9 May 2008.

26. Kenneth M. Goldstein, *Interest Groups, Lobbying, and Participation in America* (New York: Cambridge University Press, 1999).

27. Mark Kesselman, "The Conflictual Evolution of American Political Science: From Apologetic Pluralism to Trilateralism and Marxism," in *Public Values and Private Power in American Democracy*, ed. J. David Greenstone (Chicago: University of Chicago Press, 1982), 34–67.

28. Frank R. Baumgartner, Jeffrey M. Berry, Marie Hojnacki, David C. Kimball, and Beth L. Leech, *Lobbying and Policy Change: Who Wins, Who Loses, and Why* (Chicago: University of Chicago Press, 2009).

29. John Broder and Jad Mouwad, "Energy Firms Find No Unity on Climate Bill," *New York Times,* 19 October 2009.

30. Schlozman, Verba, and Brady, *The Unheavenly Chorus,* 575.

31. Pepper D. Culpepper, *Quiet Politics and Business Power: Corporate Control in Europe and Japan* (New York: Cambridge University Press, 2010).

32. Jeffrey M. Berry, *The New Liberalism: The Rising Power of Citizen Groups* (Washington, DC: Brookings Institution, 1999).

33. Alexis de Tocqueville, *Democracy in America* (New York: Knopf, 1946), 106.

34. James Q. Wilson, *Political Organizations* (New York: Basic Books, 1973).

35. Theda Skocpol, *Diminished Democracy: From Membership to Management in American Civic Life* (Norman: University of Oklahoma Press, 2003).

36. Schlozman, Verba, and Brady, *The Unheavenly Chorus,* 267.

37. Ibid.

38. Kay Lehman Scholzman et al., "Inequalities of Political Voice," in *Inequality and American Democracy,* eds. Lawrence R. Jacobs and Theda Skocpol (New York: Russell Sage Foundation, 2005), 55–57.

39. Mark S. Bonchek, "Grassroots in Cyberspace: Using Computer Networks to Facilitate Political Participation," paper presented at the Midwest Political Science Associations, Chicago, Illinois, April 1995, 1.

40. Bruce Bimber, "The Internet and Political Transformation: Populism, Community and Accelerated Pluralism," *Polity* 31, no. 1 (September 1998), 133–66.

41. Kay Lehman Schlozman, Sidney Verba, and Henry E. Brady, "Weapon of the Strong? Participatory Inequality and the Internet," *Perspectives on Politics* 8, no. 2 (June 2010), 487–509.

42. Mark A. Smith, *American Business and Political Power: Public Opinion, Elections and Democracy* (Chicago: University of Chicago Press, 2000), 173.

43. Ibid., 194.

44. Herbert McClosky and John Zaller, *The American Ethos: Public Attitudes Toward Capitalism and Democracy* (Cambridge: Harvard University Press, 1984).

45. Ibid., 7.

46. Calvin F. Exoo and Alan Draper, "Alternative Cultures, Autonomous Institutions," in *Democracy Upside Down: Public Opinion and Cultural Hegemony in the United States,* edi. Calvin F. Exoo (New York: Praeger Publishers, 1987), 189–225.

47. David Leonhardt, "Young vs. Old," *New York Times,* 22 June 2012.

48. Taylor Branch, *Parting the Waters: America in the King Years, 1953–63* (New York: Simon and Schuster, 1988), 105–206.

49. Sidney Tarrow, *Power in Movement: Social Movements, Collective Action and Politics* (New York: Cambridge University Press, 1994).

50. Ibid.

51. Lawrence Goodwyn, *The Populist Moment* (New York: Oxford University Press, 1978).

52. Branch, *Parting the Waters*, 139–141.

53. E. E. Schattschneider, *The Semi-Sovereign People: A Realist's View of Democracy in America* (New York: Holt, Rinehart and Winston, 1960).

54. Robert H. Zieger, *American Workers, American Unions*, 2nd ed. (Baltimore: Johns Hopkins University Press, 1994), 26–62.

55. J. David Greenstone, *Labor in American Politics* (New York: Knopf, 1969); Alan Draper, *A Rope of Sand: The AFL-CIO Committee on Political Education, 1955–68* (New York: Praeger, 1989).

56. Hardman is quoted in Nick Salvatore, "A Brief Ascendancy: American Labor after 1945," *The Forum* 10, no 1. (2012), 2.

57. Fraser is quoted in Taylor E. Dark, *The Unions and the Democratic Party: An Enduring Alliance* (Ithaca, NY: Cornell University Press, 1999), 113.

58. Chris Rohmberg, *The Broken Table: The Detroit Newspaper Strike and the State of American Labor* (New York: Russell Sage, 2012), 262.

59. Thomas A. Kochan, Harry C. Katz, and Robert C. McKersie, *The Transformation of American Industrial Relations* (New York: Basic Books, 1986).

60. Chris Rhomberg, "The Return of Judicial Repression: What Has Happened to the Strike?," *The Forum* 10, no. 1 (2012), 1.

61. Quoted in Steven Greenhouse, *The Big Squeeze* (New York: Knopf, 2008), 82.

62. See http://stats.oecd.org/Index.aspx?DataSetCode=UN_DEN for comparative figures on trade-union density (accessed September 3, 2012).

63. Steven Greenhouse, "More Lockouts as Companies Battle Unions," *New York Times*, 22 January 2012.

64. A statewide referendum restored public-sector collective-bargaining rights in Ohio after the governor and legislature removed them.

65. Salvatore, "A Brief Ascendancy," 2.

66. Timothy J. Minchin, *Forging a Common Bond: Labor and Environmental Activism during the BASF Lockout* (Gainesville: University Press of Florida, 2003).

67. Steven Greenhouse, "Occupy Wall Street Inspires Unions to Embrace Bold Tactics," *New York Times*, 8 November 2011.

68. Richard B. Freeman and Joel Rogers, *What Workers Want* (Ithaca, NY: Cornell University Press, 1999).

69. Peter L. Francia, "Do Unions Still Matter in U.S. Elections? Assessing Labor's Political Power and Significance," *The Forum* 10, no. 1 (2012), 13.

70. Catherine Harmois, "Re-presenting Feminisms: Past, Present, and Future," *National Women's Studies Association Journal* 20, 1 (Spring 2008), 120–54.

71. Steinem is quoted in Tauna S. Sisco and Jennifer C. Lucas, "I'm Your Girl: Gender and Feminism in the 2008 U.S. Election," paper presented at the New England Political Science Association convention, Portsmouth, N.H. (April 2012), 24–25.

72. Ibid, 24–25.

73. Michael Kazin, *Populist Persuasion: An American History* (New York: Basic Books, 1995).

74. Theda Skocpol and Vanessa Williams, *The Tea Party and the Remaking of Republican Conservatism* (New York: Oxford University Press, 2011), 204.

75. Ibid., 204.

76. Ibid., 150.

77. Adam Rome, "Give Peace a Chance: The Environmental Movement and the Sixties," *Journal of American History* 90, 2 (September 2003), 525–54.

78. Matt Grossman, "Environmental Advocacy in Washington: A Comparison with Other Interest Groups," *Environmental Politics* 15, 4 (August 2006), 626–38.

79. John S. Drysek, David Downes, Christian Hunold, and David Schlosberg, *Green States and Social Movements: Environmentalism in the United States, United Kingdom, Germany, and Norway* (New York: Oxford University Press, 2003), 96.

Part III

1. Morton Grodzins, *The American System: A New View of Government in the United States*, ed. Daniel J. Elazar (Chicago: Rand McNally, 1966).

2. Robert Dahl, *A Preface to Economic Democracy* (Berkeley: University of California Press, 1985), 2.

Chapter 6

1. Stephen Skowroneck, *The Politics Presidents Make: Leadership from John Adams to George Bush* (Cambridge, MA: Harvard University Press, 1993), 6.

2. Michael Schudson, *The Good Citizen: A History of Civic Life* (Cambridge, MA: Harvard University Press, 1998), 206.

3. Jeffrey K. Tulis, *The Rhetorical Presidency* (Princeton: Princeton University Press, 1987).

4. Joseph Cooper, "The Twentieth-Century Congress," in *Congress Reconsidered*, 7th ed., eds. Lawrence C. Dodd and Bruce I. Oppenheimer (Washington, DC: Congressional Quarterly Press, 2001), 335.

5. Sidney M. Milkis and Michael Nelson, *The American Presidency: Origins and Development, 1776–1990* (Washington, DC: Congressional Quarterly Press, 1990), 260.

6. Clinton Rossiter, *The American Presidency*, rev. ed. (New York: Harcourt, Brace, 1960), 15–44.

7. Thomas E. Cronin, "Presidents as Chief Executives," in *The Presidency Reappraised*, ed. Rexford G. Tugwell and Thomas E. Cronin (New York: Praeger, 1974), 235.

8. Aaron Wildavsky, "The Two Presidencies," *Trans-action* (December 1966), 7–14.

9. Quoted in Arthur Schlesinger, *The Imperial Presidency* (Boston: Houghton Mifflin, 1973), 42.

10. Cecil V. Crabb and Kevin H. Mulcahy, "George Bush's Management Style and Desert Storm," *Presidential Studies Quarterly*, 25 (Spring 1995), 262.

11. Louis Fischer, "Teaching the Presidency: Idealizing a Constitutional Office," *PS: Political Science and Politics* 45, 1 (January 2012), 29.

12. Gary Orfield, *The Reconstruction of Southern Education: The Schools and the 1964 Civil Rights Act* (New York: Wiley and Sons, 1969), 307.

13. The different agencies in the Executive Office are described by Bradley H. Patterson, Jr., in *The Ring of Power: The White House Staff and Its Expanding Role in Government* (New York: Basic Books, 1988).

14. John P. Burke, "The Bush Transition," in Gary L. Gregg and Mark J. Rozell, eds., *Considering the Bush Presidency* (New York: Oxford University Press, 2004), 29.

15. Robert Draper, "Obama's BFF," *The New York Times Magazine* (July 26, 2009), 34.

16. Helene Cooper, Marc Landler, and Jeff Zeleny, "In Shifting Staff Duties, Obama Seeks More Cohesive White House," *New York Times*, 8 November 2011.

17. Binyamin Appelbaum, "Nominees at Standstill as GOP Flexes Its Muscles," *New York Times*, 19 June 2011.

18. Hugh Heclo, *A Government of Strangers: Executive Politics in Washington* (Washington, DC: Brookings Institution, 1977).

19. Thomas E. Cronin, "'Everybody Believes in Democracy Until He Gets to the White House. . . .': An Examination of White House–Department Relations," *Law and Contemporary Problems* 35 (Summer 1970), 575.

20. James P. Pfiffner, "Organizing the Obama White House," *Obama in Office*, ed. James P. Thurber (Boulder, CO: Paradigm Publishers, 2011), 76.

21. Mackenzie is quoted in Michael A. Fletcher and Brady Dennis, "Obama's Many Policy 'Czars' Draw Ire from Conservatives," *Washington Post*, 16 September 2009.

22. Jacob S. Hacker and Paul Pierson, "Presidents and the Political Economy: The Coalitional Foundations of Presidential Power," *Presidential Studies Quarterly* 42, 1 (March 2012), 101–31.

23. Ibid.

24. Ibid.

25. Thomas E. Cronin, "'Everybody Believes in Democracy Until He Gets to the White House'" 575.

26. Martha Joynt Kumar, *Managing the President's Message: The White House Communications Operation* (Baltimore: Johns Hopkins University Press, 2007).

27. David Leonhardt, "Obamanomics: A Counterhistory," *New York Times*, 29 September 2012.

28. George C. Edwards, "Bill Clinton and His Crisis of Governance," *Presidential Studies Quarterly* 28 (Fall 1998), 755.

29. Thomas Friedman, "Dancing Alone," *New York Times*, 13 May 2004.

30. Quoted in James P. Pfiffner, "Introduction: Assessing the Bush Presidency," in *Considering the Bush Presidency*, eds. Gary L. Gregg II and Mark J. Rozell (New York: Oxford University Press, 2004), 13.

31. Derrick Bell, quoted in the *New York Times*, 14 June 1997.

32. Francis Fox Piven and Richard A. Cloward, *Regulating the Poor: The Functions of Public Welfare* (New York: Vintage, 1971), xiii.

33. Wilson is quoted in Louis Fischer, "Teaching the Presidency," 21.

34. E. S. Corwin, *The President: Office and Powers*, 3rd ed. (New York: New York University Press, 1957), 2.

35. Wilson is quoted in Thomas E. Cronin, *On the Presidency: Teacher, Soldier, Shaman, Pol* (Boulder, CO: Paradigm Publishers, 2008), 49.

36. Barber is quoted in Gary L. Gregg II, "Dignified Authenticity," in *Considering the Bush Presidency*, eds. Gary L. Gregg II and Marc J. Rozell (New York: Oxford University Press, 2004), 89.

37. Bruce Miroff, "Monopolizing the Public Space: The President as a Problem for Democratic Politics," in *Rethinking the Presidency*, ed. Thomas E. Cronin (Boston: Little, Brown, 1982), 220.

38. Richard E. Neustadt, *Presidential Power: The Politics of Leadership* (New York: Free Press, 1963), 5.

39. Richard S. Gilmour, "The Institutionalized Presidency: A Conceptual Clarification," in *The Presidency in Contemporary Context*, ed. Norman C. Thomas (New York: Dodd, Mead, 1975), 155.

40. Charlie Savage, "Obama's Embrace of Bush Tactics Criticized by Lawmakers from Both Parties," *New York Times*, 9 August 2009.

41. Ibid.

42. Richard Pious, "Obama's Use of Prerogative Powers in the War on Terrorism," in *Obama in Office*, ed. James Thurber (Boulder, CO: Paradigm Publishers, 2011), 255–69.

43. Truman is quoted in Neustadt, *Presidential Power*, 9.

44. Edwards is quoted in Ryan Lizza, "The Obama Memos," *New Yorker*, 30 January 2012, 49.

45. Skowronek, *Politics Presidents Make*, 55.

46. James P. Pfiffner, "Decision Making in the Obama White House," *Presidential Studies Quarterly* 41, no. 2 (June 2011).

47. Lloyd Grove, "Obama's Incredible Poker Face," *Daily Beast*, 2 May 2011.

48. O'Connor is quoted in David Stout, "Supreme Court Affirms Detainees' Right to Use Courts," *New York Times* 28 June 2004.

49. Skowroneck, *Politics Presidents Make*, 37.

50. Cronin, *On the Presidency*, 2.

Chapter 7

1. John Locke, *Two Treatises of Government*, ed. John Laslett (Cambridge: Cambridge University Press, 1960), 355–56.

2. Woodrow Wilson, *Congressional Government: A Study in American Politics* (New York: Meridian Books, 1958), 25.

3. Real Clear Politics average for the month of February: www.realclearpolitics.com/epolls/other/congressional_job_approval-903.html#polls; Rasmussen Reports, July 2011: www.rasmussenreports.com/public_content/politics/general_politics/july_2011/new_high_46_think_most_in_congress_are_corrupt; Rasmussen Reports, December 2011 poll: http://townhall.com/tipsheet/helenwhalencohen/2011/12/31/poll_congressional_performance_down_to_5.

4. Robert S. Erikson, Michael B. MacKuen, and James A. Stimson, *The Macro Polity* (New York: Cambridge University Press, 2002).

5. Elizabeth Sanders, *Roots of Reform: Farmers, Workers, and the Administrative State, 1877–1917* (Chicago: University of Chicago Press, 1984), 396.

6. Quoted in Jeffrey Tulis, "The Two Constitutional Presidencies," in *The Presidency and the Political System*, ed. Michael Nelson (Washington, DC: Congressional Quarterly Press, 1984), 68.

7. John R. Hibbing and Elizabeth Theiss-Morse, "What the Public Dislikes about Congress," in *Congress Reconsidered* (6th ed.), eds. Lawrence C. Dodd and Bruce I. Oppenheimer (Washington, DC: Congressional Quarterly Press, 1997), 77.

8. Quoted in Merrill Jensen, *The Making of the American Constitution* (Malibar, FL: Krieger, 1979), 47.

9. Robert Dahl, *Democracy in the United States: Promise and Performance*, 2nd ed. (Chicago: Rand McNally, 1973), 151.

10. Jensen, *The Making of the American Constitution*, 58.

11. Elaine K. Swift, *The Making of an American Senate: Reconstitutive Change in Congress, 1787–1841* (Ann Arbor: University of Michigan Press, 1996).

12. Quoted by Newt Gingrich in William F. Connelly, Jr., and John J. Pitney, Jr., "The House Republicans: Lessons for Political Science," in *New Majority or Old Minority: The Impact of Republicans on Congress*, eds. Nicol C. Rae and Colton C. Campbell (Lanham, MD: Rowman and Littlefield, 1999), 186.

13. Arend Lijphart, *Patterns of Democracy: Government Forms and Performance in Thirty-Six Countries* (New Haven, CT: Yale University Press, 1999), 208.

14. Malapportionment and its consequences are examined thoroughly in Frances E. Lee and Bruce I. Oppenheimer, *Sizing Up the Senate: The Unequal Consequences of Equal Representation* (Chicago: University of Chicago Press, 1999), 2.

15. Gary C. Jacobson, *The Politics of Congressional Elections*, 4th ed. (Washington, DC: Congressional Quarterly Press, 1997), 11.

16. On the advantages of small states in the Senate and the benefits whites derive from this at the expense of minorities, see Lee and Oppenheimer, *Sizing Up the Senate*, 21–23.

17. Samuel Huntington, "Congressional Responses to the Twentieth Century," in *The Congress and America's Future*, ed. David B. Truman (Englewood Cliffs, NJ: Prentice-Hall, 1965), 23.

18. David W. Rohde, *Parties and Leaders in the Postreform House* (Chicago: University of Chicago Press, 1991).

19. See David R. Mayhew, *America's Congress: Actions in the Public Sphere, James Madison through Newt Gingrich* (New Haven, CT: Yale University Press, 2000).

20. *New York Times*, 30 May 1978.

21. *New York Times*, 17 August 1998; www.Senate.gov (accessed March 8, 2013).

22. David R. Mayhew, *Congress: The Electoral Connection* (New Haven, CT: Yale University Press, 1974).

23. Julia Ritchey, "Senators Debate Merits of Earmarks in Spending Bill," *Voice of America*, 9 March 2009.

24. Morris Fiorina, *Congress: Keystone of the Washington Establishment* (New Haven, CT: Yale University Press, 1977), 36–37.

25. Richard F. Fenno, Jr., *Home Style: House Members in Their Districts* (Boston: Little, Brown, 1978).

26. Quoted in Sherrod Brown, *Congress from the Inside: Observations from the Majority and the Minority*, 3rd ed. (Kent, OH: Kent State University Press, 2004), 199.

27. Quoted in John G. Nicolay, *Abraham Lincoln: A History, Volume 1* (Teddington, England: Echo Library, 2007), 76.

28. Brown, *Congress from the Inside*, 199.

29. Jacobson, *The Politics of Congressional Elections*, 39–42.

30. Gary Jacobson, *Money in Congressional Elections* (New Haven, CT: Yale University Press, 1980).

31. Quoted in Robert B. Kuttner, *Everything for Sale* (New York: Knopf, 1996), 349.

32. www.census.gov/newsroom/releases/archives/voting/cb11-164.html (accessed March 8, 2013); www.census.gov/newsroom/releases/archives/voting/cb11-164.html (2010 election; accessed March 8, 2013); U.S. Census, 2010, Table 399. On the difference women make in Congress, see Michele L. Swers, *The Difference Women Make: The Policy Impact in Congress* (Chicago: University of Chicago Press, 2002).

33. Lester G. Seligman and Michael R. King, "Political Realignments and Recruitment to the U.S. Congress, 1870–1970," in *Realignment in American Politics: Toward a Theory*, eds. Bruce A. Campbell and Richard J. Trilling (Austin: University of Texas Press, 1980), 157–75.

34. Larry M. Bartels, "Economic Inequality and Political Representation," Princeton University, unpublished manuscript, August 2005.

35. For party unity scores of southern Democrats, see Rohde, *Parties and Leaders in the Postreform House*, 54–56. For the increasing liberalism of southern legislators, see Alan Draper, "Be Careful What You Wish For: American Liberals and the South," *Southern Studies* (Winter 1993): 309–25.

36. Charles S. Bullock III, "Congressional Roll Call Voting in the Two-Party South," *Social Science Quarterly* 66 (December 1995): 803.

37. Senator John Breaux is quoted in Sarah A. Binder, *Stalemate: Causes and Consequences of Legislative Gridlock* (Washington, DC: Brookings Institution, 2003), 69.

38. Bruce Oppenheimer, "Barack Obama, Bill Clinton, and the Democratic Congressional Majority," *Extensions* (Spring 2009), 1–6.

39. Rohde, *Parties and Leaders in the Postreform House.*

40. Ibid., 172.

41. www.opensecrets.org/industries/totals.php?cycle=2012&ind=q12 (accessed March 8, 2013); www.opensecrets.org/industries/totals.php?cycle=2012&ind=q15 (accessed March 8, 2013); www.opensecrets.org/industries/totals.php?cycle=2012&ind=q14 (accessed March 8, 2013).

42. Quoted in C. Lawrence Evans and Walter J. Oleszek, "Congressional Tsunami? The Politics of Congressional Reform," in *Congress Reconsidered* (6th ed.), eds. Lawrence C. Dodd and Bruce I. Oppenheimer (Washington, DC: Congressional Quarterly Press, 1997), 193.

43. Congressional Quarterly, *How Congress Works*, 1st ed. (Washington, DC: Congressional Quarterly Press, 1998), 61.

44. Christopher J. Deering and Steven S. Smith, *Committees in Congress*, 3rd ed. (Washington, DC: Congressional Quarterly Press, 1997), 11–20.

45. Quoted in Congressional Quarterly, *How Congress Works*, 51.

46. McCain is quoted in Steven Weiss, "Campaign Finance Reform's Rocky Road," *Capital Eye* 7 (Spring 2001), 1.

47. Thomas Mann, Norman Ornstein, and Molly Reynolds, "Truth and Reconciliation," *New Republic*, 20 April 2009.

48. Barbara Sinclair, *Unorthodox Lawmaking: New Legislative Processes in the U.S. Congress* (Washington, DC: Congressional Quarterly Press, 1997), 7.

49. Kay Lehman Schlozman and John T. Tierney, *Organized Interests and American Democracy* (New York: Harper and Row, 1986), 67.

50. Quoted in David Vogel, *Fluctuating Fortunes* (New York: Basic Books, 1989), 196–98.

51. The Center for Responsive Politics, OpenSecrets.org, has a remarkably complete database.

52. http://parkstrategies.com/ (accessed March 8, 2013).

53. At one time, lobbyists on Microsoft's payroll included Ralph Reed, who was a senior advisor to George W. Bush's presidential campaign; Haley Barbour, former chair of the Republican National Committee; C. Boyden Gray, White House counsel to former president George H. W. Bush; and Lloyd N. Cutler, counsel to former presidents Jimmy Carter and Bill Clinton.

54. In 2009, Daschle withdrew his nomination to be the Secretary of Health and Human Services in President Obama's Cabinet amid a controversy over his failure to fully report and pay income taxes.

55. John M. Broder, "With Something for Everyone, Climate Bill Passed," *New York Times*, 1 July 2009, 1.

Chapter 8

1. Quoted in Bernard Schwartz, *A Basic History of the U.S. Supreme Court* (Princeton, NJ: D. Van Nostrand Co., 1968), 9.

2. Jill Lepore, "Benched," *The New Yorker* (June 18, 2012), 82.

3. Quoted in ibid., 15.

4. Quoted in Kenneth Vogel, "Scalia on Obama: 'What Can He Do to Me?,'" *Politico* (July 30, 2012).

5. Quoted in Richard A. Brisbin, Jr., "The Judiciary and the Separation of Powers," in *The Judicial Branch*, eds. Kermit L. Hall and Kevin T. McGuire (New York: Oxford University Press, 2005), 269.

6. Quoted in Schwartz, *A Basic History of the U.S. Supreme Court*, 15.

7. Jeffrey Toobin, *The Oath: The Obama White House and the Supreme Court* (New York: Doubleday, 2012), 7.

8. Quoted in Richard Kluger, *Simple Justice: The History of Brown v. Board of Education and Black America's Struggle for Equality* (New York: Knopf, 1976), 706.

9. David Cole, "Are We Stuck with the Imperial Presidency?" *New York Review of Books* (June 7, 2012), 62.

10. Seth Stern and Stephen Wermeil, *Justice Brennan: Liberal Champion* (Boston: Houghton Mifflin Harcourt, 2010).

11. Jeffrey Toobin, *The Nine: Inside the Secret World of the Supreme Court* (New York: Doubleday, 2007), 327.

12. For a nuanced appreciation of the role the law plays, see E. P. Thompson, *Whigs and Hunters: The Origin of the Black Act* (New York: Pantheon Books, 1975).

13. John Schwartz, "Critics Say Budget Cuts for Courts Risks Rights," *New York Times*, 27 November 2011.

14. Gregory A. Caldiera and John R. Wright, "Lobbying for Justice: The Rise of Organized Conflict in the Politics of Federal Judgeships," in *Contemplating Courts*, ed. Lee Epstein (Washington, DC: Congressional Quarterly Press, 1995), 54.

15. G. A. Huber and S. C. Gordon, "Accountability and Coercion: Is Justice Blind When It Runs for Office?," *American Journal of Political Science* 48, no. 2 (2004), 27–63.

16. Brady Dennis, "Super PACs, Donors Turn Sights on Judicial Branch," *Washington Post*, 29 March 2012.

17. David Samuels, "Dr. Kush: How Medical Marijuana Is Transforming the Pot Industry," *The New Yorker* (July 28, 2008).

18. Quoted in David M. O'Brien, *Storm Center: The Supreme Court in American Politics* (New York: W. W. Norton, 1986), 290.

19. Caldiera and Wright, "Lobbying for Justice," 54.

20. David M. O'Brien, "Clinton's Legal Policy and the Courts: Rising from Disarray or Turning Around and Around?," in *The Clinton Presidency: First Appraisals*, eds. Colin A. Campbell and Bert A. Rothman (Chatham, NJ: Chatham House Publishers, 1996), 126–63. See also Robert A. Carp and Ronald Stidham, *Judicial Process in America* (Washington, DC: Congressional Quarterly Press, 2001), 243–45.

21. Kenneth L. Manning and Richard R. Carp, "The Decision Making Ideology of George W. Bush's Judicial Appointees: An Update," paper presented at the 2004 American Political Science Association Convention, Chicago, Illinois, September 2–5, 2004.

22. John Schwartz, "For Obama, a Record of Diversity but Delays on Judicial Confirmations," *New York Times*, 21 August 2011.

23. Ibid.

24. *Brown v. Allum* 344 U.S. 443, 550 (1953).

25. Lee Epstein and Jack Knight, *The Choices Justices Make* (Washington, DC: Congressional Quarterly Press, 1998), 26.

26. Quoted in Epstein and Knight, *The Choices Justices Make*, 46.

27. Fred Vinson, "Work of the Federal Courts," *Supreme Court Reporter* (1949), cited in Emmette S. Redford and Alan F. Westin, *Politics and Government of the United States* (New York: Harcourt, Brace and World, 1968), 474.

28. Quoted in Jeffrey Rosen, *The Supreme Court: The Personalities and Rivalries That Defined America* (New York: Times Books, 2007), 223.

29. Linda Greenhouse, *Becoming Justice Blackmun: Henry Blackmun's Supreme Court Journey* (New York: Times Books, 2005), 105.

30. Bernard Schwartz, *Decisions: How the Supreme Court Decides Cases* (New York: Oxford University Press, 1996), 43.

31. Quoted in Rosen, *The Supreme Court*, 227.

32. Quoted in Adam Liptak, "As Justices Get Back to Business, Old Pro Reveals Tricks of the Trade," *New York Times*, 3 October 2011.

33. Greenhouse, *Becoming Justice Blackmun*, 116.

34. Epstein and Knight, *The Choices Justices Make*, 9.

35. Jeffrey Toobin, "Diverse Opinions," *The New Yorker* (June 8, 2009).

36. Quoted in O'Brien, *Storm Center*, 81.

37. Quoted in Schwartz, *Decisions*, 184.

38. O'Brien, *Storm Center*, 84.

39. Lee Epstein and Jeffrey A. Segal, *Advice and Consent: The Politics of Judicial Appointment* (New York: Oxford University Press, 2005).

40. *Marbury v. Madison*, 5 U.S. 137 (1803).

41. Morton Horwitz, *The Warren Court and the Pursuit of Justice* (New York: Hill and Wang, 1998), 76–82.

42. Philip B. Kurland, *Politics, the Constitution and the Warren Court* (Chicago: University of Chicago Press, 1970), 17–18.

43. Doris D. Provine, "Judicial Activism and American Democracy," in *The Judicial Branch*, eds. Kermit Hall and Kevin T. McGuire (New York: Oxford University Press, 2005), 319.

44. James Q. Wilson and John J. Dilulio, Jr., *American Government*, 7th ed. (New York: Houghton Mifflin, 1998), 444.

45. Quoted in Redford and Westin, *Politics and Government*, 498–99.

46. Quoted in William E. Leuchtenburg, *The Supreme Court Reborn: The Constitutional Revolution in the Age of Roosevelt* (New York: Oxford University Press, 1995), 103.

47. Congressman Maury Maverick is quoted in Leuchtenburg, *Supreme Court Reborn*, 176.

48. This material on *Brown* is drawn from Richard Kluger, *Simple Justice: The History of Brown v. Board of Education and Black America's Struggle for Equality* (New York, Knopf, 1976); and from Raymond Wolters, *The Burden of Brown: Thirty Years of School Desegregation* (Knoxville: University of Tennessee Press, 1984).

49. Charles Epps, *The Rights Revolution: Lawyers, Activists, and Supreme Court Cases in Comparative Perspective* (Chicago: University of Chicago Press, 1998), 28.

50. This paragraph draws on the description of the "due process revolution" in Joan Biskopic and Elder Witt, *Guide to the U.S. Supreme Court*, 3rd ed. (Washington, DC: Congressional Quarterly Press, 1997), 52–53. See also Leuchtenburg, *Supreme Court Reborn,* 237–58.

51. Mark Silverstein and Benjamin Ginsberg, "The Supreme Court and the New Politics of Judicial Power," *Political Science Quarterly* 102 (Autumn 1987), 371–88.

52. Silverstein and Ginsberg, "The Supreme Court and the New Politics of Judicial Power," 372.

53. David J. Garrow, *Liberty and Sexuality: The Right to Privacy and the Making of Roe v. Wade* (New York: MacMillan, 1994).

54. For example, witnesses testified that Rehnquist had written a memorandum as a law clerk to Justice Robert H. Jackson in which he had defended the *Plessy v. Ferguson* doctrine of separate but equal, that he had tried to intimidate black and Hispanic voters by challenging their qualifications, and that he had engaged in ethically questionable behavior by not removing himself from judging a case in which he had prior connections.

55. See James F. Simon, *The Center Holds: The Power Struggle inside the Rehnquist Court* (New York: Simon and Schuster, 1995), 144–67, for the Rehnquist Court's process of decision making in *Casey.*

56. Burt Neuborne, "Free Expression and the Rehnquist Court," in *The Rehnquist Court: A Retrospective*, ed. Martin H. Belsky (New York: Oxford University Press, 2002), 15.

57. http://en.wikipedia.org/wiki/John_Paul_Stevens#Bush_v._Gore (Accessed July 13, 2012).

58. Quoted in William Crotty, "Elections by Judicial Fiat: The Courts Decide," in *America's Choice 2000*, ed. William Crotty (Boulder, CO: Westview Press, 2001), 75.

59. Toobin, *The Nine*, 299–300.

60. Cornell W. Clayton and Lucas W. McMillan, "The Roberts Court in an Era of Polarized Politics," *The Forum* 2012 10(4), 132–146.

61. Todd S. Purdun, "The Supreme Court," *New York Times*, 29 June 2004.

62. Lepore, "Benched," 78.

63. Robert Barnes, "How Is the Roberts Court Unusual? A Law Professor Counts the Ways," *Washington Post*, 5 March 2012.

64. Quoted in Thomas E. Mann and Norman J. Ornstein, *It's Worse Than You Think: How the American Constitutional System Collided with the Politics of Extremism* (New York: Basic Books, 2012), 73.

65. Timothy P. O'Neill, "The Stepford Justices: The Need for Experiential Diversity on the Roberts Court," *Oklahoma Law Review* 60, no. 4 (2007), 719.

66. Cass R. Sunstein, "The Myth of the Balanced Court," *The American Prospect* (September 2007), 28–29.

67. Peter Baker, "Kagan Nomination Leaves Longing on the Left," *New York Times*, 10 May 2010.

68. Cornell W. Clayton and Lucas W. McMillan, "The Roberts Court in an Era of Polarized Politics."

69. Linda Greenhouse, "2,691 Decisions," *New York Times*, 13 July 2008.

70. Douglas Jehl, "Fearing Bush Will Win, Groups Plan Suit," *New York Times*, 3 December 2000.

71. Alexis de Tocqueville, *Democracy in America* (New York: Knopf, 1946), 280.

72. Benjamin Ginsberg and Martin Shefter, *Politics by Other Means: The Declining Importance of Elections in America* (New York: Basic Books, 1990), 150.

73. Paul Frymer, *Black and Blue: African Americans, the Labor Movement and the Decline of the Democratic Party* (Princeton: Princeton University Press, 2008), 72.

74. Martin Shapiro, "The Juridicalization of Politics in the United States," *International Political Science Review* 15 (April 1994), 101–12.

75. Garrett Epps, "Beware Judges with Vision," *The American Prospect* (October 2011), 11.

76. Marie Gottschalk, *The Prison and the Gallows: The Politics of Mass Incarceration in America* (New York: Cambridge University Press, 2006).

77. Gottshalk, *The Prison and the Gallows*.

78. Gerald N. Rosenberg, *The Hollow Hope: Can Courts Bring About Social Change?* (Chicago: University of Chicago Press, 1991), 338.

Part IV

Chapter 9

1. *Historical Tables* (Washington, DC: Office of Management and Budget, 2012), Table 15.3, 341–43.

2. www.oecd-ilibrary.org/sites/gov_glance-2011-en/05/01/gv-21-02.html?contentType=&itemId=/content/chapter/gov_glance-2011-27-en&containerItemId=/content/serial/22214399&accessItemIds=/content/book/gov_glance-2011-en&mimeType=text/html (accessed June 2, 2012).

3. www.nationmaster.com/graph/gov_tim_req_to_sta_a_bus_day-time-required-start-business-days (accessed September 9, 2012).

4. William Greider, *Secrets of the Temple: How the Federal Reserve Runs the Country* (New York: Simon & Schuster, 1987), 351–405.

5. Elizabeth Drew, *Showdown* (New York: Simon & Schuster, 1996), 326.

6. Daniel J. Palazzolo, *Done Deal? The Politics of the 1997 Budget Agreement* (Chappaqua, NY: Seven Bridges Press, 1999), 90.

7. Steven Waldman, *The Bill* (New York: Penguin, 1996), 74.

8. Joel Slemrod and Jon Bakija, *Taxing Ourselves: A Citizen's Guide to the Great Debate over Tax Reform* (Cambridge, MA: MIT Press, 1996), 1–5.

9. Quoted in Slemrod and Bakija, *Taxing Ourselves*, 1.

10. *Historical Abstracts Fiscal Year* 2012, Table 15.1, 340–41.

11. Lori Montgomery, "In 2009, Americans Paid Lowest Tax Rates in 30 Years to Federal Government," *Washington Post*, 10 July 2012.

12. David Kocieniewski, "U.S. Business Has High Tax Rates But Pays Less," *New York Times*, 2 May 2011.

13. David Kocieniewski, "280 Firms Paid Little U.S. Tax, Study Says," *New York Times*, 3 November 2011.

14. *Historical Abstracts Fiscal Year 2012*, Table 2.2, 32–33.

15. David Leonhardt, "Why Taxes Aren't as High as They Seem," *New York Times*, 19 January 2012; Nicholas Confessore and David Kocieniewski, "For Romneys, Friendly Tax Code Reduces Taxes," *New York Times*, 24 January 2012.

16. Jacob S. Hacker, *The Divided Welfare State: The Battle over Public and Private Social Benefits in the United States* (New York: Cambridge University Press, 2002).

17. Suzanne Mettler, *The Submerged State: How Invisible Government Policies Undermine American Democracy* (Chicago: University of Chicago Press, 2011), 123.

18. Palazzolo, *Done Deal?*, 230.

19. Ibid., 229.

20. Quoted in Greider, *Secrets of the Temple*, 55.

21. Ibid., 12.

22. Henry B. Gonzalez, "An Open Letter to the President," *Challenge* (September–October 1993): 30–31.

23. Willem H. Buiter, "Lessons from the North Atlantic Financial Crisis," at www.nbr.org/~buiter/NAcrisis.pdf (accessed March 17, 2010), 36–40.

24. Quoted in Binyamin Applebaum, "Inside the Fed in 2006: A Coming Crisis, and Banter," *New York Times*, 12 January 2012.

25. Quoted in John Lancaster, "Heroes and Zeroes," *The New Yorker* (February 2, 2009), 73.

26. Edmund L. Andrews, "A New Role for the Fed: Investor of Last Resort," *New York Times*, 18 September 2008.

27. John Cassidy, "The Anatomy of a Meltdown," *The New Yorker* (December 1, 2008), 49.

28. Quoted in Cassidy, "Anatomy of a Meltdown," 61.

29. James Gwartney, Robert Lawson, and Joshua Hall, *Economic Freedom of the World Annual Report, 2011* (Fraser Institute, 2011), 161.

30. Marver H. Bernstein, *Regulating Business by Independent Regulatory Commission* (Westport, CT: Greenwood Press, 1955).

31. Quoted in Gretchen Morgensen, "Into the Bailout Buzz Saw," *New York Times*, 21 July 2012. Barofsky oversaw the $700 billion bank bailout, the Troubled Asset Relief Program (TARP).

32. Juliet Eilperin and Scott Higham, "How the Minerals Management Service's Partnership with Industry Led to Failure," *Washington Post*, 25 August 2010.

33. David Vogel, *Fluctuating Fortunes: The Political Power of Business in America* (New York: Basic Books, 1989), 59.

34. "Investigation of Failure of the SEC to Uncover Bernard Madoff's Ponzi Scheme," United States Securities and Exchange Commission Office of Inspector General Report of Investigation, p. 21, www.scribd.com/doc/19362301/Executive-Summary-of-SEC-Madoff-Report.

35. John C. Coffee, Jr., as quoted in James B. Stewart, "Another Fumble by the SEC on Fraud," *New York Times*, 16 November 2012.

36. Project on Government Oversight, "Dangerous Liaisons: Revolving Door on SEC Creates Risk of Regulatory Capture," February 11, 2013, p. 2.

37. Andrew Ross Sorkin, "Revolving Door at SEC Is Hurdle to Crisis Cleanup," *New York Times*, 4 August 2011.

38. Quoted in John McMillan, *Reinventing the Bazaar: A Natural History of Markets* (New York: W. W. Norton, 2002),174.

Chapter 10

1. Benefits, TANF. U.S. Department of Health and Human Services, Office of Family Assistance, "TANF Eighth Annual Report to Congress," at www.acf.hhs.gov/programs/ofa/data-reports/annualreport8/ar8index.htm (accessed March 19, 2010).

2. Jacob S. Hacker, *The Divided Welfare State: The Battle over Public and Private Social Benefits in the United States* (New York: Cambridge University Press, 2002), 6.

3. www.census.gov/prod/2011pubs/p60-239.pdf (accessed March 7, 2012); Gosta Esping-Andersen, *The Three Worlds of Welfare Capitalism* (Princeton, NJ: Princeton University Press, 1990).

4. Theda Skocpol, *Protecting Soldiers and Mothers: The Political Origins of Social Policy in the United States* (Cambridge, MA: Harvard University Press, 1992), 65.

5. Gwendolyn Mink, *The Wages of Motherhood: Inequality in the Welfare State, 1917–1942* (Ithaca, NY: Cornell University Press, 1995), 33.

6. Deborah Ward, *The White Welfare State: The Racialization of U.S. Welfare Policy* (Ann Arbor: University of Michigan Press, 2005).

7. James T. Patterson, *America's Struggle against Poverty, 1900–1994* (Cambridge, MA: Harvard University Press, 1994), 42.

8. Quoted in ibid., 52.

9. "The Case against Roosevelt," *Fortune*, December 1935; quoted in Arthur Schlesinger, Jr., *The Coming of the New Deal* (Boston: Houghton Mifflin, 2003), 494.

10. Francis Fox Piven and Richard Cloward, *Regulating the Poor: The Functions of Public Welfare* (New York: Pantheon, 1971).

11. An example of the least eligibility principle can be found in the British *Poor Law Report of 1834.* For "able-bodied labourers who apply for relief," the *Poor Law Report* recommended "hard work at low wages by the piece, and extracting more work at a lower price than is paid for any other labour in the parish. . . . In short, . . . let the labourer find that the parish is the hardest taskmaster and the worst paymaster he can find, and thus induce him to make his application to the parish his last and not his first resort." Quoted in David Schmidtz and Robert E. Goodin, *Social Welfare and Individual Responsibility* (New York: Cambridge University Press, 1998), 173.

12. For an overview, see Ira Katznelson, *When Affirmative Action Was White: An Untold History of Racial Inequality in Twentieth-Century America* (New York: W. W. Norton, 2005).

13. Paul Starr, *The Social Transformation of American Medicine* (New York: Basic Books, 1983).

14. In fact, Social Security coverage expanded in the 1950s under President Eisenhower to include farmworkers and maids, who initially had been left out of Social Security at the insistence of the segregated South.

15. Quoted in Sanford M. Jacoby, "Employers and the Welfare State: The Role of Marion B. Folsom," *Journal of American History* 80, no. 2 (1993): 526.

16. *Wall Street Journal,* 24 April 1969.

17. Stanley Lieberson, *A Piece of the Pie* (Berkeley: University of California Press, 1980).

18. William Julius Wilson, *The Declining Significance of Race: Blacks and Changing American Institutions* (Chicago: University of Chicago Press, 1978).

19. Laurence E. Lynn Jr., "Ending Welfare Reform as We Know It," *American Prospect* (Fall 1993): 83–90.

20. U.S. Bureau of the Census, *Measuring Fifty Years of Economic Change Using the March Current Population Survey,* table C23, C-40 to C-41; www.census.gov/prod/2011pubs/p60-239.pdf (accessed March 7, 2012).

21. September 2011 U.S. Census report, Income, Poverty and Health Insurance in the United States, 2010, issued September 2011, 15; data from 2010 Current Population Survey and 2011 Annual Social and Economic Supplements; www.census.gov/prod/2011pubs/p60-239.pdf (accessed March 7, 2012).

22. Ibid.

23. Barbara R. Bergmann, *Saving Our Children from Poverty: What the United States Can Learn from France* (New York: Russell Sage Foundation, 1996).

24. James C. Sundquist, *Politics and Policy: The Eisenhower, Kennedy, and Johnson Years* (Washington, D.C.: Brookings Institute, 1968).

25. AFL-CIO Convention *Proceedings* (1965), 2: 1–6.

26. Patterson, *America's Struggle against Poverty,* 136.

27. Sar A. Levitan and Robert Taggert, *The Promise of Greatness* (Cambridge, MA: Harvard University Press, 1976), 20.

28. For the consequences of the 1966 election for the welfare state, see Alan Draper, "Labor and the 1966 Elections," *Labor History* (Winter 1989): 76–93.

29. Quoted in Levitan and Taggert, *The Promise of Greatness*, 3–4.

30. Michael K. Brown, *Race, Money, and the American Welfare State* (Ithaca, NY: Cornell University Press, 1999), 325.

31. Thomas Byrne Edsall and Mary D. Edsall, *Chain Reaction: The Impact of Race, Rights, and Taxes on American Politics* (New York: W. W. Norton, 1991).

32. James Midgeley, "Society, Social Policy and the Ideology of Reaganism," *Journal of Sociology and Social Welfare* (March 1992): 24–25.

33. David Stockman, *The Triumph of Politics* (New York: Harper and Row, 1986), 394.

34. Levitan and Taggert, *The Promise of Greatness*, 200–01.

35. John E. Schwarz, *America's Hidden Success: A Reassessment of Twenty Years of Public Policy* (New York: W. W. Norton, 1984).

36. *New York Times*, 3 September 1995.

37. Mark Rank, *Living on the Edge: The Realities of Welfare in America* (New York: Columbia University Press, 1994), 5.

38. Randy Albelda, Nancy Folbre, and the Center for Public Economics, *The War on the Poor: A Defense Manual* (New York: New Press, 1996), 82.

39. Eliot Liebow, *Tally's Corner: A Study of Streetcorner Men* (New York: Little, Brown, 1967), 223.

40. See Lee Bawden and Frank Levy, "Economic Well-Being of Families and Individuals," in John L. Palmer and Isabel V. Sawhill, eds., *The Reagan Experiment* (Washington, D.C.: The Urban Institute, 1982) table 16–5, 460.

41. Howard Jacob Karger, "Responding to the Crisis: Liberal Prescriptions," in *Reconstructing the American Welfare State*, eds. David Stoesz and Howard Jacob Karger (Lanham, MD: Rowman and Littlefield, 1992), 92–93.

42. Quoted in "Moynihan Turns Up the Heat," *The Economist*, 11 November 1995, 32.

43. In *Goldberg v. Kelly* (1970), the Supreme Court ruled that beneficiaries, once eligible, could not lose their grants without a due-process hearing.

44. *New York Times*, 11 April 1999; U.S. Department of Health and Human Services, "Welfare Rolls Drop Again," at www.hhs.gov/news/press/2004pres/20040330.html (accessed March 19, 2010).

45. "Welfare Rolls Up after Years of Decline," *United Press International*, 22 June 2009.

46. U.S. Department of Education, "Overview: 10 Facts about K-12 Education Funding," www.ed.gov/about/overview/fed/10facts/index.html (accessed March 19, 2010); GPO Access, "Budget of the United States Government: Historical Tables Fiscal Year 2010," at gpoaccess.gov/usbudget/fy10/hist.html (accessed March 19, 2010).

47. CNN, "Kennedy: 'Iraq Is George Bush's Vietnam" at www.cnn.com/2004/ALLPOLITICS/04/05/kennedy.speech/ (accessed March 19, 2010).

48. "Remarks of Senator Barack Obama: National Education Association Annual Meeting," Philadelphia, Pennsylvania, July 5, 2007.

49. Helen Levy and David Weir, "Take-Up of Medicare Part D: Results from the Health and Retirement Study," NBER Working Paper No. 14692 (Washington, DC: National Bureau of Economic Research, January 2009).

50. www.ahrq.gov/research/oct11/1011RA18.htm (accessed March 7, 2012); cited in Jonathan Oberlander, "Through the Looking Glass: The Politics of the Medicare Prescription Drug, Improvement, and Modernization Act," *Journal of Health Politics, Policy, and Law* 32, no. 2 (2007): 187–219.

51. George W. Bush, "Excerpt of President's Radio Address on SCHIP Legislation," White House, Office of the Press Secretary, 28 September 2007, at http://georgewbush-whitehouse. archives.gov/news/releases/2007/09/20070928-9.html (accessed March 19, 2010).

52. Michael Tomasky, "The Money Fighting Health Care Reform," *New York Review of Books,* 8 April 2010.

53. David Leonhardt, "In the Process, Pushing Back at Inequality," *New York Times,* 24 March 2010, 1.

54. Richard Scase, *Social Democracy in Capitalist Society* (Totowa, NJ: Rowman and Little-field, 1977).

55. John D. Stephens, *The Transition from Capitalism to Socialism* (Urbana: University of Illinois Press, 1986).

56. Jacob S. Hacker, *The Great Risk Shift: The New Insecurity and the Decline of the American Dream,* rev. ed. (New York: Oxford University Press, 2007).

Chapter 11

1. Department of Defense, Base Structure Report, 2010 Fiscal Year Baseline.

2. Stockholm International Peace Research Institute (SIPRI) Yearbook 2012.

3. This figure is an estimate that includes the past and future costs of conducting these wars, including finance costs and payment for veterans' disability and medical care. The report documenting these costs was prepared by Brown University's Watson Institute for International Studies and is available at www.costsofwar.org.

4. This statistic is contained in a press release dated December 5, 2006, of the World Institute for Development Economics Research of the United Nations University.

5. OECD, Statistics on Resource Flows to Developing Countries; Table 1. DAC Members' Official Development Assistance in 2010.

6. For a discussion of the diverse strands of U.S. foreign policy, see Walter Russell Mead, *God and Gold: Britain, America, and the Making of the Modern World* (New York: Vintage, 2008).

7. The term *soft power* was coined by Harvard University's Joseph Nye, Jr., in the late 1980s. For an extended discussion, see Joseph S. Nye, Jr., *Soft Power: The Means to Success in World Politics* (Cambridge, MA: Perseus, 2004).

8. Fareed Zakaria, *The Post-American World* (New York: W. W. Norton, 2008).

9. Andrew J. Bacevich, *The Limits of Power: The End of American Exceptionalism* (New York: Metropolitan Books; Henry Holt, 2008), 20.

10. Richard W. Van Alstyne, *The Rising American Empire* (Chicago: Quadrangle, 1965), 99.

11. Bacevich, *The Limits of Power*, 20.

12. Dahr Jamail and Jason Coppola, "The Myth of 'America,'" October 12, 2009, at www. truthout.org/1012091 (accessed March 19, 2010).

13. Michael H. Hunt, *The American Ascendancy: How the United States Gained and Wielded Global Dominance* (Chapel Hill, NC: University of North Carolina Press, 2007), 56.

14. Stephen Kinzer, *Overthrow: America's Century of Regime Change from Hawaii to Iraq* (New York: Times Books; Henry Holt, 2006), 2.

15. Seymour Melman, *The Permanent War Economy: American Capitalism in Decline* (New York: Simon and Schuster, 1974); also see Melman, *Pentagon Capitalism: The Political Economy of War* (New York: McGraw-Hill, 1970).

16. Aaron B. O'Connell, "The Permanent Militarization of America," *New York Times*, 5 November 2012. O'Connell, a professor at the United States Naval Academy and a Marine reserve officer, points out that although military spending has increased in absolute terms since the height of the Cold War, it has substantially declined as a proportion of GDP. However, he writes, "Our culture has militarized considerably since Eisenhower's era. . . ."

17. Michael Parenti, "The Logic of U.S. Intervention," in *Masters of War: Militarism and Blowback in the Era of American Empire*, ed. Carl Boggs (New York: Routledge, 2002), ch. 1.

18. David Callahan, *Between Two Worlds: Realism, Idealism, and American Foreign Policy after the Cold War* (New York: HarperCollins, 1994), 30.

19. Graham Allison, "Cool It: The Foreign Policy of Young America," *Foreign Policy* 1, no. 1 (Winter 1970–71): 144–45.

20. Richard K. Betts, "The Soft Underbelly of Primacy: Tactical Advantages of Terror," *Political Science Quarterly* 117, no. 1 (Spring 2002), reprinted in *Conflict after the Cold War: Arguments on Causes of War and Peace* (2nd ed.), ed. Richard K. Betts (New York: Pearson, 2005), 522.

21. Robert Gilpin, *U.S. Power and the Multinational Corporation: The Political Economy of Direct Foreign Investment* (New York: Basic Books, 1975), 161.

22. Carl Boggs, ed., *Masters of War*.

23. Harry Magdoff, *The Age of Imperialism: The Economics of U.S. Foreign Policy* (New York: Monthly Review Press, 1969), 43.

24. For a sobering account of the role petroleum has played in U.S. foreign policy, and the extensive damage that results from this situation, see Michael T. Klare, *Blood and Oil: The Dangers and Consequences of America's Growing Dependency on Imported Petroleum* (New York; Owl Books; Henry Holt, 2005).

25. Ibid., 11.

26. James R. Alm and Jay A. Soled, "Filling Up on Your Dime," *New York Times*, 15 November 2012.

27. William Greider, *One World, Ready or Not: The Manic Logic of Global Capitalism* (New York: Simon and Schuster, 1997). For other influential analyses and defenses of globalization, see

Thomas L. Friedman, *The World Is Flat* (New York: Farrar, Straus and Giroux, 2005); and Jagdish Bhagwati, *In Defense of Globalization* (New York: Oxford University Press, 2004).

28. Organisation for Economic Co-operation and Development, "OECD Factbook 2009: Economic, Environmental and Social Statistics," at http://lysander.sourceoecd.org/vl=3489091/cl=21/nw=1/rpsv/factbook2009/03/01/01/index.htm (accessed March 19, 2010).

29. See, e.g., Geoffrey Garrett, *Partisan Politics in the Global Economy* (Cambridge: Cambridge University Press, 1998); David Held, Anthony McGrew, David Goldblatt, and Jonathan Perraton, *Global Transformations: Politics, Economics and Culture* (Stanford, CA: Stanford University Press, 1999); and Dean Baker, Gerald Epstein, and Robert Pollin, eds., *Globalization and Progressive Economic Policy* (Cambridge: Cambridge University Press, 1998).

30. Leo Panitch and Sam Gindin, *The Making of Global Capitalism: The Political Economy of American Empire* (London: Verso, 2012), 1.

31. Michael V. Gestrin, Rory F. Knight, and Alan M. Rugman, "Oxford Executive Briefing: Templeton Global Performance Index 2001," Templeton College, Oxford, 2001.

32. Organization for International Investment, "Insourcing Statistics," at www.ofii.org/insourcing-stats.htm (accessed March 19, 2010).

33. Huntington first put forward the claim in Samuel Huntington, "The Clash of Civilizations?" *Foreign Affairs* 72, no. 3 (1993). He developed the argument more fully in *The Clash of Civilizations and the Remaking of World Order* (New York: Free Press, 1996). Peter J. Katzenstein described the impact of Huntington's book in his presidential address to the American Political Science Association, "'Walls' between 'Those People'? Contrasting Perspectives on World Politics," Annual Meeting of the American Political Science Association, Toronto, Canada, August 28, 2009.

34. Both quotes are from Amartya Sen, "Democracy as a Universal Value," *Journal of Democracy* 10, no. 3 (July 1999), reprinted in *Readings in Comparative Politics: Political Challenges and Changing Agendas* (2nd ed.), ed. Mark Kesselman (Boston: Wadsworth Cengage Learning, 2010), 192.

35. Paul Rogers, "The U.S. Military Posture: 'A Uniquely Benign Imperialism'?" in *The New Imperial Challenge: Socialist Register 2004*, eds. Leo Panitch and Colin Leys (New York: Monthly Review Press, 2003), 149.

36. George Easterbrook, "Apocryphal Now," *New Republic*, 24 September 2000, 24.

37. Mary Kaldor, "Beyond Militarism, Arms Races, and Arms Control," in *Understanding September 11*, eds. Craig Calhoun, Paul Price, and Ashley Timmer (New York: New Press, 2002), 165–66.

38. Ibid., 167.

39. Greg Miller, "Plan for Hunting Terrorists Signals U.S. Intends to Keep Adding Names to Kill Lists," *Washington Post*, 23 October 2012.

40. Editorial, *New York Times*, 30 November 2012.

41. Stephen Glain, "The American Leviathan: The Pentagon Has All But Eclipsed the State Department in Setting U.S. Foreign Policy," *The Nation*, 28 September 2009, 18–23.

42. See Lester R. Brown, *World on the Edge: How to Prevent Environmental and Economic Collapse* (New York: W. W. Norton, 2011) for a fine description of the inter-relationship between environmental, economic, and security issues. Our analysis draws heavily on Brown's account.

43. Ibid., 15.

44. Interview with Zbigniew Brzezinski, *The Charlie Rose Show*, PBS, September 14, 2004; also see Brzezinski, *The Choice: Global Domination or Global Leadership* (New York: Basic Books, 2004).

45. The White House, "National Security Strategy of the United States," at www.whitehouse.gov/nsc/nss.html (accessed March 19, 2010).

46. Richard A. Clarke, *Against All Enemies: Inside America's War on Terror* (New York: Free Press, 2004), 30–32. Ron Suskind writes that former treasury secretary Paul O'Neill reported that planning to remove Saddam Hussein began immediately after President Bush's inauguration; several high-level meetings were devoted to the project well before September 11, 2001. Ron Suskind, *The Price of Loyalty: George W. Bush, the White House and the Education of Paul O'Neill* (New York: Simon and Schuster, 2004), 72–75, 82–86, 129; also see Suskind, *The Way of the World: A Story of Truth and Hope in an Age of Extremism* (New York: Harper Perennial, 2009).

47. Clarke, *Against All Enemies*, 246.

48. David Cole, "Bush Law Continued," *The Nation*, 6 April 2009, 8.

49. Ronald Dworkin, "The Threat to Patriotism," in *Understanding September 11*, eds. Calhoun, Price, and Timmer, 273.

50. Ibid.

51. Dahlia Lithwick, "Tyranny in the Name of Freedom," *New York Times*, 12 August 2004.

52. *New York Times*, 21 December 2004; also see the results of an army investigation reported in the *New York Times*, 10 September 2004; Seymour Hersh, *Chain of Command: The Road from 9/11 to Abu Ghraib* (New York: HarperCollins, 2004); Mark Danner, *Torture and Truth: America, Abu Ghraib, and the War on Terror* (New York: The New York Review of Books, 2004); and Danner, *Stripping Bare the Body*.

53. Michael Isikoff, "2002 Memo Reveals Push for Broader Presidential Powers," *Newsweek*, 18 December 2004.

54. Anthony Lewis, "A President beyond the Law," *New York Times*, 7 May 2004.

55. Editorial, *New York Times*, 26 October 2009, A20.

56. Lawrence C. Reardon, "Shifting Global Paradigms and Obama's Adaptive Foreign Policy," in William Crotty, ed., *The Obama Presidency: Promise and Performance* (Lanham, MD: Lexington Books, 2012), ch. 5.

57. David E. Sanger, *Confront and Conceal: Obama's Secret Wars and Surprising Use of American Power* (New York: Crown Publishers, 2012), xiv.

58. Ibid., 421.

59. Ibid., xiv.

60. Ibid., xv.

61. Ibid., xvii.

62. Martin S. Indyk, Kenneth G. Lieberthal, and Michael E. O'Hanlon, *Bending History: Barack Obama's Foreign Policy* (Washington, DC: Brookings Institution Press, 2012), 139.

63. Thomas J. Sugrue, "Empire and Revolution," *The Nation*, 15 October 2012, 35.

64. For an argument that the U.S. can be considered an empire, see Andrew Bacevich, *American Empire: The Realities and the Consequences of U.S. Diplomacy* (Cambridge, MA: Harvard University Press, 2002). For a strong defense of American empire, see Niall Ferguson, *Colossus: The Price of America's Empire* (New York: Penguin Press, 2004); also see Ferguson's *Empire: The Rise and Demise of the British World Order and the Lessons for Global Power* (New York: Basic Books, 2003); and "The Empire Slinks Back," *New York Times Magazine*, 27 April 2003. For critiques of American imperialism in the recent period, see David Harvey, *The New Imperialism* (New York: Oxford University Press, 2003); and Panitch and Leys, eds., *The New Imperial Challenge*.

65. Bacevich, *The Limits of Power*; Parag Khanna, "Waving Goodbye to Hegemony," *New York Times*, 27 January 2008; and Zakaria, *The Post-American World*.

66. National Intelligence Council, *Global Trends 2025: A Transformed World* (Washington, D.C.: U.S. Government Printing Office, 2008), at www.dni.gov/nic/PDF_2025/2025_Global_Trends_Final_Report.pdf (accessed March 19, 2010).

67. John M. Broder, "Climate Change Seen as Threat to U.S. Security," *New York Times*, 9 August 2009, A1.

68. Khanna, "Waving Goodbye to Hegemony."

69. Joseph S. Nye, Jr., "Soft Power and American Foreign Policy," *Political Science Quarterly* 119, no. 2 (Summer 2002): 263.

70. Quoted in Gideon Rachman, "Think Again: American Decline: This Time It's for Real." *Foreign Policy*, January–February 2011, 5.

71. Francis Fukuyama, "The End of History?" *The National Interest* 16 (Summer 1989). Reprinted in Kesselman, ed., *Readings in Comparative Politics*. Fukuyama's book was entitled *The End of History and the Last Man* (New York: Free Press, 1992).

Chapter 12

1. Richard C. Levin, George J. Mitchell, Paul A. Volcker, and George F. Will, "The Report of the Independent Members of the Commissioner's Blue Ribbon Panel on Baseball Economics" (July 2000), at www.bizofbaseball.com/docs/2000blueribbonreport.pdf (accessed March 19, 2010).

2. An important confirmation of the growing tolerance among Americans is the study by Alan Wolfe, *Moral Freedom* (New York: W. W. Norton, 2001).

3. Herbert McClosky and John Zaller, *The American Ethos: Public Attitudes toward Capitalism and Democracy* (Cambridge, MA: Harvard University Press, 1984), 18–61.

4. Ibid., 74.

5. Ibid., 120, 123.

6. Ibid., 7.

7. For a particularly thoughtful discussion, see Jennifer L. Hochschild, *Facing Up to the American Dream: Race, Class, and the Soul of the Nation* (Princeton, NJ: Princeton University Press, 1995), esp. chs. 1–4.

8. Martin Gilens, *Why Americans Hate Welfare: Race, Media, and the Politics of Antipoverty Policy* (Chicago: University of Chicago Press, 1999), 28.

9. Robert A. Dahl, *Dilemmas of Pluralist Democracy* (New Haven, CT: Yale University Press, 1982), 184.

10. McClosky and Zaller, *American Ethos*, 176, 177, 179.

11. Christopher A. Preble, *John F. Kennedy and the Missile Gap* (De Kalb, IL: Northern Illinois University Press, 2004); Edwin E. Moise, *Tonkin Gulf and the Escalation of the Vietnam War* (Chapel Hill, NC: University of North Carolina Press, 1996); Report of the Congressional Committees Investigating the Iran-Contra Affair, S. Report No. 216; H.R. Report No. 433 (Washington, D.C.: United States Government Printing Office, November 11, 1987); Seymour M. Hersh, "Who Lied to Whom?" *The New Yorker*, 31 March 2003.

12. V. O. Key, Jr., *Public Opinion and American Democracy* (New York: Knopf, 1963), 557, 555.

501(c)4 Organizations known by the provision of the federal tax code creating them. These organizations are intended to promote public discussion of issues involving social welfare. In reality, since these organizations are authorized to make unlimited contributions to PACs and super PACs, their funds are used to finance political candidates and campaigns. Citizens and corporations can provide anonymous tax-deductible contributions of any amount to 501(c)4 organizations. The bulk of 501(c)4 organizations support Republican candidates and conservative causes.

Aid to Families with Dependent Children (AFDC) In effect from 1935 to 1997. A program of financial transfers, funded by the states and the federal government, to support children in poor families. Commonly known as welfare.

all-directional lobbying Efforts by interest groups to influence not only policy makers, but also the wider public.

Anti-Federalists Those Founders who opposed the adoption of the 1787 Constitution for the United States, preferring a weaker federal government and stronger state governments. They also objected to the absence of a Bill of Rights in the Constitution before it was amended. Later, the anti-Federalists became an important part of the political faction led by Thomas Jefferson during the administration of President George Washington.

Articles of Confederation America's first written constitution, established by the original thirteen states as "a plan of confederacy for securing the freedom, sovereignty, and independence of the United States." Drafted by the Continental Congress in 1776–1777 and ratified by each state by 1781, it offered limited power to the central government, leaving most responsibilities to each sovereign state, but it did create a government that could wage the Revolutionary War.

Bill of Rights The first ten amendments to the Constitution of the United States, which guarantee American's freedom of religion, the right to bear arms, *habeas corpus,* a speedy trial by a jury, and other aspects of due process of law, as well as protection from unreasonable search and seizure by public authorities.

budget deficit The product of the government spending more than it collects in taxes.

budget surplus The product of the government collecting more money in revenues than it spends in outlays.

Bush Doctrine The informal foreign-policy approach sponsored by George W. Bush when he was president. It asserted the right of the United States to launch a preemptive military attack if the president decided that an opponent was planning an attack.

cabinet The group of key administrative officials appointed by the president to direct the major departments of government. The president may convene the cabinet to discuss and provide advice on major policy issues, but rarely asks the cabinet to make major policy decisions.

capitalism An economic system based on the private ownership of property in which profit is pursued through the investment of capital and the employment of labor.

capitalist class The group that owns and controls business firms.

checks and balances The system by which, in order to prevent undue concentrations of power, each branch of the federal government has independent standing. This institutional design enables the president, Congress, and the judiciary to check and balance possible abuses by the other two. A possible disadvantage of this situation is institutional gridlock or stalemate, since any one branch can hinder action by the others.

civil liberties Fundamental freedoms guaranteed by the Constitution or law with which governments are constrained from interfering, including the freedom of speech, the press, religion, and assembly.

civil rights Rights against discrimination based on characteristics such as a person's race, religion, gender, or national origin.

coalitions Different groups that ally to pursue a shared interest. A coalition may be a political party or government, or may come together on an ad hoc basis to achieve a particular ideological or policy goal.

Cold War The period of hostile relations just short of open war that prevailed between the United States and Soviet Union from 1947 to the late 1980s.

collective bargaining Type of bargaining that occurs when unions negotiate on behalf of workers with employers over wages, hours, fringe benefits such as health insurance, and working conditions.

competitive capitalism An economy dominated by many small firms that produce for local markets.

competitive sector Portion of the economy that includes small businesses that serve local markets.

conference committee A committee composed of members of both the House of Representatives and Senate to reconcile any differences between versions of a bill passed by each chamber.

constitution The fundamental principles, establishing rules and institutions, that shape how a country is governed and by whom, for what ends, and with which limitations. A constitution may be set down in a written document, as in the United States, or it can be unwritten, the result of long-accepted laws and the development of precedent, as in Great Britain.

containment A term that designates a multidimensional American strategy—using diplomacy, economic power, and military means—to limit the influence and potential for expansion of the Soviet Union during the Cold War.

corporate campaign A tactic unions use to pressure recalcitrant employers through third parties, such as members of the firm's board of directors or its creditors, suppliers, or customers.

corporate capitalism An economy dominated by large firms that produce for national and international markets and are able to dictate prices to suppliers and retailers as well as wages to their workers.

corporate complex The close relationship between corporations and the federal government. Together, they shape key features of public policy that organize and regulate how economic affairs are conducted.

critical or realigning election An election in which a long-dominant party is defeated by a party with a different social base and ideological outlook. For an election to be considered critical or realigning, the new party must succeed in governing for a significant period and in sponsoring a distinctive new policy orientation.

democracy A form of government in which sovereign authority ultimately rests with the people, who choose their leaders in competitive elections.

deregulation The removal of rules that constrain economic actors.

divided government A circumstance in which one or both houses of Congress is controlled by a majority party that differs from the party of the president.

dual court system The system in which state and federal court systems exist alongside one another.

earmarks Legislative designations that appropriate funds or provide tax relief for specific projects and programs in particular states or districts, thus circumventing any competitive process based on criteria of merit. Earmarks are sponsored by individual members of the House and Senate, but they are not publicly identified.

ecology The study of how people and other life-forms relate to their environment.

economic regulations Regulations that set standards for all firms in an industry.

Electoral College The institution created by the Constitution to elect the president. Each state is allotted as many delegates to the Electoral College as it has total senators and representatives. According to the unit rule used for most states, the presidential candidate who receives a plurality of votes in the state is awarded all the state's Electoral College delegates. The presidential candidate who obtains a majority of the delegates in the Electoral College (i.e., at least 270 votes) is declared the winner. (Also see *unit rule.* By contrast, see *popular vote.*)

electoral connection The institutionalized manner in which constituents and members of Congress are linked in the system of representation by regular elections (every two years for members of the House, and every six years for senators). The incentive to get reelected powerfully helps shape the preferences and decisions of legislators.

entitlement programs Programs that guarantee benefits to people who meet certain requirements.

equality A situation in which all people have the same access to crucial resources, such as civil rights, opportunities, and material benefits. The framers aimed to create a political system that guaranteed citizens equal civil liberties and rights. But they opposed government promoting economic equality on the grounds that doing so would be tyrannical.

Executive Office of the President (EOP) The set of key executive officials who are close advisers to the president on major policy areas, including the budget, social and economic issues, intelligence, and security.

executive orders Binding directives issued by the president, within areas in which the president has constitutional authority, to members of the executive branch and private citizens and groups.

externalities Costs involved in production that a firm avoids paying by transferring them to government, consumers, and the wider society. Because such costs don't affect the firm's balance sheet, the firm has no incentive to find ways to minimize them, even when they may be extremely costly for the society.

extraordinary rendition The practice of sending prisoners to foreign countries for interrogation, where torture is often used in an attempt to extract information.

extreme market capitalism A form of capitalism, such as that prevailing in the United States, in which there is relatively little state provision of social benefits and business regulation.

federalism A political system in which governing authority is shared between the national government and subordinate units (the fifty states in the United States).

Federalist Papers The 85 articles written by James Madison, Alexander Hamilton, and John Jay between October 1787 and August 1788 to explain the new Constitution and promote its ratification, especially in New York. Read together, they constitute an enduring work of political theory.

Federalists Those Founders who favored a much stronger federal government than had existed under the Articles of Confederation, and thus strongly supported the adoption of the new Constitution of the United States. Later, the term was applied to the emerging political faction led by Alexander Hamilton during the Administration of President George Washington.

filibuster A technique to stop the progress of a piece of legislation by continuing debate and thus not permitting a vote. The Senate permits members to talk as long as they wish until 60 out of 100 senators vote for cloture to bring the filibuster to a close.

fiscal policy The use of the budget and the process of running deficits or surpluses to manage the economy.

free-rider problem The situation that occurs when people take advantage of some public good or common resource without paying their fair share for it.

free spaces Organizations that are free or insulated from elite control so that they can develop and disseminate alternative value systems.

golden age The period from 1945 to 1973 when wages, productivity, and economic growth all rose together. Inequality declined and the average American's standard of living increased.

Great Compromise Passed at the Constitutional Convention of 1787 by a one-vote margin, the arrangement that created a Congress in which "the proportion of suffrage in the 1st. branch [the House of Representatives] should be according to the respective numbers of free inhabitants; and that in the second branch or Senate, each State should have one vote and no more."

gross domestic product (GDP) A country's total economic output, which includes the amount of goods and services consumed, invested within the country, spent by the government, and the amount of exports over imports.

gunboat diplomacy The practice of sending the U.S. Navy to Latin American ports to ensure that governments in the region support U.S. policies and protect American political and economic interests.

head of government The official who directs the day-to-day work of government. In a presidential regime, the president is head of government; in a parliamentary regime, it is the prime minister.

head of state The official who symbolizes the unity and majesty of the state. In a presidential regime, the president is head of state; in a monarchy, it is the king or queen.

impeachment The procedure specified by the Constitution for removing a government official from office for what the constitution specifies as "high crimes and misdemeanors." (The term is sufficiently vague that it is unclear what it precisely means.)

independent regulatory commissions (IRCS) Administrative agencies with authority to issue rules and regulate specific economic sectors, such as air travel, telecommunications, and stock-exchange transactions.

interest groups Groups that citizens form to influence public policy.

isolationism Doctrine that U.S. interests are best served by minimizing U.S. involvement in international affairs.

judicial review The power of the courts to overturn laws that they find are unconstitutional.

Keynesianism The theory that government can use its budgetary authority to tame the business cycle in order to maintain full employment.

liberty A condition wherein individuals have the freedom to pursue their goals and interests without restrictions imposed by governments, save for governmental regulations aiming to ensure that others also have the freedom to pursue their goals and interests.

lobbying The attempt to influence what members of Congress and the executive branch do and what they decide in matters of public policy. Lobbyists are people who exercise this influence.

mandatory spending Government spending that is required by law, in which people qualify for benefits because they meet some criterion, such as age or income.

market The institution of trade and exchange, where commercial transactions of buying and selling take place and where the chance to seek deals and make profits exists.

Marshall Plan A program of economic assistance after World War II provided to European states to enable them to rebuild their devastated economies; named after U.S. Secretary of State George Marshall.

Medicaid A program funded by the states and the federal government that offers health care to low-income persons.

Medicare A social insurance program that provides health care for citizens who reach the age of 66.

monetary policy The effort to stabilize the economy by controlling interest rates and the money supply.

Monroe Doctrine The proclamation that President James Monroe issued in 1823 warning European countries to refrain from intervention in Latin America. In effect, the Monroe doctrine claimed the right for the United States to dominate the entire hemisphere.

multilateral Joint cooperative action by several states in pursuit of common goals. (Also see *unilateral*.)

nation building The attempt by one or several states to develop a viable state in a country where the state is weak or nonexistent.

New Deal A series of policies associated with President Franklin Roosevelt's response to the Great Depression. Such policies included Social Security, unemployment insurance, minimum-wage laws, public-works programs for the unemployed, and laws protecting workers' right to organize unions.

New Jersey Plan Design for Congress proposed at the Constitutional Convention of 1787 in which the legislature would have just one chamber, with one vote for each state, thus giving an advantage to small states.

North Atlantic Treaty Organization (NATO) The organization created during the Cold War by most democratic states of Western Europe and North America. Its members pledged a common military response if any one of them was attacked. For decades, NATO was primarily designed to safeguard against a possible Soviet attack.

oversight Congress's responsibility to monitor, supervise, and review how the executive agencies of the federal government conduct their affairs. Most congressional oversight occurs within congressional committees with relevant substantive responsibilities.

Patient Protection and Affordable Care Act The 2010 law passed by Barack Obama that significantly expanded the U.S. health-care system. Among its most controversial elements was a mandate that all individuals obtain health insurance.

political action committees (PACs) Groups championing particular issues that seek to influence the election of candidates sympathetic to their point of view. PACs rely on private political contributions to finance their activities.

political economy A classical term in political thought referring to the institutions and arrangements that govern how goods are produced, distributed, and consumed within a country's economy and, more broadly, across the globe.

political entrepreneurs Activists who promote new issues around which to organize a constituency.

political machines A term that designates the situation in which a political party is informally controlled by a group that maintains its leadership of the party by distributing patronage and other benefits to supporters.

popular sovereignty The idea that the ultimate and supreme source of political authority lies not with rulers but with the people, the citizens of the republic.

popular vote The votes for a candidate cast by all participating citizens. (By contrast, see *Electoral College*.)

poverty The circumstance of not having sufficient material possessions or income to afford to secure adequate necessities of life, including housing, food, and health care.

preferences The motivating desires and wishes that persons use to make choices among given alternatives.

preventive detention The practice of imprisoning suspects indefinitely without trial and depriving them of legal counsel and other judicial protections.

progressive Tax rates that increase as people's income goes up so that people who earn more pay a higher proportion of their income in taxes.

proportional representation (PR) a system of voting in which several lists of candidates compete in each district (thus, the term *multimember districts*). The number of winning candidates on each list is determined by the proportion of votes that the list receives. (Also see *single-member-district plurality system*.)

public-assistance programs Welfare-state programs that transfer funds to needy persons and families to help them secure a decent standard of living and become more self-sufficient.

public government The set of institutions that exercises binding legitimate authority within a territory.

reconciliation A budgetary procedure under which Congress considers how revenues, spending, and debt limits should be made to conform to the annual budget resolution that already has been passed. Debate on reconciliation bills is limited to twenty hours in the Senate and requires a simple majority for passage, thus bypassing the filibuster.

regressive Tax rates in which the rich pay a lower proportion of their income in taxes than the poor. As income increases, tax rates decline.

representative system A political system in which citizens elect officials to represent them in government. This is as opposed to a system of direct democracy, in which citizens rather than representatives participate in making governmental decisions.

republic A political regime in which governmental officials do not obtain office by inheritance (as in an aristocracy or monarchy).

roll call voting Voting in Congress that concerns the content and passage of legislation, in which members of the House of Representatives and the Senate declare whether they are voting positively or negatively.

rule of four The number of justices needed for the Supreme Court to hear a case. This is not required by the Constitution but is a custom observed by the Court.

securitization The practice of combining assets, such as mortgages, into a security that is marketed and sold to investors. A principal cause of the 2008 recession was that poor-quality mortgages (known as subprimes) were securitized. Since the mortgages underlying these securities were of questionable quality, the security itself lost considerable value when mortgage holders defaulted.

separation of powers A term used to describe the national government in the United States in which the constitution grants the presidency, Congress, and judiciary independent (separated) powers. This situation differs from the system of cabinet government, in which the powers of the cabinet and parliament are fused.

signing statements Documents that recent presidents have sometimes issued when they sign bills passed by Congress. A signing statement sets out the president's interpretation of the meaning of the bill and is designed to offer guidance to administrative officials and the courts.

single-member-district plurality system A system of voting in which candidates compete in single districts and the candidate gaining a plurality wins the election. This is also known as the single-member-district system or the winner-take-all system. (Also see *proportional representation [PR]*.)

social insurance Government social-policy programs that are funded by premiums paid by people in the labor market to support the benefits given to participants.

social movements Collective action by citizens that goes beyond the normal channels of electoral or interest-group activity.

social regulations Regulations that are designed to protect social interests, such as health and safety and the environment, and that apply to all firms across industries.

Social Security The social-insurance program passed in 1935 that offers income in old age and protection against disability and unemployment.

stagflation The simultaneous appearance of high inflation and unemployment.

State of the Union The annual speech delivered by the president to a joint session of Congress that reports on how well the country is doing, and outlines the administration's legislative program. This report is mandated by Article II, Section 3 of the Constitution.

structural power of business Political influence business enjoys through its ownership and control of the means of production.

suffrage The right to vote.

super PACs Organizations that bundle political contributions from many sources, the result of which is to considerably increase the total funds supporting the election of specific candidates and parties.

superpower A country that combines a far greater degree of power and might than other nations, and thus develops a dominant position in world affairs.

supply-side economics A theory that holds that cutting tax rates will lead to such growth that total tax revenues will remain steady.

swing (or battleground) states The handful of states that are evenly divided in presidential elections, such that the presidential vote is neither stably red nor blue.

tax expenditures Favored tax treatment given to certain activities that the government wants to promote.

Temporary Assistance to Needy Families (TANF) Beginning in 1997, the successor to AFDC; TANF has provided cash assistance to the poor. Largely administered by the states with funds provided by federal block grants, TANF has a 60-month lifetime limit on eligibility and a requirement to actively seek work.

transnational corporations (TNCs) Firms with significant foreign operations.

unanimous consent The situation in which no member of Congress objects to a proposal, and it can thus pass without a roll call vote.

unemployment insurance A program that provides money to people who lose their jobs, as a temporary cushion.

unified government A circumstance in which both houses of Congress and the presidency are controlled by the same political party.

unilateral The pattern in which a state acts alone within the international sphere rather than consulting or acting with other states. (Also see *multilateral.*)

unit rule The rule that specifies that a state's delegates to the Electoral College must vote as a unit (unanimously) for the candidate who receives a plurality of popular votes in the state in the presidential election. Most states use the unit rule in presidential elections. (Also see *Electoral College.*)

Virginia Plan Design for Congress proposed at the Constitutional Convention of 1787 in which the legislature would contain two chambers, with representation for each to be determined by the size of a state's population, thus giving an advantage to large states.

veto The president's constitutional power to withhold his or her signature from a bill passed by Congress, thus preventing its passage into law. When the president has vetoed a bill, in order for it to become law, each house of Congress must override the veto by a two-thirds majority vote.

voter suppression Techniques used to create barriers to voting, such as requiring citizens to produce photo IDs and limiting the hours that polling stations are open. While the stated goal of the party sponsoring these restrictions is to prevent voter fraud, the real aim is to limit access to the ballot by qualified citizens who are likely to vote for the opposing party.

War on Poverty The label for an array of "Great Society" legislative proposals and laws supported by President Lyndon B. Johnson in 1964 and aimed at reducing the poverty rate by expanding social-welfare programs and creating programs geared to increase the political participation of poor people.

welfare state Government protection of citizens' economic and social well-being through instruments of social insurance and transfers to the needy.

CREDITS

p. 2: Ullstein Bild/The Granger Collection

p. 30: Bob Krist/Corbis

p. 49, Figure 2.2: "Number and Percentage of U.S. Manufacturing Industries in which Largest Four Companies Accounted for at Least 50 Percent of Shipment Value in Their Industries, 1947–2007" from "Monopoly and Competition in Twenty-First Century Capitalism," by John Bellamy Foster, Robert W. McChesney, and R. Jamil Jonna, *Monthly Review,* 62, No. 1 (April 2011). Reprinted with permission.

p. 52: AP Photo/PRNewsFoto/PepsiCo

p. 61, Figure 2.4: Reprinted with the permission of Simon & Schuster, Inc., from *Winner-Take-All Politics: How Washington Made the Rich Richer—and Turned Its Back on the Middle Class* by Jacob S. Hacker and Paul Pierson. Copyright © 2010 Jacob S. Hacker and Paul Pierson. All rights reserved.

p. 73: AP Photo

p. 88: AP Photo

p. 123, Figure 4.3: "Distribution of Political Inputs: Percentage of Activity from SES Quintiles, 1990" from *The Unheavenly Chorus: Unequal Political Voice and the Broken Promise of American Democracy* by Kay Lehman Schlozman, Sidney Verba, and Henry E. Brady. Copyright © 2012 by Princeton University Press. Reprinted by permission of Princeton University Press.

p. 126: Richard B. Levine/Newscom

p. 132, Figure 4.4: Fig. 9.4, p. 257: "Transformation of the National Parties." Reprinted with the permission of Simon & Schuster, Inc., from *Divided America: The Ferocious Power Struggle in American Politics* by Earl Black and Merle Black. Copyright © 2007 by Earl Black and Merle Black. All rights reserved.

p. 148: http://occupywallst.org

p. 165: Bettmann/Corbis

p. 176: AP Photo

p. 195: © Pete Souza/Corbis

p. 203: AP Photo/Doug Mills

p. 211: © Olivier/Pool/Corbis

p. 234: AP Photo/Michael Dwyer

p. 239: CQ Roll Call/Newscom

C-2 CREDITS

p. 258: Roll Call/Getty Images

p. 277: Bettmann/Corbis

p. 284: Larry Downing/Reuters/Newscom

p. 320: Gu Xinrong/XinHua Press/Corbis

p. 333: Bettmann/Corbis

p. 350: AP Photos/Charles Dharapak

p. 366: Joan Silva/The New York Times/Redux

p. 374: AP Photo

p. 380: Dept. of Defense, Petty Officer 1st Class Shane T. McCoy, U.S. Navy

INDEX

AARP, 158, 256
abortion
    public opinion on, 133
    Roe v. Wade and, 271, 280, 281, 288
Abramoff, Jack, 155
Abu Ghraib prison, 378
Acegmolu, Daron, 55
Adams, John, 236, 273
Adams, John Quincy, 360
ADC (Aid to Dependent Children), 332
Adelson, Sheldon, 129
advocacy groups, professional, 159–60
AFDC (Aid to Families with Dependent
    Children), 332, 336, 343, 344
affluenza, 34
Affordable Health Care Act (2010), 109,
    257, 258–59, 266, 283, 326–27, 345
Afghanistan
    military presence in, 356, 372, 381, 390
    military prisons in, 378
    nation building in, 372–73
    war in, 229, 303, 363
AFL (American Federation of Labor), 74,
    168–69
AFL-CIO, 170, 340
Africa
    immigration and, 7
    Monroe Doctrine in, 365
    nationalism in, 361–62
    pharmaceutical companies and, 41
    proxy wars in, 363
African Americans
    congressional representation and, 237,
        238
    education and, 264, 276–78
    2008 election and, 109–10
    2012 election and, 113, 119
    on government intervention, 164
    incarcerations and, 289

income and wealth of, 5
political parties and, 23
poverty and, 336–37
Social Security program and, 333–34
voting rights of, 7, 20, 100, 104, E–23n54
Agnew, Spiro, 270
Agricultural Adjustment Act, 275
Agriculture Department, 201
Aid to Dependent Children (ADC), 332
Aid to Families with Dependent Children
    (AFDC), 332, 336, 343, 344
AIG, 312, 314
AIPAC (American Israel Public Affairs
    Committee), 359
air pollution, 35
Akin Group, 155
Alabama, 40
Alito, Samuel, 282, 285
all-directional lobbying, 156
Allison, Graham, 364
Al Qaeda, 21, 358, 371, 372, 376, 377, 380,
    381–82
Amazon, 153, 155
American Bar Association, 280
American Enterprise Institute, 162
American Family Association, 262
American Federation of Labor (AFL), 74,
    168–69
American Federation of Teachers, 346
American Israel Public Affairs Committee
    (AIPAC), 359
American Petroleum Institute, 145, 156,
    317
American Political Science Association
    (APSA), 24, 130, 137
American Samoa, 385
Americans for George, 147
Americans for Prosperity, 178
Angola, proxy wars in, 363